GENERAL
PHILOSOPHY

GENERAL

PHILOSOPHY~

DAVID ELTON TRUEBLOOD, *1900*—

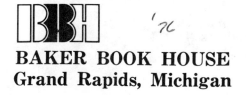

BAKER BOOK HOUSE
Grand Rapids, Michigan

Paperback edition
First printing, May 1976

Contents ✑

Part II Problems

Part III Values

Appendixes

Preface ❧

THERE ARE AT LEAST THREE TESTS WHICH WE SHOULD APPLY TO A BE-
ginning work in philosophy. The first is that it should serve to
bring students into contact with the ideas of the great philosophers
in such a way that the works of these philosophers are studied at
first hand. "The best way toward greatness is to mix with the
great." Because there is no substitute for the direct encounter with
noble minds, the contemporary book should never attempt to
provide an alternative to this encounter. It should, instead, perform
the humble role of introducing the minds of the greatest thinkers,
thereafter allowing the contagion to work for itself. It is better to
read Plato's *Dialogues* than it is to read a textbook about Plato, but
the hard truth is that many will not realize this possibility unless
some teacher points the way. Whether the work of the teacher is
spoken or written makes no great difference; interest is not likely
to be aroused without some assistance.

The beginning book must help the reader to approach renowned
works in a mood that is truly philosophical. The mood must be
critical without being condescending, and it must demonstrate
humility without adoration. Though we must always refer to the
great philosophers of the past and present, we must never be satis-

fied with a merely literary study of what they have written. This was recognized by Epictetus, in the first century A.D., when he wrote, "If I study philosophy with a view only to its literature, I am not a philosopher, but a man of letters."

The second test of a beginning book is whether it succeeds in producing questions which the student might not otherwise ask, and also in shaping those which are already dimly felt but are not precisely stated. It is not the task of the author to seek to provide stereotyped answers, because the most important questions have no valid answers of this kind, but it is part of his responsibility to mention some of the answers that have been given at various stages of human reflection and the reasons for the superiority of some of these answers over others. Perhaps the greatest help which the author can give in regard to problems is to cause the reader to be puzzled about the familiar or the commonplace. Though answers are never final, it is only fair that the teaching author, far from trying to maintain a pose of Olympian detachment, should allow the reader to know what his own personal convictions are.

The third test, and in some ways the most important one, is whether the book leads the reader to *philosophize*. We are terribly mistaken if we think of philosophy as a deposit of doctrine. It is an intellectual process, an exercise in thinking. The book must encourage a continual dialogue between reader and author. If what is presented is an *exercise in* philosophy, rather than a *treatise about* philosophy, the book can become the launching pad for the student's own intellectual orbit.

Philosophy is something which a man must do for himself. No one can do it for him. Philosophy is thinking, and only the individual can think. But this does not mean that the professional teacher of philosophy is without value. He is of assistance in that he can show where the traps are; he can save time by pointing out long-recognized fallacies; he can suggest authors whose work might otherwise be unknown. The teacher is like the golf professional. Although it is the player who must hit the ball, the coach can tell him how to stand and how to hold the club. Teaching is a great art, an art in which there is never complete success, yet which is perpetually exhilarating, because it deals with what is intrinsically.

important. This is my vocation and I love it, though I freely admit that it is often humbling.

Once we become aware of the nature of our purposes, the right method of achieving them becomes more clear. Our three tests are not likely to be successful unless we undertake a creative combination of methods. There is a place for a book which is devoted solely to the history of philosophy, and there is also a place for a book which is devoted solely to the problems of philosophy, but neither approach meets the deepest needs of the beginning student. There is little value in giving the historical answers unless the problems are already felt, and there is little value in facing the problems unless there is a direct acquaintance with the ways in which these problems have been faced in the past.

If there is anything original or unique about the approach to philosophy represented in this volume, the originality lies in the concept of order, an order which is fundamentally *dialectical*. This may, of course, be very different from the order of chronology. The idea is to present a difficult subject in such a manner that the student is ready for Chapter 2, once he has studied carefully the substance of Chapter 1, and so on to the end. We must always reject the mere book of essays, in which the order is like that of beads on a string, with the consequence that the order may be altered or reversed without loss. Much of the real dignity of thought is hidden until we find a sequence in which a leads to b and b leads to c. This is the essence of all dialectic, that cannot be altered without resulting confusion. Order is the greatest single secret of clarity.

It is hoped that this book will have a dual use, being addressed equally to those who are now enrolled in universities and colleges and to those who are carrying on their learning alone. For both groups, the book is intended as an instrument of self-instruction. If anything is clear in contemporary education, it is that, because learning need never come to an end, some of the best study goes on quite outside college halls. The book is directed, not merely to the young, but to people of any age who desire to study philosophy seriously: its purpose is not to make the work of such persons easy, but to make it possible.

The number of the people who have helped me in the writing of this book is very large. It includes many of my students, who have, by their questions, prompted further clarification. One of my students, David Rayfield, has provided valuable assistance in the preparation of the Appendix. Especial thanks are due to Mr. Robert Pitman and to my wife, who have typed and retyped these chapters.

Though this book has naturally been contemplated a long time, and though in one sense it has been in the process of composition for thirty-five years, all of the actual writing has been done in the last year and a half. The first notes were put down, under exceedingly happy circumstances, on April 16, 1961, on the *philosophen-weg*, above Heidelberg. There the decision to write was made, and the symbolism of that day has remained in my consciousness. Philosophy, because it is fundamentally a process, flourishes best on the Philosopher's Way. We did not construct the path, but we can tread it, conscious of the many who have trod it before. In one sense we walk with them, but in another sense each walks alone. If each can put up one or two signs, he thereby pays his toll on the ancient path.

D.E.T.

Richmond, Indiana
January, 1963

GENERAL
PHILOSOPHY ∽

Chapter 1 ∽ THE HERITAGE OF SOCRATES

Man is obviously made to think. It is his whole dignity and his whole merit; and his whole duty is to think as he ought.

BLAISE PASCAL

THE CHIEF FUNCTION OF A PHILOSOPHER IS TO TRY TO PERFORM the extremely difficult but manifestly important task of logical reasoning. In the nature of the case the task must always be twofold. The philosopher must not only reason about the world; he must also reason about reasoning itself. It is because of this twofold vocation that philosophy differs from all other human undertakings. In each of the natural sciences we engage in reasoning, but always about a particular sector of experience. We do not, as scientists, concern ourselves with the underlying presuppositions of all science nor do we examine critically the reasoning process itself. There are, of course, men called scientists who think with care about the interconnections and also about the processes by which some insights are rendered more probable than are any alternatives, but when they are so engaged they are acting philosophically rather than scientifically.

1

Although there is a sense in which a thinker can become a professional philosopher, it must never be supposed that the task of philosophizing is limited or ought to be limited to such professionals. There is also a deep sense in which every thoughtful person philosophizes. He may not be paid to do so, but neither was Socrates. Also, like Socrates, he may never have taken a course in philosophy, but this is no absolute deterrent. The person who frequently examines the unargued assumptions of his own and other people's thought, who has a constant sense of wonder which keeps him from thinking of anything in the world as simple or as fully known, who has a love of wisdom without claiming to be wise, who challenges his own conclusions—such a man is a philosopher, even though he occupies no professional chair and though he is not the recipient of academic degrees. When Judge Learned Hand died, an editorial in *The New York Times*, which depicted the famous jurist as really a philosopher, stated the essence of the matter by saying, "He was a philosopher, ever probing the easy assumptions of the unthinking with a passionate devotion to dispassionate truth."

The necessity of instruction in philosophy arises from the universality of philosophy. If, as is undoubtedly true, all people tend to philosophize, even though in fragmentary and patently inadequate ways, the question is not *whether* but *how*. We think, if we are truly human; the problem then is to learn how to think carefully and well.

Although it is the custom in writing introductory books in philosophy to start with a number of definitions, there is reason to suppose that this is not the best way to start. The trouble with the definitions is that they are so different from one another that they add to confusion rather than to clarification, and, furthermore, they come too soon. Definition is far more suitable at the end of a process than it is at the beginning. This is why most authors find that actually they compose the preface after the manuscript of the book has been finished. Not until they have completed the work are they able to say with precision what it was that they were trying to say or to accomplish. We move from vagueness to sharpness by experience, and particularly by the experience of intellectual creation. If our literary convention were not so deeply intrenched, it would be sensible to put what we now call the preface at the end. In any case some careful effort in the definition of the philosophical enterprise will be made in the last chapter of this book.

One method of clarification (which is both possible and profitable at this early stage) is that of pointing to a person. We get to business quickly in any enterprise by starting with denotation rather than with connotation.[1] Even while we are still struggling to see what we mean by philosophizing, there may be some historical person to whom we can point, a person who will be universally recognized as an embodiment of what we mean. Yes there is, and that person is Socrates of Athens (469–399 B.C.), who is the recognized father of western philosophical thought and who, through his pupil Plato, made an indelible imprint on all subsequent thought. Socrates lived during the great days of Athens, when some of the noblest structures were being erected; he fought with notable courage in the debilitating war against Sparta; he influenced, without pay, the lives of many young Athenians; and he was condemned to die when a small majority of the 500 who tried him, found him guilty of the double charge of impiety and corruption of the minds of the youth. Plato and others were so outraged by the injustice of the execution that they set themselves to the task of seeing to it that succeeding generations would know the true worth of the condemned man. A modern philosopher has eloquently expressed the essence of the tragic yet glorious development: "Socrates owes his immortality of fame as the martyr of philosophy not to any sentiment on the part of an emotional democracy, but to the Providence which gave him as younger friend and follower the one man in history who has combined supreme greatness as a philosophic thinker with equal greatness as a master of language, and so has been, directly or indirectly, the teacher of all thinking men since his own day."[2]

There is no better introduction to the practice of philosophy

[1] For denotation and connotation see John Stuart Mill, A System of Logic, Longmans, Green and Company, 1900, p. 19.

[2] A. E. Taylor, Socrates, Doubleday & Company, Inc., Anchor Books, 1956, p. 129. This small but intensely scholarly book is the best work in English on the life of Socrates. For another helpful view see Edith Hamilton, Witness to the Truth, W. W. Norton and Company, 1948, Chapter II. See also Encyclopedia of Religion and Ethics, Hastings House, Inc., Vol. XI, for the article on Socrates by John Burnet.

than a slow reading of the lesser dialogues of Plato, beginning with the *Laches, Charmides, Euthyphro,* then the *Apology* and *Crito.* If the reader is sensitive and willing to learn he will, as a result of this experience, begin to see what philosophy is. He will then understand that it has more affinity to verbs than it has to nouns. It is, in short, something which people can *do,* as it was something which Socrates did and did superbly well.

In one sense Socrates was a gifted amateur, while in another sense he was certainly a professional. He jealously guarded his amateur standing by not taking fees for tuition, even though he was never in good financial circumstances, but he was at the same time a true professional, because he understood what he was talking about. Socrates was the master of any intellectual situation. He was never philosophizing off the top of his mind, but thoroughly understood what the pitfalls were.

A study of the life of Socrates and a firsthand acquaintance with the dialogues in which he appears constitutes the best possible introduction to philosophical study, because the experience provides an immediate and concrete encounter with the life of reason. Socrates was reasonable because he assumed, as all thoughtful men must, that nothing happens by accident or is true without involving implications, that two contradictory propositions cannot both be true, and that the world is shot through with connections, even though some of them are hard to see. Rationality, for Socrates, involved the anticipation of consequences and acting in the light of them. It was appropriate therefore that in the lifetime of this man the term philosopher, i.e., a lover of wisdom as contrasted to one who claims to be wise, became current.

Socrates is the superb example of the philosopher because he combined, as A. E. Taylor so clearly shows, four important roles. He was first, *an eager lover,* in many senses of the word; second, he was *a religious mystic,* always avoiding the mood of the cynic; third, he was *a rationalist,* peculiarly tough-minded in hunting down error; and fourth, he was *a humorist.*[3] The third role is one which all literate people understand in part, but it is equally important to understand the other three. Without them it would not have been possible for Socrates to have become such a gifted

[3] Taylor, *op. cit.,* p. 50.

teacher. He really cared for the young men, and he cared enough not to be wanton or cruel in criticizing some deeply held faith or belief. Though he was always willing to give a reason for his position, and to defend it, he was scrupulous in doing so "with gentleness and reverence."[4] In particular it was important that he could laugh a great deal, some of his laughter being directed at himself. In one sense he was a disciple of Democritus, for Democritus was known as "the laughing philosopher."

Once we have the figure of Socrates firmly before us we can never suppose that philosophy is something separated from life. Socrates helps us to understand a great sentence from the pen of Josiah Royce when he said, "You philosophize when you reflect critically upon what you are actually doing in your world."[5]

The greatest reason for devoting this first chapter to Socrates is that the book is devoted to the teaching function, and the final greatness of Socrates is as teacher. Because of his good fortune in having both Xenophon and Plato to write down his ideas and to illustrate his method, he is our teacher almost as truly as he was the teacher of the fortunate young men of Athens. He taught superbly because he made men think of their own experiences and their own ideas, yet to think of them with a certain objectivity. He taught men to be self-conscious in the sense that they try to look at their own reasoning with the same fairness which they pride themselves on exhibiting when examining the ideas of others.

The teacher does not take students into some strange world of speculation, with no possible relation to ordinary facts; instead he starts from where they are and helps them to see the connections between experiences which otherwise are separated and wholly baffling. The extremely valuable biographical fragment in the Phaedo (96a–100c) is the chief source for our knowledge of how Socrates, after he had become discouraged by the way his predecessors, including even Anaxagoras, dogmatized about Nature, determined to strike out on a new path of his own, the path which, in the entire western world, has been continuously profitable. The new path starts from the recognition that direct inspection of

[4] See I Peter 3:15.
[5] Josiah Royce, The Spirit of Modern Philosophy, Houghton Mifflin Company, 1892, pp. 1–2.

Nature is not a fruitful method. Man understands even Nature better if he begins by considering himself, the one door into reality which he is privileged to open. If we were forced to look on other men and consider their thoughts wholly from the outside, as we must with electricity or rocks or trees, our intellectual predicament would be well-nigh hopeless, but we are not, fortunately, so limited. "There is one thing, and only one, in the whole universe which we know more about than we could learn from external observation," writes C. S. Lewis with great insight. "That one thing is Man. We do not merely observe men, we are men. In this case we have, so to speak, inside information; we are in the know."[6]

There is some excellent evidence which convinces us that Socrates experienced a great change in his life, at roughly the midway point in his mature career. The assumption that he experienced what can only be called a conversion accounts for the striking difference between the picture of the philosopher, of his name, whom Aristophanes caricatures and pillories in *The Clouds*, and the figure who emerges partly in the writings of Xenophon and fully in the major dialogues of Plato. The earlier picture is that of a natural scientist, concerned primarily with the physical world, but the later picture is one of a man concerned wholly with the ideas of men. The picture given by Aristophanes is thus not necessarily erroneous or vicious, as some have supposed, if there was a real change. It is quite possible that the crisis of change came during military service, when Socrates was in a quiet trance for a long time. Whatever Socrates was in his early life, there is little doubt that in his most fruitful years he was a man with a mission, wholly dedicated to the task of helping all who were willing to be helped in learning of their own ignorance, and in tending their own souls.

It was Socrates' decision about method that made him the founder of moral philosophy. Socrates' brilliant idea was that he should begin, not with stars and the shape of the earth, a topic about which there was great controversy between the then East and West, but with the statements or theories or hypotheses which men make about the world. Even to this dray the shift in method is justified in many ways, one being that modern natural

[6] C. S. Lewis, *Mere Christianity*, The Macmillan Company, 1960, pp. 18, 19.

science never moves forward by mere observation, but always by theories which are carefuly formulated and then tested. The Ionian physicists, who were the chief intellectual predecessors of Socrates, did not know this and were, accordingly, comparatively unproductive. The contrast between them and Socrates is analogous to that, at the beginning of the modern age, between Bacon, who supposed that the facts are there to draw a theory from, and Newton, who saw facts in a wholly different light. To Newton, facts were materials by which a theory may be tested. We all admire Newton's way more than we admire Bacon's.[7]

Socrates neither wrote a book nor held any scholarly position, but he knew superbly how to sharpen the thinking of other minds. He taught men to examine their prejudices, always emphasizing the fact that "The unexamined life is not worth living." (Apology, 38.) He admitted that in one sense he was not teaching at all, since the student either had the ideas or he did not. If he already had them, there was no need to introduce them, whereas if he did not have them he would not recognize them when they were presented.[8] Teaching, therefore, would seem to be a hopeless or impossible task, yet everyone knows that it occurs. The solution of the paradox, according to Socrates, lies in the recognition of the fact that the teacher is really acting in the modest role of the midwife. The teacher does not produce the ideas, but he can serve the useful function of helping the existent ideas to be born, i.e., to come clearly into the light where they are recognized and acknowledged.[9]

Since we do not need to be slavish adherents of an ancient figure, we can profitably alter it in the light of subsequent teaching experience. Actually there seem to be several distinct stages in the development of ideas, so far as the teacher-student relationship is concerned. The first stage is conception, and the obvious fact is that conception does not occur in isolation. The conception of ideas,

[7] See Augustus De Morgan, A Budget of Paradoxes, 2nd ed., The Open Court Publishing Co., 1915, pp. i, 88.

[8] The predicament is stated in the Meno.

[9] The well-known reference of Socrates to his inheritance of his mother's occupation is in Theaetetus, 149 a. Socrates says that Phaenerete, his mother, had great skill in helping other women to have their babies born. She was probably helpful in this way as many other good women have been, but it is an anachronism to suggest that she was a professional midwife. Socrates makes the point in an obviously humorous vein.

like the conception of children, is a joint process. We need other minds, particularly in the early stages of mental creation. That minds actually impregnate one another can be verified by noting what goes on in a modern symposium. We often put ten times as many new ideas into our notebooks while participating in a real class, as we do on other or lonely occasions. And the ideas are not merely copies of what others, including the teacher, have expressed. They are truly our own, but they do not normally occur to us in our solitude.

The second major stage may be called *development*, and this, as in the pregnancy parallel, may go on profitably when the individual is alone. The ideas conceived in the company of the professor and the other students may be refined slowly in private. Indeed, they are not likely to be refined with any success unless the thinker has the privilege of a good deal of privacy. This may, in our figure, be termed the period of gestation. The time of profitable solitude may then be followed by a third stage, a contrasting time of *public experience*, in which we gain by the criticism of others, including our teachers. Thus it is wrong for the student to be always dependent upon his teacher, just as it is wrong to be never dependent upon his teacher. A great part of wisdom in the intellectual enterprise consists in willingness to live one's life in chapters and to know which chapter is which.

All three stages of the growth of ideas are immensely helped by immediate confrontation with philosophical classics. The best way to learn to philosophize, in contrast to secondhand knowledge about philosophy, is to meet the best minds at first hand. This is why the beginning student is well advised to start immediately with the earlier dialogues of Plato, thus getting at once into the excitement of the clash of ideas in the Athens of 400 B.C. There was a time when, in our colleges, it was common to use a contemporary textbook about philosophy and to leave the matter there. Today this is not done in any first-rate institution. The multiplicity of the reprints and the excellent translations have made the direct encounter with the great minds possible for all who are willing to undertake the task. In this really productive development of the teaching art the golden text of our generation has been the words of Alfred North Whitehead when he wrote, "Moral education is impossible apart from the habitual vision of greatness."[10] This habitual vision is possible as students wrestle at first hand with the arguments of Plato, of Aristotle, of Descartes, of Kant, and so many more. These men did not say the last word on any subject, but there is a deep sense in which we can honestly say that their reputations are not on trial. It is hard to see how a person can consider himself educated if he has not struggled with the ideas of these intellectual giants. The purpose of a book such as this one is not to take the place of confrontation with the great minds, but to entice students into the experience of direct encounter with them. The hope is that enough can be said in this chapter about Socrates to cause students to read his words as recorded by his famous and loyal pupils.

Reading the Socratic dialogues gives us a foretaste of the entire philosophic adventure of ideas. In the characteristic dialogue an idea is put forward with confidence, though usually in a naïve form. It is accepted by Socrates with enough seriousness to cause him to examine it carefully. The position adopted is, for the purpose of the inquiry, assumed to be a sound one. Then Socrates asks where this position will lead. What are the implications which follow if the original proposition is affirmed? Often these implications are found to be truly alarming. If the implications of the idea are found to be patently false, ridiculous, or self-contradictory, then the original idea must be abandoned, and we must start all over again. The logical formula is as follows:

If p is assumed,
And p implies q,
And q is false,
Then p is false.

In short, the denial of the consequent leads inevitably to the denial of the antecedent. The basic rule of philosophy is, therefore, *It is not intellectually honest to hold a position after it is known that the position leads inevitably to other positions which are recognized as false.* The respect for honesty involves, thus, the respect for consistency. This presumably is accepted by all; if it is not accepted,

[10] A. N. Whitehead, *The Aims of Education and Other Essays*, The Macmillan Company, 1929, p. 106.

intelligent discourse may as well come to an end. The vocation of Socrates, as of any philosophical teacher, is to help the student to see clearly what he may not see for himself, namely, the implications of a position taken. The philosopher helps himself and others by seeing connections which may ordinarily be obscure, but he serves primarily by asking always the pertinent question, "What follows?"

The dialogues in which Socrates is the chief character serve as a model for the entire history of philosophy, a history which is not ended, but is continued by us. The purpose of the teacher (in this case the book) is to help by suggesting materials and techniques and questions, but the student must always reach his own conclusions. This is the great difference between teaching and indoctrination or, in extreme cases, brainwashing.

The knowledge of what others have thought is extremely helpful. The student sometimes feels alone; then suddenly he realizes that von Leibniz or Kant struggled long ago with the same ideas and difficulties which now seem so fresh and important to him. As he observes how an earlier thinker handled them, he begins to see difficulties and possibilities in his own answer which he did not see earlier, alone. He is really beginning to philosophize when he enters into the history of ideas and when he shares, however modestly, in the unfinished dialogue.

No philosopher of our time has stressed more thoroughly the dialogic character of human thinking than has the late Professor A. O. Lovejoy of Johns Hopkins University. His main point is made as follows in the Preface to his greatest work.

The practice of philosophizing *in vacuo* I have always regarded with a distaste and suspicion. Philosophy seems to me essentially a collective and cooperative business. Effective cooperation among philosophers consists, it is true, primarily in disagreement. For, given a sufficiently well-defined problem, philosophy can really get forward with it only by bringing together in their logical interconnection all the considerations which have occurred, or are likely to occur, to acute and philosophically initiated minds as significantly pertinent to that problem. These considerations will always, during the progress of any philosophical inquiry, be conflicting, and they must be contributed by many minds of diverse types and different training and preconceptions.[11]

If we meditate on the wisdom of such an approach we begin to see why philosophy is, in the nature of the undertaking, a *process* rather than a fixed object. It is not something finished or static. Its essence lies in the continuing dialectic and the student is part of the process which he studies. Therefore it can truly be said that philosophy, as a serious intellectual undertaking, is "a Platonic dialogue on a grand scale, in which the theses, proposed proofs, objections, rejoinders, of numerous interlocutors are focused upon a given question, and the argument gradually shapes itself, through its own immanent dialectic, to a conclusion."[12]

The student who begins to understand that philosophy is a process rather than a fixed body of knowledge may find this conception exhilarating, but he may also find it subtly discouraging in the realization that nothing is ever finally settled. In this connection it is relevant to give a warning. It is true that nothing is settled with absolute finality and that for two reasons. First, the evidence is never complete, and second, no human being is sufficiently perfect, even in his reasoning ability, to be infallible. We are all in the finite predicament and will continue to be in it. Nevertheless, there are some points which can be brought to a relatively decisive issue. Though the history of philosophy is naturally unfinished, the result of the long history is not the complete frustration of the situation sometimes alleged, in which all thinkers cancel out the ideas of all the others. The philosophic situation is neither that of complete finality nor of complete confusion. On some issues, including a good many which are examined in this book, the discussion has been carried on for a sufficiently long time and in a sufficiently disciplined manner, by a sufficient variety of minds, to make the resultant answers reasonably clear and convincing. The fact that we do not have absolute certainty in regard to any human conclusions does not mean that the task of inquiry is fruitless. We must, it is true, always proceed on the basis of probability, as will

[11] A. O. Lovejoy, *The Revolt Against Dualism*, The Open Court Publishing Company, 1955, p. ix.
[12] *Ibid.*, p. x.

be made plain in a later chapter, but to have probability is to have something. What we seek in any realm of human thought is not absolute certainty, for that is denied us as men, but rather the more modest path of those who find dependable ways of discerning different degrees of probability.

Philosophy, in the heritage of Socrates, is always dialectic. Dialectic is the way in which one idea leads to another, carried on either among different people with competing opinions and judgments, or within one man's own consciousness. This is why we should be grateful when our ideas are sharply or even rudely challenged. We are not likely to note the error mixed with the truth except for such a challenge. The place where we come out may not be identical with the position of any one individual in the debate, but we shall never arrive at the final stage unless we start the encounter somewhere. This is why A. E. Taylor can speak of philosophy as something "created by the function of minds employed in the joint pursuit after truth."[13]

Philosophy, in the tradition and mood of Socrates, has many characteristics, but among them are three which, if they are understood, will help the student of philosophy to see what it is that he is trying to do when he attempts to philosophize.

1. *The first mark is a beneficent skepticism.* Philosophy is impossible apart from doubt. It was partly because Socrates spread doubt in the minds of the young men who heard him gladly that he was condemned to death. He made them doubt, not only the wisdom of a democracy which blurred distinctions of excellence, but he caused them to doubt the wisdom of leaders who were not really wise, and he made them doubt the soundness of their own callow opinions.

Philosophy begins by raising questions which otherwise would not be raised. Some of these are about the external world, where men are not usually conscious of illusions until they are brought to their attention, while others are about human conclusions, which are often based upon inadequate or contradictory evidence. Sometimes the skill of a teacher of philosophy is demonstrated more by the questions he raises, than by the answers which he gives. One reason for this is that the answers must be primarily

[13] Taylor, *op. cit.*, p. 149.

those which the student arrives at himself, while the problems will not even occur to him if they are not introduced by his teacher. Even today many students have no doubts about the excellence of democracy until ancient and modern difficulties are mentioned. Above all, the teacher must avoid trying to provide answers until the problems are truly felt. One reason why students understand so little at the beginning of a course, and do not even hear what is said, is that the answers have been given too soon.

Philosophy in the Socratic tradition involves a certain sophistication in that we become critical of all naïve judgments. We begin to test facile generalizations, to see if we can think of exceptions and, if we can think of them, we realize that the generalization is thereby lessened in value. One mark of a philosopher is that he is aware of problems which do not appear ordinarily to the lay mind. Some of these have to do with knowledge and truth and evidence. The fact of knowledge does not seem strange until we think about it very carefully, and then it is positively mystifying. One consequence is that the area of wonder is vastly increased. Philosophers may not show much agreement in the answers which they propose, but they demonstrate remarkable unanimity in the way in which they raise the questions. A modern historian of philosophy has stated the point brilliantly:

Valuable as philosophy's answers are, they are not as important as the questions philosophy asks. In fact, we may say that the chief function of philosophy is to ask questions, rather than to answer them. Its function is to rebuff all forms of dogmatism and intolerance, to keep before the mind a sense of possibilities unrecognized, and to help man grasp his place in the universe by giving him at once a proper humility at his finitude and a proper pride at what he accomplishes with his limited powers.[14]

Perhaps the most important feature of the quotation from W. T. Jones is the way in which this eminent scholar sees that the emphasis on questions is bound to make men humble. We tend to suppose that we know a great deal until we ask what we really know, and then we realize that we have no more than scratched the surface. The immature person may seem cocky in his questions, as the

[14] W. T. Jones, A History of Western Philosophy, Harcourt Brace & World Inc., 1952, p. 995.

students of Socrates sometimes appeared, but the cure for this disease is a bigger dose of the same medicine. That Socrates was really humble and not merely acting a farce of humility we are forced to conclude, as we look at all of the available evidence. His humility came not from comparing himself with other men, but from a comparison with his own developed ideal. This was his solution of the paradox of the words of the oracle about his being the wisest of men.

That some humor was connected with Socrates' search for men wiser than himself is not surprising. Humor comes partly from not taking oneself too seriously, and often turns on a sudden righting of the balance which has been disrupted by human conceit or overseriousness. It is easy to imagine what the reaction of Socrates would have been to Sigmund Freud who boldly compared his own work to that of Copernicus and Darwin, or to the early phase of logical positivism when we were solemnly told that the work of nearly all preceding philosophers was rendered obsolete by the new positivistic doctrines and methods. It is important to note that a great many of the leading philosophers have been skilled in humor and have proved themselves to be brilliant tellers of stories. "Really a man ought not to be allowed to be a philosopher," said Archbishop Temple, "unless he has a sense of humor."[15]

If the humility born of skepticism is genuine, it will save men from an arrogant contempt for the thinkers of the past. The immature are tempted to look superciliously on the judgments of men who, living centuries ago, had never gone faster than a horse could run, and had never heard of Einstein's equations, but a deeper skepticism makes them also skeptical of the supposed advantages of contemporaneity. We realize, if we are wise at all, that the insights of men of the past are only partial insights, but they are nevertheless of immense value, because they are steps in the historical dialectic, just as our insights may be. We are not engaged in the philosophic task until we face the minds of Plato and Descartes and Kant and Hegel with a certain reverence born of humility, which arises from skepticism about our own relative merits. Not many of the considered ideas of the greatest minds are absolutely

<hr/>

[15] F. A. Iremonger, *William Temple*, Oxford University Press, 1948, p. 41.

silly or worthless. Therefore, though we live today, we dare never neglect the history of ideas.

2. *The second mark of philosophy in the classic tradition is catholicity.* Sectarianism is one of the chief enemies of philosophic competence, because it blinds the individual to some of the richness of experience which gives us our closest approximation to the truth. The true philosopher understands not only that wisdom did not originate with him and his generation, but also that it is probably not identical with the position of his particular party. A philosopher is a person who, though his experiences may be varied and numerous, is not satisfied with their separateness, but has a passion to connect. We are not likely to do this adequately if we become satisfied with membership in a philosophic sect, with its own standard of orthodoxy and with contempt for those who differ.

The tendency to narrowness is particularly great in the modern world, partly because we are awed by the impossibility of knowing all there is to know, and partly because of the popularity of specialization necessitated by science. But, though a certain amount of specialization is required, the specialist who is also something of a philosopher will always be aware of the danger involved in it. Arnold Toynbee's warning is highly appropriate:

And even the disinterested pursuit of science becomes sterile if it runs in narrow ruts. Specialization in particular branches of natural science soon runs dry if it is cut off from its source in comprehensive and philosophical scientific thinking.[16]

One of the points at which ecumenicity is greatly needed is in the relationships between scholars in the humanities and scholars in the natural sciences. Sometimes today the chasm between the two is so great that the two groups, far from appreciating each other, do not even know what the other is saying. To the men in the humanities the scientists seem childlike and naïve in their estimate of the human situation, while to the scientists the men of the humanities seem to be out of touch with contemporary realities.[17]

[16] E. D. Myers, *Education in the Perspective of History;* with a concluding chapter by Arnold J. Toynbee, Harper and Row, 1960, p. 275.

[17] See C. P. Snow, *Two Cultures and the Scientific Revolution,* Cambridge University Press, 1959.

If philosophy is really ecumenical rather than sectarian, it has a chance to become the bridge between these two competing cultures of our day. A philosopher, if he knows his business, understands, for example, the second law of thermodynamics almost as well as a scientist does and may even explain it more clearly. An excellent illustration of this possibility is A. N. Whitehead's use of the principle of increasing entropy in *The Function of Reason*.[18]

The deepest reason for the catholicity of philosophy is that we need each other. The realist can learn from the idealist and vice versa. We are not so rich in rational resources that we can afford to neglect any. Therefore we need the work of the philosophical analyst, but we also need the metaphysician and scholar who is concerned with values. The student who understands this will not be overimpressed with current fads. Some of them may have valid points to make, but the probability that any of them contains the whole truth, as some seem to claim, is very slight.

One corollary of the need for catholicity is how we are to present positions of which we are critical. The philosophical rule is: *Never caricature your opposition.* Sometimes positions which authors seek to demolish are presented in such an absurd way that the student has difficulty in believing that anyone ever seriously proposed the view which is being criticized. Perhaps the student is right. In any case we ought to present each position in its strongest, rather than its weakest form, and we ought never to try to minimize the difficulties of any position. Because each position has difficulties, the task of philosophy is not to find one with no rough edges, but rather to make a fair balance of comparative difficulties among competing positions. Always we are looking for some new position which has fewer or less serious difficulties than have any of the known positions. It is by this sort of search that we advance, but the broader our vision becomes the greater is the probability of our finding a better way.

3. *The third mark of a philosophy in the spirit of Socrates is that it is practical.* Pragmatism, of the kind upheld by William James, involves many logical difficulties, particularly in its doctrine or doctrines of truth, but pragmatism is certainly on the right track when its holds that philosophy must make a practical difference in

[18] A. N. Whitehead, *The Function of Reason*, The Beacon Press, 1958.

human life. The pragmatist, says James, "turns towards concreteness and adequacy, towards facts, towards action and towards power."[19] The point is similar to that made by one of William James's successors at Harvard, A. N. Whitehead, when he warned against what he called dead notions and inert ideas. The purpose of the philosopher can then be both theoretical and practical, in the sense that he is trying to get ideas clear and to reach sound conclusions, always in the hope of making a difference in human life.

What this means, in part, is that philosophy is not a parlor game. Sometimes we sneer at those who live and work in ivory towers, but if we are wise we shall pay attention to what goes on in such towers. There is a sense in which the British Museum was for Karl Marx an ivory tower, but his philosophizing in that secluded spot has made a tremendous difference, for good or ill, in the history of mankind. We may also note the vast difference made by Albert Einstein as a result of his philosophizing in Harnack House in Berlin.

That philosophy is bound to affect conduct is obvious to all who think. It is not really surprising that philosophical training has often provided an excellent education for those going into politics. R. G. Collingwood, referring to this at Oxford, points out that the practical effect is nothing of which we need to be ashamed. "The school of Green," he says, "sent out into public life a stream of ex-pupils who carried with them the conviction that philosophy, and in particular the philosophy they had learnt at Oxford, was an important thing, and that their vocation was to put it into practice."[20]

The best philosophers seek to live in such a way that they have a fair balance of theory and practice, theory being a guide to actual work in the world and practice being a laboratory test on theory. When Plato left the work of the first university of Europe, the Academy, and went to Syracuse to try to influence the government there, he was not departing from his vocation, but fulfilling an integral part of it. The fact that his effort at Syracuse was not successful is irrelevant. What is relevant is that the great man understood that it was not enough to philosophize *in vacuo*. He had to

---

[19] W. James, *Pragmatism*, Longmans, Green & Co., Inc. Courtesy of David McKay Company, 1907, p. 51.

[20] R. G. Collingwood, *An Autobiography*, Oxford University Press, 1939, p. 17.

take his chance when it came, if he really meant what he had already said.

It is not by accident or caprice that our highest earned degree, in any field of knowledge, including the natural sciences, is that of Doctor (Teacher) of Philosophy. This is because philosophy aims at the acquisition and propagation of a certain kind of knowledge, but also because this knowledge and the thinking which brings it about tend to produce a practical end. There is no necessary incompatibility between truth for its own sake and truth for a practical end, because the former leads to the latter.

It was reserved for Aristotle, the intellectual grandson of Socrates, to state more perfectly than anyone else the ideal balance of thinking and working. True happiness, he taught, is to be found "in the life of the philosopher, the life of scientific and philosophic contemplation," but this, as he conceived it, is a life of intense activity or energizing. The life of the philosopher, as he understood it, is happy, because it is a life of ceaseless intellectual activity. Happiness does not come by emphasis on amusement, but by "working in the way of excellence."[21] If it is true that the philosopher without a sense of humor is suspect, it is even more true that the philosopher is suspect if he is not happy.

The philosophical correlate of a scientific laboratory is a working library, in which students can match ideas of one generation with those of another. The only way to share ideas accurately with a great many people of different ages and nations is to put them into written form; many philosophers have used this method. One of the ablest of Oxford professors, Henry Sidgwick, said, "It ought to be regarded as the primary duty of an academic teacher, in relation to the class of students for whom advanced teaching is mainly provided, to supply the best possible instruments of self-instruction in the form of books and papers." This seems to be true, but the experience of Socrates makes us wonder.

Because we never forget that Socrates did not write, we are bound to ask seriously if philosophy should or can be written at all. The late T. E. Hulme saw the writing as something essentially unavoidable. "For I take it," he said, "a man who understands philos-

[21] Aristotle, *Nicomachean Ethics*, trans. W. D. Ross, *The Basic Works of Aristotle*, Random House, 1941, Bk. X, vii.

ophy is inevitably irritated into writing it." Then, in a bitter tone, he added, "The few who have learnt the jargon must repay themselves by employing it."[22] Whether a philosopher should write his deepest thoughts was seriously debated by Plato, with an indication in the *Epistles* that his conclusion was clearly negative. In the Second Letter, addressed to Dionysius, he said, "It is a very great safeguard to learn by heart instead of writing. It is impossible for what is written not to be disclosed. That is the reason why I have never written anything about these things, and why there is not and will not be any written work of Plato's own." However hard it may be to make this dictum consistent with the existence of great works like the *Timaeus and Laws*, which seem to represent the thought of Plato, rather than merely that of his revered teacher Socrates, he made the point again in the celebrated Seventh Letter, addressed to the friends and companions of Dion, after Dion's death. The relevant paragraph is:

For this reason no serious man will ever think of writing about serious realities for the general public so as to make them a prey to envy and perplexity. In a word, it is an inevitable conclusion from this that when anyone sees anywhere the written work of anyone, whether that of a lawgiver in his laws or whatever it may be in some other form, the subject treated cannot have been his most serious concern— that is, if he is himself a serious man. His most serious interests have their abode somewhere in the noblest region of the field of his activity. If, however, he really was seriously concerned with these matters and put them in writing, 'then surely' not the gods but mortals 'have utterly blasted his wits."[23]

We are grateful for the fact that so much of the heritage of Socrates was written and is thus transmissible to us today, but this does not mean that we have it all. We know that in the Academy there were unwritten doctrines taught. Professor Morrow of the University of Pennsylvania has helped us to see why this is so. "We learn," he says, "that these doctrines remained unwritten, not because they were regarded as a corporate possession which it was disloyal and perhaps sacrilegious to divulge, but because of the

[22] T. E. Hulme, *Speculations*, Harcourt Brace & World, Inc., 1924, p. xvi.
[23] *Thirteen Epistles of Plato*, trans. L. A. Post, Oxford University Press, 1925.

intrinsic difficulty of putting them into writing, and of learning them in any other way than by the close association between Plato and his pupils which prevailed in the Academy."[24]

In his conclusion that the most important truths cannot be put into a book Plato was probably right. The best ideas ordinarily arise in the swift give-and-take of oral dialogue and lose something when embalmed in printers' ink. But that there are some things which can be said in written form Plato evidently believed, inasmuch as he wrote a great deal. In any case it is worth while to try, for, whether the writing stimulates the reader or leaves him cold, it does tend to sharpen the mind of the author. In this vein C. S. Peirce wrote to Lady Welby to say "it is not likely to be altogether profitless for you to set down for the benefit of another what you so often ruminate on yourself; since one generally gains some new aperçu in putting one's personal meditations into shape for communication."[25]

[24] Plato, *Epistles*, G. R. Morrow, The Liberal Arts Press, Inc., 1962, p. 67.
[25] C. S. Peirce, *Values in a Universe of Chance*, Stanford University Press, 1958, p. 416.

Part I ~ METHOD

Chapter 2 ∽ *THE MYSTERY OF KNOWLEDGE*

I cannot make out to my own satisfaction what knowledge is.

SOCRATES

WHATEVER ELSE MAN IS, HE IS CLEARLY, BY HIS VERY NATURE, AN epistemological animal. When Aristotle began his most famous book with the affirmation that all men have a natural impulse to get knowledge, he was starting at the central point. Man is a creature who claims to *know*, who is deeply concerned to know more, and who is conscious of the need to distinguish between genuine and spurious knowledge. The moment we become truly aware of the possibility of error, in regard to either the objects or the processes of knowledge, we are forced, if we wish to be reasonable, to ask how genuine knowledge is possible. Some thinkers profess to reject epistemology, or the discussion of knowledge, claiming that they find it dull, but they cannot be serious about this point since each obviously has an epistemology of his own, tacit or implicit. Whenever a person makes a knowledge-claim, as all men do continually, he is assuming some thesis or theses about knowledge and consequently about himself and the external world, about his relation to that world, and about his relation to his fellows who also claim to know.

The Claim to Knowledge

Human beings habitually claim to have knowledge of a great variety of objects. Among the physical objects some are near at hand, but most are far away, some of them millions of light years away. Some are no longer existent. We talk, for example, of the great Temple in Jerusalem, even though it was destroyed by the Roman conquerors in A.D. 70. We claim to have knowledge of ancestors who are no longer living and whose bodies we have never seen. We talk confidently of the composition of bodies, such as the sun, which we have never touched and no part of which we have ever analyzed in a chemical laboratory. We have no hesitation in telling one another what occurred on our own planet when life as we know it was new. We speak of dinosaurs, though no living person ever saw one in the flesh.

What we habitually assert is that the experience called knowledge is so remarkable that it can bridge, in some sense, the chasm between the self and the other, between knower and known, between the present and the past, between the immediate locality and the remote area. Normally we see nothing strange in all this, because the claim to know is continuous, but when we begin to think seriously about it we are filled with the sense of wonder which both Plato and Aristotle said were intrinsic to philosophy.

Perhaps the most amazing fact about knowledge is the variety of alleged "objects." It should be obvious that when we speak of objects we are not meaning physical objects necessarily, for that would be begging a very important question and accepting an unsophisticated materialism. Object, as normally used in this connection, means that which we claim to know, whatever its character may be, the term being meaningful by contrast with the subject or the knower. The acceptance of this contrast between knower and known is called epistemological dualism and has been the position, in one form or another, of most philosophies, though it received its most familiar defense in what A. N. Whitehead has called "the century of genius," i.e., the seventeenth century. The emphasis of Descartes and Locke upon this analysis is largely in harmony with what the ordinary man supposes to be true, that is, that the human mind may have more or less accurate judgments of what is other than itself.

The supposed objects of human knowledge are many and various, but six have been most prominent among those considered by philosophers.

1. *The first class of alleged objects of knowledge is that of bodies.* By a body, in this connection, we mean something which has location and mass. Thus a body may be a stone, the body of an animal, the body of another human being, a planet, a tree, or anything of such a nature that it could conceivably be weighed, measured, and analyzed in a scientific laboratory. On the surface it appears, therefore, that the mind is able to achieve an important relationship between itself and something of a vastly different character. Descartes spoke of the realm of bodies as *res extensa*, in contrast to *res cogitans*, the latter having, as one of its characteristics, the capacity to become aware of the former. The mystery is that what has mass and length, can, by means of sensory impressions, give rise to thoughts which are marked by neither mass nor length. But, however great the mystery, it is the almost universal consensus of mankind that men do have knowledge of bodies, including their own.

2. *The second class of alleged objects of knowledge is that of minds other than our own.* Here we assert that we have genuine commerce with objects which are as truly independent of ourselves as are planets and stones, yet of a character wholly different from that of planets and stones. We normally suppose that we know something, though never everything, of the minds of our neighbors, by means of the motions and the sounds which are connected with their bodies. We hear voices, we read marks put on paper by other men's hands, we observe artistic effects, perhaps in stone or on musical instruments, and we infer intentions from what seem, in the order of bodies, to have been the effects of intentions.

The supposed knowledge of other minds is not limited to the minds of our fellow human beings, since many of the animals, particularly those which we call the higher animals, appear to think and to know. Though the highest of the animals other than man do not give evidence of knowledge of what is remote in time or remote in space, we realize that we are dealing with minds in animals because they seem to be aware of at least part of their environment, and to give evidence of this by what we are forced to call conscious reactions and decisions.

It is important to observe that, on the whole, we know other minds far better than we know other bodies. We know physical objects only by a great effort of the imagination. After all, I have never been a tree, and consequently, I cannot conceive what a purely vegetable existence is. Because I am a mind, it is relatively easy for me to appreciate other minds, on the fair assumption that they operate somewhat as mine does. Knowledge of other minds is less mysterious than is knowledge of other bodies, because the kinship is so much closer, but the problem is nevertheless great, in that we never seem to know other minds directly, but always through physical or sensory media. This accentuates the mind-body problem, a problem to which an entire chapter must be devoted later in this book.

3. *The third class of alleged objects of knowledge is a class with only one member, namely, one's own mind.* Man is not only the epistemological animal par excellence, he is also the self-conscious animal. There is no evidence that the other animals reflect on the act of knowing, but there is abundant evidence that man does, and that this provides one example out of many of the ways in which man is conscious that he is conscious. We can ascertain in the world at least three significant levels of reality, the *unconscious*, the *conscious*, and the *self-conscious*. Most of the external world, including that of the sidereal universe, manifestly belongs to the first or the unconscious level. A great many of what we call the higher animals belong to the second level. Without awareness, most of them would not be able to survive. Man alone is the truly self-conscious animal, criticizing his own acts, examining his own decisions, studying his own thoughts, and sometimes rejecting his own conclusions when they appear to be erroneous. Here, in knowledge of the self, there is a marked contrast to both of the classes of knowledge already outlined. Not only are we dealing here with an object which has neither mass nor length (a *res cogitans*), but also

one in which we are no longer dependent upon the mediation of sense experience. The other man's thoughts cannot be known by me, apart from my physical senses, as I listen to sounds which could be recorded in a physical laboratory or look at marks on paper, but in knowledge of myself I am free from dependence upon such media. A. N. Whitehead, in a celebrated passage, has made this point with such clarity that it is difficult to deny it.

In human experience, the most compelling example of nonsensuous perception is our knowledge of our own immediate past. I am not referring to our memories of a day past, or of an hour past, or of a minute past. Such memories are blurred and confused by the intervening occasions of our personal existence. But our immediate past is constituted by that occasion, or by that group of fused occasions, which enters into experience devoid of any perceptible medium intervening between it and the present immediate fact. Roughly speaking, it is that portion of our past lying between a tenth of a second and half a second ago. It is gone and yet it is here. It is our indubitable self, the foundation of our present existence.[1]

In so far as there is consciousness at all, there is direct awareness of something which does not reach us by the deliverances of eye or ear or tactual sensations. My recent sense of shame is something which I know better than I know almost anything, yet this is, by no stretch of the imagination, to be called sensory knowledge. Man is a creature who not only claims to know, but one who claims to know that he knows.

4. *A fourth class of alleged objects of knowledge is that of historical events.* In one sense these are forever gone. Certainly they cannot be verified by being reenacted. The vast majority of events that we claim to know are of the class which, in the nature of things, are no more. In fact, the moment we begin to discuss an event it is already gone. Our knowledge that the Prime Minister made a speech yesterday and that the army of Julius Caesar entered Britain in 60 B.C. belong to the same classification, in that both have to be known, if known at all, *indirectly.* We infer that such events occurred because of secondary evidences which we are forced to take seriously. I infer that my great-grandmother gave birth to

---

[1] A. N. Whitehead, *Adventures of Ideas,* The Macmillan Company, 1933, p. 233.

my grandfather, but I lack real proof. Obviously my evidence is exceedingly indirect, depending upon assumptions which I certainly cannot prove, yet I refer to the birth of my grandfather as an event which I somehow claim to know. It is possible that there is an inferential element in all knowledge, but this element is particularly obvious in our alleged knowledge of the past.

5. *A fifth class of alleged objects of claimed knowledge is made up of universals.* Nearly all of the advance of intellectual life has arisen from the fact that man is not satisfied to know mere particulars. Thus we claim to know the distance to remote stars, but this alleged knowledge depends upon the prior knowledge of principles of triangulation. We think we can know the height of a tree without climbing it, and that we can know the distance to the moon without going there in a rocket, but we are dependent in both instances upon a wholly generalized knowledge of the relation between angles and intermediate sides and projected perpendiculars. We claim to know that, in any triangle, whether made of chalk or of wood or of stone or of imaginary lines, the sum of any two sides is longer than the third side, and that, if the triangle has a right angle in it, the other two angles are, together, equal to it. We think we know that a square projected upon the hypotenuse, however long or however short, is equal to the combination of the squares projected upon the other two sides.

Now, on the face of it, this is an odd kind of knowledge. It does not arise from the senses, though the senses may provide a certain kind of verification. The serious scientist is seldom concerned with particulars, but is greatly concerned with laws. In this regard he is close to classic philosophy. From the time of Socrates, and even before that, the greatest thinkers have been concerned with norms and principles and values, including the laws of logic as well as the laws of things. Plato's famous doctrine of ideas is only one illustration out of many of the enduring concern for universals, by means of which order is brought into our understanding of otherwise confusing experience. Every person who uses a common noun is thereby claiming to have some knowledge of universals.[2]

[2] One of the most intelligible and persuasive arguments for knowledge of universals is that written by Bertrand Russell in *Problems of Philosophy*, Oxford University Press, 1959, p. 93. "It will be seen," says Russell, "that no

6. *The sixth class of alleged objects of knowledge is God.* As in the case of self-knowledge, we encounter here a class with presumably only one member, but the differences between the two kinds are sufficiently great to require a separate treatment of this possible referent. Knowledge of God, in this connection, belongs to general philosophy and not merely to a particular intellectual discipline called the philosophy of religion, because the claim is clearly epistemological. It has been asserted by millions of human beings that they have knowledge of a Being Who is of the nature of another Mind yet not a finite mind, that knowledge of Him does not come by the senses, as in the case of physical referents, and that, in sharp contrast to knowledge of the self, the awareness is of One who is objectively real and independent of our knowing. It is freely alleged, furthermore, that such knowledge is not a matter of mere speculation, but is verifiable by the way in which the awareness makes a difference that is observable by others and is conformable to the ordinary tests of agreement. This claim has been made, not merely by the ignorant or the thoughtless, but by some of the most careful minds known in human history, such as Blaise Pascal. It is knowledge which asserts itself to be of the immediate present, to be deeply personal, to be nonsensory, and to be concrete rather than abstract. These claims have been made by so many of such high qualifications that no philosophy can afford to neglect them. If the claims are valid our world is far more complex than we have assumed in less thoughtful moods.

Criticism of Naive Realism

Until somebody raises disturbing questions, the ordinary person believes that the world revealed to him by his senses is essentially in the form which it appears to him. The simple judgment is that the objects around us are in themselves colored, solid, and of a certain objective weight and texture. They are in no sense depend-

---

sentence can be made up without at least one word which denotes a universal. The nearest approach would be some such statement as 'I like this.' But even here the word 'like' denotes a universal, for I may like other things, and other people may like things. Thus all truths involve universals, and all knowledge of truths involves acquaintance with universals."

ent upon our power of perceiving them, but would be exactly as they seem even if there were no observers at all. The great ferns which marked the primeval forests before men appeared to see and to touch them were just as green and just as luxuriant as though knowing subjects had been there to appreciate them. This position may be called *naïve realism*, a position almost universally adopted, until philosophers begin to ask embarrassing and disturbing questions.

When any thoughtful person reflects seriously upon the knowing situation, he realizes that naïve realism cannot be justified. What is the locus of the senses? Upon reflection, we realize that all of them are centered, not in the external objects, which seem so obvious, but in the knowing mind. I watch a boat sailing away from me, as I believe, on the lake. It seems to me to be of the same size as it sails, but when I think of it I realize that the size of the image on the retina of my eye has changed constantly, and that at the end of ten minutes the boat is by no means as large as it was at the beginning of the view. The senses are clearly providing me with some materials for knowing, but they are by no means the only factor. There may be, and I think there is, an actual boat on the lake, but my experience of it is wholly within me. My past experience, my rational processes, my present expectation, influence enormously what I suppose that I "see."

Consider the top of an ordinary table. Normally we think that we experience it as a perfect rectangle, the four corners being right angles, but actually we almost never have a physical image of this kind. Instead, we have an image in which some corners are obtuse angles and some acute, depending on the perspective from which we look. The only point from which the image of the table top would be an actual rectangle is from straight above the middle, a most unusual place of observation. In a similar way we "see" the coin lying on the table and suppose that we experience it as round, but almost never is this the case. We find out, when we try to draw it, that the coin actually appears in the shape of an ellipse, the thickness changing with our approach to it. We all believe that the coin is round, but our reasons for this are not the reasons of naïve realism.

Not only the experience of sight, but every other sensory experience is fundamentally subjective. Let us say that we seem to see, at a distance, what looks to be some kind of spider. Having had some illusions before, we go over to the spot to see if we can touch the apparent object. We have sufficient sophistication to understand that we may have exercised too violently and have burst a tiny blood vessel in the eye, causing us to project a spiderlike object that is not really there. We know that vision is notoriously open to illusion, because we have frequently seen mirages. While driving on a hot day, we have seen lakes ahead of us on the highway, but have found nothing but dry surfaces as we proceeded. So we test one fallacious sense organ by using another. But we do not get out of our subjective sight or hearing, since these occur in us. If I wonder whether the object is there and go to touch it, I am not escaping from my prison of inwardness, for the sense of pressure is just as inward as is the sense of sight, and could be equally deceptive. We may do well to check one sense by using another, but the evidence which results is of the same fundamental kind.

The world may actually be quite different from the way in which we experience it. This we begin to understand when we think of color blindness or of the fact that some animals experience only blacks and grays. There are certainly potential sounds which we do not "hear" and there may be beauties of which we have never dreamed, any more than a faithful dog can imagine the depth of the conversation between his master and his master's associates. The position of the naïve realist is sound when he believes that the external world really is;[3] but he is almost certainly wrong in many of his conclusions about what the external world is.

As scientists, and particularly physicists now view matter, we are told that it is, in fact, far different from what we normally suppose that we observe. The table top, instead of being solid, as it appears, is really a whirling set of electrons and protons with vast relative spaces between them. Are the electrons yellow? Do the whirling constellations of the rose petals smell sweet? We do not know. All that we know is that they look yellow to us and smell sweet to us. But always we must distinguish between the external physical situa-

[3] The heart of all realism, whatever its degrees of sophistication, is the conviction that the external world exists independently and is not dependent upon being known.

tion, which we posit by a kind of abstraction or act of faith, and the experience, which is something of a totally different character. The old childish conundrum about the tree falling in the uninhabited forest, leading to the question whether there is "sound," arises only because, in the beginning, we fail to distinguish between object and subject. There would, we believe, though we cannot prove it, be "motions" in the forest, but there would not be "sound," if by sound we mean an experience in a perceptive subject, either animal or human.

The mystery of perception is greatly deepened if we study carefully the mechanism of sense. Sound waves travel through the atmosphere and make vibrations in our eardrums, and these vibrations are transmitted by delicate devices to the fluid of the cochlea. The swaying of hairlike threads, which results from the agitation of this fluid, sends neural impulses to the brain and then, suddenly, there is experienced sound or consciousness. "Consider," says Sir Arthur Eddington, "how our supposed acquaintance with a lump of matter is attained. Some influence emanating from it plays on the extremity of a nerve starting a series of physical and chemical changes which are propagated along the nerve to a brain cell; there a mystery happens, and an image or sensation arises in the mind which cannot purport to resemble the stimulus which excites it."[4]

A student has hardly started to think philosophically if he does not recognize the truth of Eddington's remark about the dissimilarity of the experience and the physical situation which is its natural cause. Indeed, this understanding is the beginning of sophistication on the problem of the relationship between minds and bodies, a relationship which involves problems so great that we shall need to consider them in a separate chapter.[5] Though physiological research may help by pointing out where the change occurs, in some part of the physical object called the brain, this does not solve the mystery, only locates it more precisely. No word on this topic is more profound than that of Robert Bridges, when he says in a line of poetry that "when the waves have passed the gates of ear and eye

[4] Sir Arthur Eddington, *Science and the Unseen World*, Allen and Unwin, 1929, p. 22.
[5] See Chapter 7.

all scent is lost."[6] Though behaviorism and other fundamentally simple philosophies engage in efforts to avoid this mystery, it remains with us. It is part of the stuff of which a mature philosophy must be made.

As we human beings meditate on the mystery of knowing, particularly upon the knowing of that which is fundamentally alien to ourselves, we are forced to two elementary conclusions. The first is that we know minds better than we know bodies. The analysis presented by Descartes may be criticized at many points, but he is certainly correct in his conclusion that our systematic doubt cannot include our own mind. Even when I doubt that I doubt, I am still asserting my own mental process. There is no possible way of avoiding the egocentric knowing situation. Every proposition, i.e., every statement capable of being true or false, assumes the preliminary statement, "I judge that."

The second elementary conclusion to which we are forced, when we begin to deal with epistemology is that our knowledge of the external world is intrinsically imperfect. We may be sure that many of the features of the world are very different from our suppositions about them. Our knowing apparatus is wonderful, but there is little reason to suppose that it is adequate to the need of perfect reflection of what is. It is as certain as anything can be, that our view is distorted at many points by our perspective. There are many things which we realize that we do not know, but there must be many others of which we are unaware and do not realize that we are ignorant of. We do not know now, for instance, whether there are epistemological creatures on any other planet, though it is conceivable that we may find out some day. Accordingly, the path of wisdom is to recognize our ignorance and not waste time by arguing questions on which we have no relevant evidence.

Epistemological Dualism

Modern philosophy began with the firm conclusion that knowing is indirect. What is called epistemological dualism was accepted

---

[6] R. Bridges, *The Testament of Beauty*, Oxford University Press, 1930, Bk. III, lines 669, 670. Reprinted by permission of The Clarendon Press.

by Descartes (1596-1650), and was carefully expounded and defended by John Locke (1632-1704). The student must not confuse epistemological dualism with psychophysical dualism, though both converged in seventeenth-century philosophy in the hypothesis of *ideas* and both were accepted by Descartes and Locke. It is possible to defend each of these dualisms in separation from the other because different arguments are involved, even though the two can be combined and often are. We shall have an opportunity to consider carefully the claims of psychophysical dualism in Chapter 7.

The central point of epistemological dualism is the conviction that what is given in perception, or other cognitive experiences is not identical, as a particular existent, with what is known. We know, Locke argued with great cogency, not directly and simply, but *indirectly*, i.e., by means of representative ideas. It must not be assumed that the representative theory was the peculiar doctrine of one or two men; instead it was the accepted position of the majority of thinkers in the "century of genius." It was espoused by Galileo and Hobbes, and by many others.

The doctrine rests in part upon the recognition of a radical difference between primary and secondary qualities. There is an obvious sense in which color does not belong to an object in the same sense that molecular structure does. For one thing we know that color changes with the changing light, and may actually arise from a colored light thrown upon the object. The primary qualities, *solidity, extension, figure,* etc., are those which are inseparable from the body and not dependent in the least upon their being observed. Locke's point is that the extension of a body is the same when known and when unknown. Colors, sounds, and tastes, on the other hand, are not in the object, but are potential reactions in the observer, and are therefore termed secondary qualities. In a celebrated passage Locke explains the difference as follows:

The particular bulk, number, figure and motion of the parts of fire, or snow, are really in them, whether any one's senses perceive them or no; and therefore they may be called real qualities, because they really exist in those bodies: but light, heat, whiteness or coldness, are no more really in them, than sickness or pain is in manna. Take away the sensation of them; let not the eyes see light, or colours, nor the ears hear sounds; let the palate not taste, nor the nose smell; and all colours, tastes, odours, and sounds, as they are such particular ideas, vanish and cease, and are reduced to their causes, i.e., bulk, figure, and motion of parts.[7]

In our own day Bertrand Russell has said essentially the same thing, even though he professes to hold a view that is "quite different." He is, in fact, not sure about the status of primary qualities, but he is very clear about the status of secondary qualities. "In places," he says, "where there are no eyes or ears or brains there are no colors or sounds, but there are events having certain characteristics which lead them to cause colors and sounds in places where there are eyes and ears and brains."[8]

Sensation, thought Locke, provides us with the raw materials of knowledge, but we never experience these in the raw because the mind is always performing operations of reflection upon this basic material. What we have in consciousness is not the hot *thing*, for it is remote, but the idea or representation of the *heat* of the hot thing. What the mind knows is, therefore, a world of ideas which represents real things, but is never identical with real things. If the ideas were real things, error in perception would be impossible, and we have abundant reason to know that error is widespread.

We are forced to agree with Locke and his contemporaries on the essentials of the knowing situation when we realize that there are many intermediary steps between the bare existence of an object and the consciousness of it. If it is a star, the light has come through great space, has been conditioned by the atmosphere of our particular planet, and has activated the optical equipment of at least one individual before consciousness occurs. It is wholly possible, in view of the time lapse, that the star we see may be no longer shining. Moreover, what we experience is greatly influenced by what we have been led, by means of former experiences and reflection on them, to expect. Many in our day cry out against the "bifurcation of nature" as though this were some malevolent invention of the great seventeenth-century philosophers who set the stage for the thinking of all of their successors, but when we face the hard realities of the knowing process, we find some bifurcation

[7] J. Locke, *Essay Concerning Human Understanding*, Bk. II, chap. 8, sec. 17.
[8] B. Russell, *Philosophy*, W. W. Norton & Company, Inc., 1927, pp. 157–158.

impossible to avoid. It is hard to see what is evil about it, if it happens to express what seems to be the case. Not all that the great John Locke taught is beyond criticism, but the center of his teaching is as sound as it was when it was first presented three hundred years ago. With him we can say that "it is evident that the mind knows not things immediately, but by the intervention of the ideas it has of them."[9]

One of the most important developments of modern philosophical scholarship is the late A. O. Lovejoy's examination of all of the main contemporary efforts to avoid dualism, and his showing that each phase of the "revolt against dualism" has failed to make its case. His own statement of the two main parts of the knowing situation, parts which cannot be made into one, is of great potential value to any serious student of philosophy. The twofold picture involves:

An organism confined at each moment within its own spatial bounds; in its field of awareness certain data or sense-objects which are private, transitory, conditioned by both the generic nature and the individual character of the percipient event, and existentially dependent upon this event; over against these sense-objects a world of reals not thus conditioned or relative, numerically distinct, and in all probability qualitatively different from the sense-objects; between the organism and the external realities such a relation that the latter partially determine the character of the sense-objects, though only as terminal products of a long series of intervening events; and these terminal products apprehended by the percipient as somehow "signifying" the external reality and affording him the only basis for any knowledge of its existence and of the pattern of spatio-temporal and causal relations which characterizes it.[10]

It is obvious that this classic epistemological dualism leads necessarily to a certain degree of agnosticism. Because dualism is a far cry from naïve realism, the essentials of external reality may be very different from what we tend to suppose them to be. Dualism is always on the verge of lapsing, implicitly or explicitly, into phenomenalism or subjectivism.[11] If all that we know we know by

[9] Locke, *Selections*, Charles Scribner's Sons, 1928, p. 253.
[10] A. O. Lovejoy, *The Revolt Against Dualism*, The Open Court Publishing Company, 1955, pp. 233, 234.
[11] The danger of going down the subjectivistic sliding board, until only the

means of representative ideas or *sensa*, perhaps these are all that are. Since we do not know *what* the external world is, how can we be so sure that it *is*?

As we share in the historical dialectic it is important to note the intellectual honesty of Locke. Locke had used his epistemology as a weapon to oppose those in theology and metaphysics who were reluctant to admit that, in speaking dogmatically, they were only arguing about their own ideas. But if this is true in theology and metaphysics, why is it not also true in science? It is! Locke had the courage to draw the full skeptical conclusions concerning all knowledge based on sensory experience. Like Descartes, he accepted two points of certainty in the area of knowledge, knowledge of self, which comes intuitively and therefore directly, and knowledge of God, which comes by necessary rational demonstration. All else is, by the nature of the knowing process, he held, merely *probable.* "We are so far from being admitted into the secrets of nature, that we scarce so much as ever approach the first entrance towards them." Like Descartes, Locke accepted the assumption which science seems to require, that nature is a highly ordered and inter-related system, in which each element necessarily implies each other element. But he could not accept the second Cartesian assumption which science seemed to require, the conviction that the human mind was equipped to know what the order of nature is. "We are," wrote Locke, "so far from being able to comprehend the whole nature of the universe, that we are not capable of a philosophical knowledge of the bodies that are about us, and make a part of us. . . . As to a *perfect science* of natural bodies (not to mention spiritual beings), we are, I think, so far from being capable of any such thing, that I consider it lost labour to seek after it."[12]

The most celebrated system at the beginning of the modern age, a system which has given its successors a multitude of problems as well as an honest appraisal of the human situation which it is hard to surpass, was not so much a rejection of the position of Descartes as a refinement of it. This classic position is a combination of empiricism and rationalism, the latter being necessary because sensory

immediate experience remains, with no memory, no cause, and no enduring personal identity, is shown vividly in the development through Berkeley and Hume. All good histories of philosophy include chapters on this.

[12] J. Locke, *Selections, op. cit.,* p. 251.

experience provides only the material for critical reflection. The natural fruit of this combination is dualism, subjectivism (to a degree), and a skepticism which necessitates humility in anyone who claims to know.

The Necessity of Realism

There is a sense in which we are driven, by an analysis of the facts of knowing, to the acceptance of a certain subjectivism, yet the working out of the historical dialectic makes us realize that subjectivism involves an unacceptable inference. There is in each of us an element of subjectivism, but there is also in us an element of warning against it. Part of the knowing situation is contributed by the subject, but if there is nothing other than what is given by the subject, we may as well abandon the entire enterprise. Unless there is some objective factor, i.e., some factor which *is*, whether we recognize it or not, it is difficult to see how even the dialogue can go forward. All communication is impossible if each person is locked, without means of escape, in the privacy of his own subjective consciousness. Since communication is something which we will not, and indeed cannot give up, we must ask what view of reality there is which makes genuine communication logically possible.

Because of the obvious weaknesses of all subjectivism, there has been a near consensus of opinion among twentieth-century thinkers which, without any necessary denial of the existence of subjective factors in knowing, has emphasized the reality of objective factors. Early in the century there appeared a number of arguments, of which G. E. Moore's is the most celebrated,[13] rejecting subjective idealism as an adequate account of the knowing process and affirming basic realism. The majority of philosophers in our generation, though they may differ in many concrete ways, are realists in the sense that they deny the ancient dictum that *to be is to be perceived*. They hold that there is a real world waiting to be known and that this world would *be*, even if all men and other percipient

[13] The essay, "The Refutation of Idealism" is available in G. E. Moore, *Philosophical Studies*, The Humanities Press, 1951. The original publication of the famous essay was in *Mind*, New Series, 1903, Vol. xii.

subjects were by some calamity removed from it. Nearly all believe that there are flowers blooming in deserts which have never been seen (something which the strict subjective idealist is forced to deny), and that much of the world, including stars and rocks, existed before there was any conscious perception of them. The evolutionary evidence for this conclusion seems to be overwhelming. If our reasonable inferences are correct at all, our earth existed for millions of years before it was populated by conscious inhabitants. In short, there is abundant reason to conclude that cognition exists in the world rather than the world in cognition. If this is accepted, *esse est percipi* is simply false.

Though considerations based upon the apparent history of the world are important in driving us to some minimum realism, they do not stand alone. Another important consideration is the contrast, which no one seems able to reject, between the subjective experiences of perception and those of remembering or imagining. If the object is in my mind, in the same sense that my apprehension of it is in my mind, there can be no difference between the two, yet every reasonable person admits that there *is* a difference. David Hume's effort to account for the difference by intensity will not stand examination. Since we cannot accept the consequent of the confusion of perception and imagination, we must reject the antecedent of identification of object and apprehension. The only way out of the logical difficulty is the postulation of an object that is *real*, not necessarily in the sense that I know it perfectly, but in the more modest sense that I must assume that it is not dependent for its existence on me or on others like me, and then see what epistemological picture can include this postulate without inconsistency.[14]

Part of our immense debt to A. O. Lovejoy is for the way in which he clarified the items of the epistemological faith which every man, whether he calls himself a philosopher or not, actually finds unavoidable in common life, as even Hume admitted. Whatever they may say or write when they are trying to debate some

[14] Professor John McMurray proposes a new start where we begin, not with the self as thinker, but with the self as agent. An agent necessarily has something beyond himself on which to act. See his two volumes of Gifford Lectures, *The Self as Agent*, Harper and Row, Inc., 1957, and *Persons in Relation*, Harper & Row Inc., 1961.

point, there seems to be a primary and universal faith of men to the effect that all men are living in the midst of realities which are not themselves or shadows of themselves and that, without in any way harming the transcendence of these realities, whether they be sticks or stones or other minds, men can somehow reach beyond the confines of their own restricted existences and bring some of these external existences within the orbit of their own lives, so that they are really known. A great part of wisdom about life lies in the decision to accept thoughtfully what cannot, by any intellectual legerdemain, be avoided.

The fundamental epistemological assumptions are, according to Lovejoy, five.[15] All of these assumptions relate to cognoscenda, i.e., to things-to-be-known-if-possible. Let the student, as he ponders, ask himself if he finds it possible really to reject any of the following:

1. *The assumption regarding space.* This is that many cognoscenda are at places in space external to the body of the percipient. Perception at a distance is involved in nearly all vision. "Man may be described biologically as an animal whose habitual and paradoxical employment is the endeavor to reach outside his skin."[16]

2. *The assumption regarding time.* This is that many of the things we claim to know are *not*, because they are already in the past or have not yet come to be. I contemplate today what time has, in one sense, forever extinguished. Man is habitually employed in exceeding his temporal reach.

3. *The assumption of independence.* This is that objects have a real existence and character which are not relative to the cognitive situation. Even our effort to find what things really are, which may be in contrast to how they appear, is a meaningless effort unless there already is some independent reality which we are trying desperately to understand.

4. *The assumption of social realism.* This is the assumption that the knowing and thinking person is surrounded by others of his kind, who are also engaged in knowing and in making decisions. The notion that we are surrounded by automata is merely a queer

[15] See Lovejoy, *op. cit.*, pp. 15 ff.
[16] *Ibid.*, p. 15.

affectation which there is no reason to suppose that anyone takes seriously. It is important to see that every time we argue with another person we are engaged in pure epistemology, since there is no point in arguing with another unless there is some sense in which we know him. Such social realism

seems to be one of the specific characters of *homo sapiens*, as properly a part of his zoölogical definition as his upright posture or his lack of a tail. It is implicit in all his most distinctive modes of feeling and behavior—his elaborations of language and art as a means of expression, his craving for affection, the curious and immense potency over the individual's conduct which is possessed by his belief about the thoughts and feelings of others about himself, and his occasional ability to recognize the interests of other sentient creatures as ends in themselves.[17]

5. *The assumption of verification.* This is the assumption that what I perceive and know is potentially, if not actually, "apprehensible by other knowers." My individual experience, though in one sense private, is in another sense *public*. Every man really believes in a category of publicity, in that there is a common verifiability. In short, we are forced to believe, as all of our argument assumes, in a world of objects for common knowledge. We cannot, without some perverse act of the mind, avoid the conviction that common verifiability is the ultimate criterion of the independence of the known object, the final way of distinguishing between imaginary and real objects.

It should be noted that, given these five articles of the spontaneous creed of mankind, reflection leads inevitably to some kind of dualism. This is because, if we accept the inevitable assumptions of daily life, the *cognoscendum*, the thing we seek to know and claim partly to know, is certainly separated by a chasm, whether temporal or spatial or qualitative, from the knowing event. I have my experience here, but I claim to have commerce with what is there. You have your epistemological experience in your immediate present, but you claim to have commerce with what is in sharp contrast to the present. We are minds, but we claim to know what are not minds. The precise character of the dualism to which a sound philosophy is driven may be open to debate, but the general con-

[17] *Ibid.*, p. 17.

viction that ours is a bifurcated world is inescapable. It is no wonder that Plato was a dualist in almost every important sense of the term. By epistemological dualism we mean the conclusion that knower and known are not identical. The difficulties which face a thinker who believes that a real physical world exists and who, nevertheless, fails or refuses to distinguish between *datum* and *cognoscendum* are enormous.

Critical Realism

To be a realist is to be convinced that there is a real world of independent events. The fire is not recreated when I come back into the room after an hour's absence. That it was still burning while I was away is indicated by the fact that so much of the fuel is now in ashes. The difficulty of believing that the fuel disappeared without burning or that the room comes back into existence when we see it again is really too great to be acceptable. Most of us, like Alice, cannot believe several impossible things before breakfast. But, though the case for basic realism is good, this does not mean that there is not also a case for the main contentions of historic idealism. The important thing to know is that there is a way in which both cases can be accepted without contradiction and without compromise.

The central strength of historic idealism is the recognition that, in the familiar and everyday experience of knowing, there have to be *ideas* as well as *things*, and that knowledge, accordingly, is not simple or direct. The moon, says the realist, would exist without perception, but our knowledge of the moon's true character, says the idealist, is the end term of a series of slow and painful efforts in which what we see is dependent upon our inner expectations and reflections. We know the moon only by ideas, and these ideas belong to a completely different order from that of lunar existence.

It would have been impossible for science to develop if men had not recognized that there is a realm of objects which do not satisfy the rules of membership in the physical system. Early man had much experience with "fires" that leave no ashes and "animals" that require no food. Before long, these objects which are said to exist only in dreams or hallucinations or imaginations, came to be assigned to a special category of "mental entities." If they had not been so assigned, the conception of a reign of law, on which science depends, would have been impossible of universal application. If I shut my eyes, I can, in my imagination, have a visual image of my friend entering the room, but if this is assigned to the external world, the result is total confusion. "My image, therefore, is regarded as an event in me, not as having that position in the orderly happenings of the public world that belongs to sensations."[18]

What is true, in the experience of illusion, about the subjectivity of the experience, is true in a lesser degree of all experience in which there is reason to posit an objective existence to which my idea refers. We know that the datum is not identical with the object, because the datum changes, whereas the common assumption is that the object does not thus change. The datum regarding the moon is very different in childhood from what it is in maturity, but the moon is supposedly constant. This means that there is a strong subjective element in the claim to know; this is the very point on which the idealist has always insisted.

The precise ways in which, according to a careful analysis of familiar experience, there is genuine difference between the datum and its objective referent are many, but at least five are of compelling significance.

First, there is a difference between datum and object whenever, as is usually the case, some element of memory is involved. If I say I know now that the walls of the room are darker than they were last year, my knowledge is potentially genuine, but it is certainly mediate. It is mediated by photographs, by my own fallible remembrance, by the testimony of other observers. In any case the present awareness is distinct from the past memory-object on which the present comparison depends.

In the second place, there is a difference between datum and object in the inevitable time lag between the external object and the percept. This comes in two ways, the time it takes for the external event to be reported to our sense organs and the further time, however brief, which it takes for the neural impulse to reach the cortical center, without which arrival the experience of perception does not occur. Even as early as the time of Francis Bacon the

18 B. Russell, *The Analysis of Mind*, George Allen and Unwin, 1924, p. 153.

possibility was recognized that astronomical events may have both a real time and an apparent time.[19] What we always have, in sense experience, is a more or less belated report of what may already be gone when known. The retinal image I have tonight is a far cry from the now extinct star whence the light which strikes my eye once emanated.

In the third place the existential duality is demonstrated by the well-known fact that objects differ in appearance under different conditions, some of which, like dust in the air, are outside our bodies and others, like drugs, are within our bodies. Objects differ in appearance, depending upon the cleanliness of our spectacles or even upon the fatigue of our eyes. The fact that the basic and elementary relativity of knowledge occurs to almost everyone in infancy does not keep it from being an important philosophical discovery. Even a child sees the fallacy of naïve realism.

In the fourth place is the discrepancy between datum and object which is demonstrated by conflicts of reports among different observers, when all are claiming to have the same referent. The same object cannot, in the same sense, be spherical and flat, but the representative knowledge of different observers so reports it. When the observations are contradictory somebody is wrong. The one who supposedly envisions the object correctly, might be supposed to do so by some monistic identification of knowing experience with known object, but in that case, all of those who claim to know and have a different report must have their knowing experience mediated by data which are not identical with the object.

Fifth, there is the type of separation between datum and object which we call error or illusion. At a very early age we learn that the handle of a spoon in the glass half-filled with water appears bent, though we *believe* that it is really straight. Error is so widespread that a full and careful consideration of it is important for any philosophy which seeks the truth about our world. Suffice it to say now that the thing about which we err cannot be a thing immediately present to our consciousness. The experience cannot be erroneous, since it is what it is; error has no significance unless it

[19] Francis Bacon, *Novum Organum,* II, 46. The point was established by Roemer in 1675.

is possible for there to be a contrast between our experience and that to which it refers.

We conclude, then, as a point from which we must proceed as our dialectical process develops, that knowledge is highly complex, involving both an inner subject and an outer object. Realists we must be, for realists we inescapably are, but our realism must never be simple and naïve. Our realism must be critical, because we can never escape the predicament in which we, as knowing subjects, bring our own presuppositions into the total process. Since we cannot alter this situation, we must find ways in which our knowledge is made relatively more genuine. If this means that we can never know anything perfectly, in its total objectivity, that is something to be accepted with humility, for that is the way things are.

Chapter 3 ∽ THE NATURE OF TRUTH

Truth is never created.

W. P. MONTAGUE

THOUGH, IN ORDINARY SPEECH, WE FREQUENTLY USE CERTAIN GREAT words, such as "truth," "knowledge," "meaning," and "reality" almost interchangeably, there is value in trying to make a clear distinction between them. Even though we are frequently forced to use these terms in conjunction, the combination is more fruitful if the denotation of each particular term is kept carefully in mind.

Knowledge, as we have argued in the preceding chapter, arises when the mind, having subjective experiences or impressions, refers these to objects which the mind is then said to "know." This knowledge is of various degrees of refinement, depending in large measure upon particularized methods of verification, most of which are possible only by means of communication with other knowing minds. Many of these communications exist by means of statements which we soon recognize as being either misleading or trustworthy or a mixture of the two. If we have reason to believe that they are trustworthy, we say that the statements are true. If the objects with which we seem to have contact turn out to be merely imaginary, we say that they lack reality, that they are fanciful, and therefore not real. Knowledge has meaning only in reference to *minds*; truth has meaning only in reference to *propositions* which are created and judged by minds; reality has meaning only in reference to *objects*, these being said to be real when there is reason to believe that they exist independently of being known. There is no reason to suppose that real objects are limited to the physical. The following formula may be a means of clarification:

> *Minds* may be knowing or ignorant.
> *Propositions* may be true or false.
> *Objects* may be real or imaginary.

The order of consideration is important. The consideration of reality inevitably comes late, because there is a profound sense in which the effort to distinguish the real is the final purpose of all philosophizing. Knowledge comes early, because the claim to know is that with which we ordinarily start any fundamental inquiry. But we hardly start before we realize that some supposed knowledge will not bear full examination. We are therefore forced to proceed to an examination of the meaning of truth, which is that upon which the genuineness of knowledge depends.

The Fact of Error

If we follow the method of Descartes, resolutely doubting all that it is possible to doubt, and retaining only that which is indubitable, we soon come to the realization that it is the lot of men to make mistakes. The fact of error is so obvious that we often fail to note it or to see its deep significance. Day after day in the newspapers some statement of fact is confidently made, only to be denied on a later day. Of course it is still possible that the original story is the true one, but in that case the denial is itself false. Thus, in any case, there is a falsity, because somebody is in the wrong. The heart of the principle of noncontradiction, on which we are forced to depend, since we affirm it even when we try to deny it, is that, when two propositions are in diametrical opposition, somebody is wrong. When two men argue about the number of persons in the room at a given moment, we may not be sure which reporter is wrong, but we can be sure that one reporter is wrong. Therefore error is of the very stuff of daily life and communication, because propositions which are diametrically opposed are of distressingly common occurrence.

Error appears in all kinds of human situations, including those which involve judgment. Even the wisest of men make some glaring mistakes. It is hard to believe, but we must accept it as a fact, that Dr. Samuel Johnson held that Milton's poem beginning: "Methought I saw my late espoused saint" was a poor sonnet. The sharp contrasts in judgment of the character of public men are well known and some of these are involved in intimate portraits. One of the wives of Brigham Young said, "A kinder, more indulgent, more affectionate husband than mine cannot be seen," but Ann Eliza, his twenty-seventh wife, called him "a cruel despot." It will generally be conceded that each lady reported on the aspect of the great man which she saw, somewhat after the manner of the blind men of Hindustan, but in so far as each lady turned her observation into a universal judgment of Young's character, one of them was in error.

Every claim to progress involves the assertion of error. If I move to a position which is a better position on any subject, this is possible only because of my recognition of previous error. And the earlier propositions were erroneous at the moment when they were made, not merely now. If it is an improvement in truth to affirm the spherical character of the earth, the ancient propositions about the flatness of the earth were erroneous when made. If it is a moral improvement for a community to move over to the rule of law from the rule of mob violence, then it follows that those who formerly approved mob action were in error.

We mentioned, in Chapter 2, the well-known errors of perception which are undoubtedly more numerous than we can ever realize. But error also appears in memory, the form in which most of our mediate or representative knowledge appears. Nearly everything we discuss involves memory experience, since the immediate perception is already in the past by the time it is possible for us to discuss it. But here error creeps in at all points. I "remember" that I put the keys in my coat pocket, but I am demonstrably self-deceived, for the keys are not in the pocket, and there has been no possibility of theft or removal, for no human being, including myself, has been in the closet in the period subsequent to the alleged deposit. Therefore, I was wrong.

In most cases of error which is established, and therefore partially transcended, the original affirmation of the erroneous proposition had a certain amount of justification. *The New York Times,* in printing the retraction of the now rejected story says, "We secured the story from generally reliable sources." When people believe something, they obviously believe it *for a reason.* The human recognition that the apparently good reasons may not be good enough is a philosophical step forward in the consciousness of the race. One of the most instructive examples of widespread acceptance of error as truth is that of the Piltdown "man." Many contemporary adults remember vividly the experience in school and college of discussing, in a supposedy learned manner, the evidence which the skeleton, found in southern Britain, allegedly provided for the antiquity of man. Once this "man" was the subject of several paragraphs in the standard scientific textbooks, especially those concerned with human evolution. Later we had reason to conclude that the whole story was a giant hoax. If this does not increase our skepticism about other evidences in other fields of inquiry, we have not progressed very far in philosophy. Error, we conclude, is something of which we can be sure, and our certainty of this can be stated dialectically. Either there is error or there is not. If there is not, then the judgment that there has been error is itself erroneous; therefore, in any case, there is error.

It is part of the great and often unrecognized merit of the philosophical position of Josiah Royce that he had the wisdom to start with the fact of error and to ask, persistently, what view of reality the universal recognition of error requires. To find a point of universal agreement is a very great thing. The common assumption which skepticism, far from rejecting, only serves to emphasize, is that truth implies an objective order. We cannot be wrong unless there is something to be wrong *about!* On the basis of sheer subjectivism, error would be impossible, for then there is no referent. Being sure is not a mark of truth, for the writers of the textbooks were sure about the Piltdown man. Error, if accepted, necessitates the affirmation of an objective situation to which the erroneous proposition refers and about which it is wrong.

The Objectivity of Truth

The dialectical step by which we move from the ubiquity of error to the objectivity of truth is one of the most important which the human mind can take. It provides us with a complete answer to the naïve relativism in which we assume that truth is conformity to our own judgments or that it is wholly a matter of perspective. All thought, including all of the criteria which we develop in order to criticize our thought, must, in the nature of things, be subjective, but the very effort to create means of self-criticism entails the notion that our thought *refers* to that which is more than subjective. The paradox is that, on the one hand we can never escape from our own self-consciousness and that, therefore, all evidence is finally judged by our own inner certitude, but on the other hand our certitude is concerned characteristically with something which it is trying to discover, that is, something which, of itself, is independent of our own perspectives. Every thinker who is humble enough to know that he may be wrong, i.e., that his own perspective is inadequate or partial, is demonstrating this paradox, and tacitly affirming the truth of the proposition. The man who affirms that the physical world was created out of nothing in 4004 B.C. is making a proposition which may be true and may be false, but the truth or falsity is not relative to his own perspective or to his wishes or his beliefs; it depends upon whatever truly occurred. That we cannot in our finitude know what occurred, does not alter the situation in the least. Methodological limitations of knowledge have nothing whatever to do with the truth of propositions and they do not depend upon the propositions being uttered. The truth (or falsity) of a proposition does not depend upon the operation by which it is verified (or rejected).[1]

Only by the acceptance of such a dictum is it possible to maintain any distinction between appearance and reality. This follows

[1] W. P. Montague, *The Ways of Knowing*, The Macmillan Company, 1925. This is still the most advanced work available in defense of the objectivity of truth, with clear recognition of alternatives and the various difficulties involved.

from the fact that each philosopher regards his position as true and that of his opponents as erroneous. Unless truth is objective, there is nothing but confusion. In the degree to which all relativist thinkers have made us realize that each of us sees the world from his own personal or socioeconomic viewpoint, we can be glad, but whenever popular relativism goes on beyond this modest observation, to the claim that there is no objective truth to be known, the entire validity of thought is undermined. G. D. Kaufman begins his important book by the following reference to the contemporary tendency:

Many contemporary writers take for granted that the relativity of truth and value is a demonstrated fact. Objective descriptive studies in history and the social sciences appear to have revealed wide variations in valuation, judgment, and cognition between different cultures and even between individuals within a given culture. From this fact it is often inferred that values and even truth are relative to the historical context or to the individual personality. Not even the prestige of natural science has preserved it immune from relativistic analysis.[2]

The task of a philosopher is not to accept the popular relativism and not to reject it, but to analyze it as carefully as possible, in the light of the probability that part of it can be accepted, while another part of it is rejected. Popular relativism is in a strong position when it points out the limitations of the particular culture in which each man stands, thus warning him against absolute judgments. It is always important to realize that Gulliver looks large to one race and small to another. In short, no people can achieve a complete transcendence of its starting point, though all scientific or rational thinking constitutes an effort to move in this direction. Whenever relativism reminds men that they inevitably look at the world from a particular vantage point it is performing a useful purpose. This is particularly the case when we are engaged in making value judgments. The problem of West Berlin, for example, looks differently when viewed from the East and from the West.

Valuable as all relativism is in the development of a certain humility about our judgments, it represents a glaring non sequitur when it goes on to assert that, consequently, there is no objective

[2] G. D. Kaufman, *Relativism, Knowledge and Faith*, University of Chicago Press, 1960, p. 3.

truth. Our failure to know the truth perfectly about any subject is no evidence whatever that there is no truth about it. Indeed, the more we contemplate, the more we realize that, unless there is a truth, there is no point whatever in trying to overcome our relative failures to achieve it. The only advantage of pointing out the limitations of a particular perspective lies in the expectation of becoming partially liberated from it.

We think it is true, for example, that Adolf Hitler died in a bunker near the Brandenburg Gate during the siege of Berlin in 1945, but we are not absolutely sure. It is conceivable that we may some day learn that our belief has been wrong. Will this mean that the truth about Hitler's death is thereby shown to be relative to our changed position? Not at all. Our belief is relative to our position because belief is always subjectively conditioned; it always occurs in minds. But the truth about Hitler's death is whatever it was. Here is something utterly independent of our wishes or of our changes in ideology. The history of World War II may be very different when written by a Russian or by a scholar of the West, but unless there is an objective truth which both are trying to discover, their very efforts to be scholarly are themselves ridiculous.[3]

As finite men we are not in a position to talk with any competence about *absolute* truth, though this may, in the long run, be a meaningful expression, but we are in a position to talk about *objective* truth. By this we mean the truth in any situation which we discover rather than invent. We do not possess it beyond a shadow of doubt, but all of our efforts to possess it are based on the intelligent assumption that it *is*. Whenever we try to find which propositions among several are true, and which are false, we are proceeding on the assumption that there is a genuine difference between the two conditions and that, with sufficient care, we can learn to make the distinction. Anyone who carries his relativism so far that he denies the objectivity of truth is, of course, free to do so, but he cannot do so without, at the same time, destroying the entire motivation, not only of philosophy but also of science. If

[3] Lord Acton believed that one mark of the development of history into a true science would be a situation in which a life of Martin Luther, written by a Roman Catholic, would be substantially the same as one written by a Protestant.

the objectivity of truth cannot be rationally defended, this might as well be the end of the book.

In the vast literature of philosophy one passage stands out above all others in the support of the objectivity of truth, by means of the dialectical analysis of subjectivism and the consequent exposure of its self-contradiction. The passage occurs in the *Theaetetus*, one of the most mature of all of Plato's writings and one apparently written when the author was at the height of his powers. Socrates is presented as trying to be utterly fair to the famous position upheld by Protagoras in his book called *Truth*, which we know only by references to it. The much-quoted maxim of Protagoras, "Man is the measure of all things," was intended to hold that each man sees the world from his own subjective point of view and that objective truth, consequently, cannot even be discussed. Those who wish to appreciate philosophical method should study the following segment of the celebrated conversation between Socrates and Theodorus, the outcome of which applies equally to contemporary and to ancient subjectivism.[4]

Soc. Just think, Theodorus; would any follower of Protagoras, or yourself, care to contend that no person thinks that another is ignorant and has false opinions?

Theo. No, that is incredible, Socrates.

Soc. And yet this is the predicament to which the doctrine that man is the measure of all things inevitably leads.

Theo. How so?

Soc. When you have come to a decision in your own mind about something, and declare your opinion to me, this opinion is, according to his doctrine, true to you; let us grant that; but may not the rest of us sit in judgement on your decision, or do we always judge that your opinion is true? Do not myriads of men on each occasion oppose their opinions to yours, believing that your judgement and belief are false?

Theo. Yes, by Zeus, Socrates, countless myriads in truth, as Homer says, and they give me all the trouble in the world.

Soc. Well then, shall we say that in such a case your opinion is true to you but false to the myriads?

Theo. That seems to be the inevitable deduction.

Soc. And what of Protagoras himself? If neither he himself

---

[4] Plato, *Theaetetus*, trans. Fowler, Loeb Classical Library series, Harvard University Press, 1928, pp. 109, 111.

thought, nor people in general think, as indeed they do not, that man is the measure of all things, is it not inevitable that the "truth" which he wrote is true to no one? But if he himself thought it was true, and people in general do not agree with him, in the first place you know that it is just so much more false than true as the number of those who do not believe it is greater than the number of those who do.

Theo. Necessarily, if it is to be true or false according to each individual opinion.

Soc. Secondly, it involves this, which is a very pretty result; he concedes about his own opinion the truth of the opinion of those who disagree with him and think that his opinion is false, since he grants that the opinions of all men are true.

Theo. Certainly.

Soc. Then would he not be conceding that his own opinion is false, if he grants that the opinion of those who think he is in error is true?

Theo. Necessarily.

Soc. But the others do not concede that they are in error, do they?

Theo. No, they do not.

Soc. And he, in turn, according to his writings, grants that this opinion also is true.

Theo. Evidently.

Soc. Then all men, beginning with Protagoras, will dispute—or rather, he will grant, after he once concedes that the opinion of the man who holds the opposite view is true—even Protagoras himself, I say, will concede that neither a dog nor any casual man is a measure of anything whatsoever that he has not learned. Is not that the case?

Theo. Yes.

Soc. Then since the "truth" of Protagoras is disputed by all, it would be true to nobody, neither to anyone else nor to him.

The Answer of Pragmatism

In the long dialectic of intellectual history the thesis of objectivity has been challenged by many antitheses, one of the most persuasive of these being the general answer which we know as pragmatism. Pragmatism, without the name, has been with us a long time and is indeed, as William James said, a new name for an old way of thinking. The term was given wide publicity, chiefly though not solely, by American thinkers near the end of the nineteenth century and at the beginning of the twentieth century. The term *pragmatism* was introduced by C. S. Peirce (1839–1914) in an article, "How to Make Our Ideas Clear," published in 1878 in a most unlikely place, *The Popular Science Monthly*. The article was not widely influential at the time, but is well known to philosophers today, partly because it influenced William James and, through him, helped to inaugurate a conscious movement.

Peirce did not claim to be saying anything fundamentally new, and indeed would have been very doubtful of it if it had been. It was his firm conviction that "any philosophical doctrine that should be completely new could hardly fail to prove completely false."[5] While pragmatism, in the teaching of James, soon became a doctrine of truth, for Peirce it was primarily a doctrine of *meaning*. His most influential insight was to the effect that we frequently argue, not because we differ, but because we have not made clear what we mean. We cannot know what we mean unless we establish a way to say what we mean. Now the only meaning of a term, he contends, is the difference it makes in some experience. To say that an object is soft means only one thing—it can be easily scratched or indented. Weight means absolutely nothing except the fact of falling in the absence of support. If two doctrines cannot make any conceivable operational difference, they are the same doctrine, whatever words may be employed.

To illustrate his theory of meaninglessness Peirce points to the conflict between Roman Catholics and Protestants over the doctrine of transubstantiation. The Roman Catholics hold that the elements become *actually* the flesh and blood of Christ, when appropriately blessed, but admit that they continue to demonstrate the operational characteristics of bread and wine. A difference which does not *make a difference*, says Peirce is really no difference. The central affirmation is: "If one can define accurately all the conceivable experimental phenomena which the affirmation or denial of a concept could imply, one will have therein a complete definition of the concept, and *there is absolutely nothing more in it*."[6]

The theory of meaning which Peirce promulgated might just as

[5] J. Buchler (ed.), *The Philosophical Writings of C. S. Peirce*, Dover Publications, Inc., 1955, p. 269.
[6] *Ibid.*, p. 252.

well be called "futurism," for it involves the idea that "The rational meaning of every proposition lies in its future." This is because meaning is found in conduct, and future conduct is the only conduct subject to self-control. This leads to certain paradoxes, one of which is that at the end of history no proposition is meaningful, for there is then no future.

It is important to remember that, whatever seeds of relativism Peirce sowed, he was himself an orthodox realist and an epistemological dualist.[7] The development of pragmatism as a conception of truth arose with Peirce's contemporaries, particularly William James (1842–1910). James proposed the pragmatic approach as giving, not only the meaning of meaning, but finally, the meaning of truth itself. "What difference would it practically make to anyone," he asks, "if this notion rather than that notion were true? If no practical difference whatever can be traced, then the alternatives mean, practically the same thing, and all dispute is idle."[8] Here we find meaning and truth being subtly combined. Without fully realizing that he was doing so, James soon championed a number of ideas which got him into philosophical hot water. Truth is that which "works"; "a truth is anything which it pays to believe." These possible conclusions opened the door to critics who seemed to James to be unfair because he thought that they were attacking a caricature of his doctrine, but it cannot be doubted that he invited such attack by his exuberant and epigrammatic way of writing.

Often it is hard to know which of two contradictory positions James espoused. Thus, in a single passage, he seems to uphold, on the one hand, the position that truth is objective and unalterable, while on the other, he makes truth into a changing function of our own experience. First he wrote, "Truth . . . is a property of certain of your ideas. It means their agreement as falsity means their disagreement with reality. Pragmatists and intellectualists both accept this definition as a matter of course." But a few lines below he wrote, "Truth *happens* to an idea. It *becomes* true, is *made* true by events."[9]

[7] *Ibid.*, Chapter 19.
[8] W. James, *Pragmatism*, Longmans, Green & Company, Inc., 1928, p. 45. Courtesy of David McKay Company.
[9] W. James, *The Meaning of Truth*, Longmans Green & Company, Inc.,

At first the average student tends to be drawn enthusiastically to the doctrine that truth means that which works. We seem here to be dealing with the warm life of everyday experience and to be far removed from dull intellectual arguments. But as the student advances he begins to ask embarrassing questions. Two important philosophers were especially effective, early in our century, in phrasing for students these questions better than they could phrase them themselves. One of these was Bertrand Russell, then at the height of his great powers as a philosophical analyst. He examined ruthlessly the attractive epigrams: Do we really mean that the useful is the same as the true? How about Rousseau's social contract? It is surely a myth, for no reputable historian believes that a contract of this kind was ever made. But, since Rousseau's idea was undoubtedly useful in stirring up revolution, James would seem to be forced to accept it as true. In more recent times Adolf Hitler promulgated the idea of the innate superiority of the Nordic man. No true philosopher seriously accepts the doctrine as valid, but it certainly was useful in so arousing the German people that they held off the combined power of many other nations for nearly six years. We have to face the fact that there are useful falsehoods, but the moment we face this, we realize that the doctrine that that which works is true is too simple. Furthermore, we soon realize that it undermines the augustness of truth in that the truth changes with our changing success. Was the Nordic myth true in 1941 and false in 1945?

The bearing of the pragmatism of James on our most important beliefs is now obvious. When a believer says that "God exists" he does not mean that the hypothesis is one which works satisfactorily, in the sense that it brings peace and power. Such a belief would make wholly unnecessary the arduous pursuit of religious truth. Russell, though himself a religious unbeliever, sees this perfectly. He says that "what religion desires is the conclusion that God exists, which pragmatism never even approaches."[10]

1909, p. v. Courtesy of David McKay Company. In an address before the American Philosophical Association at Cornell in December, 1907, James, speaking on "Truth" said, "My account of truth is realistic and follows the epistemological dualism of common sense."

[10] B. Russell, *Philosophical Essays*, Longmans, Green & Company, Inc., 1910, p. 135. Courtesy of David McKay Company.

The strongest attack on pragmatism from the American side of the Atlantic was centered, and continues to be centered, on the fundamental ambiguity of the pragmatic doctrine. What is meant precisely by the popular word "works"? Does it refer to emotional satisfaction or mere expediency or survival value or cash value or what? The most careful of all known expositions of the multiple possibilities of the pragmatic formula was provided by A. O. Lovejoy in his celebrated article on the ambiguity of pragmatism. The article is both an important step in the dialectic, since it presents questions which pragmatists must answer if they wish to be taken seriously, and provides an admirable example of the valuable philosophical habit of making distinctions when distinctions exist.[11]

Because pragmatism appears to the average man so promising, the exhibition of its logical shortcomings seems often to be an unkind blow, yet the blow is unavoidable if we are to carry on the beneficent dialectic. Pragmatism seems hopeful because it appears to be down to earth and to provide an escape from unprofitable questions, but deeper reflection is sure to cast doubt.

Pragmatists subsequent to William James have tried to restate the position with care, in the effort to avoid the most obvious mistakes of the earlier formulation. John Dewey tended to avoid the word "truth" because of its overtones suggesting the fixed and the eternal and proposed, and instead, to speak of "warranted assertability." Dewey used illustrations to show that there are propositions which have no antecedent truth, but become true only by the process of verification after a completed action. Suppose we ask the truth of "X is elected." This has no truth until the election actually has occurred and therefore, in James's phrase, "becomes" true.

Dewey's mistake is that of essentially limiting himself to problems of this particular kind, those in which the event is still undecided or undetermined. What is really strange is that he did not give equal attention to problems of another kind, which we constantly face in ordinary experience. For example, "There is a usable stamp in my desk drawer." Everyone will recognize that the truth or falsity of the proposition about the existent stamp cannot be

[11] A. O. Lovejoy, "The Thirteen Pragmatisms," *Journal of Philosophy*, 1908, Vol. V.

ascertained until I open the drawer, but it is surely obtuse to claim that my opening the drawer makes it true. If we do not admit the truth of the statement that there was a stamp here all of the time, it is difficult to see how we can proceed with any intelligent discussion at all.

Or consider, from the point of view of Dewey, a question of historical composition. Many Biblical scholars mention a compilation which they designate by the neutral term "Q," and which they believe was used by the authors of both Matthew and Luke in producing their gospels. Though some speak confidently of this document, supposedly devoted to oral discourses, no person has claimed to have seen it. It is conceivable that we might find this document, as we have found the Dead Sea Scrolls. The instrumentalist of the Dewey persuasion would be forced to say that the proposition "Q was in writing" only became true upon the act of discovery. Such a position is intrinsically absurd.

In this, as in so many hard situations, we gain light by making distinctions. There are questions in which the truth is futuristic, as pragmatists have always claimed, but there are other truths which are established, as common sense has always claimed. The truth about human flight to other planets is, at this writing, futuristic and still to be determined, but the truth about the number of moons encircling Jupiter is established and our propositions about them are already either true or false. Pragmatists are not justified in adhering to a meaning of truth which rules out meaningful problems in which millions of thoughtful men and women are reasonably interested.

Another variant on the pragmatic position is that of F. C. S. Schiller. He upholds the dictum "all truths are useful," but denies that this position is a definition and therefore convertible. In this, his separation from James is extreme, for James held that the propositions "It is useful because it is true" and "It is true because it is useful" must be understood to "mean exactly the same thing."[12] Schiller is more moderate and careful. "Pragmatism," he says, "does not affirm that whatever is useful or works is true. To assert this would be to ignore the existence of lies, fictions, errors, methodological assumptions and other varieties of truth claim, which

12 James, Pragmatism, op. cit., p. 204.

are not generally called truths." Schiller's variation on the pragmatic theme is an emphasis on the relativism of truth as well as of
right and good. The truth, he insists, may be different for different
persons. It must be "developed by the continuous correction of
errors and the substitution of better and more satisfactory views
for worse."[13] This, he holds, is highly conducive to toleration and
social harmony, but it is hard to avoid the conclusion that it makes
for absolute confusion. Perhaps the truth about what ought to be
done about a divided Germany is one thing for the Communists
and another for the West. Since the convictions are contradictory,
the only reasonable conclusion is that there is no truth at all. When
does tolerance become fuzziness?

The seed of logical relativism, with its resulting confusion, was
sown by William James when he said, "The truth of the idea is one
relation of it to the reality, just as its date and place are other
relations."[14] Now, date and place are obvious relations. We are
forced, if we are to discuss them, to set purely arbitrary zero
points in latitude and time and to measure from these. But truth is
completely different. Truth refers to propositions which are resultant, not of some arbitrary establishment, but of what is—
whether we like it or not, and whether we know it or not. There
cannot be a false date, for we can follow any system of dating we
happen to like. We can call this A.D. 17, if we so choose. This
would not be false, but merely silly. But to say, "Caesar never
existed," is to say something of a totally different character. It is
to say something false. Truth does work, of course. It has fruits, but
the fruits follow from the truth; they do not constitute it.

Correspondence

The plain man has what seems to him a perfectly clear conception of the meaning of truth. What I say, he will insist, is true if
it corresponds to the fact, and it is false if it conflicts with the fact.
When I speak of living chestnut-trees the truth of what I say is

---

[13] F. C. S. Schiller, "Pragmatism," Hastings House, Encyclopaedia of Religion and Ethics, Vol. X, p. 150.
[14] James. The Meaning of Truth, op. cit., p. 234.

dependent wholly on whether all chestnut-trees have died. The fact that I may not know whether any are living has no bearing at all, the plain man supposes, on the truth of my statement. Truth, he believes, is wholly a matter of correspondence with fact and never with knowledge or belief, both of which may be falsely claimed.

This straightforward conception of truth is not only the view of the plain man, but also of a great proportion of the professional philosophers of the past and present. The most famous of early exponents of what is called the correspondence doctrine of truth was Aristotle, who made his reasoning on the subject explicit in his *Metaphysics*. "A false account," Aristotle said, with the clarity which comes from profundity, "in so far as it is false, is the account of things that are not."[15] What this means is that there is an objective situation and that men make propositions about the various details of the situation. Truth, then, belongs to propositions which in themselves refer to what is or is not.

The correspondence theory of truth has been upheld with great conviction by leading philosophers of the twentieth century, including men who differ widely on other subjects. Among these are Bertrand Russell and the late Arthur O. Lovejoy. At the same time strong objections occur to them as they study the problem. The strongest objection is that correspondence between judgment and fact is absolutely impossible, because we never know a raw fact. How can you test the correspondence between two elements, in this case the judgment and the fact, if you can never line them up for comparison? I judge that my fire is still burning, so I investigate to see whether my judgment is a true one. I look and see flames, but I am still unable to isolate the fact from the subjective experience, because the vision and the sense of warmth are still experiences of the observing subject. This, in the nature of the case, is a predicament from which I shall never escape. It follows from this that we cannot defend the simple notion of correspondence as the assertion that our ideas are copies of reality. We have reason to believe in objective reality, but we never encounter it in the raw. We talk much of facts, but we need to be reminded that every alleged fact

[15] Aristotle, *Metaphysics*, trans. R. Hope, Bk. Delta, 1024, University of Michigan Press, 1960, p. 120.

of which we speak is actually the way the situation appears to some individual mind.

The defense of common sense correspondence is possible, providing we are more precise about both ends of the correspondence. It is too vague to say that truth is the "correspondence of our ideas with reality," since both idea and reality tend to be ambiguous. The correspondence we claim, in ordinary life, is that between propositions and the precise situations to which they refer. It is not necessary that these propositions be uttered, in order for such a conception of truth to make sense. The proposition, "The earth is essentially spherical in shape," was true long before the proposition was put into a sentence, and it was true because the earth really is of that shape. How we know it is of that shape is another question. It was true before it was believed. This becomes clear when, with Lord Russell, we make a valuable distinction and point out that "beliefs (a) depend upon minds for their existence, (b) do not depend on minds for their truth."[16] The falsity or truth of a proposition arises not from the intensity with which it is asserted, but from the existence or nonexistence of that to which it makes reference.

This kind of analysis helps us to see that the difficulty raised by William James and others, to the effect that judgment and fact cannot be compared, is not as serious a difficulty as it appears to be. The opinion that it is a difficulty arises from the failure to distinguish between the tests of truth and the meaning of truth. There may be many valuable tests of truth, but absolute confusion reigns unless truth means just one thing, real agreement between what is believed and what is. The pragmatic test of utility may be one important test, but it cannot be the whole meaning of truth, because there has to be something which is being tested. The correspondence conception of what we mean by truth is the only philosophical antidote to the subjective relativism which Aristotle both feared and denounced. He was well aware of the subjective factors in perception, and knew that emphasis on these led some thinkers to assert that everything that appears is true. But he saw

[16] B. Russell, The Problems of Philosophy, Oxford University Press, 1959, p. 129.

that this would make nonsense out of all discussion of what is. The crucial statement is "For perception is surely not of itself, but there is something else besides the perception, and that is necessarily prior to the perception."[17] That which is necessarily prior to the perception is that to which we refer when we endeavor to tell the truth. It is not something which we make; it is something which we claim to discover.

Coherence

The theory of truth which seems most often to present a live alternative to correspondence is that of coherence. This theory has been defended with great persuasiveness by idealist philosophers, the most competent in our generation being Professor Brand Blanshard of Yale University. The theory begins with the common sense observation that we normally test the truth of empirical statements by their consistency with other statements which we already know to be true. Since, with a little sophistication, we realize that we cannot go beyond judgments to unexperienced fact, our only recourse is to see one judgment in the light of others. Though I cannot avoid the egocentric predicament, in asking whether my fire is burning, I can add deliberately to my experiences of vision or warmth, or both. I can have new experiences of my own, and I can ask other human beings about their experiences. If the various reports corroborate one another, if they are mutually consistent, and if there are no experiences which bring in inescapable contradiction, we say in practice that the truth has been discovered. The principle which affirms that two contradictory propositions cannot both be true is not only accepted but is thus made indispensable to the entire intellectual undertaking.

In court we use the principle of coherence all of the time. We are forced to depend upon testimony, since it is really all that we have. There is no way in which the court can reach the fact directly, even though it is that for which a search is being made. For one thing, the fact is already in the past. Even fingerprints do not obviate the necessity of depending upon witnesses. It may be a

[17] Aristotle, op. cit., p. 81.

working assumption that no two people have the same fingerprints, but no one *knows* that this is the case. Accordingly, we bring in a variety of witnesses and all that the lawyers can do is to try to see whether the testimony is coherent. If a lawyer for the opposition believes that a witness is lying, he tries, tirelessly, to catch him in a contradiction, his questions being phrased with this purpose in mind.

The philosophy back of this legal procedure involves the conviction that the truth is something which can be explicated endlessly, without contradiction. The liar may avoid getting caught, but the effort to keep his false propositions consistent with one another is terribly demanding. Only a very intelligent man can present a false story coherently over a long period. This is because he must remember everything which he has said, and this is far more difficult than sticking to the simple truth of what has occurred.[18]

The strength of the coherence theory of truth is evident when we realize that no fact stands alone and isolated from its context. How, for example, can we know the truth about what transpired at the Yalta Conference, unless we know the state of President Roosevelt's health at the time, the extent of promises already made, the cleverness of Stalin, and the general conditions of the end of World War II? The truth on many subjects is amazingly complex. This is what gives credence to the statement that truth depends upon consistency. "Any judgment is true," wrote the late Professor Edgar S. Brightman of Boston University, "if it is both self-consistent and coherently connected with our system of judgments as a whole."[19] It should be noted that the idealist philosopher, in holding this position, is not a mere subjectivist. He is saying that truth refers to more than the experience of the individual; his extrapersonal reference is to the entire set of other judgments. The greatest strength of his position lies in the recognition we have already noted, that never do we go beyond judgments to the unjudged fact. The upholder of coherence may therefore say that he is appealing to all that there is to appeal to.

[18] For an incisive examination of the significance of witness and testimony see Gabriel Marcel, *The Philosophy of Existence*, trans. Manya Harari, Harvill Press, 1948.

[19] E. S. Brightman, *An Introduction to Philosophy*, Holt, Rinehart and Winston, Inc., 1925, p. 61.

Attractive as this line of argument is, we are not satisfied. Coherence is wonderful as a test, just as the utility of the pragmatist is, but the more we analyze the situation, the more we realize that coherence is not what we mean by truth. Coherence is merely one, probably the most important or inclusive, of the ways of knowing, however imperfectly, what the truth is. Coherence, in short, is instrumental, but it does not tell us the nature of the end sought.

Consider an important and difficult court case, that of the death, in December 1954, of Mrs. Samuel H. Sheppard, the pregnant wife of Dr. Sheppard. The surgeon was found guilty of murder and is now serving his sentence, though he still maintains his innocence, and though many believe him. A recent book by a veteran reporter goes into the case fully.[20] The case is important, philosophically, because it emphasizes the extreme difficulty of knowing what the truth is. Everyone who argues it uses coherence as a test, yet all agree that there is an objective truth, even though most men do not know what it is. Here we see the striking difference between our *methods* of ascertaining and that which we seek to ascertain. Either Dr. Sheppard killed his wife or he did not. Presumably at least one person knows what the objective truth is: Dr. Sheppard, if he is really guilty, or, if he is innocent as he claims, the actual murderer. Some day, when the coherence argument is concluded, we may know; if so, we shall know what has been true all along.

The main reason for rejecting coherence as the *meaning* of truth, rather than merely a test, is that it leads inevitably to a doctrine of degrees of truth. Since we never know the entire context or all of the implications of any act, we never know the truth really, and, what is worse, we cannot say of two contradictory propositions that at least one of them *is* the truth. This involves, not merely the necessity of relativism, so far as our own judgments are concerned, but a far more fundamental relativism concerning the status of the very propositions we discuss. It is not sufficient to say that truth resides in the absolute, for the experience of the absolute is totally alien to finite creatures such as we are. There may be degrees of truth about many subjects, but there are surely some subjects in which the notion of degrees makes no sense at all. There cannot be degrees of truth about the Sheppard Murder Case. If the sur-

[20] P. Holmes, *The Sheppard Murder Case*, David McKay Company, 1961.

geon killed his wife, that is the truth, and it is not a matter of degrees at all.

The fact that we have difficulty in knowing the truth does not mean that there is a lack of truth waiting to be known. The careful student of Aristotle's *Metaphysics* is amazed to find the way in which this ancient thinker dealt with so many subjects that seem relevant now, including that of the relativity of truth. He points out that we may get nearer to the truth, inadequate as we may be, and sees that the act of getting nearer necessarily implies an objective truth which is approached if not reached. The crucial paragraph is as follows:

In any case, whether things be so or not, still things are more or less; for we could not say that two and three are both even, and if we say four is five we are less mistaken than if we say it is a thousand. If, then, not all are equally mistaken, it is clear that one is less mistaken, and therefore more right. If, then, one quantity is more nearly right, something must be true to which the more true approximates. And even if this truth does not exist, still some things must be more certain and truer than others; and we are far from that irresponsible doctrine which would prevent us from making definite judgments.[21]

Thus it is possible to combine in our philosophy a genuine humility about our ability to know the truth with absolute certainty, and a conviction that there is an objective truth which we are trying, with relentless effort, to ascertain. In so far as we have the beginning of wisdom we resist, equally, the notion that we have arrived, and the notion that there is no place to go. Truth is waiting to be discovered, even though we approach it stumblingly. The idea that truth is independent of our ability to grasp or even to verify it was expressed in a forthright manner by that most original of American philosophers, Charles S. Peirce. "By belief," he wrote, "I mean merely holding for true—real, genuine practical holding for true—whether that which is believed be the atomic theory, or the fact that this ink is pretty black, or what you will."[22] Peirce was a sophisticated thinker, but in regard to the meaning of truth he sided with the plain man. It was in this same sense that Peirce believed

[21] Aristotle, *Metaphysics*, op. cit., Bk. Gamma, 1008b and 1009a.
[22] C. S. Peirce, "Letters to Lady Welby," *Values in a Universe of Chance*, Stanford University Press. 1958, p. 397.

in God. He knew he could be wrong about God, as he could about the blackness of the ink, but he did not believe that his judgment, in either case, could alter *what is*. He was a genuine philosopher in that he exhibited a passionate devotion to a dispassionate truth.

Chapter 4 ~ THE LIFE
OF REASON

Mankind have a great aversion to intellectual labor.

SAMUEL JOHNSON

THE SPIRIT OF PHILOSOPHY IS THE SPIRIT OF THOSE WHO RECOGNIZE that they may not be right. It is because philosophers, when they are worthy of the name, realize that they may be wrong in their conclusions, that philosophical methods of careful inquiry have been developed through the centuries. Philosophers ask, in relation to every assertion, whether made by themselves or by others, what the rational basis of each conclusion really is. It is not enough to assert a statement confidently; each belief requires support. A great part of serious thinking, therefore, is devoted to the criticism of beliefs, in the hope of discarding the unworthy and corroborating the worthy. Our recognition of the danger of error leads, if we are at all wise, not to the abandonment of the struggle for intellectual integrity, but to its accentuation. This accentuation is what is meant by the life of reason.

Experience

There is always something healthy-minded about the emphasis on experience. After men have speculated for a long time about an event, it is extremely refreshing for someone to bring in the testimony of the firsthand report of the event. The actual voyage of Christopher Columbus outweighed, in convincing quality, any amount of geographical speculation. The astronomical speculations about the existence of Neptune were intricate and valuable, but the sighting of the distant planet by means of a telescope was far more valuable. In a very important sense the discussion about the possibility of artificial earth satellites was both transcended and outmoded by the first Sputnik flight. Firsthand experience does not make speculation unnecessary, but helps to keep it honest. No sensible man ever claims that his area of belief must be identical with his area of experience. In that case he will be condemned to live in a restricted and impoverished world. We do not deny the existence of atoms, for example, merely because we have never seen any atoms. The wise man knows that reality is bigger than his experience of it, but he will depend upon experience whenever he can. The necessity of rational belief in the unseen does not, therefore, deny the importance of firsthand experience at some point in the series. We believe in atoms, not by sheer unsubstantiated faith, but because we are forced to posit the existence of what we do not see, in order to make sense out of what we do see. At some point in the series, if we are to avoid living in sheer fantasy, there must be dependable experience on the part of some dependable person.

The importance of experience, in contrast to mere argumentation, accounts for the significance which we rightly attach to the famous experiment conducted at Pisa by Galileo (1564–1642). Instead of merely arguing about falling bodies, Galileo dropped the balls from the top of the leaning tower and thereby changed an intellectual fashion. Of course it would be naïve to suppose that the dropping of the balls, or any other single experiment, is sufficient to establish a case. Seeing is not necessarily believing! There is always the possibility of deceit, of optical illusion, or of the presence of peculiar circumstances which are effective though unrecognized. But seeing helps!

One evidence of the degree to which we all tend to be empiricist at heart is shown by our hearty response to Jean-Paul Sartre in his kind of empiricism. "Before there can be any truth whatever," he writes, "there must be an absolute truth, and there is such a truth which is simple, easily attained and within the reach of everybody; it consists of one's immediate sense of one's self."[1]

William James called such philosophy "radical empiricism." In a key sentence he wrote, "The only things that shall be debatable among philosophers shall be things definable in terms drawn from experience."[2] If we pay close attention to the formation of this sentence we can support the contention of James, for the vital word is "drawn." We may, and must, go far beyond experience, but unless we use it as a way of touching reality there is nothing to keep us from imagining any kind of dream we like and the dream will be absolutely worthless. An example of a system which spins its own web, without the tough-minded checking by experience, is what is called astrology. The requirement of experience is part and parcel, on the other hand, of astronomy. That is why we say astronomy is a reliable science, while astrology is not a science at all.

A great part of the life of reason lies in the consideration of the fruitful relationship between experience and thought. The mere experience, though necessary, is never sufficient, for it must be analyzed and developed by a rational process of ordered thinking. One excellent illustration is that of the work of garage mechanics, who are often thoughtful men. I go to a garage because of an irregularity in the operation of the direction signals of my car. The mechanic, having had much experience, begins to analyze this situation. He sees at once that the trouble is limited to the left side; by testing the electric bulb he learns that it is not burned out; he therefore guesses, out of a rich background of similar experiences, that the difficulty is in the grounding device and looks for a loose bolt, which he finds and fastens. The whole operation, though rapid, is precise and admirably successful. But we must notice that the success arises from a combination of experience and thought. If the

[1] J.-P. Sartre, in Existentialism from Dostoevsky to Sartre (ed.), W. Kaufmann, The World Publishing Company, Meridian Books, Inc., 1956, p. 302.
[2] W. James, The Meaning of Truth, Longmans, Green & Company, Inc., 1909, p. xii. Courtesy of David McKay Company.

mechanic had not had experience he would not have known what points to check, and therefore, would not have been effective so soon, but, if he had had only experience, he would not have been effective at all.

The great tradition in modern philosophy, stemming from Locke and his contemporaries, is that of rational empiricism. All of our knowledge *begins* in experience, but it does not end in experience, because reason is required to bring order into experience. The mind is wonderfully active and productive, but it must have some raw material on which to work, and it is experience which provides this raw material. Thought is efficacious, but it does not work in a vacuum. That Locke's central thesis is essentially correct most subsequent philosophers have agreed. This does not mean that there are not points to criticize and to elaborate. Kant agreed that all of our knowledge begins with experience, but denied that "it all arises out of experience." Unless some other source is added we have nothing but confusion.

Perhaps the worst mistake of historic empiricism has been the arbitrary limitation to sense empiricism. Even to this day there are thinkers who, when they use the word *empirical* assume, without argument or defense, that the only experience to which reference can thus be made is that which comes to us by means of the sensory organs. They do not, of course, limit their attention to the traditional five senses, but they do limit themselves to experience which follows the same organic pattern as that demonstrated in sight, touch, and hearing. The serious philosopher is bound to ask the reason for such an arbitrary limitation. Why should not the empirical approach be broad enough to include any alleged experience of any kind? Since we use thought to criticize experience, why not accept all alleged experience for analysis and judgment? Our knowledge of the world is poor at best; why then rule out in advance something which might give us new understanding?

If we require an example of a widened use of the appeal to experience, it can be provided by reference to direct religious experience. Now it is undeniably true that great numbers of people, including some of the most thoughtful who have ever lived, have reported a direct experience with the divine, but not in connection with physical sight, sound, or touch. Among these is the philosopher and mathematician Blaise Pascal, whose report of his encounter with the Living God on November 23, 1654, is one of the most moving in all autobiographical literature. His testimony does not stand alone, but is merely one peak in a great range. Nearly all of the classic journals of the acknowledged saints, such as that of John Woolman, add impressively to the abundance and richness of the witness thus made. What is a philosophically minded person to do with such testimony? He can elect, as some do, to rule out this impressive claim to experience as invalid and unworthy of examination, merely because it does not claim to come by sensory experience. But it is hard to see how any genuine philosopher could do this. Who knows enough to be able to say with finality what the limits of objective experience may be?

The truly philosophical mood is that which extends the meaning of empiricism to what its historical derivation suggests, i.e., to all claims to experience in contradistinction to interpretation of experience. In every case there ought to be a complete openness of approach. Perhaps it can be shown that some nonsensory claims to experience are unreliable. That would not be very surprising, in view of the fact that even some sensory claims can be shown, when tested, to be unreliable. If we have anything of the spirit of intellectual humility which resists dogmatism, we shall make no prejudgment of what is possible and what is not possible, but shall submit all experiences which come into our ken to the same tests of validity.

It will never be said by a genuine philosopher that he rules out experiences because they are subjective. Of course they are subjective; no experience can be anything else. If the love of God is subjectively experienced by Blaise Pascal it is equally true to say that the heat of the fire is subjectively known by John Jones. Since all experiences are subjective, the path of reason lies in submitting these experiences to tests in order to try to learn, to the best of our ability, which of them have objective reference and which do not. The animals in the zoo are experienced quite as subjectively as are the "animals" which torment the patient suffering from delirium tremens, but there are good reasons for making a distinction between the two forms of subjectivity and for coming to the conclusion that the zoo inhabitants enjoy objective existence while those of the hospital do not. The crucial point is that an experience which is subjectively known may have, but need not have objective reference. Whether we believe that it has objective reference depends, not on some means of escaping from the subjective predicament, which no one ever does, but rather in noting certain types of agreement within the subjective realm. The most impressive of these are the interpersonal agreements which drive us to the conviction that we are talking about a common public world. The chief reason for the cogency of this approach is that the alternative to objective reference is the miracle of coincidence, in which we have no good reason to believe.

The Method of Comparative Difficulties

We begin to understand why the late Judge Learned Hand was called a philosopher when we see how he arrived at his juridical conclusions. To a notable degree, he recognized that the weight of evidence is seldom all on one side in a decision. Important decisions are inevitably complex, because, of two alternatives, neither one is free from difficulties. The mood of philosophy is not that of the person who waits until he finds a solution utterly free from difficulties; it is rather the mood of one who knows very well that the best available is itself imperfect. It is one of the marks of the life of reason to know this and to proceed accordingly. Hand's decision in favor of free discussion, in spite of the dangers of the Communist conspiracy, illustrates admirably the philosophic method of comparison and consequent acceptance of something which is less than perfect, because the alternative is worse. "Risk for risk," he said, "for myself I had rather take my chance that some traitors will escape detection than spread abroad a spirit of general suspicion and distrust which accepts rumor and gossip in place of undismayed and unintimidated inquiry."

A thoughtful person, who understands human finitude, recognizes that he is not likely to have a perfect answer to any question. Our ultimate position is likely to include elements which are intellectual liabilities, but we accept the answer because any conceivable alternative is worse. Thus we introduce problems when we refuse to limit, in advance, the scope of valid experience to the sensory, but we make the refusal because the advance limitation introduces even more damaging problems. Philosophy in this, as in so many intellectual decisions, is the art of balancing imperfect alternatives.

The great practical advantage to be gained by expecting difficulties, even in the best answers, is that we do not discard an answer merely because it is imperfect. Instead of discarding, we examine the field as carefully as we can to see whether there is any alternative in which the liabilities are less numerous or less damaging. Here, as in connection with so many other aspects of philosophy, the record of autobiography is extremely helpful. "I remember well," says the late Professor John Baillie, of Edinburgh, "how during my study of philosophy as an undergraduate one of my teachers wrote the following words (or their like) on the margin of an essay in which I had criticized a certain accepted theory: 'Every theory has its difficulties, but you have not considered whether any other theory has less difficulties than the one you have criticized.' And I remember that the further reflection set up in my mind by that simple remark was, in that particular instance, enough to lead me back to the received doctrine."[3] Professor H. G. Wood, formerly of the University of Birmingham, makes a similar and equally profound witness in his Hulsean Lectures at the University of Cambridge, for the year 1933–1934.[4]

Philosophy, far from avoiding recognition of difficulties, thrives on them, and actually seeks new ones that have not been generally noticed. Philosophy is created by the friction of minds which are employed in the joint pursuit after truth. Often that friction must be artificially produced. It was one of the chief marks of the greatness of Josiah Royce as a teacher that, when strong objections were made by students, he would restate the objections with greater force.

A clear understanding of the philosophic method known as that of comparative difficulties explains why it is that thought so often advances by means of attack. Both Marxian and Freudian thought are filled with attacks on positions inconsistent with their doctrines, and this is perfectly satisfactory, but the right response to them is

[3] John Baillie, *Invitation to Pilgrimage*, Charles Scribner's Sons, 1942, p. 15
[4] H. G. Wood, *Christianity and the Nature of History*, Cambridge University Press, 1934.

never that of mere defense. The role of the philosopher is to unearth and to examine the difficulties inherent in the attacking systems. That they have problems of their own is thoroughly obvious,
and it is our duty to explore them. If, after careful examination, we
conclude that their difficulties are fewer than those of any known
alternative, loyalty to the truth requires that we accept these systems. Thus the process of intellectual survival goes forward by a
certain ruthlessness of selection. The history of ideas advances by
the survival of the less unfit. It is right that there should be struggle
and apparent harshness of attack and counterattack, for there is no
other way by which the balance of difficulties between alternatives
can be accurately ascertained. The good philospher is seldom satisfied with mere defense of his own position; he adopts the posture
of attack as soon as he can. If he thinks that logical positivism in
its contempt for metaphysics is unsound, he does not rest satisfied
with defending metaphysics; instead he explores the possible metaphysical basis of positivism to see whether it will bear full examination.

The student of philosophy is often surprised to learn how much
of philosophy is engaged in criticizing other positions. This ceases
to be a surprise, however, when we begin to see how thought
progresses. It progresses, in great measure, by the exposure of weaknesses, by noting hidden contradictions, by revealing inconsistencies. Much of this is, perforce, negative in nature, but it is not
for that reason lacking in benefit to the human mind. We must
tear down false positions if there is to be openness for more sound
positions. Unfortunately, yet truly, it is easier to see what is wrong
than it is to know what is right. We may not know where the
hidden pot of gold is, but it is not very hard to know when we
have missed finding it. While the presence of contradiction shows
that a position is erroneous, the absence of contradiction does not
show that a position is a true one. It is because man has learned, by
long experience, of the high probability of error that he has found it
necessary to invent means of avoiding error, at least in some measure. Thoughtful men have concluded, and concluded rightly, that
the unexamined position is not worth holding. The life of reason
progresses as the means of examination become more precise and,
accordingly, more dependable.

Dialectic

The great historical method of the examination of positions is that known as dialectical. In the simplest sense this means by the method of dialogue. The dialogue represents the way in which, in common life, one person's thought can correct and supplement that of another, until, in the end, all participants in the interchange come to joint conclusions not held by any of them at the beginning. We can frequently see the exceptions to our own generalizations more clearly in conversation, than in working alone. The philosophical dialogue is an imagined conversation in which mutual correction, supplementation, and consequent progress are demonstrated with only a minimum of extraneous material.

Plato appears to have been the inventor of the literary form known as the Socratic dialogue. The fact that Xenophon wrote dialogues does not make this judgment really doubtful, for Xenophon's literary work, according to the best evidence, is later than the early work of Plato. The probability is that Xenophon's account of the defense of Socrates was written after reading the *Apology*, written by Plato. The important conclusion is that Plato accomplished more than he intended. His manifest purpose was to preserve the memory of a great thinker and of a great age. Although he did accomplish this, he also accomplished much more: he invented a philosophic form which has been prized and copied, though without conspicuous success, in succeeding generations. He found a way, not merely to honor his teacher, but to present brilliantly the teacher's ideas and his own. The dialogue is more successful, as a way of intellectual expression, than is the essay or the oration. This is because valid thought is more akin to a process than to a fixed conclusion.

The experience of dialogue leads to the concept of dialectic. In the Socratic dialectic, when some position is espoused, the characters, particularly Socrates, ask questions about it. These questions are sometimes like scalpels which cut away the excess fat and reveal what is being said, in fact, rather than merely what is said in appearance. This process nearly always reveals hidden, unstated, or deliberately suppressed assumptions. Dialectic may therefore be de-

fined as "repeated and thorough criticism of our assumptions."[5]
Even the simplest human act or decision involves assumptions. For
example, we go into a church building and find a baby being bap-
tized, in the absence of the parents. What does this mean? Clearly
this is not a ceremony undertaken with the hope of encouraging
the parents to bring up the child as a Christian, for they are not
there to be encouraged. The ceremony is nonsense, except upon the
assumption that baptism is a performance which has objective or
even magical efficacy. Certainly there is no suggestion that the
child is conscious of the event. Do the parents and the clergyman
understand the assumptions of their act, and would they approve if
they did?

The truth of assumptions, once they are nakedly revealed, is by
no means self-evident and is, in fact, often very doubtful. In short
an argument is frequently more persuasive before it is analyzed
than it is afterwards. Let us say that a person, noting the act of
another, concludes that his neighbor's action could not have been
one of free choice because, he says, there was a "reason" why he did
it. This often passes as valid, but its validity is by no means obvious
once we smoke out the hidden assumption to the effect that whatever is caused is, therefore, unfree. This assumption may, in the
end, be a sound one, but our world is not so simple that it can be
accepted in advance, without careful substantiation. In short, the
assumption seems obvious until it is examined.

Dialectic is based on the recognition that no proposition stands
alone. On the one hand, it depends for its worth upon prior propositions and, on the other hand, it leads to implications which
are integral to its total meaning. The basic rule is that it is never
intellectually respectable to accept an idea unless one is also ready
to accept all that the idea entails. To affirm a position without
affirming its implications is cheating. One of the chief ways, in
Plato's dialogues, of making men see their error is to show them
what else their ideas involve. If these other things are absurd, then
the original position is itself absurd. If p involves q and q is unacceptable, then p is unacceptable. Thus it is not intellectually

[5] A. E. Taylor, The Faith of a Moralist, The Macmillan Company, 1931,
Vol. I, p. 24.

honest to stand for absolute freedom of action and at the same time, refuse to accept the necessary conclusion that one cannot, then, raise any objection to the actions of those who claim their freedom to cheat, to malign, to steal, and even to kill. Dostoevsky made excellent use of this dialectic in *The Brothers Karamazov*. Applying the test of consistency, he asks of the man who asserts that "everything is lawful," "What is wrong with murder?" Complete tolerance makes logically impossible any moral judgment of any kind.

Because truth is almost always complex, and therefore difficult to know, we need, not a single light, but many lights. This is what dialectic achieves, by probing from a variety of directions. A single light might leave some shadows, but the shadows are removed if the light comes from all angles. This is the philosophy on which our court trials in western civilization are based. The accused man is more likely, we think, to receive justice if there is a fierce struggle, both for prosecution and defense. A single lawyer, with impartiality, might supposedly be far enough above the battle to make sure that objective justice is done, but, unfortunately, this is not the way in which human beings are made. A government is more likely to provide stable justice if it has built into it a system of checks and balances: these are needed because even the best of men are never wholly impervious to the interests of themselves, their families, and their parties. The price we pay for our human imperfection is the system of cross-lights in the courtroom, of opposing parties in the government, and of continuing dialogue in the practice of philosophy. Because the truth is complex, and because men are partially blind, we need to entertain claim and counterclaim, each of these being presented as persuasively as possible. Dialectic is needed in the life of reason, not because men are always reasonable, but because there is so much chance of their being unreasonable.

The best way to expose a position as erroneous is to show, by dialectical development, that it leads to self-contradiction. There is reason to believe that no false premise can be consistently elaborated; at some point or other its weakness will become evident. We proceed, necessarily, on the conviction of Socrates, that error is eventually obvious, but we must remember that it is not likely to appear obvious until we examine the problem. It is the emphasis on the role of contradiction that binds together the work of three of the greatest thinkers of ancient Greece: Socrates, Plato, and Aristotle. Socrates employed the principle in oral discourse, Plato made it the key instrument of his dialogues, and Aristotle provided a clear argument in its defense. Aristotle's argument is given in its more careful form in his *Metaphysics*. The person who denies the law of noncontradiction is seen by Aristotle to be ruling himself out, in advance, of any intelligible discourse. Aristotle shows why:

For if contradictories apply to anything, one thing will not differ from another; for if it differs, this will be something true and peculiar to it. So what has been said follows if whoever makes a distinction speaks truly. It would follow, besides, that all men may be speaking truly and all men may be speaking falsely, and therefore our opponent must admit that he speaks falsely.[6]

Throughout the history of philosophy the method here used by Aristotle has been employed in rational argument. It is a method in which the person who seeks to engage in the practice of philosophy must become adept. The best way to start is to ask of any position, what would be involved *about itself*, if it were taken seriously and therefore consistently. If a psychologist of a particular persuasion holds that all human conclusions are to be explained by irrational impulses, even the beginner in dialectic is encouraged to inquire what this dictum does to itself. What irrational impulses led the scholar to affirm that all conclusions come from irrational impulses? Or we may contemplate the odd situation of the behaviorist who denies consciousness, yet claims to be conscious of the fact that his brand of behaviorism is true and its alternatives false.

Dialectic has taken different forms in different generations, even though all forms are based on the notion that truth is revealed better in process than in any other way. The most famous interpretation of dialectic, after Plato's, is that of G. F. Hegel.[7] This great German philosopher has been in and out of fashion many times during the last one hundred and fifty years, but his enduring

---

[6] Aristotle, *Metaphysics*, trans. R. Hope, Bk. Gamma, University of Michigan Press, 1960, p. 74.
[7] The Hegelian dialectic is described carefully in Hegel's *Logic*, but is assumed in his other works, especially *The Phenomenology of Mind*.

contribution seems to be that of the threefold dialectic. What Hegel taught in this regard was that thinking, on any important subject, tends to move over to its opposite. We start, inevitably, with a *thesis*, but as we examine it, we begin to see its intrinsic weaknesses. The thesis might, in a historical situation, be the widespread spiritualism of ancient Greece, with its implicit belief in the Olympian gods and the conviction that spiritual powers were everywhere effective. The weaknesses and inconsistencies of this position were so great that thoughtful men, beginning with the school of Miletus, tended to become sheer naturalists, denying the role of the spiritual forces and concerning themselves primarily with material factors. This position, in the terminology of Hegel, we may call the *antithesis*. But, as men meditated upon it, the antithesis came to appear quite as inadequate, in its way, as was the thesis in its way. The second moment in the dialectic avoided some erroneous features in the thesis, but introduced, at the same time, new and different ones of its own.

The recognition of the inadequacies of both the first moment and the second moment led Socrates and his immediate successors to the search for a third way, which Hegelians would call a *synthesis*. Anaxagoras had made a start on this, but did not carry his start to its logical conclusion. In the thinking of Socrates, however, we find a true synthesis. It reasserts the central position of the thesis that spiritual forces are real and effective, but also, after the manner of the antithesis, denies that effective forces are arbitrary in their operational procedures. There must be a genuine order and it must include a logical order. Socrates' invention of the idea of the soul, so different from any that had preceded him, sought to include the values of the preceding positions without their defects and their limitations.

It is astonishing to learn how wide is the area of experience in which the Hegelian dialectic can be applied. Our thought is always in process, providing it is genuine, but the process is seldom a direct movement comparable to a straight line between two points. In the great majority of problems we are forced to move, if we move at all, by indirection, tacking against the wind. We cannot normally go straight from a to c, but must go through b. The average citizen of the West tends to start life, in his father's home, believing in free enterprise, but without any examined reason for his faith. Later, with a little education, he tends to move for a while to the left and becomes something of a radical. Later, still, with the responsibilities of home and job upon his shoulders, he tends to move back to free enterprise, but with some recognition of its difficulties. The synthesis, in human thought, tends to re-establish the thesis, but with the advantage of the criticism which the antithesis has provided. Then the synthesis becomes a new thesis and the process continues, if thought continues.

It is not to be supposed that the use of dialectic is reserved for great philosophers or for great ideas. It can be used in daily life and must indeed be used if a person expects to engage in the practice of philosophy. Though it is harder to work alone than with others, it is possible for a man to provide his own criticism. He states his hypothesis in the form of a generalization and immediately, as the next step, tries to find exceptions to his own rule. If he finds any exceptions, he goes back to the starting point and states his conclusion in a more acceptable, because more limited, formulation. He tries in fact to go through all three moments of the dialectic. This process can continue for days and even for years. It does not, in the end, give any insurance of absolute certainty of correctness of judgment, but it does provide a means of eliminating many particular mistakes. To be on the road is not tantamount to arrival, but it is better than never starting.

Implication

Though there are many ways in which the cogency of thought may be consciously improved, no way is more valuable than the way of implication. Implication is deeply involved in scientific method and philosophic method, but not in exactly the same way for both. Indeed, the different uses of implication represent the greatest distinction between the two methods. The beginning student is often confused by the apparent ambiguity of the word *implication*, sometimes feeling that it is used one way in formal logic and another way in ordinary life. He is not sure whether he ought to say, "Rain implies wet ground," or "Wet ground implies rain." It helps to realize that, in ordinary speech, it is almost always the latter. This is because we are concerned, not with a temporal sequence, but with a logical sequence. In scientific procedure we can concern ourselves with temporal sequence by the device of prediction and verification, but it is the logical sequence that is most fundamental.

We are lost in the mountains and desire to find a path to some human habitation. We find paths, but they may be animal paths which merely lead from one wilderness to another. Finally, on one path, we see marks evidently made by iron shoes. We infer at once that there must have been horses here recently. We do not see the horses or their riders, but the marks imply riders, for normally horses in the wilderness are not shod. We move from an observed position to what the position is said to imply. If there is a baby born one month after a marriage, we say that this implies conception out of wedlock. This is different from the use of implication in laboratory science, since there is no possibility of a planned experiment. Planned experiment is never possible in facilitating the understanding of a single or unique event which has already transpired.

The examples of the use of implication in common life are legion. Almost always implication is a significant factor in medical diagnosis. Does the patient have mononeucleosis or not? If he has, we can expect a particular change in his blood. Accordingly we set up the modest experiment of testing to see whether the change has occurred. If it has not, the diagnosis is wrong and we try again. The television repair man comes to the house, looks at the machine which is not operating and quickly deduces a number of possible reasons for its failure to operate. Is a fuse blown out? Is the plug connection faulty? Is a tube worn out? Any one of these would be sufficient to cause the result. Consequently the repair man performs a series of tests to see which source of trouble is the one. This he does by reference to *other consequences*.

The essence of reasoning lies in the ability to connect what, without intellectual effort, seems separate, and to see accurately what follows from the connection which is observed. Though there are many kinds of connection, starting with mere compatibility or conjunction, the most powerful instrument of connection is that expressed by the words "if . . . then." This is what, in general, we mean by implication. We soon observe many connections of this kind in ordinary experience and we quickly learn, on the basis of these connections, to infer more than we observe. We learn very early, for example, that the coming of rain makes the ground wet (if it is uncovered). If, then, the ground is not wet we infer that there was no rain (in that particular area). It is by an extension of this method that we claim to know millions of things which we have never observed at first hand. Nearly all of our alleged knowledge is based on reasoning rather than upon direct perception, and the bulk of our reasoning involves the principle of implication. A people who cannot meaningfully say "if . . . then" cannot advance in intellectual stature.

The principle becomes clearer if we see the precise relation which obtains between the antecedent, which we may call p and the consequent, which we may call q. The formula is:

If p then q;

$p \; \therefore \; q$;

Not $q \; \therefore \;$ not p.

Once the relation of "follows from" is firmly established we can proceed logically, either by affirming the antecedent, in which case it is possible and necessary to affirm the consequent, or by proceeding to negate the consequent, when we are enabled, with confidence, to negate the antecedent. In strict logic, nothing whatever follows from the negation of the antecedent nor from the affirmation of the consequent.

To make this clear we may use the illustration of a murder case where we do not know the truth, but which we are investigating. We can begin with the basic proposition, "If the accused were the murderer, he would have been in the murder premises when the murder occurred." If it can be shown conclusively that the consequent here is false, we conclude that the antecedent is false and the man is judged to be innocent. The most common way of establishing the falsity of the proposition is by means of an alibi, to the effect that the man was known to be in another location at the time when the murder occurred. Of course we realize that this procedure involves many unargued assumptions. One assumption is that murder cannot be accomplished at a distance; another is that a person cannot be in two places at one time. Admittedly these assumptions cannot be proved, but the probability of their truth seems to us so great that we do not bother to examine them, and our action seems, accordingly, to be justified.

It is a matter of great importance to remember that, while the negation of the consequent leads to significant conclusions, the affirmation of the consequent leads to *nothing*. The presence of the accused in the house where the murder occurs does not lead, logically, to conviction,[8] though absence leads to acquittal. The fallacy of the "affirmation of the consequent" leads to a serious problem for all inductive reasoning, a problem which we shall try to face in the succeeding chapter. Suffice it now to say that we seek to reduce the effect of the fallacy, in contemporary science, by a great multiplication and refinement of the process of testing consequents. This process is normally called *verification*.

The chief difference in the use of implication in science and in philosophy is that science tends to reason forward and philosophy tends to reason backward. In a great deal of natural science implication is used in the sense of prediction. We do not know whether a certain hypothesis is justified. Accordingly we set up an experiment, producing artificially and by conscious intent, a situation in which the expected results of the hypothesis, if it is a sound one, will appear. Thus the relationship involved is temporal as well as logical. This is why we say the implication points forward. Therefore, if we conduct the experiment many times, with many minor variations, we say that the original hypothesis is verified. If, on the other hand, the implied or expected event fails to occur, great doubt is cast upon our hypothesis. We say, "great doubt," to distinguish our conclusion from absolute rejection, because we realize that it is always possible (a) that our original inference of what ought to follow was erroneous, or (b) that alien and unnoticed factors have entered the picture. There might be more than one reason for failure.

In philosophy, and in everyday life, the great use of implication

---

[8] If, however, we can show that, not only was he present, but that he was the only person present, the case for the prosecution is sound, but to prove that no one else was present is an extremely difficult task. To prove a negative of this kind is almost impossible.

lies in reading backward from what we experience to enable us to infer what we do not perceive. The reasoning on which we necessarily depend most is that from effect to cause, from consequent to alleged antecedent. That such reasoning does not give absolute certainty is obvious, because we can never know beyond a shadow of doubt that the assumed connection is a necessary one. A seems to be necessary as a prerequisite of B, but we do not know absolutely that this is the case. Thus probability enters into our highest reasoning.

What we do, in ordinary life, is to reason from the relatively well known, or observable, to the relatively unknown or unobservable. I never saw my paternal grandfather, but I reason back to his existence from effects which cannot be understood except on the basis that he once was. We are really doing this in physics when we reason back, not temporarily but logically, to the existence of atoms which we do not see, from the consideration of observable factors which are part of the predicted consequence if the existence of atoms is assumed. Thus, though science is unique in the way in which predicted consequences can be tested experimentally, it is not really unique in the basic logical operation. Many a scientist is also a philosopher, and he is always a philosopher to the extent that he raises questions about the hidden assumptions of his procedure.

One of the most fruitful ways in which the principle of implication enters into philosophy is by means of what are called *postulates*. This conception was given wide and significant use by Immanuel Kant, particularly in his *Critique of Practical Reason*. Kant, in this famous book, centered his attention on certain experiences which we find it virtually impossible to doubt and then asked the pertinent question: *"What else must be true if this is true?"* Kant found the sense of oughtness to be indubitable, both in himself and other men. Perhaps this is not a clue to reality, but if it is not, what else is? It is as easy to doubt sensory experience as it is to doubt moral experience. Therefore, the life of reason requires that we ask what kind of world it must be which gives rise to a sense of obligation.

Kant reasoned that, in order to make intelligible the sense of obligation, he was driven to affirm three postulates, freedom, immortality, and God. He knew that he could not prove any of the three directly or conclusively, but in this they did not differ from other objects of our belief. What is there, in which men believe, that can be proved directly and conclusively?

But why postulate *freedom?* Because, reasons Kant, a sense of ought is utterly meaningless if action which is supposedly required is impossible. It is not my duty to do what I cannot do. I do not have a duty to enter the footrace if I am so handicapped that it is impossible for me to run. The formula which appears over one of the doorways at Harvard is, "You can because you should." If man is a mere pawn in the hands of external forces, moving as unfreely as a billiard ball, it is certainly nonsense to hold him responsible, or to blame him, or to ask him to ponder seriously what he ought to do. Decision is nothing unless choice is real. Kant thus poses the alternative, "Either man's life is necessitated and morality is ridiculous, or there is an area of freedom and our sense of obligation is reasonable."

The postulate of *immortality*, Kant reasons, arises in a similar way. No man's sense of oughtness can ever find fulfillment in this short life. We are driven to seek justice, but justice is not fully done. Therefore, unless the very urge to justice is a fundamentally absurd one, there must be life after death, a life in which the frustrations known in finite existence can be fulfilled in infinite time. Finally, the moral experience requires God, if it is to make sense. Though the drive of oughtness is always a drive in the direction of justice, that is, a union of happiness and goodness, this is something which no men, either singly or in conjunction, ever achieve. Therefore, if the urge is not deceptive, there must be, somewhere in reality, a Power able to produce what is required. This Power is God.

The contribution which Kant thus made to the general practice of philosophy is by no means limited to these particular postulates, but lies primarily in the refinement of the method itself. The student of philosophy, if he understands this method, has a new tool in his hand, a tool which can be used in the attack on a multitude of problems. Each life has a little window through which we may look out on reality, a window severely limited by time and space and experience. It is not much, but it is something. The way of wisdom is not to complain about our limitation, but to try to reason from this starting point. If I have evidence that something is true, and if I am anything of a philosopher, I do not rest satisfied with what I know. Instead I ask, restlessly, rigorously, and continuously, what else *must* be true, to make the little that I have intelligible. In short I must use the method of implication in order to escape from my finitude in any measure and the most potent of all implications are postulates.

Self-Evidence

The methods of extending knowledge by the careful use of thought are concerned for the most part with the development of valid chains of reasoning. Thus, in most dialectic, we move back and back until we reach something upon which we think we can depend. Whenever we use the word *because* we are reaching for some basis of credibility which the other person or persons of the dialogue will be willing to accept. We discuss, for instance, the practice, in certain American states, of denying the privilege of voting to Negroes, even when they are well-educated persons. When asked why it is that we object, we may say that the practice is unjust. But, why, asks the defender of the system, is it unjust? Because, we say, it denies equality of rights. We have moved from a concrete practice to an abstract principle, in the hope that the debating opponent will accept the principle. And this, indeed, is the only way in which anyone can argue. If, when we hit bedrock, the opponent refuses to recognize it as sound, there is not much more that we can do. We can try again, but there is no certainty that we shall succeed the second time better than the first. The point to notice most clearly is that all reasoning of this type is undertaken in the hope of reaching, by argument, something so firm and so obvious that it requires no further argument or defense. The fact that so many disputes are inconclusive only shows that the discovery of a mutually accepted ground is extremely difficult. It does not, however, show that we ought to give up the effort to find such a ground.

Our reasoning shows that there must be, at some point, self-evident propositions. Unless some are self-evident, the others are not evident. The hardest problem arises when we try to provide examples of what these propositions that require no demonstration may be. Thomas Jefferson, in writing the Declaration of Independence, appealed confidently to self-evidence, in reaching for a solid base of argreement; in this he may have been justified, but he was not dealing with propositions which seemed, at that time, self-evident to the English king or to the French king. These gentlemen simply did not accept the principle of equality of rights.

The common procedure at one time was to use, primarily, mathematical truths as examples of self-evidence. These are no longer as appropriate, partly because we know that there can be different geometries, depending on different axioms, and also partly because we now realize that such propositions can be interpreted as mere tautologies. It is true that $2 + 2 = 4$ because we mean the same thing on both sides of the equation. We might as well say $4 = 1 + 1 + 1 + 1$. We have long used the example "The whole is greater than any of its parts," but this loses some of its self-evidence when we begin to deal seriously with numbers extended to infinity.

The fact that it is difficult to find valid examples of self-evidence does not, of course, mean that there are none. Aristotle's best illustration, that of the law of noncontradiction, may still be our best. He called it, we must remember, "the most certain of all principles." One reason for thinking that his judgment in this regard is correct is that almost anyone can see that the law is the necessary condition of intelligible discussion, and most people evidently want to discuss. That which is necessarily involved in all considerations of evidence is inescapable. Another good example is "Knowledge is possible." This is self-evident because to deny it is to affirm it, in that the very denial involves the claiming of a certain kind of knowledge. A similar example is, "There is error." In this case, as in that about knowledge, the principle is affirmed even when it is denied, for to deny error is to say that the proposition is itself in error. It is therefore inevitable; it provides a stable fulcrum by which we can lift the intellectual load.

There has been a vast amount of discussion, in the history of philosophy, about a priori propositions. These are propositions, the truth of which can be supposedly known in advance of experience, and are therefore contrasted with those which are known a posteriori. In contemporary language the chief argument is about propositions which are synthetic and those which are merely analytic. An analytic proposition is one in which it can be shown that the predicate is contained already in the meaning of the subject, even though this may not be superficially obvious. Thus when we say "All men are mortal" we are, essentially, telling about our use of the word man and not, as appears, making a factual statement. If there should be a creature with some human characteristics, which, over a period of many centuries, is impervious to death, we should probably claim that he is not a man. Synthetic judgments are those in which the predicate provides new information. Kant has been widely criticized for holding that mathematical propositions arc synthetic.[9]

A fresh approach to the controversy comes when we note a third class of judgments, which is not purely analytic and not synthetic, in the sense of dependence on experience. This third class was explained carefully by the late W. P. Montague in what became something of a philosophical classic even before his death. There are, he reasoned, propositions which are necessary in the special sense that any denial of them would land us in self-contradiction.[10] "We find this new criterion," he wrote, "in the notion of self-contradiction as applied in the following way: The truth of a given proposition is proved to be necessary when its contradictory implies self-contradiction." It is not easy to find propositions which meet this rigorous standard, but unless there are such we have no firm basis for subsequent reasoning. On the whole it is a distinct gain to think of self-evidence as belonging only to that which can be shown to be necessary.

The life of reason involves the construction of a chain, but the chain, to be effective, cannot be endless. Most propositions must be demonstrated, but nothing is demonstrated unless by ultimate reference to something which does not require demonstration. Infinite regress, in such a procedure, is absolutely worthless, for an infinite chain, fastened to nothing at the end, gives no more stability than does a chain which is only one inch long. Aristotle realized

[9] For a reliable study of the Kantian a priori contention, see M. R. Cohen, A Preface to Logic, World Publishing Company, Meridian Books, Inc., 1959, p. 35.

[10] W. P. Montague, The Ways of Knowing, The Macmillan Company, 1925, p. 90.

this and said it with great clarity in the following sentence: "For there cannot be demonstration of everything altogether; there would then be an infinite regress, and hence there would still be no final demonstration."[11]

Since your opponent may not be willing to accept the principle to which you, by careful steps, make ultimate appeal, it is up to him to say what principle he is willing to accept. Otherwise, all profitable conversation is at an end. Sometimes conversation is unprofitable and might as well be avoided. If you appeal ultimately to logical relations and say to your neighbor, "Can't you see that if x implies y, and y implies z, then x has to imply z?" and he answers, "No, I can't see it, and I don't accept it," you have come to the end of one road. Not everything can be argued or defended on other grounds; some things have to be seen.

The task of the philosopher is not to force people to accept a principle (which he could not do even if he would), but rather to present so clearly the steps, that those who listen are shown a reason which they may see, providing they are both able and willing to look. We cannot change the innate powers of men, but we can provide men with the means of insight. It is good to remember the celebrated encounter in which Dr. Johnson said to a man whom he had led along carefully, and who did not see, "Sir, I have found you an argument; but I am not obliged to find you an understanding."[12] Certainly the teacher, which is what a philosopher of the Socratic tradition hopes to be, must discipline both his thought and his speech so that he can make clear. If this does not succeed, there is no more that he can do.

In our emphasis upon clarity, an emphasis given vivid expression by Descartes, we must never confuse clarity with simplicity. We do not search for simple answers, because, in a world amazingly complex, simple answers are almost sure to be wrong. But simplicity and clarity are far from identical. Some philosophies give the appearance of depth to the unwary, merely because they are turgid. We understand that there is no reason why depth and clarity should be incompatible when we note that some of the greatest

[11] Aristotle, Metaphysics, op. cit., Bk. Gamma, 68, 69.
[12] James Boswell, Life of Samuel Johnson, John B. Alden, Publisher, 1887, Vol. IV, 375.

minds have been amazingly clear, as that of Socrates evidently was. But this kind of clarity comes at a great price, the price of intellectual discipline.

The high price of clear vision is indicated in Plato's *The Republic*, by the enormous emphasis that is placed on the right kind of education. The future leaders are to be trained in the hope of their becoming sufficiently sensitive to see what is waiting to be seen, though it is hidden from the unprepared. This is the major purpose of the entire life of reason. The aim is not to enable men to prove what they already believe; it is to enable them to become aware of what they otherwise might miss. Dialectic, when rightly understood, is not a method of winning arguments, but the method by which the eye of the soul is converted.[13]

---

[13] See Plato, *The Republic*, trans. F. M. Cornford, Oxford University Press, 1960, Bk. VII, 518.

Chapter 5 ∽ *THE LIMITS OF PROOF*

That which is used to prove everything else cannot itself be proved.

JEREMY BENTHAM

MAN IS A CREATURE WHO IS DEEPLY INVOLVED IN BELIEFS. HIS BELIEFS are not only numerous, but differ markedly from one another in character. Sometimes belief means *belief in*, when it is actually the equivalent of commitment, while at other times it means *belief that*, which amounts to assertions about the occurrence of events or the existence of objects. One of the first marks of human sophistication is the recognition that beliefs can be wrong, that there is a vast difference between what is merely asserted and what is truly substantiated. It is one thing to assert, for example, that there are communists who have infiltrated the government of the United States; it is quite another matter to provide support to this claim.

The difficulty and importance of the substantiation of belief are both so great that they require the development of a philosophical discipline which is devoted to the examination of problems which arise when substantiation is attempted. This philosophical discipline is generally known as logic. All men recognize that it has something to do with proof, and a famous logician, John Stuart Mill, even defined logic as "the science of proof." Such a science must go beyond belief to the ground upon which defensible belief rests. "In so far," wrote Mill, "as belief professes to be founded on proof, the office of logic is to supply a test for ascertaining whether or not the belief is well grounded."[1] There is little doubt that this is what the general public expects of that part of philosophy known as logic. What the world wants is proof and what it asks of the philosopher is a clear answer to the question of how proof is to be achieved. Whether this hope can be realized is a matter which we must now examine with care.

The Problem of Proof

The popular demand for proof is the sound instinct that an unsupported assertion is not merely worthless—it may be positively vicious as well. If we are told that an acquaintance has been guilty of embezzling funds, we rightly ask the informer whether he has any proof of the allegation, because, if he has none, we recognize that he is indulging in malicious gossip. In short, the problem of the support of assertions often has an ethical as well as a logical aspect. The recognition of this phase of the matter has influenced many areas of our common life, including our legal system. Thus, if a newspaper prints a story which is damaging to a man's reputation, and the story cannot be adequately verified, the publisher of the paper can be convicted of libel.

All who seek to be philosophers in the modern world have reason to be grateful to W. K. Clifford (1845–1879) for his vivid insistence upon the evil of belief without sufficient evidence.[2] A man who lets other men sail on a vessel which is known not to be safe is not to be congratulated on his faith; he is, says Clifford, to be denounced as guilty of the death of the men when disaster comes. Belief, unless it is well grounded, has a moral aspect; a man must ask himself, not merely whether he believes, but also *whether he has*

---

[1] J. S. Mill, *A System of Logic*, Longmans, Green and Co., 1900, p. 5.
[2] W. K. Clifford, "The Ethics of Belief," *Lectures and Essays*. The Macmillan Company, 1879, Vol. II, 178.

a right to believe. And the guilt of the shipowner is not diminished in the slightest, when, because of favorable weather and other circumstances, the potential disaster does not actually occur. Such considerations led Clifford to enunciate a much-quoted dictum in the following terms, "It is wrong always, everywhere, and for anyone, to believe anything on insufficient evidence."

Clifford made such a vivid point in his celebrated essay that all who are seriously concerned with philosophy must deplore his untimely death, which no doubt robbed posterity of valuable additions to literature. But Clifford's point is only a step in the historical dialectic and by no means the final answer. The problem which remains to be solved arises from the ambiguity of the phrase, "insufficient evidence." How much is sufficient? Must we delay action until a course is proved, in advance, or beyond a shadow of doubt? Shall we deny every scientific observation that is not proved? Certainly we hear, regularly, requests for this kind of proof in many areas. Many say, for example, that they will not believe in God unless God's existence is proven or demonstrated. What such people often fail to recognize is the obvious inconsistency of demanding absolute demonstration in one realm, while accepting belief with less than this in another. It is part of the ethics of belief to accept a single standard! If, upon careful examination, we find that we have to operate in this life with something less than the kind of evidence which Clifford demanded, this is something which we shall have to accept, and it may lead to a salutary humility, even though it does not provide a neat solution to our problems. The human situation may turn out to be paradoxical in that, on the one hand, it is wrong to accept any belief without proof of its correctness, yet, on the other hand, proof is denied to finite mortals, who must nevertheless proceed to act on that of which they cannot be sure. Often our hands are forced. As Pascal has taught us, and William James has repeated, there are times when we are forced to decide on insufficient evidence, because no decision is itself a decision.

The practical importance of the problem of proof may be noted in connection with the difficult question of disarmament. Can we be certain, for example, that bombs are not being tested on the other side of the earth? How do we know that there has not been underground testing already, in addition to those tests which have been detected by our scientists? As soon as we ask this question seriously we understand the impossibility of a categorical negative. The truth is that we do not know, and that we have no way of being sure that there is not something which we have missed.

Man is equipped to think, but there is no guarantee that he will think well. In fact, it is obvious to us, when we consider the matter with any care, that human experience involves a vast amount of shoddy thinking. Not only do men and women draw conclusions without any apparent evidence, they draw contrasting conclusions from the same evidence. Different groups of Americans differ sharply, for example, about the testing of atomic weapons. Some declare that America should eliminate all atomic testing, while others hold that such elimination would be criminally dangerous, in that it could lead to an imbalance of power and consequent destruction, both of ourselves and other nations. Here is a clear disjunction in which somebody is wrong. The group that is wrong is wrong in either or both of two ways: (a) about the facts of the case, or (b) about the proper deductions to be made from the facts.

We have some idea of the difficulty of proof in important decisions which bear on the welfare of millions of contemporary and future inhabitants of the earth when we see how sharp the contrast is in the judgments of men of genius and learning. Two of the most eminent of living thinkers, who are both persons of wide and long experience, are Lord Bertrand Russell of England and Professor Karl Jaspers of Germany. Russell is the leading figure on the Committee of One Hundred, which brings pressure on the government of the United Kingdom to adopt unilateral atomic disarmament. Jaspers, by contrast, argues that unilateral disarmament would be completely irresponsible, because it would remove the only effective deterrent to naked aggression.[3] Where is proof when the experts differ? Because the evidence they give is conflicting, it cannot be conclusive.

The agonizing decisions which the President of the United States has had to make are necessarily those in which the evidence is never conclusive because it never is complete. There are dangers in testing

[3] See K. Jaspers, *The Future of Mankind*, University of Chicago Press, 1961, p. 52.

and there are dangers in not testing. The President naturally collects all of the evidence he can, but finally he is forced to operate on insufficient evidence because life and destiny do not stand still. He takes the public into his confidence and explains the basis on which the decision is made. Though the wisdom of his decision cannot be proved in advance, the indefinite postponement of decision might produce a situation in which the very possibility of any decision is removed.

The paradox of belief is rendered even more paradoxical when we face the fact that sometimes evidence cannot come until after belief. Herein lies the deep wisdom of the famous dictum, *credo ut intelligam*. We do not now know any cure for leukemia and certainly we cannot prove that it is curable, but the men engaged in medical research really believe that a cure is possible and that it will be found. Except for such belief there is no strong likelihood of any important advance in this field of research. Thus the ancient dictum, which has often appeared to represent the height of absurdity, is actually most reasonable.[4] The medical illustration, moreover, is by no means unique, for the same logical process is illustrated in any successful marriage as well as in any vocation. Perhaps the best contemporary expression of the ancient paradox is that men must venture in order to know, but "venture" always implies belief in advance of proof.

The more careful our philosophical inquiry becomes, the more we realize that the relationship between belief and proof is not simple. The clearest way of denying simplicity is to point to the existence of paradox. If philosophy can make men understand this paradox it will be performing a significant service in telling the truth about the human situation, even though it will not be performing the impossible service which men seem to desire.[5] In the light of the almost pathetic desire for proof, in so many areas, it comes as a

[4] C. S. Peirce, in a letter written in May, 1911, underlined the following sentence: "Nobody will try new experiments without a leaning to an unsupported hypothesis." *Values in a Universe of Chance*, Stanford University Press, 1958, p. 430.

[5] An example of how the central paradox leads to the profitable continuation of the dialogue is shown by the way in which Clifford's famous essay led directly to the production of the equally famous essay by William James, "The Will to Believe" (*The Will to Believe*, Longmans, Green and Co., 1897). Though neither essay is final, each is a valuable step in the historical dialectic.

rude shock to learn that complete proof is not possible anywhere, but philosophy is not faithful to her vocation unless this shock is administered. If we are careful with our words we have to admit that sufficient evidence is something which we almost never possess. Is the guilt of an alleged criminal ever really proven? It is hard to see how. Confession certainly does not constitute proof, inasmuch as some crimes have been claimed by several men. The identification of fingerprints is not proof, since the assertion that the fingerprints of no two persons are identical is itself an unproved and unprovable assertion, even though we accept it on faith.

We tend to suppose that demonstration, particularly in science, is reasonably easy—until we try it, but when we really attempt to complete it we discover that every kind of proof has problems of its own. Pascal saw this with great clarity three hundred years ago, particularly when he wrote, "How few things are demonstrated! . . . Who has demonstrated that there will be a tomorrow and that we shall die?"[6] Cardinal Newman took up the same theme a century ago. "If it is difficult," he wrote, "to explain how a man knows that he shall die, is it not more difficult for him to satisfy himself how he knows that he was born? His knowledge about himself does not rest on memory, nor on distinct testimony, nor on circumstantial evidence. Can he bring into one focus of proof the reasons which make him so sure?"[7]

If it is difficult to know for certain about contemporary events at a physical distance, it is even more difficult to be certain about events remote in time. In our elementary textbooks we talk blandly about the origin of life, about beginnings in single cells, etc., but the reader, unless he is unusually alert, will fail to realize that he is dealing with vast speculations requiring many assumptions, of which proof is intrinsically impossible. Some of the evolutionary theories may be true, but we do not know that they are true. If Clifford's dictum is taken seriously, a great deal that passes for natural science will necessarily be discarded. Sometimes good philosophy appears in unlikely places, such as a column of a newspaper. Thus, James Reston brings the clear light of criticism to bear

---

[6] B. Pascal, Pensées, trans. W. F. Trotter, J. M. Dent and Sons, 1931, p. 73.
[7] J. H. Newman, A Grammar of Assent, Burns & Oates Ltd., 1870, Pt. VIII, Bk. 2, 1.

on our gullibility in the presence of scientific terms, such as *extrapolation.* "Extrapolation," he says, "is a seventy-five-cent word for an educated guess. It is a calculation from a fact about what preceded that fact or is likely to follow it."[8]

The problem of proof becomes acute whenever we seriously consider the nature of historical evidence. In one sense we face an insuperable barrier in all search for historical evidence, because the past is forever gone and cannot be verified in any conceivable re-enactment. There is a special advantage which appears in what we call the physical sciences, particularly chemistry and physics, in which, for many purposes, the element of time can be eliminated or at least neglected, whereas this can never be done in consideration of events in the historical sciences. The strength, and also the abstractness, of the physical sciences is that, in their experiments, it is always possible to operate in the present tense. Every historian and every expert witness at a criminal trial is forced to limit himself to circumstantial evidence, for the simple reason that, about events which are forever gone, there is literally no other kind.

The differences between the sciences, in regard to proof, become obvious when we distinguish the following:

1. The things which occur.
2. The things which recur.
3. The things which endure.

Physical science is based on the conviction that there are recurrences, not in concrete events, but in features which reappear in new contexts. Therefore, if one chemical experiment fails, another can be tried. It is, of course, not identical in time or in particular substances, but this is unimportant for the purpose, since what is being tested is recurring or enduring relationships. It is quite otherwise when we seek to deal scientifically with datable events, such as the production of the Dead Sea Scrolls or the Battle of Marathon. "What recurs," says Stebbing, "must be a set of properties, or characteristics, capable of belonging to more than one thing. Whenever we are concerned with the particular as such, *date* is relevant. We may say, conversely, that whenever date is relevant we

[8] J. Reston, "The Scientific Revolution and Democracy," *The New York Times,* March 7, 1962, editorial page.

are concerned with that which cannot as such be repeated."[9] The historical event is unique because it is located in a determinate place at a determinate time. History cannot, therefore, be approached by the methods which are suitable when we are dealing with repeatable characteristics.

The historian seeks, with careful effort, to ascertain what once happened. This he does by means of written records, by archeological remains, by oral reports, when these are available, and by the use of witnesses, when contemporary events are in question. What he cannot do is observe what has happened. It follows that every bit of our knowledge of historical fact is indirect. The primary objects of our search are inferred, since they cannot be observed. Historical knowledge is therefore probable.

The Imperfection of Logic

In the study of formal logic, if nowhere else, we naturally expect to find ways in which proof can be demonstrated. It must be admitted that some logicians, including John Stuart Mill, have encouraged this faith in what they have to offer.[10] But the more we examine the structure of logic the more we come to see that it is not, in fact, the science of proof at all. In neither of its main branches, deduction and induction, is there a way of complete substantiation of any belief.

Deduction appears to provide proof that is beyond cavil or dispute. This seems most clear in the use of the syllogism. A syllogism, as invented by Aristotle and as defined by him, is a set of propositions in which the truth of two assertions necessitates the truth of a third, which is called the conclusion. The syllogism, so understood, has three and only three propositions, which jointly employ three and only three terms, each of which appears twice. The term

[9] L. Susan Stebbing, A Modern Introduction to Logic, 2nd ed., Harper & Row, Inc., Torchbooks, 1961, pp. 383, 384.

[10] Perhaps the greatest mistake of Mill was his failure to understand that the canons of experimental inquiry gave only probability. Modern logicians tend not to share Mill's faith. Miss Stebbing speaks for many when she says that "we must admit that the principles of probability alone cannot enable us to reach inductive conclusions that have any considerable degree of probability." (Ibid., p. 410.)

which appears in both premises, and thus connects them, is called the middle term. There are four possible figures of the syllogism, depending upon the location of the middle term. If P represents the predicate of the conclusion and S represents the subject of the conclusion, while M represents the middle term, the four possible figures are as follows:

1	2	3	4
M – P	P – M	M – P	P – M
S – M	S – M	M – S	M – S
S – P	S – P	S – P	S – P

Thus the syllogism:

> All men are animals;
> Americans are men;
> Therefore, Americans are animals.

is a syllogism in Figure 1, with "men" as the middle term. Given the rules, such a chain of reasoning is either valid or not, the one above being valid. The rules, which are in addition to the elements of definition already given, are:

1. The middle term must be distributed in at least one of the premises. (A term is distributed when we refer to all members of a given class.)
2. No term may be distributed in the conclusion unless it was distributed in its own premise.
3. From two negative premises no conclusion follows.
4. If one premise is negative the conclusion is necessarily negative, and if the conclusion is negative, one premise is necessarily negative.

Here is a system so clear and so comprehensible that it is bound to receive the admiration of thoughtful persons. Thus von Leibniz could say, "I hold that the invention of the form of the syllogisms is one of the most beautiful which the human mind has made, and even one of the most considerable." Though the syllogism does not represent all possible forms of valid reasoning, it does provide a system of necessary involvement which is so definite that it can be

put on a calculating machine, called a Validoscope.[11] The electrical
Validoscope can, by a system of lights, show instantly which combination of premises leads to a valid conclusion. Fallacious inference can thus be detected instantly.

"Truth and falsity," wrote Aristotle, "imply combination and
separation."[12] By this he meant that the art of sound reasoning is
the art of connection, particularly the right kind of connection. Being the founder of logic as a science, Aristotle was eager to show
carefully what the right connections are, by which we avoid some
of the errors to which the human mind is liable. In some ways
subsequent philosophers have carried the process of validation of
beliefs farther than Aristotle did, but no philosopher in his senses
would even think of denying his great debt to Aristotle's foundation work. All that we can add, even in the period of symbolic logic,
is superstructure.

The place to begin with logic is the clear distinction between the
conception of truth and that of validity. Both conceptions are involved, but they are not used well if they are confused with each
other. Truth, as we have already seen, in Chapter 3, refers to whatever is the case. If it is true that there are only three people in the
room, it is false that there are more than three people in the room.
Normally we find out how many there are by counting, though
sometimes we find out in other and less direct ways. In the great
majority of situations we are forced to use less direct ways. I think
that it is true that I had a paternal grandfather, but, since I have
been told that he died before I was born, I certainly do not ascertain this truth directly. Yet, whatever the means available, we mean
the same thing about truth in both instances. We mean the same
when we affirm that God is; namely, we affirm something about
which we may be right and also about which we may be wrong.

Validity is utterly different from truth. Instead of referring to
what is the case it refers to a particular quality in a chain of reasoning. A chain of reasoning is called valid if the connection between
links is such that what supposedly follows really follows. The conse-

---

[11] Two forms of the Validoscope are in use at Earlham College.
[12] Aristotle, *De Interpretatione*, trans. E. M. Edghill, *The Basic Works of
Aristotle*, Random House, 1941, p. 40.

quence is that it is possible to form a chain of reasoning which is perfectly valid, though the individual propositions involved are untrue. For example:

All Russians are atheists;
The Pope is a Russian;
Therefore, the Pope is an atheist.

In this there is nothing wrong with the validity, for, if the first two propositions are accepted, the third must be accepted, but it is easy to see that the effort is worthless, inasmuch as the basic assertions are false.

On the other hand it is possible to have a combination of truth and *invalidity*, in which we have true premises and a true conclusion, but no validity of connection. For example:

All Hoosiers are Americans;
All residents of Indianapolis are Americans;
Therefore, all residents of Indianapolis are Hoosiers.

If we employ the usual meanings of "resident" and of "Hoosier" these three propositions tell what we know to be the case, but the first two propositions could be true without the third being true at all. This we see immediately if we keep the same logical form but employ different propositions.

It is important, once we recognize the sharp distinction between truth and validity, to know that logic, as an intellectual discipline, is primarily concerned with validity. This is not because logicians are unconcerned about truth, but because they are so deeply concerned about it that they seek to learn *how* it may be reached. The goal is the presentation of valid steps arising from the foundation of true propositions so that *other* true propositions may be confidently asserted. What is desired is to start with truth and then to extend it validly, so that the conclusion is true. The ideal is the arrival at propositions which are true because they really follow from other propositions that are known to be true. Therefore, though validity and truth are vastly different conceptions, they come to completion only when they are combined with each other.

The formal method of testing validity in syllogisms depends upon the Aristotelian square of opposition, which classifies propositions in terms of quality (affirmative and negative) and quantity (universal and particular). Thus every possible proposition of a syllogism is one of the following:

A   universal affirmative.
E   universal negative.
I   particular affirmative.
O   particular negative.

Combinations of A, E, I, and O propositions which may provide valid inference in one of the four figures may not provide it in another. Though there are sixty-four possible combinations of the premises, only nineteen of these lead to valid conclusions. Invalidity is, accordingly, far more common than validity. It is easier everywhere to be wrong that it is to be right. Examples of invalidity are easy to find. For example:

Members of the John Birch Society are conservative;
Many college students are conservative;
Therefore, many college students are members of the John Birch Society.

It is important to see, not only that this particular conclusion is invalid, but also that the combination of the two premises does not lead to any conclusion at all. It does not lead to a conclusion because we do not know that we are talking about the same conservatives in the two instances. This is what we mean when we say that we are illustrating here the fallacy of the undistributed middle.[13]

Now the important feature for us to notice in this deductive system is the sharpness and completeness of the proof, *within the system*. If, in a valid syllogistic procedure, the premises are true, then it follows necessarily that the conclusion is true. So far as the form itself is concerned we have transcended probability and have reached certainty. This is well illustrated by the various proofs that are possible. For example, we can prove that, in a third-figure syllogism, every valid conclusion is a particular proposition and never a universal one. In short, it is always either an I or an O and never

[13] The student who wishes to go fully into these matters has many excellent choices. See, in the Bibliography, "Books on Logic and Epistemology."

an A or an E. The way in which such proof is made is instructive, because it is elegant and clean. The minimum steps are as follows:

1. If a valid conclusion is universal, its subject (the minor term) is distributed.
2. If the minor term is distributed in the conclusion, it must also be distributed in the corresponding premise. (Rule 2.)
3. The corresponding premise (the minor premise) must then be negative, since no affirmative proposition ever has a distributed predicate, and, in Figure 3, the minor term is necessarily a predicate.
4. If the minor premise is thus negative the conclusion must be negative. (Rule 4.)
5. If the conclusion is negative the major term (the predicate of the conclusion) is distributed, since all negative propositions distribute all predicates.
6. If the major term is distributed in the conclusion, it must also be distributed in the major premise. (Rule 2.)
7. The major premise, like the minor premise, is thus necessarily negative.
8. But from two negative premises there is no valid conclusion. (Rule 3.)
9. Therefore a valid conclusion in Figure 3 must be particular.

This is the sort of proof which gives delight to many minds, especially when it is applied to mathematical theorems. There is no doubt that it provides genuine proof, but it is a proof which is limited to a special logical context. The proof is possible only because the rules of the syllogism and the truth of the premises are taken on faith. The deductive development does not tell *whether* the original premises are true, but only the truth of what follows, *providing* the original premises are true. In short the system is concerned with validity rather than with truth. That which follows validly from what is true is itself true, but how do we know whether the starting points are true? The premises must come either from experience, which, as we have seen, is highly vulnerable to doubt, or from arbitrary assumptions, or as deductions from previously affirmed propositions. Not one of these can provide certainty. If we go back and back, by a series of deductions, we do not improve our logical position, because a long deductive chain is no stronger than a short one, and infinite regress is no answer at all.

We are, therefore, driven to the conclusion, so far as deduction is concerned, that proof, in the strict sense, is not our portion. However neat the intermediate steps of proof are, they rest back inevitably on postulates, axioms, and unsupported convictions which we cannot prove at all. This is the point of Miss Stebbing's brilliant conclusion when she says, "The notion of proof is relative to something unproved; what is taken as unproved determines what can be proved."[14]

The realization that the provable depends upon the unprovable is not the pet theory of one particular school of philosophy, but is agreed to by the great majority of philosophers, ancient and modern. The Spanish thinker, Ortega y Gasset speaks for the great tradition when he says:

Therefore, in order to affirm the existence of certain objects by means of inference or proof one must start with a more basic and primary certainty in the existence of other objects; a type of certainty which needs neither proof nor inference. There are, then, things whose existence we neither can nor need to prove.[15]

It is important for the student of philosophy to know what logic can do and also to know, with equal clarity, what logic cannot do. Because a valid conclusion is involved in a particular connectedness of the premises, it follows from them, as the night the day, but the strength of the conclusion thereby attained is no greater than is the strength of that upon which it rests. This does not mean that formal logic is to be disregarded. Formal logic is extremely valuable. The educated person needs to know what processes are valid and what processes are fallacious, but logic is not thereby rendered an infallible system for knowing or for defending the truth. We are helped immensely if we can spot an undistributed middle or an illicit process, but this does not release us from the human predicament of finitude and consequent potential error. However long the valid chain may be, it is anchored somewhere in

14 Stebbing, op. cit., p. 473.
15 Ortega y Gasset, What Is Philosophy?, trans. Mildred Adams, W. W. Norton & Company, Inc., 1960, p. 137.

an assumption or in an experience, and these provide no way of absolute insurance against error.

There is further difficulty in deductive logic in that it never escapes completely from the taint of tautology and circular reasoning. Consider the classical syllogism in Figure 1:

> All men are mortal;
> Socrates is a man;
> Therefore, Socrates is mortal.

This seems intellectually respectable until we ask seriously how we know the truth of the major premise. Can we really know that all men are mortal, *unless* we have already included in our study the man Socrates? He is surely part of the relevant evidence. Either we have considered him or we have not. If we have considered him, the conclusion is redundant. If we *have not* considered him the major premise is unjustified. The critics of syllogistic reasoning tend to admit that people do actually reason in this inferential way, but they deny that we learn anything which we did not already know, because, they say, the major premise is really dependent upon the conclusion. If it is not true that Socrates is mortal, it would be impossible to say truly that all men are mortal. By this analysis the syllogism certainly seems to be guilty of the fallacy of *petitio principii*, or begging the question. This is a serious charge and one that can be met only by a careful consideration of how the truth of the major premise is established. If the mortality of the human race is established by considerations of human physique, and not by counting all persons, the charge of circularity is effectively answered. Actually, of course, this is how the proposition is supported. In any case it could not rest on a counting of everybody, including the unborn as well as the unknown. Since the major premise may be affirmed, without knowing the conclusion, the conclusion may be *epistemically* independent of the major premise. Only in that case can the charge of *petitio principii* be avoided. Although it can thereby be avoided, it must be admitted that much syllogistic reasoning *is* actually question begging.

Inductive logic is that in which the conclusions follow from preceding propositions, not necessarily but probably. Thus, from many reported observations of the temperature at which water is changed from a solid to a liquid state, we draw a conclusion about the melting point that is universal. All progressions from particular events to laws are of this character. Since the conclusion is usually far larger in scope than the supporting propositions, either individually or collectively, it is obvious that the movement of thought within an inductive system is only probable and by no means necessary or inevitable. Each inductive conclusion is a leap, but it is a leap which it is reasonable to take, because the alternative is no conclusion at all.

If genuine proof is limited in the system of deduction, it is even more limited in a system of induction. The entire principle of induction rests, of necessity, on probability and therefore never escapes it. From the mere observation that a thousand men have died, or a million men, for that matter, I cannot infer with certainty that all men will die. The leap from some to all is so great that it is always full of dangers, yet, if this leap is not made, there is no inductive process. The upshot of the matter is that induction has no perfect right to its conclusion, as deduction has no perfect right to its starting point.[16]

Fact and Idea

Not all that has come into contemporary philosophical thinking as a result of the recovery of admiration for David Hume is good, but one feature has been extremely good. That is the way in which we have learned to appreciate Hume's distinction between "relations of ideas" and "matters of fact."[17]

Of the first kind are the sciences of Geometry, Algebra and Arithmetic; and in short, every affirmation which is either intuitively or demonstrably certain. That the square of the hypotenuse is equal to the square of the two sides is a proposition which expresses a relationship between these figures. That three times five is equal to the half of thirty expresses a relation between these numbers. Propositions of this kind are discoverable by the mere operation of thought, without

---

[16] One of the clearest statements of this twofold predicament is provided by W. Temple, Nature, Man and God, The Macmillan Company, 1956, p. 90.
[17] D. Hume, An Enquiry Concerning Human Understanding, Sec. II, Pt. I.

dependence on what is anywhere existent in the universe. Though there never were a circle or triangle in nature, the truths demonstrated by Euclid would forever retain their certainty and evidence.

Matters of fact, which are the second objects of human reason, are not ascertained in the same manner; nor is our evidence of their truth, however great, of a like nature with the foregoing. The contrary of every matter of fact is still possible.

If we take this distinction seriously we see why there is, in our understanding, an area of proof and an area of mere probability. Real proof is always limited to relations of ideas. If we understand what we mean by two and if we understand what we mean by square, then it follows necessarily that the square of two is four. This is proof within a system of agreed postulates and is similar in character to the proof, given earlier, that all valid conclusions in the third-figure syllogism must be particular.

As soon as we begin to deal with fact, however, we are in another logical situation and realize with Hume, that *what is may not be.*[18] When we deal with electrons or with the laws of *things* (as contrasted to relations of symbols) we can be wrong! We collect all of the evidence we can, and in some simple matters we approach certainty as a limit, but we never fully reach it. We can be wrong about the future, as we are wrong about the past, because we do not know all of the relevant factors. Though many persons have strong reason to believe that God is, not as a mere idea but in objective reality, the evidence for this belief is never coercive. The philosophy of religion may be a very careful and intelligent discipline, but it cannot, in the nature of the case, produce demonstration, for doubt is always possible, and it is possible for the precise reason that we are dealing with the realm of fact. Fact does not permit of perfect proof, but it is the realm of fact about which men care and rightly care.

To know that proof about matters of fact is not available to finite men is not really discouraging. Though we do not have proof, we do have evidence, and our intellectual duty is to try to learn what the degrees of probable evidence are. Though the use of logic will not do what many expect it to do, it can do something of great human value. Perhaps the very best thing that logic can do for us is

[18] *Ibid.*, Sec. VII, Pt. III.

to develop the habit of clarity in the expression of a problem, and the habit of looking for the evidence everywhere.

Some of the most brilliant logic is found, not in textbooks where the illustrations seem to the student to be mostly trivial, but in great works of the imagination such as *The Brothers Karamazov*. In this magnificent work Dostoevsky uses logic in many subtle ways. In the examination of the evidence of the central murder, Ivan's failure to act is fastened upon as being fully as significant as an overt action. Smerdyakov says:

> Then you ought, as your father's son, to have had me taken to the lock-up and thrashed at once for my words then . . . or at least, to have given me a punch in the face on the spot, but you were not a bit angry, if you please, and at once in a friendly way acted on my foolish word and went away, which was utterly absurd, for you ought to have stayed to save your parent's life. How could I help drawing my conclusions?[19]

The philosopher, like the detective of the Sherlock Holmes variety, must discipline his mind to watch for the evidence which is present, though not immediately obvious. In listening to a man's defense of a position, there is great value in watching for what may be inadvertent evidence of the weakness of his case. A. E. Taylor advises us that "we must never forget the principle . . . that the most valuable statements of the apologist are just those incidental admissions which are incompatible with the case he is putting forward."[20]

Though some parts of logic can be represented mechanically, most cannot, and the parts that can be so represented are the least important. What is most important is a habit of mind which watches for revealing details and which learns, by experience, to know what the weight of evidence is.

Antidote to Misology

The demand for absolute proof, when, as a matter of fact, such is not possible, is obviously a practical as well as a theoretical danger

---

[19] F. M. Dostoevsky, *The Brothers Karamazov*, The Modern Library, 1929, Random House, Pt. IV, Bk. XI, vii.

[20] A. E. Taylor, *Socrates, The Man and His Thought*, Doubleday & Company, Inc., Anchor Books, 1956, p. 24.

to mankind. The essence of the danger is that which is involved in all perfectionism. The evil of perfectionism arises when the ideal best becomes the enemy of the concrete good. The person who will not act without perfect proof will, unfortunately, not act at all, and will therefore fail to do the modest act which, though imperfect, is often better than none. Gandhi made this mistake when, speaking of Satyagraha he said, "It excludes the use of violence because man is not capable of knowing absolute truth and therefore not competent to punish." Logically this unwillingness to act short of absolute certainty would leave the innocent at the mercy of the ruthless marauder. Perfection serves, in practice, to cut the nerve of the modest moral effort of which we may be capable. The danger of insistence on perfect proof is the danger so brilliantly explained by Plato in the *Phaedo*, the danger of misology. There is always a temptation, as Plato saw, for those who first become aware of the conflicting nature of human reasoning, including the inconclusive character of all evidence, to desert the entire enterprise and to declare it hopeless. There is a tendency of men who are shocked by the recognition that they cannot know perfectly, to leap to the conclusion that they cannot know at all, and thereby to give up the entire effort. This, Socrates is made to say, is the worst thing that can happen to a man. The celebrated passage is:

But first let us take care that we avoid a danger.

Of what nature? I said.

Lest we become misologists, he replied: no worse thing can happen to a man than this. For as there are misanthropists or haters of men, there are also misologists or haters of ideas, and both spring from the same cause which is ignorance of the world. Misanthropy arises out of the too great confidence of an experience:—you trust a man and think him altogether true and sound and faithful, and then in a little while he turns out to be false and knavish; and then another and another, and when this has happened several times to a man, especially when it happens among those whom he deems to be his own trusted and familiar friends, and he has often quarrelled with them, he at last hates all men, and believes that no one has any good in him at all.[21]

After showing that there can be an experience with untrustworthy arguments comparable to that with untrustworthy men, with a

[21] Plato, *Phaedo*, trans. Jowett, *The Dialogues of Plato*, Oxford University Press, 1871, Vol. II, 89, 90.

similar general refusal to trust any, Socrates is represented by Plato as concluding with the following important words: "Let us then, in the first place, be careful of allowing or of admitting into our souls the notion that there is no health or soundness in any arguments at all. Rather say that we have not yet attained to soundness in ourselves, and that we must struggle manfully to do our best to gain health of mind."[22] The problem about proof is to recognize the inherent limitations of all probatory evidence without, at the same time, falling into the fallacy of absolute skepticism which inevitably cuts the nerve of intellectual effort. The great tradition in philosophy is the tradition which, while it enforces humility, avoids the kind of skepticism which is self-defeating. No finer expression of this middleground can be found than that which appears in the conversation of one who was a contemporary of both Butler and Hume, Dr. Samuel Johnson. "There are," said he, "innumerable questions to which the inquisitive mind can in this state receive no answer."[23] Five years later he completed the balance by saying, "Sir, I considered myself as intrusted with a certain portion of truth. I have given my opinion sincerely; let them show where they think me wrong."[24]

[22] *Ibid.*
[23] James Boswell, *Life of Samuel Johnson*, John B. Alden, Publisher, 1887, Vol. IV, 47.
[24] *Ibid.*, 186.

Chapter 6 ∽ THE SCIENCE OF EVIDENCE

Probability is the guide of life.

BISHOP BUTLER

PROOF, WE AGREE, IS SOMETHING THAT, IN THE STRICT SENSE OF THE word, is not part of man's portion. But this does not mean that we are bereft, nor that one opinion is as good as another. There is something which we do have, and that is evidence. The fact that evidence never amounts to perfect proof does not alter the fact that there are degrees of evidence. It is these degrees which it is the duty of the philosopher to examine. The elimination of the hope of absolute proof, which we have considered in the preceding chapter, is really a source of encouragement rather than of disappointment, because it is only when we have given up the false hope of absolute proof that we are willing to give ourselves fully to what is possible. The fact that we cannot be absolutely certain makes it all the more important that we try to be relatively certain. Though proof is impossible, some chains of reasoning are relatively more dependable than others. To seek these chains may be a modest endeavor, but it is worth following and, morover, it is man's only

112

alternative to that wild and unsupported assertion which is worthless. We must use our minds, both individually and as an intellectual community, to try to ascertain what constitutes warrantable assertability.

As philosophy is not concerned with what is undeniably true, so is it not concerned with what is patently false. It is concerned, rather, with what there is good reason to believe and with what the substantiations of sound belief are. As philosophers we are not called upon to ascertain the truth of particular observations, but rather to examine the principles upon which all substantiation of belief may rightly depend.

Every contradiction about fact indicates that somebody is wrong, though we cannot, at least at first, know which one is wrong. This constitutes a powerful incentive to further examination of the nature of evidence. Beliefs depend upon evidence, and because beliefs are important, evidence is also important. What is evidence? What is good evidence? How may we know what follows from evidence? What do we mean by probability? These have always been, and presumably will always be, central questions in the quest which we call philosophy.

Cumulative Evidence

If the analysis suggested in Chapter 5 is justified by the facts as we know them, it is clear that we are forced to depend on probable evidence, at least in regard to those beliefs which have to do with existence. This may not be all that we could desire, but it is part of the inescapable human predicament. What we must understand, at the outset, is that we have an alternative to absolute certainty, on the one hand, and to sheer guess, on the other. It is this to which Butler referred in his famous aphorism as the "guide of life."

The fact that, in our human finitude, we are forced to act on the basis of probabilities need not cut the nerve of intellectual effort. The recognition that we are limited to the realm of probabilities is a strong incentive to thoughtful people to learn to distinguish between the degrees of probability. We must agree with Temple that "the most important of mental disciplines for almost all purposes is not that which distinguishes between certainty and uncertainty, but that which leads to discrimination between the degrees of probability, and especially between degrees of justification attaching to unproved assurances."[1]

The classic treatment of probable evidence is that of Joseph Butler (1692–1752) who ended his scholarly life as the Bishop of Durham. Realizing that he believed in God, but that he had no demonstrable proof of God's existence, Butler set his life to the examination of evidence in other realms and discovered that his failure to have demonstration in the religious realm was by no means unique. He found that he was in the same human predicament in science and in practical decisions, a point already noted briefly by John Locke. If this seemed to ally the good Bishop with implicit skepticism, then the implications of this alliance would have to be faced with resolution, for this, he concluded, was the nature of human understanding and an inevitable consequence of our finitude.

Direct and circumstantial evidence, Butler held, make up one argument by their necessary combination. "For it is the kind of evidence upon which most questions of difficulty, in common practice, are determined: evidence arising from various coincidences, which support and confirm each other, and in this manner prove, with more or less certainty, the point under consideration."[2] Butler was not satisfied merely to fall back on revelation because he saw that evidence needed to be given for it, but when he examined the possible evidence he found that it was strikingly similar to evidence for other alleged facts in that the conclusion rests, not on a single line, "but on a great variety of circumstantial things also."

The heart of Butler's contention was that "though each of these direct and circumstantial things is indeed to be considered separately, yet they are afterwards to be joined together; for that the proper force of the evidence consists in the result of those several things, considered in their respects to each other, and united into one view."[3]

[1] W. Temple, *Nature, Man and God*, The Macmillan Company, 1956. p. 84. The passage quoted appears in a brilliant chapter, "Mathematics and Logic," which no serious student of logic should overlook.
[2] J. Butler, *The Analogy of Religion, Natural and Revealed*, J. M. Dent, Everyman Library, p. 217.
[3] *Ibid.*

No philosopher has seen more clearly the point about cumulative evidence than did Butler. Butler's central insight was his recognition, not merely that separate lines of evidence support and confirm an original hypothesis, but that they "support and confirm each other."[4] The careful thinker, then, does not watch for a single, definitive proof, which is seldom or never available, but for a combination of probative factors. He must learn, as he becomes more skilful, to estimate the force of evidence which never consists in simple addition. The total force is always greater than is the sum of the individual constituents, considered separately, in their aloneness. Proofs which, separately, are manifestly inadequate, achieve in conjunction a remarkable adequacy. This is the point of Butler's famous conclusion which he stated in such aphoristic form that any student who really grasps it cannot forget it. "Probable proofs," he said, "by being added, not only increase the evidence, but multiply it."[5]

Butler's great contemporary, David Hume, differed from him in important ways, particularly in his religious convictions, but Hume's view of cumulative evidence is similar and escapes attention only because it is not put so memorably. "This concurrence of several views in one particular event," wrote Hume, "begets immediately, by an inexplicable contrivance of nature, the sentiment of belief."[6]

Probability has been the subject of many penetrating studies, particularly in the twentieth century.[7] Since the term is widely used in popular speech it is not a surprising fact that it involves, ordinarily, a great deal of ambiguity. In one sense of the word, probability can be exactly defined, because in this sense it is a branch of mathematics, a branch which owes much of its early development to Pascal. It would not be suitable to give much space here to a purely mathematical conception, but the student should know that it has been worked out elaborately in a number of contemporary treatises. In the ordinary system certainty is represented by 1

[4] *Ibid.*, p. 217.

[5] *Ibid.*, p. 231.

[6] D. Hume, *An Enquiry Concerning Human Understanding*, Sec. II, Pt. IV, 144.

[7] See J. M. Keynes, *A Treatise on Probability*, The Macmillan Company, 1921.

and impossibility by 0. If the favorable factors are denoted by r and the unfavorable factors by r', then the odds in favor of an event's happening will be expressed by $\frac{r}{r'}$ while the odds against its happening will be expressed by $\frac{r'}{r}$. What is really amazing is the degree to which a discipline which seems to be a branch of mathematics actually applies to the world of events. The possibility of such application underlies the entire development of life insurance.

One of the areas of common life in which the calculation of probabilities is a familiar feature is the opinion poll. The principle used here is that of fair sampling, which means that only a few opinions need to be examined in order to know the general truth, providing the opinions are rightly spaced in regard to sex, race, education, geography, etc. The prestige of such polls, which have been widely used in forecasting election results, received a severe blow in 1948, when President Truman was actually elected for another term, even though the public opinion experts, including Dr. Gallup, claimed to be able to demonstrate, by their strictly scientific methods, that Mr. Truman would be overwhelmingly defeated. The setback was really a beneficent development because it destroyed some of the public credulity concerning methods which seem impressive and scientific, solely because they involve statements expressed in numerical percentages.

The idolatry of mathematics is shown whenever there is a tendency to honor whatever can be stated in terms of graphs and tables. Apart from this idolatry it is hard to understand the generally favorable reception of the Kinsey reports. The study might ignore the researches of psychiatrists and psychoanalysts over the last fifty years, but it seemed impressive because the results could be stated in percentages. The use of polls at elections involves an area of experience which can be checked by future results, but a study of the past has no such check upon its accuracy or inaccuracy.

It is important to note that probability in ordinary experience, which is what concerns the philosopher as distinguished from the mathematician, is not something which can be put into a precise formula. We mean something which is distinct from certainty, at one extreme, and from impossibility, at the other. It is in this broad middleground that experience normally occurs. On one side we have extremely high probability, which approaches certainty. Most of us would say that this is so when we consider an astronaut's many orbits of the earth. At the other extreme are claims so preposterous that most thoughtful people reject them. In all this we must be alerted to a danger to which Butler sometimes fell victim, the danger of accepting *possibility* as probability. Thomas Hobbes, in the seventeenth century, had already warned against this by saying, "He that believes a thing only because it may be so, may as well doubt it because it may be otherwise."[8]

The immense significance of the point about the cumulative nature of evidence is that it shows us how we may have practical guidance, not only in our beliefs, but in the affairs of ordinary life. The interior certainty of a syllogistic system is not to be despised, and we must use it as an aid to clarity, but it is seldom applicable to experience except by a manifest abstraction. Logic in practice is primarily the logic of the coherence of many little parts into one whole. Cardinal Newman had this in mind in his emphasis on informal inference.

It is plain [he said] that formal logical sequence is not in fact the method by which we are able to become certain of what is concrete; and it is equally plain, from what has been already suggested, what the real and necessary method is. It is the cumulation of probabilities, independent of each other, arising out of the nature and circumstances of the particular case which is under review; probabilities too fine to avail separately, too subtle and circuitous to be convertible into syllogisms, too numerous and various for such conversion, even were they convertible.[9]

This practical logic of noting convergence of evidence is a skill which is needed in questions of every kind. It applies to moral questions as well as to scientific ones, for concerning what men ought to do in regard to anything in the world, we are denied the luxury of absolute certainty. It applies to the knowledge of God as truly as it applies to atoms. Whether God is or is not is a question

[8] Thomas Hobbes, *Last Sayings, or Dying Legacy of Mr. Hobbes of Malmesbury*, in *Somers Tracts* (1812), VII, 369.
[9] J. H. Newman, *A Grammar of Assent*, Burns & Oates Ltd., 1870, p. 281.

of tremendous significance, but we cannot answer it with the certainty which would give comfort to so many.

However interesting the relationships between ideas may be, it is not these that matter most. What concerns us deeply is fact, and it ought to concern us, providing we are interested in knowing what kind of world it is that we inhabit. It is reasonable to ask whether God is, or whether belief in Him is a mere projection of our wishes; it is reasonable to wonder whether atoms are or whether they are merely a useful scientific fiction; it is reasonable to wonder whether the earth has been in existence for millions of years or only for a few thousand years. If anyone says that he is not interested in such questions, that is his personal privilege, but he is not representative of the bulk of mankind. Aristotle was speaking for most thoughtful persons when he said, at the beginning of the *Metaphysics*, "All men by nature desire to know." But the only way to know is to learn to estimate the weight of evidence. This cannot be estimated mechanically, but we can make advance as we practice the science of evidence in all of its parts.

If proof is never complete, especially in a court of law, how, we may ask, are we ever justified in sending a man to prison for a crime of which he is the alleged perpetrator? Since there is a sense in which all evidence is circumstantial, are we justified in this world in making any judgments at all? Yes, we are justified because the alternative, of no judgments whatever, is manifestly worse and would make practical life impossible. We must proceed on the weight of evidence and this comes, in most instances, by the joint impact of several lines of evidence, each of which is inadequate alone, while the cumulative effect is almost overwhelming.

A California doctor is put on trial for the murder of his estranged wife. Did he kill her? He says he did not. But the jury, after much deliberation, finally decided that he was, in fact, guilty. There was a monetary motive; there was the relationship to the other woman; there was the weapon; there was the escape from the scene. Not one of these was adequate alone, for each single line of evidence might have another and innocent explanation, but two converging lines are far stronger than a single line, while three are many times stronger than two, and four are almost overwhelming in their cumulative effect. Thus Butler's dictum is of immense practical application.

Charles S. Peirce supported the idea of cumulative evidence, not, as did Bishop Butler, through an analysis of the human predicament, but through his understanding of the success of modern science. He saw that in so far as science advances, it does so by the cumulative combination of different probabilities. A good philosopher, he concluded, would follow a similar procedure. Thus, in science or anything else worthwhile, Peirce saw that wisdom lies in the frank acceptance of the twin doctrines of fallibility and probability. We are prone to error; our evidence is only probable at best; therefore let us make the strongest possible combination, which may be compared to a cable rather than a chain. Peirce's key passage is the following:

> Philosophy ought to imitate the successful sciences in its methods, so far as to proceed only from tangible premises which can be subjected to careful scrutiny, and to trust rather to the multitude and variety of its arguments than to the conclusiveness of any one. Its reasoning should not form a chain which is no stronger than its weakest link, but a cable whose fibers may be ever so slender, provided they are sufficiently numerous and intimately connected.[10]

The understanding of the nature of evidence and the practical need of corroboration is important in a society in which there is a jury system, requiring ordinary untrained people to decide the fate of their fellow men who are accused. It is a fearful thing to decide on life or death for another human being, especially when we recognize that proof is never complete or demonstrable. But, fearful as it may be, the obligation cannot be evaded, for the failure to decide on the weight of evidence may occasion an even worse injustice than that produced by making that decision.

We tend to distinguish between evidence that is direct and evidence that is circumstantial, but, in reality, the distinction is difficult to maintain. Since the supposedly direct evidence is given on the witness of a person who is himself a fallible human being, even

[10] C. S. Peirce, *Values in a Universe of Chance*, Stanford University Press, 1958, pp. 40, 41.

this direct evidence is only probable, and thus needs corroboration. Often in a court of law we have strong competing witnesses. Each might be lying, each might be mistaken. This is why our only certainty is what is called "moral certainty." Even the use of the expert, in line with the principle of authority which we shall soon defend in this chapter, provides no perfect insurance that justice will be done. In a given case, the witness of the expert is itself fallible. For example, the evidence seems to indicate that the accused actually shot his estranged wife on a given day at a given place. Now we bring in a skilled psychiatrist who is presented with the evidence and asked whether, in his judgment, the accused was sane and responsible (i.e., able to distinguish between right and wrong) at the time of the alleged murder. The psychiatrist may be assumed to be doing his scientific best, but he is judging an event which is forever gone and which he did not personally observe. The same would be true of any other expert, be he locksmith, photographer, or criminologist.

It is the recognition of the cumulative nature of evidence that causes us to prize the practice of cross-examination. If a single witness were adequate, cross-examination could be abandoned without significant loss, but we know that we need the corroboration which standing up under cross-examination provides. In many states we carry this so far that we do not allow testimony to bear weight if a witness dies during the trial and his testimony has thus been unchallenged. The general principle is that unexamined and unsubstantiated evidence is not worthy of acceptance.

Scientific Method

It is one of the misfortunes of recent academic history that some studies are termed sciences while others are supposedly nonscientific. The misfortune lies in the fact that the outside observer immediately concludes that science is a matter of special subjects, like those of chemistry or geology, and is consequently limited in scope. We avoid much confusion if we think of science as a matter of method, which can be applied, with suitable variations, to a great variety of subjects. The absurdity of our conventional division is made obvious when we realize that the study of the Dead Sea

Scrolls, though not ordinarily listed among the sciences, can be fully as scientific as the study of the earth's surface. What is important is a special way of looking for the evidence and a special way of handling the evidence. If subject matter were enough to produce a science, then astrology would be a science, but clearly it is not. Scientific method may be applied by a host of men who would feel it presumptuous to call themselves scientists, even though their skill is astonishing.

Familiar illustrations of scientific method are noted, almost constantly, among plumbers and automobile mechanics. Without feeling self-conscious about it the mechanic uses at once the main steps of scientific method when he faces a problem of failure of some part of a car. He *observes, he forms a preliminary hypothesis, he thinks what would follow if the hypothesis were true, and he tests* to see whether the expected results are actually found. Frequently he employs a whole series of hypotheses. If the lights are not burning he quickly tests the following educated guesses:

1. The power is lacking.
2. The connection is broken.
3. The bulbs are burned out.

He finds whether each of these is a false hypothesis by noting other results, in addition to the original problem, to see whether they occur. If they do not, then he must seek some further hypothesis. The best mechanic is usually the one who can think of new and possibly fruitful hypotheses.

Much that goes on in science is logically identical with what goes on in philosophical thinking and in ordinary human experience. One of the most important differences between scientific mentality and ordinary common sense is that science tends to analyze the obvious. To do this, as A. N. Whitehead has taught us, requires a very unusual cast of mind. Furthermore, the scientific mind is keenly conscious that isolated facts are worthless. We make progress only when events are observed and men use reason to try to guess at some prior situation which will explain the observed events. A good illustration of such progress is seen in the problem of the Dutch elm disease in the United States. The location of the dead and dying trees was carefully observed in the hope that some pattern might appear. Finally, after the suspicion was aroused that disease-carrying beetles were being imported, the logs which had been brought to Baltimore from France were examined and the harmful beetles were found. It is clear that all diagnosis necessarily is an estimate of the causes of observed facts.

What is new in modern science is not this highly valuable use of backward inference, which men have used as long as they have been consciously rational, but rather the kind of *forward* reasoning which is made possible by the use of *experiments*. The introduction of experiment makes it possible to move deliberately from *a* to *b* by setting up artificial conditions. By means of experiment we can transcend the observatory and move on to the laboratory. We can opine that a certain consequence *should* appear under certain explicit conditions, so we set up the conditions and *wait to see*. The thinking is still of the if . . . then variety, but a method has been found which accelerates the speed of learning enormously. This may involve untold good for human life, as Dr. Jonas Salk has demonstrated in his experiments with polio vaccine.

There are some scientists who are so impressed with the value of experimental reasoning that they tend to have contempt for all other ways of operating. Thus they feel superior to those who do not work in laboratories. A little more care would convince such men that, though experimental method is good, it has definite limitations. By common consent we cannot engage, for example, in coerced human vivisection. There are some experiments which we might like to make, but which, providing we are decent persons, we never make. Moral experimentation is clearly unsuitable, partly because it involves a certain element of self-contradiction. To experiment with what is intrinsically valuable is to deny the value. Experiment is possible when the materials involved are of such a nature that they can be discarded without serious loss, but experiment cannot be performed with a sense of integrity when the worth of the human individual is jeopardized by our experiment. The task of wisdom is to know when experimentation is acceptable.

There is a widespread tendency to suppose that science succeeds almost wholly by physical experimentation, when actually the crucial part of most advanced science is pure theory, such as that in which Einstein engaged so fruitfully in the early work which made atomic fission possible. To think that a man can observe the facts inductively and that induction leads automatically to significant conclusions is to falsify the scientific process almost completely. Einstein himself provided an excellent antidote to the popular mistake when he said, "In error are those theorists who believe that theory comes inductively from experience."[11]

The classic example of the way great intellectual activity, especially of a deductive nature, is necessary for science is that of the discovery of the planet Neptune. After Uranus had been discovered in 1781, it was possible to determine its orbit through its eighty-four-year revolution about the sun. The critical observation, however, was that the calculated orbit did not agree exactly with the observed positions. It was recognized that the orbit of each planet is influenced by the other planets in orbit. The disturbing fact was that the orbit of Uranus could not be accounted for by known factors. A thinking astronomer, convinced of the truth of the general law and unwilling to admit chaos, even in details, was forced to conclude that there must be some other planet, as yet unobserved. The French astronomer, Leverrier, was able to assign the particular region of the heavens where the hitherto unknown planet ought to be. When the high-powered telescope was directed to this precise region, the planet was discovered. It is clear to anyone that the intellectual process involved in this classic scientific victory is essentially deductive. The crucial step is the formulation of the hypothesis, "The discrepancy is due to the existence of an unknown planet."

Because ours is an age of scientific success, there is a great danger of the idolatry of science, and it is part of the task of philosophy to point out this danger. Scientists are men, with all of the dangers and foibles of men, and consequently they do not agree. Note the wide disagreement, already mentioned, about the wisdom of testing atomic weapons. It ought to be shattering to the idolatry of science in the popular mind to realize that the division among professional

[11] Contemporary studies are available to the student who wishes to consider carefully the phenomenon of genius in the creation of fruitful hypotheses. Important works written in recent years are: Jacques Hadamard, *The Psychology of Invention in the Mathematical Field*, Princeton University Press, 1945, and Norwood Russell Hanson, *Patterns of Discovery*, Cambridge University Press, 1958.

scientists on this question is quite as sharp as is the division among the general populace. Science is a potential good and sometimes an actual good, but it is by no means the panacea which it is popularly supposed to be. Gilbert Highet has pointed out the danger vividly:

There are naïve people all over the world—some of them scientists—who believe that all problems, sooner or later, will be solved by Science. The word Science itself has become a vague reassuring noise, with a very ill-defined meaning and a powerful emotional charge: It is now applied to all sorts of unsuitable subjects and used as a cover for careless and incomplete thinking in dozens of fields. But even taking Science at the most sensible of its definitions, we must acknowledge that it is as unperfect as all other activities of the human mind.[12]

An important point which is often neglected in the popular estimate of scientific method is its inclusion of a recognized logical fallacy. Ordinarily scientific method involves four separate steps: (1) observation, (2) the formation of a hypothesis, (3) the recognition of what the hypothesis implies, and (4) verification. The chief logical problem appears in the fourth and final step and involves us in committing the fallacy of "the affirmation of the consequent." The logical form is

a implies b;
b is true;
Therefore a is true.

This form may be given substance in countless practical ways. For example:

If John has been drinking to excess he weaves as he walks;
John does weave as he walks;
Therefore, John has been drinking to excess.

Illustrated in this form, that the fallacy is the affirmation of the consequent is obvious to almost anyone. There may be other reasons, quite different from excessive drinking, to render a man unable to walk a straight line. In short there may be a plurality of causes having the same effects. More than one antecedent may lead to a particular consequent. Therefore the reasoning backward, which is the essence of verification, is full of the possibility of error.

[12] G. Highet, *Man's Unconquerable Mind*, Columbia University Press, 1954, p. 106.

"A theory whose consequences conflict with the facts cannot be true, but so long as there may be more theories than one giving the same consequences, the agreement of the facts with one of them furnishes no ground for choosing between it and the others."[13]

The problem involved in the fallacy of verification is a serious one, inasmuch as the method is inherent in the scientific procedure. Many of the objects of which we speak, in scientific language, are never observed at first hand, but are only inferred, and they are inferred by the method just outlined. The entire atomic theory, for example, is supported in this manner. Scientists do not observe atoms, but they use their minds to predict what ought to result, that is be observable, if the atomic theory is true. Thus the theory is confirmed. In many intricate problems of knowledge, there is no other way of reaching a definite conclusion. Meanwhile, we do all that we can to overcome the formal fallacy and this we do by testing the consequent, not in just one way, but in as many ways as is feasible. The paradox is that we overcome the fallacy by *committing it in a refined fashion, many times instead of once.* The logical form then is not the simple one of

a implies b

with the subsequent verification of b, but rather

a implies b, b^1, b^2, b^3, b^4, etc.

We check as many of these varied and complicated resultants as we can, under a great variety of conditions. If all of them appear, the fallacy is still that of the affirmation of the consequent, but the probability of truth is vastly increased by the multiple coincidence. In short, the miracle of coincidence, without adequate reason, is theoretically possible, but we do not expect it in any particular situation. This brings us back to Bishop Butler and his insistence on the principle of accumulation. We depend upon science, not because it has a foolproof method, which it does not, but because of our primitive and unproven faith that the miracle of coincidence does not occur.

[13] H. W. B. Joseph, *An Introduction to Logic*, Oxford University Press, 1916, p. 523.

The faith which is necessary to science can be made explicit. Science, as we understand it, is not possible unless at least two distinct articles of faith are accepted and made the basis of operation. The first is that the natural world is *ordered*. The fact that this order is often not apparent is, for the faithful scientist, only an incentive to deeper probing. If he finds the same causes producing different effects he operates on the assumption that, in his analysis, he is missing something important. He believes, and must believe, that closer scrutiny will reveal differences in either the alleged cause or the alleged effect. If the scientist really believed that anything can happen chaotically in this world his entire motive to research would be undermined.

The second article is associated with the first, but logically distinct from it—the belief that the order of nature is *intelligible*. It is conceivable that there might be laws, but laws of such a nature that they could not be discovered by creatures like ourselves. The order of nature might indeed be one of unimaginable complexity. If laws of nature were not intelligible to finite men, all extension of generalization beyond a particular experience would be impossible. If, in spite of some appearances to the contrary, the order is such as to be intelligible, then man's position is not so exceptional that he cannot generalize beyond the limits of human experience. The very fact of science is a tremendous fact for the philosopher. In so far as it is justified it means that there is some kinship between reason, even the finite reason of men, and the fundamental order of the world.

Authority

Man as a thinking creature who knows that he is liable to error, must engage in the task of discovering methods by which his liability to error may be reduced. It is important to know that, in pursuing the science of evidence, man cannot rely on any single method, since no single method is adequate. Neither are all the methods used together adequate; but a combination of certain methods provides a result which is *less inadequate*. It is a corollary of our humility that we must explore all possible methods of proof or of quasi-proof. One of these methods of proof is the appeal to authority.

Sometimes we hear people say that, whereas former generations depended upon authority, in our enlightened age we have outgrown such dependence, and we now appeal directly to facts. The naïveté of this remark becomes clear whenever we recognize that the central problem is that of knowing *what the facts are*. Is it a fact that Socrates died by drinking poison in 399 B.C.? I think so. But why do I think so? Only because of a complicated chain of authorities, including that of Plato. The choice is not between dependence upon facts and dependence upon authority, because authority is one of the chief ways in which facts are to be ascertained. Facts are known only through the report of persons, others or ourselves. Trust is a great conception, but it is essentially meaningless except as applied to the judgment of persons. "Instead of trusting logical science," says Newman, "we must trust persons, namely, those who by long acquaintance with their subject have a right to judge."[14]

Since there are many things we need to know, and since most of these are not open to direct observation, reliance on the authority of the expert is the path of intelligence. Few have expressed this significant point better than Alexis de Tocqueville:

If man were forced to demonstrate for himself all the truths of which he makes daily use, his task would never end. He would exhaust his strength in preparatory demonstrations, without ever advancing beyond them. As, from the shortness of his life, he has not the time, nor, from the limits of his intelligence, the capacity, to accomplish this, he is reduced to take upon trust a number of facts and opinions which he has not had either the time or the power to verify for himself, but which men of greater ability have sought out, or which the world adopts. On this groundwork he raises for himself the structure of his own thoughts; he is not led to proceed in this matter by choice, but is constrained by the inflexible law of his condition. There is no philosopher of so great parts in the world, but that he believes a million of things on the faith of other people, and supposes a great many more truths than he demonstrates.[15]

The principle of authority, as de Tocqueville explains with his usual clarity and distinction of language, is inescapable, if we seek to extend our boundaries of knowledge. Authority does not give

[14] Newman, *op. cit.*, pp. 334, 335.
[15] A. de Tocqueville, *Democracy in America*, trans. H. Reeve, New American Library of World Literature, Mentor Books, 1956, Bk. I, chap. 2.

absolute certainty, for the authorities may be wrong and have frequently been shown to be wrong, in the light of subsequent experience, but in many areas the only alternative to reliance upon the authority of the experts is *reliance on nothing*. If anyone proposes to reject the reliance on authority because it is only probable, he is free to do so, but it is the task of a philosopher to help him to see the necessary price—poverty of mind—which this decision entails.

Since the question whether we are to rely on authority is not really one which represents a valid option, we are driven to the question of how we may know which authority we are to trust. Some are obviously more reliable than others; a man is not a dependable authority in any field merely because he declares himself to be such. What we want to know, primarily, is whether the person whom we are asked to trust gives evidence of being trustworthy. Does he, for example, have wide and deep experience in a particular field? The well-known statement of Aristotle about trusting men of age and experience is relevant here. "We ought," he said, "to attend to undemonstrated sayings and opinions of experienced and older people or of people of practical wisdom not less than to demonstrations; for because experience has given them an eye they see aright."[16] We accept the authority of the physician or of the dentist, when his judgment conflicts with our own, chiefly because, in the first place, he has engaged in years of study and of practice. It is not certain that his judgment is sounder than ours, but it is highly likely that it is.

In testing the dependability of authority we must recognize the fallacy of any belief in the factual equality of men. Here, more than almost anywhere, we see the relevance of Plato's dictum that our valid interest is in the judgment of the few rather than of the many. If a million persons selected at random were to have an opinion about a star, while five men from great observatories were to have a contrary opinion, the judgment of the five would far out-

[16] Aristotle, *Nicomachean Ethics*, trans, W. D. Ross, *The Basic Works of Aristotle*, Random House, 1941, Book VI, Chap. 11. Note a similar emphasis on age and experience in *Republic* I, 328. "To tell the truth, Cephalus, I answered, I enjoy talking with old people. They have gone before us on a road which we too may have to travel, and I think we do well to learn from them what it is like, easy or difficult, rough or smooth."

weigh, in evidential value, the judgment of the million.[17] Consequently, when we examine the credentials of a supposed expert, what is important is not his general popularity so much as his standing in the eyes of his fellow experts.

Herein lies the evidential value of Nobel prizes, honorary degrees from first-class institutions, membership in learned societies, and outstanding honors of all kinds. These are valuable, not in the degree to which they minister to pride, but in the degree to which they contribute to a reasonable basis of trust. There are, in any country, many men who sound convincing, though we may not be sure whether they are pretentious fools. If we know, however, that a man, even though his ideas seem shocking, is a member of the American Philosophical Society, we have reason to believe that he is at least someone to whom we should listen. The intense screening on the part of other scholars, to which men must submit before election might let an irresponsible man pass the test, but this outcome is most unlikely.[18]

The pattern of authority is intricate, and is never the same in two situations. For the medical man the pattern includes the diploma from a reputable graduate school of medicine, involving the combined judgment of many other medical men who have been his teachers and examiners. It includes also membership in a county medical society, participation in advanced work at clinics, such as that instituted at Rochester, Minnesota, acceptance by hospital staffs, and much more. The chance that the charlatan or the quack can pass this entire series of demanding tests is not great.

Since reliance upon authority is not a perfect way to know the truth, but is often the only alternative to a poorer way, we must transcend it whenever we can. We must examine credentials relentlessly; we must remain skeptical when we have some good

---

[17] In this connection we may consider the foolishness of the kind of newspaper reporting which picks out persons at random and solemnly prints their judgments on important questions. Usually the opinions are entirely worthless because they are not based on either a broad induction or serious analysis. Such reporting is a waste of newsprint and the reader's time.

[18] One of the best tests of credibility is provided by publication, which necessarily involves submission to criticism at the hands of an author's supposed equals or superiors. In learned discussions we have a wonderful chance to expose pretentious quackery, as the adversary system in court exposes false witness.

reason to doubt what the authorities say; and we must engage in a personal test whenever possible. Because printed airplane schedules can be erroneous, we may find it wise to check actual departure and arrival times in person. In religious experience we must seek firsthand evidence when available, rather than accounts which are still secondhand, even when they come from the devout and the good. But however hard we try, reliance upon authority will never be outgrown by the human thinker. It will always be reasonable because it is one among the relevant evidences concerning what the truth is. We do not know now and presumably we shall never know anything about an infallible authority, just as we shall never have absolute certainty, for these are inconsistent with any clear recognition of the finite predicament of man. Even if there were an infallible authority we should require some infallible means of knowing that it is so, and this, if our analysis is correct, is denied to mortals. But probability as a guide to life is far better than nothing, and the right use of authority increases it.

When Aristotle, the founder of the science of logic, came to the climax of his inquiries at the end of the *Posterior Analytics* he expressed clearly the conviction that there was no escape from dependence upon the intuitions of dependable men. How, he asks, can we know the basic premises? The only hope, he says, lies in paying attention to men of disciplined insight who have followed careful steps, which he outlines. Dependable insight or intuition comes, not at the beginning, but at the end of the disciplined process. "The soul," he says, "is so constituted as to be capable of this process." The modern student can profit much from a slow and careful examination of Aristotle's compact statement:

From these considerations it follows that there will be no scientific knowing of the primary premises, and since except intuition nothing can be truer than scientific knowledge, it will be intuition that apprehends the primary premises—a result which also follows from the fact that demonstration cannot be the originative source of demonstration, nor, consequently, scientific knowledge of scientific knowledge. If, therefore, it is the only other kind of true thinking except scientific knowing, intuition will be the originative source of scientific knowledge.[19]

[19] Aristotle, *Posterior Analytics*, trans. G. R. G. Mure, *The Basic Works of Aristotle, op. cit.*, Bk. II, chap. 19.

Part II ~ PROBLEMS

Chapter 7 ∽ MIND AND BODY

The world is not merely physical, nor is it merely mental.
                                ALFRED NORTH WHITEHEAD

TRADITIONALLY METAPHYSICS HAS BEEN CONCERNED WITH THE HARD-
est questions men can ask. The answers to these questions are
never wholly satisfactory, for they are subject to continual review
and criticism, even on the part of the persons who propound the
best answers they know how to give. Thus, in the *Sophist*, Plato
puts into the mouth of the Stranger, who is presumably Plato himself, criticisms of "Friends of the Forms" who, of course, are the
Platonists. The fact that we can find difficulties in all positions,
including our own, does not mean that the metaphysical quest is
fruitless. To ask the right question is to be already on the way to an
answer and, though we may not have perfect answers, we have good
reason to conclude that some answers are relatively better than
others. The glory of philosophy is that it trains men to ask, and to
ask in a disciplined manner.

A gifted thinker, Professor Highet of Columbia University, has
expressed trenchantly the enormous difficulty of the major questions. "I suppose," he says, "there are not a hundred men in the
history of mankind who have ever understood time. Very few have

fathomed the connection of body and spirit. Very few have been able to explain what death is. And as for the nature of God—it is almost by definition inexpressible, incomprehensible though Absolute. We know that There Is. We do not know What Is."[1]

The proper attitude to employ in any consideration of the basic questions is always one of humility touched with wonder. One of the greatest dangers of science, especially in its popular aspect, is that, in its search for laws, it tends to oversimplify. The wise scientist will always be also a philosopher, in the sense that he will resist this temptation. In one of the highest points of the Platonic corpus we learn that the sense of wonder is the mark of the philosopher, and that, indeed, philosophy has no other origin.[2] No one is truly wise, but almost anyone, if he stops to think, can realize that both the outer world of things and the inner world of the mind represent ultimate mysteries. No man really knows what matter is and no man really knows what his own mind is. But he can be very sure that the simple answers are the ones most wrong, because it is at least clear that the natures in question are complex. The most obvious complexity is that which is involved in the connectedness which each person experiences every day of his life.

The Socratic Position

In the Phaedo we are given one of the first attempts at philosophical autobiography, in the effort of Socrates to tell of the growth of his own thinking. Socrates explains his excited hope concerning the ideas of Anaxagoras about the ultimacy of mind:

Then I heard some one reading, as he said, from a book of Anaxagoras, that mind was the disposer and cause of all, and I was delighted at this notice, which appeared quite admirable, and I said to myself: If mind is the disposer, mind will dispose all for the best, and put each particular in the best place; and I argued that if any one desired to find out the cause of generation or destruction or existence of anything, he must find out what state of being or doing or suffering was best for that thing, and therefore a man had only to consider the best for himself

[1] G. Highet, Man's Unconquerable Mind, Columbia University Press, 1954, p. 105.
[2] Plato, Theaetetus, 155d.

and others, and then he would also know the worse, since the same science comprehended both. And I rejoiced to think that I had found in Anaxagoras a teacher of the causes of existence such as I desired.[3]

But the hope of Socrates soon faded into disappointment when he went further into the new book. The importance of his disappointment is so great that the account of it must be given.

What expectations I had formed, and how grievously was I disappointed! As I proceeded, I found my philosopher altogether forsaking mind or any other principle of order, but having recourse to air, and ether, and water, and other eccentricities. I might compare him to a person who began by maintaining generally that mind is the cause of the actions of Socrates, but who, when he endeavored to explain the cause of my several actions in detail, went on to show that I sit here because my body is made up of bones and muscles; and the bones, as he would say, are hard and have joints which divide them and the muscles are elastic, and they cover the bones, which have also a covering or environment of flesh and skin which contains them; and as the bones are lifted at their joints by the contraction or relaxation of the muscles, I am able to bend my limbs, and this is why I am sitting here in a curved posture—that is what he would say; and he would have a similar explanation of my talking to you, which he would attribute to sound, and air, and hearing, and he would assign ten thousand other causes of the same sort, forgetting to mention the true cause, which is, that the Athenians have thought fit to condemn me, and accordingly I have thought it better and more right to remain here and undergo my sentence; for I am inclined to think that these muscles and bones of mine would have gone off long ago to Megara or Boeotia—by the dog they would, if they had been moved only by their own idea of what was best, and if I had not chosen the better and nobler part, instead of playing truant and running away, of enduring any punishment which the state inflicts.

There is surely a strange confusion of causes and conditions in all this. It may be said, indeed, that without bones and muscles and the other parts of the body I cannot execute my purposes. But to say that I do as I do because of them, and that is the way in which mind acts, and not from the choice of the best, is a very careless and idle mode of speaking.[4]

[3] Plato, Phaedo, trans. Jowett, The Dialogues of Plato, Oxford University Press, 1871, Vol. II, 97d.
[4] Ibid., 98d.

Partly because of the hint given by Anaxagoras, but imperfectly followed by him, and partly because of his own original effort, Socrates established, for western man, the tradition of what is generally known as psychophysical dualism. This position is marked by (a) the conclusion that minds and bodies, though often united, are distinct referents, and (b) the conclusion that the mental operations are true causes, both of other mental events and of physical events. This position, far from denying the reality of the physical order, is at pains to emphasize the existence of the material order and to show that minds operate within it. The greatest emphasis is on the conclusion that the actions of a living human body cannot be accounted for sufficiently by merely physical causes or conditions. As Socrates said, merely physical causes might have taken his body to Megara or Boeotia, and there was no possibility of accounting for his remaining in the Athenian prison except by reference to *thoughts*, which, in his judgment, made the crucial difference. Characteristically, he appealed not to speculation, but to his own firsthand experience, which he presumably knew better than could any external observer.

We tend to assume, after the passage of more than two thousand years, that the idea of the soul, as we understand it, was an ordinary idea in ancient Greece. We know now that it was not. The idea of the soul as a unitary, nonphysical, causal factor in events was an idea which Socrates invented. The story given about Anaxagoras and the reaction to his book may reasonably be taken as factual, since Plato had had abundant opportunity to learn the relevant facts of the story both from Socrates himself and from others. The story evidently relates to events in the early life of Socrates, events which may have taken considerable time for their development. Because Socrates did so much to create the intellectual and moral tradition by which the West has since lived or has tried to live, his idea of the soul is something which every student of philosophy must try to understand. No one has put this more succinctly than has A. E. Taylor:

For more than two thousand years it has been the standing assumption of the civilized European man that he has a *soul*, something which is the seat of his normal waking intelligence and moral character, and that, since this soul is either identical with himself or at any rate the most important thing about him, his supreme business in life is to make the most of it and do the best for it. There are, of course, a minority of persons who reject this theory of life, and some of them even deny the existence of a soul, but they are a small minority; to the vast mass of Europeans, to this day, the existence and the importance of the soul is a doctrine so familiar that it seems self-evident.[5]

In the recent past, the scholarly work of John Burnet has been a significant factor in clarifying the philosophy of mind and body which the Socratic idea of the soul represents.[6] Many of Burnet's insights were taken up and developed by A. E. Taylor, who freely acknowledged his debt. One of Taylor's best descriptions of the soul is as follows:

Now that which uses all other things, even a man's body, is his soul. The soul *is* the man, and everything else that is his is merely something he has or owns. A man, in fact, is a "soul *using* a body" [this is the standing academic definition of "man"]. Hence the first condition of enjoying real good and making a real success of life is that a man's soul should be in a good or healthy state. And the good or healthy state of the soul is just the wisdom of knowledge (*sophia, phronesis*) which insures that a man shall make the right use of his body and of everything else which is his.[7]

The remarkable fact is, as Taylor points out, that this conception of mind and body, which the idea of the soul involves, is fully accepted by such diverse thinkers as Plato, Xenophon, and Isocrates, whereas "it is wholly, or all but wholly, absent from the literature of earlier times." In short, a great philosophical watershed is contemporary with the life of Socrates. Earlier writers had mentioned the *psyche*, but this did not mean the conscious personality, with potentiality for vice and virtue, which it is our business to tend deliberately and consciously. For Homer the psyche is not the man himself, but his *ghost* and the man himself is his body. Here is one of the positions which Socrates openly challenged. The departed psyche, for Homer, has no consciousness, whereas the continuation

[5] A. E. Taylor, *Socrates, The Man and His Thought*, Doubleday & Company, Inc., 1956, pp. 132–133.

[6] See Burnet, "Socrates," in *Encyclopaedia of Religion and Ethics*, Hastings House, Vol. XI.

[7] A. E. Taylor, *Plato: The Man and His Work*, The World Publishing Company, Meridian Books, Inc., 1959, p. 27.

of consciousness after the death of the body is integral to what Socrates means by immortality. It is obvious that, if mind and body are identical, in the sense of inseparable, all talk of immortality is sheer nonsense.

It cannot be too strongly emphasized that the conception of the soul which Socrates bequeathed to mankind is not, as in the Orphic religion, something appropriate to dreams and trances, but the seat of the normal personal intelligence and character, as exhibited in ordinary experience. It is that "in virtue of which we are pronounced wise or foolish, good or bad." The soul, in short, is not explained, but is identified. It cannot be observed by the senses, but it can be known in terms of its functions. Its primary function is to know, to distinguish better and worse, to direct and govern external actions. The soul, as discovered by Socrates, is what most thoughtful people today mean by the word mind when they are not limited by the popular inhibitions of contemporary psychology. The mind, as generally understood by literate people, is the seat of judgments, both in epistemology and in ethics.

The major tradition in sophisticated thought in positing a real distinction between mind and body is represented by Dr. Samuel Johnson. After his paralytic stroke Johnson wrote to Mrs. Thrale, "I was alarmed, and prayed God, that however much he might afflict my body, he would spare my understanding."[8] This makes sense to most people and, as Augustine Birrell says, "is indeed tonic and bark for the mind." The great scholar's body was so weakened that he could not talk, but he could think. The philosopher is bound to consider such a situation in forming his conception of the world order. In the light of such experience, can a fundamental discontinuity be reasonably avoided? This is one of the chief questions that philosophy faces.

The Urge to Monism

The major intellectual heritage of the West, deriving ultimately from Plato, though receiving specific modern formulation in the writings of John Locke, is that of psychophysical dualism. This is to be distinguished sharply from other forms of dualism, especially

[8] James Boswell, Life of Samuel Johnson, John B. Alden, Publisher, 1887, Vol. IV, p. 310.

epistemological dualism, though the various forms are obviously compatible with each other. Since epistemological dualism has already been considered in Chapter 2 it need not be described here. By psychophysical dualism is meant the conclusion, which is based on both empirical evidence and rational examination, that minds and bodies, though connected in our normal finite experience, really belong to different categories. This need not mean that a mind is a thing in the identical sense that a body is a thing, but it does mean that mental and physical referents are qualitatively distinct. This is what the ordinary man means when he makes the familiar distinction between *himself* and his *body*. In most moods, he refers to his body as belonging to *him* and he emphatically does *not* mean the tautologous absurdity that his body belongs to his body.

As against this longtime deposit of both ordinary experience and professional philosophy, there is a more or less constant effort to transcend the dualism by some kind of monism. Some appear to suppose that the establishment of monism would be an obvious gain and the urge to achieve this gain has recently become so great that, in certain academic circles, it is clearly supposed that dualism is somehow scandalous. Others have been so imbued with the reductive idea, which they assume to be essential to science, that they think it would somehow be a gain in explanation if mind could be reduced to matter in motion. The classic effort in this direction is La Mettrié's *L'Homme Machine* (1748).

The choice between psychophysical monism and psychophysical dualism is one which involves great complexity, but it is easy to see that the consequences are momentous. If, for example, the hypothesis of materialistic monism, in any of its many forms, is sustained, then all discussion of immortality is nonsense. If any distinction between mind and body is illicit, and if we face honestly the fact that the human body, like all other bodies, decays, then there is no logicial possibility of the continuation of the conscious being after death. Of course, if there is overwhelming evidence for monism, we shall, as thinkers who try to be honest, accept this consequence, but we shall not suppose that the issue is trivial or unimportant.

The urge to deny psychophysical dualism has taken many forms, the chief of which were described by A. O. Lovejoy, in his monumental book, *The Revolt Against Dualism*. It was Lovejoy's contention, after careful analysis of each phase of this revolt, that each fails to make its case, with the necessary consequence that the received doctrine of dualism continues in possession of the intellectual field.

The most violent form of the revolt against dualism is what is known in psychology as behaviorism. Behaviorism is by no means limited to psychologists and, within professional psychology, is not limited to those who apply to themselves this somewhat pejorative appellation. Nothing is easier than to adopt behaviorism without the name. This can be verified by even a cursory examination of introductory textbooks in psychology. Some changes have come in language since John B. Watson invented the term "behaviorism," and there has been some effort to make the doctrine less blatantly dogmatic, but much of the essential approach remains.

The inspiration for behavioristic psychology is not hard to understand. Impressed by the success of the physical and natural sciences, and suffering slightly from an academic inferiority complex, numerous psychologists wanted to be more scientific, which they supposed meant more able to limit themselves to publicly verifiable and repeatable experiments. It is possible to watch a rat as it goes through a maze, in something of the same manner that it is possible to watch the swing of a pendulum. All can see, all can check, and there is some degree of numerical measurement. It is an easy step from such experiments with rats to experiments involving human beings. Scholars who were devoted to the study of the human psyche were frustrated by the fact that no person can measure another's thought, whereas he can record and measure another's speaking voice or his muscular reactions. Why not, then, cease even to mention thinking, which seems to be intrinsically unobservable by the methods of natural science and thus reject introspection completely? Some deny to psychology the use of the term "science" because psychology seems to be necessarily introspective in at least part of its method. Those who assert that psychology is a science must then either deny that it uses introspection or maintain that the use of introspection is scientific. The behaviorists choose the former alternative, while Bertrand Russell chooses the latter. Those who accept the former alternative elect to limit themselves to what they can observe objectively. This simple procedure is indeed the original proposal of all behaviorism. Since only the overt behavior of human beings can be observed by a variety of witnesses and only it can be mechanically recorded, such overt behavior is asserted to be the entire subject-matter of psychology.

It does not require much philosophical sophistication to suspect that such an oversimplification leads to many intellectual difficulties. Thinking, as contrasted to physical acting, does not disappear by our refusal to discuss it. Purpose, which is hard to find in the index of a contemporary psychology textbook, does not disappear from human life merely because scholars do not mention it. Watson's behaviorism, because of its philosophical naïveté, was extremely vulnerable to attack; one of the most effective of attacks being that of A. O. Lovejoy in his now famous essay, in which the point is made clear by the title, "The Paradox of the Thinking Behaviorist."[9] What are we to say of a scholar who denies consciousness, yet claims to be conscious that his doctrine is true and appeals to the consciousness of others in his effort at intellectual persuasion? It must be remembered that William James, in his essay "Does Consciousness Exist?" did not deny that the word stands for a function. All that James was trying to do was deny that it stands for an entity. But of course dogmatic behaviorists are far more extreme than James is. About all that they have accomplished is so strict a delimitation of their field of inquiry that they leave to others much of the area which psychologists have investigated in earlier times. Scientists have a right to delimit their field in any way they happen to like, but they cease to be scientists and become poor philosophers when they, because of this arbitrary limitation, deny the very being of the subjects neglected.

A more sophisticated behaviorism is now represented by Gilbert Ryle, Waynflete Professor of Metaphysical Philosophy in the University of Oxford. Ryle explicitly renounces the mechanistic doctrine which has been implicit in so many denials of dualism, but he proceeds, with what he admits is "deliberate abusiveness" to

[9] In *The Philosophical Review*, Vol. XXXI, pp. 135–147. The article, though published in 1922 and written in the light of the contemporary intellectual situation, is relevant also to the challenge of a later period.

denounce what he calls "The dogma of the Ghost in the Machine." By this rather unphilosophical language he means to denote, in essence, the familiar idea that soul and body, though combined in ordinary experience, are not identical concepts. The idea he opposes, and which he claims to be able to show is "entirely false," is that which "represents the facts of mental life as if they belonged to one logical type or category (or range of types and categories), when they actually belong to another."[10]

Ryle apparently believes he can dislodge the reigning dualism by means of analogy. Thus he refers to a stranger who, at Oxford or Cambridge, can see the various colleges, but asks where the university is. The question is treated as an ignorant and confused one, since the university does not exist in the same sense or in the same way that the colleges exist. The university is only one way of looking at the same totality which the colleges jointly constitute. But, however revealing such an analogy is in various circumstances, it has no relevance at all in considering minds and bodies. The visitor who asks the innocent question about the university is indeed confused because he supposes that "university" stands for an added member of a class already observed in several instances in the colleges. Now the weakness of the analogy lies in the fact that no important philosopher has supposed mind to be an extra member of the class to which bodies belong unless we use "class" so loosely that we mean the whole class of existents. Every dualist has, of course, meant this last, because, in his denial of the possibility of reduction of minds to bodies or of bodies to minds, he naturally holds that both are.

Ryle believes that he has solved the ancient problems associated with idealism and materialism in that his particular linguistic analysis has "dissipated" the "hallowed contrast between mind and matter."[11] This astounding claim, we soon discover, rests on nothing more substantial than his private consideration of the word exist. Former philosophers have been deluded, it is indicated, by their failure to realize that existence may mean more than one thing. The key passage is as follows:

[10] G. Ryle, The Concept of Mind, Hutchinson, University Library, 1952, p. 16.
[11] Ibid., p. 23.

It is perfectly proper to say, in one logical tone of voice, that there exist minds and to say, in another logical tone of voice, that there exist bodies. But these expressions do not indicate two different species of existence, for "existence" is not a generic word like "coloured" or "sexed"! They indicate two different senses of "exist", somewhat as "rising" has different senses in "the tide is rising", "hopes are rising", and "the average age of death is rising".[12]

Ryle may have better arguments than this for his denial of the duality of mind and matter, but it is not hard to see that the above analogy is confused. What he is referring to in the use of the various meaning of "rising" is little more than a simple figure of speech. But this is clearly not the case at all when we use the word exist, for existence is vastly more fundamental than a simple verb of motion. If I say that my hand exists and I say that my mind exists I am not making the latter a figurative parallel to the former. Indeed, I mean precisely the same thing in both cases. When I say that my hand exists I am expressing my conviction that it has not been severed from my arm, that it is really a part of my body rather than an imaginary organ. When I say that my mind exists I mean that my thought is really in operation and that it is not an imaginary operation, like that of the mind of Mr. Samuel Pickwick. There are imaginary minds and there are imaginary bodies and they are imaginary in precisely the same way. We have already noted that, in many phases of human thought, there is great advantage in a negative approach. We may handle the concept of error before we are able to handle the concept of truth. We may do the same with existence.

How does one negate existence? Not by affirming something spiritual or mental, but rather by affirming the fictional, the imagined, in short the nonexistent. Monism may be a respectable philosophy, as concerns mind and body, but it cannot be upheld by the analysis of a word, particularly when that analysis is faulty or oversimple.

Statements of law are different from statements of fact, but both may be either true or false and they are true or false in the same sense, namely, that men can be right or wrong in their assertions. To say that my century-old elm is still standing is one thing and to

[12] Ibid.

say $E = MC^3$ is another, but they have the same fundamental logical character because both affirm what is false. Both point to an existent which is spurious. The fact that one referent must be known by the senses and the other by thought alone, makes no difference in the primary situation. In both cases we are dealing with what can be in error and when we do that the plain man's use of the verb *exist* is clearly defensible. The truth about existence is that it can apply equally and identically to a great variety of referents.

The Functional Contrast

Sometimes the student, in the beginning, will speak of brain and mind as identical referents. We do this largely because we are keenly conscious of the fact that the condition of the brain seems to determine the condition of the mind; it is then an easy, though an unwarranted, step to identify them. It is true, of course, that brain damage leads to errors in both speech and thought. The psychiatric literature on language provides us with all kinds of bizarre developments in aphasia, alexia, and kindred disturbances: in certain kinds of brain damage words are substituted for others whose meaning is entirely different.[13] Mrs. Langer refers to cases in which a cerebral lesion causes inability to name any inanimate object, but not inability to name living things or call people by their proper names. Clearly, the brain is important to the mind, whatever the precise relationship may be shown to be.

Even though the ancients did not understand the importance of the cerebral cortex, as modern men do, they tended to interpret experiential facts on the analogy of merely physical facts. Thus Democritus crudely explained sight, with reference to the image appearing in the pupil of the eye, as simply a process of physical reflection, similar to reflection in a pool. Aristotle recognized the crudity of this account and so was the first, according to W. K. C. Guthrie, to make the functional contrast clear. " 'Are we to suppose then,' Aristotle asks, 'that bowls of water and mirrors are capable

[13] See Susanne K. Langer, *Philosophical Sketches*, The Johns Hopkins Press, 1962, pp. 36, 37. Mrs. Langer refers to a number of detailed neurological reports.

of seeing?' It is just the difference between the two events which constitutes sensation. . . . The peculiarity of life is that when the bodily organ is materially altered by an external object, then another totally different result intervenes, which we call the sensation."[14] The distinction could hardly be more clearly expressed. It is not necessary to say brain is one thing and mind is another thing. It is sufficient to stay close to experience and to point to a contrast in function.

If we begin with experience rather than dogma we soon see that, in referring to minds and bodies, we are at least referring to contrasting functions and to operations which obey contrasting laws. Descartes, as is well known, sought to provide his fellow men with a new start in human thinking by his search for certainty. Because he could doubt so much, he sought something which he could not possibly doubt. He discovered something about which most of his successors have agreed, namely, that he could not doubt his own process of conscious thinking. He could doubt any part of his body or of his physical environment, but he could not doubt that he doubted, for, if he were to do so, he would be doing the very doubting about which he doubted. But why this certainty? Is it because of weight or motion or anything which can be observed in a laboratory? Most assuredly not. It is because of *logical* necessity.

Now the important fact to note is that such logical necessity, which every sane and thoughtful person experiences at times, is utterly meaningless and absurd except in the realm of mind. It is exemplified in the laws of thought and *only* in the laws of thought. Because Brand Blanshard has been able to express this vital point so clearly, it is worth while to ponder his sentences:

But it is only in this realm of the non-sensible that the relations of implication and consistency, or indeed any of the relations of logic, can subsist; to say that two physical things, two billiard balls or two boulders, implied each other or were mutually inconsistent, would be nonsense. Such relations as physical concomitance and collision, which the behaviorist must offer as substitutes, are totally different things. Thus if he builds on the foundation he has laid, he has no title to a belief in logic or the use of it. Of course he does use it; everyone does

[14] W. K. C. Guthrie, *The Greek Philosophers from Thales to Aristotle*, Harper & Row, Inc., Torchbooks, 1960, pp. 148–149.

and must. But the attempt to *prove* his case must proceed through an appeal to meanings and relations for which his theory has no room.[15]

Few efforts can assist the student of philosophy more than the effort to distinguish between "consciousness" on the one hand and "bodily behavior" on the other. Always we assign different attributes to them. When we speak of ideas we speak of their clarity or their confusion. A little reflection will make us realize that such terms are entirely inappropriate if applied to electrons, molecules, muscles, or larynx. When we apply these terms to speech we do so only in a recognizably figurative sense. For, while thought can be confused, speech, as a matter of sound waves, can be only loud or harsh or inaudible, and the like. Herein lies the difficult problem of the behavioristic monist. If consciousness *is* nothing but laryngal motion then we are necessarily deprived, and the monist is deprived, along with the rest of us, of all use of logical terms. Adjectives which are perfectly in order when applied to ideas are patently absurd when applied to movements of muscle or nerve.

It is hard, in the light of experience, to avoid the conclusion that ideas represent one kind of reality while objects in motion represent another. How else can we account for the radical difference in function? Movements have velocity, but thoughts have cogency. We do not avoid this vivid contrast by pointing out that the only thoughts we know are those experienced by persons who happen to be associated with bodies. *Association is not identity.* There is no good reason to deny that realities which are different can be combined. The combination according to which thought affects bodies and bodies affect thought is indeed a mystery, and no philosopher would wish to deny that it is mysterious, but this recognition does nothing to obliterate the empirical distinction.

Most of those who seek to deny the uniqueness of mind, holding that it is really nothing but physical structure, are influenced in their decision by the facts of medicine and physiology which seem to bear on the question. Thus it is noted that a blow on the head may stop consciousness and that brain surgery or a brain tumor can alter or destroy certain mental functions. This, however, is by no means a clinching proof that mind is *nothing but* a physical opera-

[15] B. Blanshard, *The Nature of Thought*, The Macmillan Company, 1940, Vol. I, pp. 333–334.

tion. All that it means, if we are careful in our reasoning, is that the kind of mental operation of which we are aware in ourselves and, by inference, in our associates, is in part at least dependent upon a physical condition. Anyone who goes farther than this in attempted reduction is substituting dogma for evidence.

What is most important for the student is the mood of skepticism which makes him question all monism that neglects the plain facts of experience according to which there is a striking difference in attributes. We need not speculate about different substances, for these we do not know, but we can hold firmly to the fact that we are acquainted, in everyday experience, with operations which are radically different. It is because these differences are so great that, in the major philosophical heritage, they have been recognized as differences in kind. No one in our century has put the case for essential dualism of process more eloquently than has A. N. Whitehead. In one of his greatest paragraphs he wrote:

> The universe is dual because, in the fullest sense, it is both transient and eternal. The universe is dual because each actuality requires abstract character. The universe is dual because each occasion unites its formal immediacy with objective otherness. The universe is many because it is wholly and completely to be analyzed into many final actualities—or in Cartesian language, into many res verae. The universe is one, because of the universal immanence. There is thus a dualism in this contrast between the unity and the multiplicity. Throughout the universe there reigns the union of opposites which is the ground of dualism.[16]

RADICAL DISCONTINUITY

However strong the intellectual urge to complete monism may be, the urge to the recognition of actual differences of level is greater. Perhaps no part of the philosophy of Blaise Pascal is now more greatly honored than that in which he outlines his conclusion of radical discontinuity. The key aphorisms are the following:

> The infinite distance between body and mind is a symbol of the infinitely more infinite distance between mind and charity.

[16] A. N. Whitehead, *Adventures of Ideas*, The Macmillan Company, 1933, p. 245.

All bodies, the firmament, the stars, the earth and its kingdoms, are not equal to the lowest mind; for mind knows all these and itself; and these bodies nothing.

All bodies together and all minds together, and all their products, are not equal to the least feeling of charity. This is of an order infinitely more exalted.

From all bodies together, we cannot obtain one little thought; this is impossible and of another order. From all bodies and minds we cannot produce a feeling of true charity; this is impossible and of another and supernatural order.[17]

In a climate of thinking much dominated by the idea of evolution that, in general, tends to obscure those elements of experience which indicate discontinuity, Pascal's observation comes with fresh and arresting force. He holds that the three orders, though connected or combined, are not, for that reason, continuous or even similar. They are discontinuous, because the higher is not implicit in the lower. The higher levels are not intelligible until they appear and even then the effort to reduce the higher to the lower is not possible except by gross distortion. This is probably Pascal's most important contribution to philosophical thought. We can agree with T. S. Eliot when he says, "In this distinction Pascal offers much about which the modern world would do well to think."[18] Though most philosophers do not seem to have taken this advice a few have done so, among them the late T. E. Hulme, whose death as a soldier in World War I, in 1917, was a tragic loss to speculative thought. Pascal seemed to Hulme to be the greatest example of a thinker whose attitude and ideology belong to a period opposed to his own. In his essay on humanism, which takes the principle of discontinuity seriously, Hulme says, "Everything that I shall say later in these notes is to be regarded merely as a prolegomena to the reading of Pascal, as an attempt to remove the difficulties of comprehension engendered in us by the humanism of our period."[19]

Perhaps the best way to begin to understand what Pascal means by his famous contrast between the frail thinker who dies, but

[17] B. Pascal, Pensées, trans. W. F. Trotter, J. M. Dent and Sons, 1931, p. 235.
[18] T. S. Eliot, Selected Essays, Harcourt Brace & World, Inc., 1950, p. 368.
[19] T. E. Hulme, Speculations, Harcourt Brace & World, Inc., 1924, pp. 56, 57.

knows that he dies, and the material world which he knows in some degree, whereas it does not know him in any degree, is to consider the glory of thought. This is often hidden from us because we are so deeply immersed in the process of thought. It is hard for the scientist, committed as he is to the study of the objective facts of the natural order, to realize that the fact of his knowledge is more wonderful and mysterious than any object of his attention, unless that object is another mind, but so it is. The most wonderful single fact we know about our world is the fact that some minds have emerged in it. And we know what minds are by what they do. Here the clarity of Highet is of great assistance.

To spend fifty or sixty years in the study of fishes, or the relation between logic and language, or the history of the Incas, or the routes of comets, or the geometry of non-Euclidean space, or the literature of Iceland, or the anatomy of the brain; to acquire and systematize and record new knowledge on any of these subjects without any expectation of benefiting mankind except by extending its range of understanding: that is to pass a happy and valuable life, usually tempered at the close by regret that another fifty years could not be added, in which to learn more, and still more. It is the purest and least selfish satisfaction known to man, except those of creating a work of art and healing the sick. And it is, as Aristotle said, to share the activity of God himself; his eternal life of pure contemplation.[20]

There has been a widespread conviction in the modern world that, though reality appears to us in qualitatively different levels, this is only an accident of our present state of ignorance, a state which will be remedied by the advances of science. Thus it is a common belief that, though our experience reveals a crucial difference between brains and bodies, the time will come when we shall bridge this chasm. A similar belief involves the conviction that the present radical distinction between what is living and what is not living will some day be transcended. This latter conviction is greatly strengthened by the hope of biogenesis, the production of life where no life has been previously. The usual argument is that, if some scientist can succeed in producing life out of nonliving matter, this will demonstrate conclusively that the theory of levels is false and that life is "nothing but" matter after all. Now, they

[20] Highet, op. cit., p. 102.

admit, life has unique characteristics which distinguish it from stones or sterile water, but all this will be changed when life arises in the laboratory.

The philosopher is not in a position to say whether biogenesis is possible, but he is in a position to show that biogenesis, if it occurs, will in no way deny the reality of a distinction in levels. All that the operation will show is that some human beings are able to observe or encourage the point at which the radical change from the nonliving to the living takes place. If I am once in the water and later I am in the air, the reality of the change of circumstances is in no way denied by the fact that I know where and when and by what manipulation the change has occurred. Once, we have good reason to believe, this earth which is now our home was completely devoid of life. Later it became the scene of life. At some point and at some time therefore, life appeared. We do not know how this came about and we are not likely to know, even though we may speculate endlessly, but our ignorance has nothing to do with the reality of novelty which undoubtedly emerged. For our present purposes, which are philosophical, whether this occurred by the immediate creative act of God or by "natural" processes makes no difference at all. If philosophy is, in the words of Pringle-Pattison, "a critical interpretation of experience," it is our task to point out that ours is a world which has radical differences of level in it. Whatever the links between them, the nonliving and the living are not the same. Our world has in it both rocks and organisms: whereas these obey some of the same laws, they also obey different laws. Whitehead's emphasis on this has been so insistent that it has been embarrassing to the conventional mind with its monistic bias.

Only inorganic things persist for great lengths of time. A rock survives for eight hundred million years; whereas the limit of a tree is about a thousand years, for a man or an elephant about fifty or one hundred years, for a dog about twelve years, for an insect about one year. The problem set by the doctrine of evolution is to explain how complex organisms with such deficient survival power ever evolved. They certainly did not appear because they were better at that game than the rocks around them. It may be possible to explain "the origin of species" by the doctrine of the struggle for existence among such organisms. But certainly this struggle throws no light whatever upon the emergence of such a general type of complex organism, with faint survival power. The problem is not to be solved by any dogma, which is the product of mere abstract thought elaborating its notions of the fitness of things.[21]

Once Whitehead has made clear the uniqueness and utter strangeness of organisms in an overwhelmingly inorganic world, he goes on to stress even more the still greater disparity between the physiological and the mental. We must agree, he says, that the main transformations of matter and energy which constitute an animal body are not, in principle, different from those which govern the activities of inorganic matter, but it would be exceedingly naïve to suppose that this observation settles the matter or denies fundamental discontinuity. The merely physical laws have nothing to say about purpose, yet purpose is intrinsic to the operation of minds. Therefore, we have the observation that "Scientists animated by the purpose of proving that they are purposeless constitute an interesting subject for study."[22] The central argument of Whitehead is so important that extensive quotation is required.

But the point to which I wish to draw attention is the mass of evidence lying outside the physiological method which is simply ignored in the prevalent scientific doctrine. The conduct of human affairs is entirely dominated by our recognition of foresight determining purpose, and purpose issuing in conduct. Almost every sentence we utter and every judgment we form, presuppose our unfailing experience of this element in life. The evidence is so overwhelming, the belief so unquestioning, the evidence of language so decisive, that it is difficult to know where to begin in demonstrating it. For example, we speak of the policy of a statesman or of a business corporation. Cut out the notion of final causation, and the word "policy" has lost its meaning. As I write this lecture, I intend to deliver it at Princeton University. Cut out the notion of final causation, and this "intention" is without meaning.[23]

The motions of bodies, whether they be ships or rocks, are, we are told, governed by purely physical laws. But how about that particular kind of body which we call the body of a man? If such a man, for example, President Lincoln, decides to write and sign the

[21] A. N. Whitehead, *The Function of Reason*, Beacon Press, 1958, pp. 4, 5. By permission of Princeton University Press.
[22] *Ibid.*, p. 16.
[23] *Ibid.*, p. 13.

Emancipation Proclamation, would his intentions be beside the question? Was Lincoln's hand, as he wrote, obeying nothing but physical laws with no consideration of his double intention of destroying slavery and preserving the Union? The suggestion is, and will be generally recognized as, preposterous. The physical movement of Lincoln's hand was as purely physical as the motion of a stone, yet it is obvious that it cannot be explained except in terms of something utterly different from the motion of a stone. Both Lincoln's hand and the stone are moved by efficient causes, but in the case of the President's hand, the truly effective cause is a final one. There is clear evidence that the actions of many animal bodies, including human bodies, but not limited to them, engage in operations which depend for their execution on the foresight of an end and a consequent purpose to attain it. As long as this is true, the distinction between minds and bodies, which is the major heritage in philosophical thought, is not likely to be superseded.

Chapter 8 ∽ *MAN AND ANIMAL*

Man is the only animal that laughs and weeps; for he is the only animal that is struck with the difference between what things are and what they ought to be.

WILLIAM HAZLITT

THE PROBLEM OF MAN IS CLOSE TO THE CENTER OF ANY SERIOUS philosophical inquiry. The question is important because of the way in which it bears on so many other questions, epistemological, metaphysical, and moral. If it should be proved that man is just one of the primates, we would have to accept the fact with due humility. If, on the other hand, he is different in kind, this fact tells us something highly significant about the world of which we are a part. The great Scottish philosopher, Andrew Seth Pringle-Pattison, made the importance of the question clear when he wrote: "The breach between ethical man and pre-human nature constitutes without exception the most important fact which the universe has to show."

Very early in the history of human inquiry man became an object of his own contemplation. Being curious about the external world and its processes, he was also curious about himself. He could see that he shared some characteristics with the animals, particularly with those which he was able to train for his use, but he could see, at the same time, that there were important differences between his own kind and all other kinds. The effort to state what these differences are appeared very early in reflective literature and has continued without abatement to the present time. Hundreds of men, both in philosophy and in general literature, have tried to state precisely what makes man different, not merely in degree, but in kind.

The problem of the *differentiae* of man comes up in the most unexpected places. Thus, even in the *Poetics*, Aristotle raises the question. "Imitation," he says, "is natural to man from childhood, one of his advantages over the lower animals being this, that he is the most imitative creature in the world, and learns at first by imitation." In the same passage, moving from imitation to learning, Aristotle says, "To be learning something is the greatest of pleasures not only to the philosopher, but also to the rest of mankind, however small their capacity for it."[1]

The question of the precise nature of difference, if there is any, is perenially interesting, especially to the portion of mankind with a specifically philosophic bent. It seems, therefore, highly appropriate that, over the doorway of Emerson Hall, which houses the department of philosophy in our oldest university, there should be inscribed the question, "What is man that thou art mindful of him?"

The Problem of Origin

When we speak of man it is important to make our denotation clear. We are using the term to refer to every individual human being, of both sexes and of every race and color, who has lived, is living now, and who will live in the future. We may have real difficulty in trying to say what is essential to man's nature, but we never have any trouble in actuality, in distinguishing men from

---

[1] Aristotle, *Poetics*, trans. I. Bywater, *The Basic Works of Aristotle*, Random House, 1941, p. 1457. See also P. Teilhard de Chardin, *The Phenomenon of Man*, Harper & Row, Inc., p. 189. "It is not in their germinal state that beings manifest themselves, but in their florescence."

other creatures. Though we speak metaphorically of some men as tigerish and others as mouselike, we never have any difficulty in knowing whether a particular living creature is, in fact, a man or a mouse or a tiger. The analysis in which the philosophical student is invited to participate is, therefore, not pragmatic, but metaphysical.

That man is, in some sense, an animal is almost too obvious to note, and certainly too obvious to deny. Like the other animals, we go on living only by the injection of food; we reproduce our kind as the mammals do; we experience similar sexual desires and satisfactions (though man has no particular mating season); we are liable to similar diseases; we have great similarities in anatomy. All this was well known to the ancients in our culture, so well known, indeed, that in both the Academy and the Lyceum man was defined, not as a non-animal, but as a particular kind of animal. In short, the assertion of similarity was universally recognized by thinkers as being wholly compatible with the recognition of vital distinctions.

This recognition of man's membership in the animal kingdom led inevitably to various speculations about some kind of evolution, a speculation which seems to go back at least as far as the time of Anaximander, in the sixth century before Christ. It is now widely supposed that man had, long ago, an animal origin, descending or perhaps ascending from other animal forms. This, of course, is a speculative concept, one which we do not really know and presumably cannot know, because so much of the relevant evidence is intrinsically unrecoverable, but it seems a reasonable guess. What is important for the philosopher is not a denial of this speculation, but a recognition that it is a speculation and the conscious effort to avoid drawing unwarranted conclusions from it.

The most common of the unwarranted conclusions of popular thought which appear to derive from evolutionary theory are three. The first is the supposition that, if man did come into existence by descent from lower creatures, the biblical conception of divine creation is thereby undermined. Nothing of the kind follows. There is just as much cogency in the idea of creation with descent as in the idea of creation without descent. If there is strong reason to conclude that divine creative power is needed to make sense out of our world, as Plato and the majority of his successors have thought, this applies just as much to a slow process as it does to a rapid one.

The second unwarranted conclusion is the notion that, if man came from a beast, he is therefore nothing but a beast now. The idea that earlier stages in development are more genuine or truer than later ones has nothing to commend it intellectually, but this fact has not deprived the idea of wide acceptance. So wide is the acceptance that we have a name for it; we call it the "genetic fallacy." Sometimes it is argued that, since religion presumably arose from superstitious animism, contemporary religion is really nothing but animism in disguise, and is to be discounted accordingly. A particularly flagrant example of the genetic fallacy, so applied, is to be found in Sigmund Freud's *The Future of an Illusion*. By this same standard, modern science, for all its success, would necessarily be identified with the primitive magic which is its intellectual ancestor. Aristotle, in recognizing this danger, laid down the far more intelligible principle that anything should be judged by its fulfillment, rather than by its origin. "A thing," he said, is more properly said to be what it is when it has attained to fulfillment." (*Physics*, II, 1, 193b). In short, origin does not entail destiny. We do not know for sure whether the first men were the descendants of apelike creatures, but if they were, that tells us nothing at all of any importance about man now. Man is to be judged by what he *is*, not what he *was*.

A third unwarranted conclusion is that, if man is biologically cousin to the primates, he is therefore merely one of them and not different in kind. The scholars who have tended most to minimize the differences between man and the other animals or to deny that there is any difference in kind, are the psychologists. It is obvious that, unless they succeed in their effort to minimize the difference, their comparison of animal with human behavior becomes a specious analogy. What we learn from observing rats may be applicable to the understanding of ourselves, but the claim that it is applicable rests upon a vast assumption of fundamental identity, which is certainly open to question. Mrs. Langer has told the story of the recent development as follows:

First biologists, then psychologists, and finally sociologists and moralists have become newly aware that man belongs to the animal kingdom. The impact of the concept of evolution on scientific discovery has been immense, and it has not stopped at laboratory science; it has also produced some less sober and sound inspirations. The concept of continuous animal evolution has made most psychologists belittle the differences between man and his non-human relatives, and led some of them, indeed, to think of *homo sapiens* as just one kind of primate among others, like the others in all essential respects—differing from apes and monkeys not much more than they differ from species to species among themselves.[2]

A whole succession of writers has tried to deny man's uniqueness and the only argument presented has been that of man's biological similarity to beasts or his supposed origin from them. A little serious reflection, however, is sufficient to make us realize that physical kinship does not necessitate spiritual identity. Since children of the same parents are sometimes remarkably different, who can tell us, with authority, that even greater differences are impossible, when the kinship is less close? The doctrine is finally rendered untenable by the fact that differences of kind can, in fact, be witnessed. If men and animals could be classed together, with no genuine differentiae, it would constitute a great gain in neatness and tidiness in the effort to understand the world, but, unfortunately for the system builders, there are many features of our world that are neither neat nor tidy. The existence of man is a great embarrassment not only to mechanists, but to simplifiers of all sorts. Whatever the nature of the world turns out to be, it must be such as to be consistent with the fact that it has men in it.

While, on the one hand, we must be on guard against drawing conclusions from evolutionary doctrine that are illicit or unnecessary, we must also beware of claiming differences which do not stand up under examination. It is not true, for example, that man is the only animal that speaks. Many of the higher animals have a number of sounds which are obviously well understood by others of their kind, and constitute rudimentary speech. This, of course, has nothing to do with written language and is therefore limited to

[2] Susanne K. Langer, *Philosophical Sketches*, The Johns Hopkins Press, 1962, p. 111.

momentary influence, with none of the cumulative effect which is necessary for the production of a conscious civilization.[3]

We must likewise beware of following Aristotle in holding that man is the only animal that reasons. Though it is only in the twentieth century that we have amassed definitive evidence of the ability of nonhuman creatures to engage in a rational enterprise,[4] the great John Locke emphasized, in the seventeenth century, the rational ability of some animals. The distinction between minds and bodies, made in the preceding chapter, is of capital importance, but it would be ridiculous to claim that man has any monopoly on mind. Assuredly, we are not the only creatures in which thought and even effective thought occurs. In short, the mystery of the union of mind and brain is not limited to the human species. Mind appears prior to the emergence of man, because its quality arises as soon as there is any response to the environment involving choice. That such experience is widespread in our world tells us something significant about the nature of the real.

Whatever the crucial difference between man and the other animals may be, it is evidently not a matter of bodily form. Man's hand is a marvelous tool, but would be worth little without certain desires of man's consciousness which the hand facilitates, though it does not initiate. Man's brain is relatively large, but the brains of some other creatures are heavier in proportion to the total body weight. The fully erect posture is an asset, in that the hands are accordingly freed from participation in locomotion, but the resulting speed of locomotion is vastly inferior to that of many fourfooted animals. Man is exceeded by other creatures in keenness of eyesight, in the sense of smell, and in the ability to distinguish sounds. His body is, in some ways, poorly adapted for survival, particularly in his relative lack of a hairy covering and his long period of infancy, which constitutes him a burden to his parents through many years before he is able to be self-sustaining. Man is not well equipped, compared with some others, with either teeth or claws.

---

[3] Animal language, all scientific observers agree, is used to stimulate action and evoke responses. Human language is used for these purposes also, but, in addition, human language may be employed to communicate thoughts and to indicate properties.

[4] Most notably in the work of Wolfgang Kohler. See *The Mentality of Apes*, Harcourt, Brace and Company, 1926.

Yet, in spite of all this, man is manifestly superior. Wherein does his superiority lie?

Differentiation

The true answer to the question of man's uniqueness is bound to come by rational analysis rather than by search for historical evidence. We may, indeed, unearth weapons and various artifacts, but these are only the most *observable* factors and not necessarily the most significant. Almost certainly they are primarily results, rather than causes. Consequently, the behaviorist is not likely to help us at all. Since he looks at man as he looks at electricity or cabbages, he is not likely to get any really significant or inside information. We shall never make any advance unless we are willing to employ the signal advantage which is ours if we will only use it.

We are likely to get our best help from men who are willing to be truly reflective on the basis of all that they know, including their self-knowledge. What is most impressive, once such an approach is adopted, is the great degree of unanimity that we find among those generally counted the most thoughtful of men. Nearly all agree that man is truly unique and that his uniqueness has something to do with his self-consciousness, his freedom, and his ability to engage in abstract thinking. Reflection is required to see the relationships between these.

The emphasis on the uniqueness of man's freedom begins far back in human reflection, but receives its greatest emphasis from the leading men of the Renaissance. Characteristic of this emphasis is the oration of Count Giovanni Pico della Mirandola, which was delivered in Rome in 1486 and entitled "The Dignity of Man."[5] Though the author was only twenty-four years of age when he delivered this oration, it "lives as the most succinct expression of the mind of the Renaissance." Man, Pico concluded, is different from all other creatures because he alone is a being of indeterminate image. God, says Pico, was still unsatisfied when He had made all of the other creatures, each having its own place and character. He needed one who could not only be, but also *know* and comprehend.

[5] For an English translation see *Oration on the Dignity of Man*, trans. A. R. Caponigri, Henry Regnery Company, 1956.

When the general work of creation was done, "the Divine Artificer still longed for some creature which might comprehend the meaning of so vast an achievement, which might be moved with love at its beauty and smitten with awe at its grandeur."[6]

Here is an intimation of Pascal's famous dictum, that man's dignity consists in his thought or comprehension. Other beings undoubtedly perform useful functions, but man observes both their functions and his own.

Man is but a reed, the most feeble thing in nature; but he is a thinking reed. The entire universe need not arm itself to crush him. A vapour, a drop of water suffices to kill him. But, if the universe were to crush him, man would still be more noble than that which killed him, because he knows that he dies and the advantage which the universe has over him; the universe knows nothing of this. . . . By space the universe encompasses and swallows me up like an atom; by thought I comprehend the world.[7]

Pico, being preCopernican, naturally thought of man as residing in the center of the universe which he is capable of comprehending, but the geographical feature of the conception is not intrinsic to Pico's thought. Therefore the change caused by the abandonment of the geocentric astronomy does not damage Pico's theory of human dignity.[8] Man is able to comprehend, not so much because of a central location, but because he has a share in the particular endowment of every other creature. By this Pico seems to mean that man's body is made of material parts, that he lives biologically as an animal, and that he shares the higher powers with the angels. Because man shares in all, he can be like any and is therefore, alone among all others, fundamentally indeterminate. The crux of the famous oration is put in the mouth of God:

We have given you, O Adam, no visage proper to yourself, nor any endowment properly your own, in order that whatever place, whatever form, whatever gifts you may, with premeditation, select, these same you may have and possess through your own judgment and decision. The nature of all other creatures is defined and restricted within laws

[6] *Ibid.*, p. 2.

[7] B. Pascal, *Pensées*, trans. W. F. Trotter, J. M. Dent and Sons, 1931, p. 97.

[8] Pascal's assertion of a similar view came after the Copernican view was generally accepted.

which we have laid down; you, by contrast, impeded by no such re-
striction, may, by your own free will, to whose custody we have assigned you, trace for yourself the lineaments of your own nature. . . .
We have made you a creature neither of heaven nor of earth, neither
mortal nor immortal, in order that you may, as the free and proud
shaper of your own being, fashion yourself in the form you may prefer.
It will be in your power to descend to the lower, brutish forms of life;
you will be able, through your own decision, to rise again to the
superior orders whose life is divine.[9]

It will be noted at once that this Renaissance doctrine of man is
sharply distinguished from any doctrine which affirms the natural
or necessary goodness of man. What is asserted is a kind of fluidity
which appears nowhere else in the natural order. Man can rise
higher than any beast and he can sink far lower. The capacities for
both good and evil are immense, as any candid observation of ourselves or others will indicate. It is important for man to know both
his potential evil and his potential excellence of character, because
the knowledge of either alone is harmful. If we know only our base-
ness we cut the nerve of moral effort in seeking improvement, while
if we know only our greatness we lose the humility which is essential
to greatness. Pascal said memorably:

It is dangerous to make man see too clearly his equality with the
brutes without showing him his greatness. It is also dangerous to make
him see his greatness too clearly, apart from his vileness. It is still more
dangerous to leave him in ignorance of both. But it is very advantageous
to show him both. Man must not think that he is on a level either
with the brutes or with the angels, nor must he be ignorant of both
sides of his nature; but he must know both.[10]

Man's essential indeterminateness amounts to a tragic ambiguity
in his character and self-consciousness. "Man is neither angel nor
brute, and the unfortunate thing is that he who would act the angel
acts the brute."[11] One of the greatest reasons for taking Pascal more
seriously than professional philosophers have usually done is that
this man, whose death left his philosophy in scraps rather than in a
finished volume saw so clearly the mistake of all simplifications of

[9] Pico, op cit., p. 3.
[10] Pascal, op. cit., 418.
[11] Ibid., 358.

the nature of the human situation. Man's nature is perhaps the supreme instance in which truth cannot be told except in the form of paradox. The recognition of the paradox is very ancient. Thus, in the Hebrew scriptures we find that, concerning man's nature, both sides of the complex picture are stressed. While the psalmist says, "Thou hast made man a little lower than the angels," a notable prophet says realistically, "The heart of man is deceitful above all things, and desperately wicked." (Jeremiah 17:9.) It is a mistake to deny man's evolutionary origin and it is a mistake to dwell upon it. Susan Stebbing is in this tradition of paradox when she says, "Human beings are manysided creatures, growing from an animal origin and capable of reason and love."[12]

Man, of course, is not wholly indeterminate, though the flamboyance of Pico's rhetoric seems to suggest that he is. There are certainly deeds which men cannot perform, but, within limits, the flexibility is very striking. There is now some reason to believe that man may eventually be able to bring the whole human enterprise to a gigantic end in planetary suicide. The constant basis of hope, which is to be distinguished from naïve optimism at one extreme and from despair at the other, is the fact that man, being the relatively indeterminate creature, is capable of improvement. Alexis de Tocqueville made this point more succinctly than it has usually been made. "Although," he says, "man has many points of resemblance with the brutes, one trait is peculiar to himself—he improves; they are incapable of improvement. Mankind could not fail to discover this difference from the beginning. The idea of perfectibility is therefore as old as the world; equality did not give birth to it, but has imparted to it a new character."[13]

No serious observer can fail to see that de Tocqueville is right in his observation. The contrast between the beaver who makes dams and the man who builds houses is not primarily that the man builds more skillfully, but rather that the beaver builds as his ancestors built, whereas the man experiments endlessly with new kinds of structures. We have been, in great measure, set free from

[12] L. Susan Stebbing, Ideals and Illusions, C. A. Watts & Co., Ltd., 1943, pp. 77, 78.
[13] A. de Tocqueville, Democracy in America, New American Library of World Literature, Mentor Books, 1956, p. 157.

the built-in behavior called instinct. Many creatures, particularly bees and ants, show great ingenuity, but this ingenuity is connected with a technique which is followed undeviatingly by each succeeding generation, allowing for no experimentation. Man, on the other hand, does not inherit such an adequate technique; instead, he is remarkably plastic. He is a creature who is poorly endowed for survival, and may now destroy himself, but he is well endowed for both progress and decay. Haldane and Huxley are speaking for a multitude of philosophical biologists when they say:

However the one great difference between man and all other animals is that for them evolution must always be a blind force, of which they are quite unconscious; whereas man has, in some measure at least, the possibility of consciously controlling his evolution according to his wishes.[14]

The long tradition which stresses man's designation as *homo sapiens* is one which is fundamentally justified. Thought is not limited to man, since other animals obviously do *some* thinking, but in man the life of thought comes to play a dominant role. Though many, in the history of philosophy, have sought to describe what this dominance involves, one of the most masterly accounts of it has been made in our own time in the following passage:

Consider our lives. All other activities we share with the other inhabitants of the planet. Animals, birds, reptiles, fish, and insects also struggle for power, as we do. They organize themselves into social groups. Many build. Some control their environment by ingenious inventions. Some of them, like some of us, collect wealth. They fight. They make love. They play games. Some have powers we shall never possess and can scarcely comprehend. Cunning and skillful that they are. Yet collectively they learn little that is new and individually almost nothing. Their skills are intricate, but limited. Their art, though charming, is purely decorative. Their languages consist of a few dozen signs and sounds. Their memory is vivid, but restricted. Their curiosity is shallow and temporary, merely the rudiment of that wonder which fills the mind of a human scientist or poet or historian or philosopher. They cannot conceive of learning and knowledge as a limitless activity administered by the power of will. Only human beings really learn, and

[14] J. B. S. Haldane and J. Huxley, *Animal Biology*, Oxford University Press, 1927, p. 335.

know, and remember, and think creatively as individuals far beyond the limitations of any single group or dominance of any single need. Knowledge acquired and extended for its own sake is the specific quality which makes us human. Our species has the hair and lungs of animals, reptilian bones and fish-like blood. We are close indeed to the beasts; often we are more cruel. But we are fundamentally different from them in that we can learn almost infinitely, and know and recollect. We are Homo sapiens: Man the Thinker.[15]

The Flair for Objectivity

Though there are still some writers who belittle the difference between man and the other animals, they have not been very convincing. The chief reason for their failure lies, not in some dogma which they have challenged, but in their conflict with observable fact. It might be supposed that the chief opposition to the essential identification of man with the animals would come from traditional religious sources, but such is not the case. Among the strongest contemporary voices raised in behalf of the recognition of a radical differentiation of man are those of Mrs. Langer and the late A. O. Lovejoy, neither of whom speaks from the standpoint of any traditional religious heritage. The question which these, and thinkers like them, raise is not one of whether man has an immortal soul, which beasts presumably do not possess; this would seem to them a matter of speculation. The hope of immortality is not unreasonable, as Plato sought to show in the Phaedo, but it is intrinsically a hope and not something observable or empirically verifiable. What concerns contemporary philosophers in regard to this significant question is not a religious doctrine but philosophical anthropology. What do we see, they ask, when we look carefully and critically?

Mrs. Langer's treatment of the subject is intended to be one which is wholly compatible with scientific mentality. "I myself," she writes, "stand entirely in the scientific camp." She is not arguing, she says, against any religious or vitalistic doctrine, and by the same token she is not arguing for them. Her observation of human and animal behavior leads her to the paradoxical conclusion that, within the evolutionary series, there is a qualitative leap. "Despite

[15] G. Highet, Man's Unconquerable Mind, Columbia University Press, 1960, pp. 7, 8.

man's zoological status, which I wholeheartedly accept, there is a deep gulf between the highest animal and the most primitive normal human being: a difference in mentality that is fundamental."[16] So fundamental does this difference appear that she compares it with the difference between plant and animal.

One fruitful way to approach the question of man's possible differentiation is through a consideration of man's needs. Whatever his physical similarity, man obviously has needs which the animals do not share. The uniqueness of his needs has led to a number of unique ways in which these needs are met. Consequently, man is the only animal who makes fires, the only one who makes pictures, the only one who prays, the only one who develops a written language, the only one who is truly penitent, the only one who invents, the only one who erects monuments, and so on, through a long and impressive list. It is hard to overcome the suggestion that these particular manifestations may be severally the consequence of something more central and generic than any of them. Perhaps so. In any case, the question is one which we need to examine with care.

Perhaps man is radically different from all other creatures, not because of a single vital attribute, but because of a complex of characteristics which go together. Most of the philosophers of the past who have mentioned the unique feature have been correct in pointing to something that does, in fact, make a differentiation, but there remains the problem of how the various features which constitute uniqueness are combined. One of the factors to be examined is self-consciousness. Some beings are unconscious; some are conscious; man alone is truly self-conscious. It is because he can turn upon himself and examine his own actions or his own decisions that his behavior is inevitably plastic. It is because man can be critical of all ways of doing and thinking, including his own ways, that he exhibits the possibility of truly moral judgment. Man can do terrible things, but, by virtue of his self-consciousness, he can know that he does them and he can be, consequently, penitent. "The greatness of man is great," says Pascal, "in that he knows himself to be miserable. A tree does not know itself to be miserable. It is then being miserable to know oneself to be miserable; but is also

[16] Langer, op. cit., p. 111.

being great to know that one is miserable."[17] Error recognized is still erroneous, but it is partly transcended.

There is no more vivid evidence of man's self-consciousness than that which is demonstrated by the perennial interest in the very question now being considered. The persistence of the question provides a significant part of the answer. Man is indeed the metaphysical animal, as Schopenhauer said, and he is the epistemological animal, as Lovejoy said,[18] but he is also the anthropological animal, if we may judge by his enormous interest in his own distinctive nature.

All living creatures shape their environment to some degree, and man as the "world-changer" is only doing in a large way what the other living creatures do in a small way; but man seems to be the only one who consciously shapes himself. A being who can really look at himself can change and he can be concerned with what he ought to do because he is capable of criticizing himself. Man seeks to reshape the world as others do, but he does not stop there; he goes on to try to reshape himself and the conduct of his fellow humans.[19] Because he sees his own inadequacy, man learns deliberately from others. His tools, accordingly, are almost always social products. It is true, as Darwin asserted,[20] that animals other than men use tools, but "the tools of animals are never the outcome of collective and historical thought."[21]

The self-conscious experience is one which everyone shares but which we seldom analyze. The experience, in its simplest form, is that in which an individual makes his own states of mind, or his own feelings, the objects of his own attention. There is a crucial difference between the experience of a creature who wants, and the experience of a creature who attends to his wanting. It is one thing to have the experience of pain; it is quite another if the pain is felt in the contemplation of one's own character. It is one thing to criticize a method of achieving a satisfaction; it is wholly another

[17] Pascal, op. cit., 397.
[18] A. O. Lovejoy, The Revolt Against Dualism, The Open Court Publishing Company, 1955, p. 12.
[19] See W. E. Hocking, Human Nature and Its Remaking, Yale University Press, 1929, pp. 5, 6.
[20] C. Darwin, The Descent of Man, D. Appleton and Company, 1871, p. 49.
[21] G. Spiller, The Origin and Nature of Man, Williams and Norgate Ltd., 1931, p. 83.

to criticize the character of the satisfaction permitted. Man became man, not when he became clever, but when he asked himself whether he was justified in performing the clever act. The sophisticated insight of the Book of Genesis in the Hebrew Bible is to the effect that the emergence of man and the recognition of moral evil were contemporary events.

When we conclude that, although man differs from the animals so greatly, it is still reasonable to speak of him as an animal, the paradox may receive clarification from the familiar analogy of figure and cube. A cube is indeed a figure, but it is more than a mere figure, because it has properties which figures in general do not have. The fact that such a situation can obtain in a familiar and accepted area of experience makes it less strange to say that man has animal propensities, yet is not *just an animal*. Man is *sui generis*, because he has propensities which mere animals do not have. We and the animals, suggests Schopenhauer, are on the same ship but we perform contrasting functions. Schopenhauer compared the animals to the sailors and man to the navigator, who may be where the others are, but who, by means of chart and compass, *knows where he is*.[22]

Part of man's ability to know where he is refers to time rather than to space. We have some idea of history, even though our knowledge of the past is always factually imperfect, and our knowledge of the future is intrinsically so. Alfred Korzybski emphasized the temporal aspect of man's uniqueness when he said:

The facts if we will note them and reflect upon them, are such as to show us that the chasm separating human nature from animal nature is even wider and deeper than the chasm between animal life and the life of plants. For man improves, animals do not; man invents more and more complicated tools, animals do not; man is a creator of material and spiritual wealth, animals are not; man is a builder of civilization, animals are not; man makes the past live in the present, and the present in the future, animals do not; man is the binder of time, animals are not.[23]

[22] See A. Schopenhauer, "The World as Will and Idea," trans. Haldane and Kemp, in W. Durant (ed.), *The Works of Schopenhauer*, Simon and Shuster, 1928, p. 15.
[23] Alfred Korzybski, *The Manhood of Humanity*, E. P. Dutton and Company, 1921, p. 186.

Korzybski distinguished among the plants as "basic-energy-binding," the animals as "space-binding," and man as "time-binding." This is probably too neat a division, because the nonhuman animals undoubtedly learn something from past experience, and they make some preparation for the future. What really demands explanation is the fact that, though other animals have some power to reason, some self-consciousness, language, and time sense, man differs so greatly in degree in all of these respects. Something is added which makes each of the differences in degree enormous.

One who faced the question in this manner was the late Max Scheler (1874–1928), whose work has not yet enjoyed an adequate reading even on the part of professional philosophers. Scheler's early death robbed philosophy of one of its most brilliant practitioners. If he had lived longer, many intellectual movements, particularly on the European continent, might have been significantly altered. Though in one sense a disciple of Husserl, and therefore a phenomenologist, he was no mere copy of his teacher, and in fact provided an intellectual bridge to the developing existentialism. Bochenski does not hesitate to speak of Scheler in superlative terms, saying that he was "beyond doubt, the most brilliant German thinker of his day."[24] His most creative period came after World War I, when he taught philosophy at Cologne. In this period he stressed both essence and existence, both objectivity and subjectivity, but he was convinced that man's flair for the objective is really the heart of the matter. The great though slim book which came out the year of Scheler's death, in 1928, called *Die Stellung des Menschen im Kosmos*, explained this flair for objectivity as the essence of human personality. The deepest problems of philosophy, Scheler maintained, are the problems involved in philosophical anthropology. Find out what man is, and the rest of the world begins to make sense.

Man, Scheler held in his final phase, is *sui generis*; he is absolutely and generically different from all animals in the fact that he is spirit, and spirit is not the same as intelligence. So far as intelligence is concerned, said Scheler, Edison and a clever chimpanzee differ only in degree, not in essence. Man, as a new creation, rad-

---

[24] I. M. Bochenski, *Contemporary European Philosophy*, University of California Press, 1961, p. 140.

ically different from nature, though associated with it, is able to separate essence and existence. Spirit, the new development which is our hope, is objectivity (*Sachlichkeit*), which is the capacity to grasp the nature of things, independent of our desires. The potential objectivity of man is so great and inclusive that he can even get outside and look at himself as part of the total scene which he observes. Man, as spirit, can see the difference between what he wants and what is. He can have a *world*, and he has it long before he explores it in full detail, which he may never be able to do. Man may be a poor, weak creature, and he may fail to do what he recognizes as objectively right, but his glory and his hope for a brighter future are involved in the fact that the distinction can be made. Every person is individual, standing over against his world.

Beyond man's capacity to make tools or laugh or weep or pray or improve himself or know or judge or reason, lies the generic capacity for discovering that he is himself involved in the world which he inhabits, yet is distinguishable from it. We cannot know perfectly what goes on in animal minds, but it is reasonably certain that they do not know that there is a world at all. Man is *sui generis* in that he is concerned with the nature of the world and his place in it. The question of the *differentiae* of man constitutes a philosophical problem, and the chief answer is the fact that man is the philosophical animal. He does not thereby lose his animal nature but, in so far as he is truly human, he can see even his animal nature in perspective. It is reasonable to suppose that, from this initial capacity of man, which makes him truly unique, have evolved all the typically human characteristics and experiences, aesthetic, cognitive, moral, and spiritual. Man is not often wise and he is not really good, but he is disturbed by needs which other known creatures do not share. He knows that he is not good and that he is not wise and he is, consequently, never really satisfied. He has powerful desires in his self-conscious experience, powers which seem ineradicable.[25] Few have equaled Susan Stebbing in her clarification of what man's strange needs entail:

Man is a strange creature. Whatever his origins, he differs funda-

[25] Note, in this connection, A. O. Lovejoy's essay "The Desires of the Self-Conscious Animal," Lecture 3 in *Reflections on Human Nature*. The Johns Hopkins Press, 1961.

mentally from the other animals. These can be ill-treated, suffer pain and neglect, be diseased and die; but they do not know the long-ranging fear of death, they do not suffer from oppression of spirit. They cannot (so I presume) regret the past nor have hopes for the future. Man, however, does not live by bread alone, nor is kindness enough to satisfy him. He has spiritual powers, creative energies, forward-looking hopes. If these be left underdeveloped and unsatisfied, nothing else that man acquires can be felt as sustainingly worthwhile.[26]

To say that man is *sui generis* because he is potentially if not actually a philosopher is to say that man, with all his liabilities, has a flair for wholeness. He can be conscious of others and of himself. The animal may have some slight memories and some expectations, but it is obvious that it lives essentially in the present. Man always escapes the specious present; he has a past in which he locates his memories and this he extends without limit. He tries to mould the future, but he does this by reference to the past; this is well demonstrated whenever we seek precedents for decisions which affect the future. Every animal lives in a circumscribed place, but man is always extending his horizons, so that he lives in a universe.

Thus we see that the many differentiating characteristics go together. We transcend time, we transcend space, we transcend individuality, we go beyond what is done to a consideration of what *ought* to be done, we transcend life by the universal recognition that we shall die. The animal experiences death, in *other* creatures, but he cannot know that he, himself, will die, because he does not experience death in himself. Man, by contrast, because he lives in a world, because he has a flair for wholeness, can reflect on his own participation in the universal tragedy. "Only a creature who can think symbolically *about* life," says Mrs. Langer, "can conceive of its own death. Our knowledge of death is part of our knowledge of life."[27]

The Emergence of Spirit

There is no chance of developing an adequate philosophy unless we keep in mind the relevant fact that ours is a world which has

[26] Stebbing, *op. cit.*, p. 25.
[27] Langer, *op. cit.*, p. 114.

persons in it. There was a time, it is evident, when there were no persons, at least so far as the earth is concerned. Whether there are persons elsewhere, i.e., on other planets around other suns, is, at this juncture of history, so entirely speculative that it cannot be intelligently discussed. Some day there may be empirical evidence on this subject, but now there is none. For all we know now, this earth may be the only part of the physical universe in which personality has appeared, and even here it has appeared very late. Once, according to our available evidence, the earth was completely barren of life, a mass of rocks and water whirling through space, as some astronomical bodies probably are now. We have good reason to believe that life appeared only after millions of years of the planet's existence and that self-conscious beings whom we call persons appeared after further millions of years. What we do know is that they finally appeared; we know this because we are persons ourselves. No philosophy can stand which does not include this fact. The only intelligible system of belief is one which is consistent with it.

To be a person is to engage in experiences which involve vast extensions of consciousness. Persons are conscious of a world of affection, of purpose, of wrong doing, and of a long time span. Though the word has often been misunderstood in the past, the best general term for these experiences, familiar to all of us, is the word "spiritual." The word so employed need not involve a narrowly religious connotation, Susan Stebbing has employed the term "spiritual excellences" in application to the present temporal world in which we live now, and without any reference to a future existence.

These spiritual excellences are intellectual and moral capacities lacking which the life of human beings would be nasty and brutish; length of days could not redeem it. The excellences I call *spiritual* include love for human beings, delight in creative activities of all kinds, respect for truth, satisfaction for learning to know what is true about this world (including ourselves), loyalty to other human beings, generosity of thought and sympathy with those who suffer, hatred of cruelty and other evils, devotion to duty and steadfastness in seeking one's ideals, delight in the beauty of nature and in art—in short, the love and pursuit of what is worth while for its own sake. In this pursuit the individual does in fact have at times to suffer pain and to surrender what it would be good for him to have were it not for the incompatible needs of others, needs which he recognizes as claims upon himself. This is another spiritual excellence. These excellences are to be found in *this* world; no heaven is needed to experience them.[28]

Because Miss Stebbing wrote as a philosopher and not as a theologian, which she was not, she avoided, in so far as possible, all speculation and sought to analyze only recognizable human experiences. This is, indeed, the best way to recognize what a spiritual being is. We are so close to it every moment that we tend to forget its wonder. It is clear that any attempt to explain it in merely physical terms is doomed to failure, because we are talking about functions which mere bodies do not illustrate. Stones are, but there is no reason to suppose that they recognize other stones or reflect upon their stoniness. The only way to understand what a person means is to use the path of denotation as Miss Stebbing has done, and that is something of which only a person is capable.

In the recent past the concept known as the theory of levels has been widely supported by thinkers who differ widely in general interests and in other conclusions. Among the most influential names in connection with the theory of levels have been those of Whitehead, Temple, Alexander, and Lovejoy. The central idea stems from the observation that our universe is also a multiverse, in that it exhibits levels of reality which are marked by utterly different laws. We know what anything is by what it does, and the things which persons do are radically different from the things which impersonal objects do. All who accept the evidence for the reality of different levels in the world as experienced are, in some important sense, upholders of emergent evolutionism. "In its very simplest form," says G. T. W. Patrick, "emergent evolution means simply this: that in the evolutionary process new qualities, new modes of action, and qualitatively new entities arise when physical structures become more complex and integrated."[29]

To face honestly the fact that our world has persons in it means to accept novelty when it appears and not to try to reduce it to

[28] Stebbing, op. cit., pp. 27, 28.
[29] G. T. W. Patrick, *Introduction to Philosophy*, rev. ed., Houghton Mifflin Company, 1935, p. 112.

something which is not itself. If we are serious observers we can hardly fail to note that, in considering personality, "we are upon a new level, among new realities, in a new atmosphere, dealing with new things having their own laws and peculiarities. Mind has emerged from matter; the spiritual has emerged from the physical. After long centuries of misuse, the word *spirit* gains a definite and profitable meaning; it means the level of the psychical as viewed from the standpoint of value."[30]

The convergence of thinkers in this general direction has been evaluated by a prominent contemporary philosopher Dorothy Emmet, as follows: "When such very different lines of thought converge on a generalization of this kind, we can be the more confident in believing that something like it can stand."[31] All who share in the convergence to which Miss Emmet points accept the speculative truth of evolution in the sense that the higher elements of reality, known to us and experienced in ourselves, have, in all probability, come to pass in a causal nexus of temporal successiveness, yet all of us refuse to allow this belief to blind us to the reality of differences.

During most of the period in which there has been serious scientific and philosophical discussion about the evolution of man as spiritual being, the unargued assumption has been that the new level has arisen by very slow degrees, over very long periods. We have held to this speculation even when it has had no support from research and we have been somewhat embarrassed by the fact that the earliest men, whose remains we are able to study, appear to have been able to engage in symbolic activity, much as we do now. But now various thinkers are beginning to ask whether this hypothesis of slow development, especially in human speech, is a necessary one. One of the most exciting phases of philosophical anthropology today is the bold suggestion that the crucial development may have come with great speed!

The factors which make human language possible, as something utterly different from animal cries, are numerous and they need to come simultaneously in order to be effective. A fortunate combination might result, not in a painfully slow process, but an extremely

30 *Ibid.*, p. 300.
31 F. A. Iremonger, *William Temple*, Oxford University Press, 1948, p. 528.

rapid one. When one creature was able not merely to evoke responses in another being, but to express ideas and thus really to communicate *about* something, he was suddenly able to do what no animal does. "From then on," says Susanne Langer, "speech probably advanced with headlong speed. . . . The new motive of communication must have driven it like wildfire. . . . Once communication got started, the use of human mentality may have been cataclysmic, a matter of a few generations wherever it began at all."[32]

What the new philosophical anthropology proposes is as much a matter of speculation as was the old, but it now comes with a great freshness and it indicates the possibility of a great hope. If there was a magnificent and cataclysmic breakthrough once before, there might be again. Man is the kind of creature in whom this could occur.

[32] Langer, *op. cit.*, pp. 52, 53. The whole of chapter 2 in this book makes exciting reading.

Chapter 9 ∽ *DETERMINISM AND FREEDOM*

Man *is condemned to be free.*

JEAN-PAUL SARTRE

CAN A HUMAN BEING, BY TAKING THOUGHT, MAKE A DIFFERENCE IN the total course of events that would not otherwise be made? If so, there is a profound sense in which man is free; if not, the freedom of which he speaks is only a delusion. Perhaps there is a wave, not only of the future but also of the present, on which we ride and which we affect no more than the foam affects the great rollers which strike the beach relentlessly. Some thinkers have supposed, either sadly or with a sense of relief, that this is the case. A person cannot be a philosopher unless he examines this question as carefully as possible.

The Argument for Determinism

A tradition among philosophers, also among men who are not professional philosophers, has involved the conviction that some of man's actions are free in the sense that they are not coerced by prior conditions, either material or mental. Most philosophers have concluded that, though some acts are determined, there are other acts which cannot be rightly understood except in terms of genuine personal choice. Some of the reasons for this general conclusion have already been indicated and others will be mentioned later, but, whatever the reasons, there is no serious doubt about the side on which the weight of thoughtful opinion rests. Aristotle was foreshadowing the major conclusion when he said, "All men know that situations call for decisions." But it is idle to talk of decision if the event is already predetermined by what has gone before.

In spite of the vast weight of judgment against absolute determinism in human actions there is, today, a widely held opinion in favor of determinism: the upholders of this opinion include some professional philosophers. The position often begins with a desire for tolerance or sympathy with other people, especially with people who are guilty of immoral acts. A young man, let us say, is guilty of murdering a girl, whom he has raped. The popular argument in many circles, including some academic circles, is that he is not really to blame, because there were conditions which led inevitably to his act. He came from a broken home; he grew up in poverty; he was rejected by society; consequently he had no choice. It would, therefore, we are told, be as unfair to blame him as it would be to blame a mousetrap for killing the mouse when the mouse nibbles the cheese and thereby springs the trap. It is obvious that much of our teaching about tenderness, with refusal to judge, buttresses what is presented as a purely intellectual argument. We seem to be embarked on this road whenever we say, "There, but for the grace of God, go I," and "Let him that is without sin cast the first stone."

Though part of the incentive is thus emotional, all philosophical determinism claims to be based on rational grounds. The central conviction is simply the combination of strict causality with metaphysical monism. Both of these need to be explained before they are examined.

The belief in strict causality seems to be a necessary element in any world view which takes science seriously, and we cannot fail to take science seriously in the light of its manifest success in the modern world. There are some scientists and some philosophers who have tried to operate without the notion of cause, but it cannot be said that they have been successful. Long ago Bertrand Russell remarked that "the word 'cause' is so inextricably bound up with misleading associations as to make its complete extrusion from the philosophical vocabulary desirable."[1] What Lord Russell hoped for, when he wrote these words more than a half century ago, was to substitute for causation the notion of function, as is done in higher physics. But this is not possible unless, as in mathematics, we eliminate the factor of time, which is something which we cannot do in dealing with the data of history. If we suddenly find that the birds of a neighorhood are sick and dying we rightly look for an adequate cause *prior* to this event, and we think we have found it when we find that DDT has been sprayed by aircraft in the area in order to kill certain insects. It is hard to see how life can go on intelligently unless causation in this practical sense is assumed. Such causation cannot, of course, be observed, and in this David Hume was right, but it is a necessary postulate of the kind described in Chapter 4. This leads Miss Stebbing to say that, "whatever may be the case with philosophy, it is not possible to expel the word or the conception from science."[2]

Now, if ours is a connected world, as it obviously is, we learn to manipulate it by finding what conditions lead inevitably or probably to particular results. If we want to kill Japanese beetles we employ the proper chemicals, but if we want to avoid, at the same time, the death of birds, we may refuse to use such chemicals. It is the great merit of John Locke as a philosopher that he speaks in clear terms, which the plain man can understand, and he does this with eminent success when he defines cause. "A cause," he says, "is that which makes any other thing . . . begin to be, and an effect is that which had its beginning from some other thing."[3] The billiard ball is at rest on the table until another billiard ball strikes it and causes it to move. Not all actions in the world are as simple as that, but there is little doubt that such relationships occur in

[1] B. Russell, *Mysticism and Logic*, Doubleday & Company, Inc., Anchor Books, 1957, p. 180.

[2] L. Susan Stebbing, *A Modern Introduction to Logic*, Harper & Row, Torchbooks, 1961, p. 260.

[3] J. Locke, "Essay Concerning Human Understanding," *The Works of John Locke*, George Bell and Sons, 1875, Bk. II, chap. 26, par. 2.

many areas of experience, including the area of our own bodies. Fundamentally, all diagnosis of disease follows this same logical pattern, no matter how complex it becomes. When I am overtired, I think that there must be a reason, so I consult with my physician to try to ascertain what the reason may be.

The other pertinent factor in human determinism is the monistic principle, which holds that laws of the same kind operate in all levels of nature. Men are part of nature just as truly as germs are and cannot therefore be exempt from the same causal nexus. The moment that we allow exceptions, we break down the scientific world view which is, intrinsically, total in its claims. The motions of muscles obey the same laws as do the motions of mechanical levers. Human bodies decay as stumps decay, and the human brain is destroyed by a collision much as a watch is. Both are intricately balanced and both can be damaged by a physical impact. Aristotle appeared to be upholding such causal monism when he said, "Now everything that comes to be comes to be by the agency of something and from something."[4]

It is easy to see that the combination of strict causation and metaphysical monism makes choice meaningless. The upholders of determinism are as well aware as anyone of their own experience of choosing, but they are forced, they believe, to the conclusion that this experience is illusory. They, like ordinary mortals, feel that they are choosing, but they are convinced that, in reality, they are not, because the outcome has already been determined by prior conditions, including the condition of their own mental events. The introduction of mental events does not ease the paradox because the prior mental events were themselves determined by earlier events, so that, ultimately, we are forced to sheer materialism. Nearly all who think about the problem realize that such a system seems to deny free will, though a few, of whom R. E. Hobart is representative, seek to hold that determinism is not only compatible with freedom, but is actually necessary if free will is to be maintained.[5] We shall consider his argument later.

[4] Aristotle, *Metaphysics*, trans. W. Ogle, *The Basic Works of Aristotle*, Random House, 1941, p. 791.
[5] R. E. Hobart, "Free will as involving determinism and inconceivable without it," *Mind*, 43, 1934, 1–27.

Perhaps the most influential philosophical determinist of the last century has been Dr. Sigmund Freud, the founder of psychoanalysis. Freud considered that he had made a revolution in thought comparable to that produced by Copernicus or by Darwin, the heart of his contribution being the recognition of unconscious determinants. If scientism is a disease, Freud had it badly. He expressed naïve positivism with no reservations whatsoever, asserting "that no knowledge can be obtained from revelation, intuition or inspiration." Such a dictum was characteristically introduced by the phrase, "Science asserts." Freud accepted the doctrine of determinism in a complete form, asserting that all acts are the inevitable outcome of prior conditions, and he thought he had evidence for such a sweeping statement by reference to the later effects of childhood experiences. His philosophic position was made clear when he wrote, "Psycho-analysis is not, in my opinion, in a position to create a *Weltanschauung* of its own. It has no need to do so, for it is a branch of science, and can subscribe to the scientific *Weltanschauung*."[6]

Freud believed that all science is one and that therefore, since determinism is applicable to chemistry or physics, it must be applicable to psychology as well. The founder of psychoanalysis did not mind being criticized by metaphysicians or theologians, but he was terribly hurt when he was criticized by scientists, for science was his religion. Though Freud was a very great psychologist, and though he and his followers have undoubtedly rendered valuable human service by the practice of psychoanalysis, it is easy to see that he was a very poor philosopher. His naïveté in philosophy is shown by his failure to investigate the consequences of his position, particularly in the denial of responsibility. Nevertheless, it is his philosophical view that has influenced modern mentality more than his psychological technique. The popular tendency, in a court trial, to absolve the prisoner of all blame often stems, upon analysis, from Freudian presuppositions.

When we ask seriously what the evidence for determinism is, we are struck by how little there is. After all, the doctrine of monistic causality is nothing but a dogma, and certainly not one which is

[6] S. Freud, *New Introductory Lectures on Psycho-Analysis*, Carlton House, 1933, p. 248.

supported by anything approaching supporting proof. In so far as the idea of levels, already mentioned in Chapter 8, is a sound one, the whole monistic hypothesis is damaged. Perhaps human actions are characterized by a causal order, yet one that is different in kind from the order represented by billiard balls. The popular belief in deterministic explanation rests on nothing more substantial than the conviction to the effect that "there must have been a reason." Even a decision, we all recognize, does not occur in a causal vacuum. But, unless all human experience is to be set aside, there must be a way to maintain a belief in decisions that are genuine and in an order that is pervasive. How to unite these two, neither of which we can reject, but which appear to be mutually contradictory, is the heart of our philosophical problem.

When we say that the only support of determinism is a metaphysical dogma,[7] we mean that there is no experimental evidence. It is easy to look back, after the event, and to say that what has occurred is the inevitable result of the prior condition which we now seek to describe, but *this* is not experimental evidence. What would be required for a clinching argument is the establishment of conditions, with definite predictions, plus verification of the predicted events. This we can have at a mechanical level, but this is precisely what we do not have at the level of human decision. It is in prediction of human actions that we are notoriously weak. The prediction of Alexis de Tocqueville about the emergence of two great powers, Russia and the United States of America, is often mentioned for the very reason that success in this field is so rare.

The precise moral conditions of many experiments simply do not exist, for they would involve a manipulation of men which is incompatible with any recognition of the worth of the individual. We cannot, in the nature of the case, experiment with a boy to see whether we can produce a criminal mentality, and even when we limit ourselves to observation rather than to experiment, our predictions are often wrong. This is true even of the most scientific

[7] The metaphysical dogma, said Lovejoy, is "that the actual determinants of those movements of organic matter which we call human behavior are those other antecedent states or movements of matter and energy, or energy alone, which consists in patterns or motions of particles or energy-quanta in the brain and nervous system." (A. O. Lovejoy, *Reflections on Human Nature*, The Johns Hopkins Press, 1961, p. 72.)

observations. All that we have, then, in support of psychological determinism is a speculation which is based on a doubtful analogy, the analogy with a mechanistic order.

The problem which arises for the determinist, because of the failure to predict accurately, is often met by saying that we could predict if only we knew all the conditions. The inability to predict, then, is held to be, not a measure of the objective situation, but merely a measure of our own ignorance. Though this argument is often employed, it is not very impressive. The fact is that we do not know all the conditions and, in view of our finitude, we are not likely to know them. Therefore we are appealing to something of which we have no experience at all. This is manifestly unprofitable. The argument from ignorance is always worthless.

The Difficulties of Determinism

As we proceed dialectically, it is our duty to examine whatever arguments there may be against determinism, after having heard the arguments for it, and then to see whether some sort of synthesis can be achieved. The most powerful argument against determinism is that it utterly destroys any logical basis of responsibility. Kant's analysis of the problem can hardly be improved upon and may, indeed, be one of his most enduring contributions to human thought. No man is responsible, said Kant, for what he cannot help doing. The tree which is blown by the wind and hits a house, crushing out the life of the inhabitants, is not morally culpable. There was no decision on the part of the tree; it was a passive agent at the mercy of wind and weather. Sometimes a man performs acts of the same nature, which are purely mechanical reactions. In that case, Kant contends, it would be ridiculous to blame him. If, on the other hand, good results were to come from a mechanical act, it would be equally ridiculous to praise him. He does what he must, and that is the end of the matter.

Now, if all acts are determined as a mechanical act is determined, there would be no logical basis of either praise or blame in the world. The universality of this conclusion involves our reactions to ourselves as well as to others, so that, on the basis of psychological determinism, there would be no meaning to penitence. How could a man blame himself if he merely did what he had to do and if decision were an illusory experience? Yet the experience of responsibility and of remorse is so deep in human life that any philosophy which fails to make room for it is immediately suspect. Kant's great contribution in regard to this problem was his decision to depend upon the moral experience as something so nearly indubitable that it must be taken seriously. We must, then, have a world view which can include the moral experience rationally. If any philosophy cannot be made compatible with the basic sense of responsibility for our own deeds, it is the philosophy rather than the sense of responsibility which is suspect. It must be noted that even the most vocal upholders of determinism admit that they feel responsible, and they extend this feeling to others, in that they condemn the decisions of others which are different from what determinists think they should have been. The probability is that there are no consistent determinists.

Some determinists recognize the need of including responsibility in a rational system, but hold that this can be done through a determinist metaphysic. The chief argument for this, best expressed by Hobart, but also accepted by such philosophers as Ayer and Raab, is that the only logical alternative to determinism is chance, which is entirely destructive of responsibility, while determinism can be interpreted in ways that save something of what most needs saving. If by free will we should mean that what I choose, I choose for no reason, there would be no important difference between my alleged decision and the tossing of a coin. If I come into court accused of a crime, I might evade, logically, all responsibility by saying that the crime was a chance action which I did last week, and that probably, by the laws of chance, I would not do it today. This would mean that I am not reacting as a moral person at all.

If the only alternative to absolute determinism is chance, then Hobart and others who have defended determinism are right. The determinist can at least show how the total past is the intricate cause and can, pragmatically, include punishment as a causal factor that would affect future events. A deterministic judge would not succumb to the popular view of leniency toward the criminal because the criminal could not help his act; he would, instead, be ready to punish brutally in order to influence the future; he would treat persons as things, and seek by his judgment to alter the course of events, as he could with a mechanical device. It is one of the chief marks of the impartiality of the late Archbishop Temple as a philosopher that he saw this so clearly. He wrote in his splendid chapter on "Freedom and Determinism":

It is noticeable that for legal or civic purposes, it is easier to associate responsibility with Determinism than with an extreme doctrine of Free Will. The difficulties created by the latter have been mentioned. So far as character is conceived as the source of conduct, an extreme doctrine of Free Will makes it uncertain whether the prisoner, though convicted of a crime, can justly be punished; for in what sense is he the same person who committed the crime? Determinism gives rise to no such difficulty. The judge may say to the convicted prisoner: "The Law, which I am charged to administer, takes no interest in the process by which you come to be what you are; but you are the perpetrator of a crime; and as such you must submit to the penalty prescribed by the Law, both that you may be thereby determined to a different course of conduct, and that others may be determined to avoid the conduct which is seen to incur such penalties."[8]

It is important to say that, though a judge might conceivably operate as Temple suggests, this is not what normally occurs. Most members of the legal profession reject the simple dichotomy of determinism and indeterminism and maintain a position similar to that which will be presented at the conclusion of this chapter. Indeed, much of the tension between jurists and psychiatrists arises from deep philosophical differences, rather than from the character of their professions. There is no doubt that, like Freud, most psychiatrists are deterministic in their approach, while most jurists are not. The resulting tension is the subject of an admirable article by Raymond L. Erickson of Whittier College, "Psychiatry and the Law: An Attempt at Synthesis."[9] The thesis that the tension is fundamentally philosophical is stated as follows:

The lack of agreement between members of the two professions of psychiatry and the law as to what constitutes the proper end of criminal justice is at least in part a result of the differing concepts of the nature

[8] W. Temple, Nature, Man and God, The Macmillan Company, 1956, p. 224.
[9] See Duke Law Journal, Vol. 1961, No. 1, pp. 30–73.

of man which are held. Simply put, the major difference is that members of the legal profession tend to picture man as a free moral agent with the capacity to choose between right and wrong acts, while most psychiatrists, by remaining true to the scientific picture of man that has been evolved during the last seventy years, conceive of man's behavior as completely subject to the influence of antecedent determining factors. They would, of course, admit that man has a conscious experience which he calls "making a choice"; but the choice that he will make has already been determined by antecedent circumstances, and his conscious experience of making a choice is merely his subjective awareness of the means whereby the influences of previous experiences and other antecedent conditions are synthesized.[10]

If the only alternative to determinism is chance, we can see easily why determinism is the less outrageous of the two possibilities, but this ought not to blind us to the real difficulties of determinism. The fundamental difficulty is that it involves the treatment of persons as though they were things. The psychiatrist, believing that the man who consults him is not really free, and that choice is a delusion, simply adds his bit to the sum total of antecedent circumstances. The popular judgment that determinism is destructive of morality is therefore not mistaken, even though the popular judgment may not entertain any fully defensible alternative.

The strangest feature of the entire complex situation is the psychiatrist's implicit elimination of himself from the total picture. If the patient's freedom of choice is delusive, so is that of the physician! Each simply does what he must do, and that is the end of the matter. But of course no psychiatrist really believes this. The other man may be passive, but not he! He deliberates; he thinks; he resists temptation; he makes a decision, not as a result of mere conditioning, but in the light of reason. All planning seems to be based on the necessity of thinking of other men as pawns to be moved by the planner, but why, then, is the planner not himself also a pawn? Since prior conditions supposedly determined his plans and since these prior conditions, including his own thoughts, were similarly produced, there is no reason to stop the regress at any point. There is thus no freedom anywhere and the whole of human history is a predetermined set of events. Actually, of course, upholders of de-

[10] *Ibid.*, pp. 32, 33.

terminism stop short of such an extreme position, but when they do so they are merely refusing to follow the logic of the position which they espouse.

The Experience of Choice

We are not likely to develop a sound philosophy unless we take seriously the importance of actual choice in human experience. Since this is an experience which appears to be universal in the human species, it cannot be lightly dismissed. It is easy to see that there are many motives for trying to dismiss it. One such motive is the desire for neatness or simplicity. If something really new takes place in the experience of choice, something that cannot be fully accounted for in prior conditions, this would be extremely disturbing to the scientific picture which has been built up with such laborious care. This is the meaning of Erickson's statement, that most psychiatrists are determinists because they seek to remain "true to the scientific picture of man that has evolved during the last seventy years." If there can be no simple equation of cause and effect, it is a blow against a system painfully constructed, and something which might possibly open the door to superstition or the willingness to be satisfied with mystery.

Another motive for denying the responsibility which genuine choice entails is the desire to avoid the burden which responsibility involves. If I can blame my acts upon my circumstances, then nobody can rightly blame me. Here was a theme which intrigued the restless mind of Albert Camus in the last years of his brilliant life. At a crucial point in the argument he makes a character say, "The question is to slip through and, above all—yes, above all, the question is to elude judgment. I am not saying to avoid punishment, for punishment without judgment is bearable."[11] Camus has hit a tender point in the human mentality. To accept responsibility is painful and often humiliating. It means that a man must stand up and say, "I did it. I am ashamed. I cannot account for it fully by

[11] A. Camus, *The Fall*, trans. J. O'Brien, Alfred A. Knopf, 1957, pp. 76, 77. In the Biblical story of the fall in Genesis, both the man and the woman refuse to accept responsibility.

the influences which undoubtedly affected me. There was something in addition to the influences, my decision, and it was, indeed, mine."

No serious thinker of our generation has stressed the painful and essential acceptance of responsibility more than has Jean-Paul Sartre. In developing what he calls "existentialist psychoanalyis," he rejects utterly the Freudian emphasis on sex, and stresses instead the reality of choice. He says that the investigator must recall on every occasion that his object is not a datum buried in the darkness of the unconscious, but a free, conscious determination—which is not even resident in consciousness, but which is one with this consciousness itself.[12] Sartre believes that a person who excuses himself by reference to the prior condition of his deed is refusing to see what it is to be truly human and is dealing with reality on the subhuman level. The total situation includes the man's choice as part of it and, indeed, a most important part. "He must assume the situation with the proud consciousness of being the author of it, for the very worst disadvantages or the worst threats that can endanger my person have meaning only in and through my project; and it is on the ground of the engagement which I am that they appear. It is therefore senseless to think of complaining since nothing foreign has decided what we feel, what we live, or what we are."[13]

This is strong meat and it comes from a surprising source. Sartre is not even a believer in God, one of his chief fears being that, if he did believe in God, he might be tempted to shift to the divine shoulders some of the august sense of responsibility which he feels, and which he ought to feel because he is a man. The weight, he believes, cannot be shifted because "man being condemned to be free carries the weight of the whole world on his shoulders; he is responsible for the world and for himself as a way of being."

It is clear that responsibility must lie somewhere and that the problem is not solved by shifting it. The popular view in regard to juvenile delinquency is to blame the parents, but, by the same logic, we should have to blame their parents and so on ad infinitum. There is no solution of a problem in infinite regress. In some way or other, someone must accept responsibility: this is precisely the

[12] J.-P. Sartre, *Existentialism and Human Emotions*, The Wisdom Library Paperbacks, Philosophical Library, Inc., 1957, p. 79.
[13] *Ibid.*, p. 53.

solution of the problem which Sartre and Camus have proposed. They make this answer, not as a mere speculation, but as a result of a careful analysis of the human consciousness, which, as Descartes has taught us, is the only possible starting point. We must have a theory if we are to operate intelligently; the existentialist theory is one which seeks to take seriously the undoubted sense of shame which means that the decision could have been different and that the failure was simply personal failure. It is not certain that Whittier's line, "It might have been" is the saddest of tongue or pen, but it is certainly one of the most revealing of the nature of the human predicament.

The pure determinist is bound to hold that choice does not add anything to the causal relationship of events; it arises simply from ineffective awareness of the sequence. It is easy to state such a position, but there is grave reason to doubt whether any man really believes in its accuracy. It is the sort of thing which we introduce into an argument for the sake of intellectual consistency or for victory, but it is never a truth of experience. This is the point of Dr. Samuel Johnson's famous outburst on the subject when he said, "A man who [does not suppose he is a free agent] should not be suffered to live; if he declares he cannot help acting in a particular way, and is irresistibly impelled, there can be no confidence in him, no more than in a tiger. But, Sir, no man believes himself to be impelled irresistibly; we know that he who says he believes it, lies."[14]

The great Dr. Johnson was probably right in his judgment about human veracity, but, of course, this does not settle the main question. We could be deluded, and this delusion could include all men. How can we know? The answer, as on other major questions, is that, since we cannot know perfectly, we must follow the weight of evidence and consider comparative difficulties. The difficulty of freedom of choice is a lack of scientific neatness; the difficulty of determinism is a conflict with experience. If, as determinists must say, no one really chooses, but only observes an irresistible process, we have to face the fact that most of the good literature of the world is thereby reduced to an assertion of what is false. What, on such grounds, can we make of the agonizing choices revealed in the great novels and great plays?

[14] J. Boswell, *Life of Samuel Johnson*, John B. Alden, Publisher, 1887, Vol. IV, p. 230.

No serious believer in free will ever claims that choice is every-thing, because all recognize that much is given. Certainly Sartre, in spite of what may seem to be his extreme emphasis on responsi-bility, sees this. There are, for example, conditions which I cannot change, and it is not part of our responsibility to do the impossible. We must remember that Christ, in the Garden of Gethsemane, prayed, "If it is possible." (Matt. 26:39.) Though a free man is responsible for the way in which he plays his hand, he is not re-sponsible for the hand which is dealt him. The central point at issue, a point of great importance in the establishment of any general philosophy which is soundly based, is whether it is ever true that even the smallest choice is meaningful and genuine. The con-sciousness of guilt provides the best indication that freedom is real.

The Fallacy of Misplaced Concreteness

When we deal with a dilemma such as that of determinism and freedom, in which the comparative difficulties on both sides are so great, we are wise to consider the possibility of some deeper trouble in our thinking. If a deeper trouble exists it is probably to be found in the idea of causation. Perhaps we are employing a conception which we need not employ. As the metaphysical inquiries of A. N. Whitehead advanced, he became increasingly convinced that this was the case. Whitehead was sure that much of our trouble starts with a wrong view of cause and that, until we alter it radically, we have no genuine way out of confusion. He held that the various schools of thought derived from Hume and Kant were "under the misapprehension generated by an inversion of the true constitution of experience."[15] If we are off to a wrong start, we shall not be helped by an attempt to tidy up the details. The view made domi-nant by Hume is that we get our information about the world by means of our sense organs and draw our conclusions solely from the aid of this information. But, as a matter of fact, says Whitehead, "No philosopher really holds that this is the sole source of informa-tion." The empiricist tries to hold his opponent to it, while he lets

[15] See A. N. Whitehead, Process and Reality, The Macmillan Company, 1929, pp. 263 ff.

in other factors by the back door "veiled under the ordinary uses of language." The use of ordinary language about responsibility, which the philosopher shares with the average man, is a case in point.

Hume, like all who have followed him, claimed to be a strict empiricist. Very well, says Whitehead, let us take empiricism seriously. What is the experience which we have to report? Consider our experience of the bodily parts. "Our bodily experience is primarily an experience of the dependence of presentational immediacy upon causal efficacy"—rather than vice versa. I have the experience of sight, but I experience my eye as "the reason for the projected sight-sensum." In the external world cause may be a speculation, but in the human person it is an experience, says Whitehead, and he argues the case with meticulous care.

Whitehead's celebrated observation, which is likely to be referred to in philosophical literature for years is that philosophers such as Hume and Kant (in that part of Kant's metaphysics expressed in *The Critique of Pure Reason*) are victims of a serious, but, of course, unrecognized fallacy. This fallacy, which Whitehead has called "the fallacy of misplaced concreteness" is the false assumption of these thinkers that their data are concrete, when, in fact, they are abstract. The presentational immediacy of the sensum is certainly an abstraction for, if it is to have any meaning at all, it must be part of a larger order. Abstraction is nothing else than omission of part of the total truth about any situation. We commit the now famous fallacy whenever we take as real something, whether it be a physical object, a sensory experience, or a scientific theory, which is abstracted, i.e., "drawn out" from reality for a special purpose. Abstractions can be useful, but they are sources of delusion if we forget that they are abstractions. A map is highly useful, but is obviously abstract, and would cease to be useful if this fact were ignored.

If we are not careful we fall into the error of believing in "simple location," i.e., believing that "in expressing its spatio-temporal relations, it is adequate to state that it [a particle of matter] is where it is, in a definite finite region of space, and throughout a definite finite duration of time, apart from any essential reference of that bit of matter to other regions of space and to other durations of time."[16] If we stay close to experience there are no objects which meet these qualifications. All objects participate in the continuity and order of our occasions of experience. If we cannot understand even a physical event or object in isolation from order, how much more is this true of moral experience! Perhaps the problems raised by determinism only represent an oversimplification of the human predicament.

Whitehead exerted an immense influence by making men see that it is more reasonable to view their own acts according to the concept of organism than according to the concept of mechanics, which represents a greater degree of abstraction. Paul Weiss indicates this debt. "Our finite natures," he says, "are in part a function of the rest; the others help determine what powers we can exert and what effect we can have. This truth was effectively underscored by that benign genius, A. N. Whitehead. He made an entire generation see that there is no thing in this world which is 'simply located,' here and not also somehow there. He saw too that what is here and what is there must somehow be one."[17] The value of Whitehead's approach is that it makes us wonder whether the principle of explanation, which seems to require that men deny the reality of choice even when they experience it, may not itself be an abstraction.

Creative Causation

Whenever we face a real dilemma the path of reason is to reconsider the situation in order to see whether there may be a new and different way of looking at it. There is no doubt that the alternatives of determinism and indeterminism constitute such a dilemma, because both, though on different grounds, undermine the moral life. Determinism undermines it by denying the reality of choice, while indeterminism undermines it by reducing decision to what is essentially chance, with no emphasis upon continuity of character. Absolute indeterminism would make intelligent prediction of human acts impossible. But it is well known that, with the

[16] A. N. Whitehead, *Science and the Modern World*, The Macmillan Company, 1948, p. 84.
[17] P. Weiss, *Man's Freedom*, Yale University Press, 1950, p. 23.

development of character, human reactions are dependable to a high degree. I do not know all that John will do, but I am morally certain that he will not steal my pocketbook. "Indeed," says Temple, "nothing is further removed from chance than strength of will, which shows itself in constancy of character, not in unaccountable variations."[18]

The most intelligent approach, when both alternatives are unacceptable, is to begin to question whether they exhaust the possibilities and to look for some new way in a new perspective. Perhaps the division into determinism and indeterminism is too simple. Let us look, not for a denial of causality, but for another kind of causal order. Charles Harteshorne, much influenced by Whitehead, suggests this in his term "creative causation,"[19] by which he means that mere chance is not the only alternative to strict determinism. The more we take decision seriously and the more it conflicts with a deterministic doctrine of causation, the more we come to doubt the sufficiency of the latter. Since we know the causal efficacy of thinking better than we know any other causation, all other causation being essentially speculative, we are wise to begin close to home. What is most needed is an analysis of this third way which, according to Whitehead, is one in which we are internally determined, but externally free. This, it may be noted, is the exact opposite of the popular view of the matter, according to which we are externally determined but internally free.

The best place to begin such an analysis is in a serious recognition of the fact that the human mind, which is the only mind we really know, operates to a large extent by reference to final causes. This is so obvious that it might seem impossible to neglect it, yet it is neglected by everyone who denies freedom in employing the billiard ball analogy of causation. Of course the billiard ball moves primarily by efficient causation, but man operates in a totally different way. Man is a creature whose present is constantly being dominated by reference to the nonexistent, but nevertheless potent future. What is *not* influences what *is*. I have a hard problem, but the outcome is not merely the result of a mechanical combination

---

[18] Temple, op. cit., p. 226.
[19] See "Causal Necessities, an Alternative to Hume," *The Philosophical Review*, 63, 1954, pp. 479–499.

of forces, which is true of a physical body; instead I think, and most of my thought is concerned with what might be produced, provided certain steps could be taken.

Whitehead's insistence on this point and his surprise that it should ever be missed need to be studied carefully. This insistence is found best in *The Function of Reason*, in which creative causation is the dominant theme. He is shocked, he says, by the prevalence of a doctrine which tries to cut down the specifically organic experiences to the measure of the inorganic, a process which is really at the heart of all determinism. "The particular doctrine in question," he says, "is, that in the transformation of matter and energy which constitute the activities of an animal body no principles can be discerned other than those which govern the activities of inorganic matter."[20] Whitehead grants, of course, that organic bodies obey physical and chemical laws which apply equally to inorganic matter, but adds that "this is a very different proposition from the doctrine that no additional principles can be involved."[21]

Whitehead's strength lies in the fact that he honors physiological method, but at the same time recognizes realities which mere physiological method cannot handle. Reconsider the following:

> But the point to which I wish to draw attention [he writes] is the mass of evidence lying outside the physiological method which is simply ignored in the prevalent scientific doctrine. The conduct of human affairs is entirely dominated by our recognition of foresight determining purpose, and purpose issuing in conduct. Almost every sentence we utter and every judgment we form, presupposes our unfailing experience of this element in life. The evidence is so overwhelming, the belief so unquestioning, the evidence of language so decisive, that it is difficult to know where to begin in demonstrating it.[22]

If we omit the element of final causation, all of our discussion of national policy or national purpose becomes meaningless. The truth is, not that mental acts are free from causation, but that they introduce the kind of causation in which the "not yet" is of great importance. Men's decisions cannot be interpreted validly after the

[20] A. N. Whitehead, *The Function of Reason*, Beacon Press, 1958, pp. 4–5. By permission of Princeton University Press.
[21] *Ibid.*, p. 12.
[22] *Ibid.*, p. 13.

pattern of physical science, which seeks always to eliminate a time factor; for creatures like ourselves the element of time is always significant. The characteristic act of decision is creative for the simple reason that it binds the past, the present, and the future, into a new and therefore creative unity.

The new kind of causation is really *self*-causation and is therefore always misunderstood when interpreted by mechanical analogies. Self-causation is one way, and perhaps the profoundest way, of expressing the Hebrew conception that man is made in God's image. This is why man is responsible and cannot even put the blame upon his Creator. Machines are essentially passive, but the self is essentially active. The alternative to determinism and to chance is, therefore, the loyal acceptance of the reality of selfhood. Decision, instead of being some oddity which requires explanation in terms of something alien, is the very stuff with which we live and the normal place to begin. Decision never ends. "Even the firmest of our decisions," says Ortega, "must constantly be receiving corroboration, must constantly be renewed, freshly charged like a gun whose powder loses force with lack of use; in short must be redecided."[23] Man, we conclude, is engaged in decision, not intermittently but constantly. We are constantly deciding what we are going to do and to be.

When contemporary philosophers speak of creative causation, they are referring to a conception of what man is, similar to that developed in Chapter 8: they are defining. Ortega defines man as "a being which consists not so much in what it is as in what it is going to be."[24] In short, they accept the essential paradox. It is not enough to say that the outcome is determined even by one's previous character, for the reality in which we share is such that genuine novelty can emerge in the very act of thinking. Thinking, as we actually experience it daily, is not merely awareness of action, as it is in all epiphenomenalist doctrine, but is a true and creative cause. Something happens, when a man thinks, which would not have occurred otherwise. This is what is meant by self-causation as a genuine third possibility in our familiar dilemma.[25]

[23] Ortega y Gasset, *What is Philosophy?*, W. W. Norton & Company, Inc., 1960, p. 224.
[24] *Ibid.*, p. 223.
[25] See, in this connection, Whitehead, *Process and Reality*, *op. cit.*, p. 373.

All life is an offensive against the repetitive mechanism of the universe, and conscious mental life in a human being is a radical extension of this offensive. Freedom of choice is always a possibility because of what man is, but the implementation of this possibility comes only with the application of intelligence to our desires. Men are not free when they are doing just what they happen to like; they are not free until they distinguish between their superficial desires and their deeper desires, the latter often involving deliberate pain. Man is a creature who can operate, not merely in accordance with physical laws, but in the light of what is supremely desirable, and what is desirable always involves an active concern for the future. Men are habitually concerned with subsequent judgments upon their actions, long after they will be gone from the human scene, and therefore not present to enjoy the public confirmation of the rightness of their acts.[26] The earliest buildings which have been preserved are not mansions, but monuments, which involve the future even more than the present. It is no wonder that the future seems so important, for, in the words of Martin Heidegger, the past is made by the future.

The development of an intelligible conception of creative causation has been one of the glories of recent and contemporary philosophy, a development in which many have shared. Karl Jaspers has dealt directly with the question in his *Introduction to Philosophy* and Professor Paul Weiss has produced an entire book on the subject, calling it *Man's Freedom*. In a critical passage he writes, "To choose is to introduce another factor, making a difference in what was there. But this factor neither of the traditional positions allows. They both antecedently define the situation to be one in which no real choice can or does occur. They fail to see that choice is a creative art in which some alternative is altered by being made inseparable from a justifying end."[27]

It is difficult to think of a better solution to the problem than that which Weiss provides. Human action is, of course, not utterly free, and no sensible philosopher has ever supposed that it is. All that philosophy can show is that, within our limitations, it is not

---

[26] A. O. Lovejoy, *Reflections on Human Nature*, The Johns Hopkins Press, 1961, Lecture 3.
[27] Weiss, *op. cit.*, p. 121.

unreasonable to maintain that there are some actions which are determinable by the self. Causality in the light of an accepted end is genuine causality, and it is creative because it produces novelty. Decision is the act of an *agent* not of an automaton. This is all that we need in order to make the concept of responsibility reasonable.

Chapter 10 ᔍ THE BEING OF GOD

God is, is a true proposition.

ST. THOMAS AQUINAS

ONE OF THE GREATEST QUESTIONS THAT CAN ENTER THE HUMAN MIND is the question of God's existence. Men of all known cultures have long believed that the world of reality includes the divine as well as the human, but such belief is by no means self-verifying. Consensus of opinion may be impressive, but it does not constitute definitive evidence, and this we know as soon as we meditate on the strong possibility of human error. When men say that they believe in God they are not expressing an obvious truism, which nobody would deny, nor an obvious falsehood, which nobody in his senses would assert. They are expressing, instead, an exciting possibility, the possibility that, in their struggles for spiritual life, men are not alone. It is the possibility that men have the potential support and guidance of One who combines with infinite goodness all the power that is consistent with such goodness. The belief which we must examine is the conviction that what is highest in value is not transitory nor local, but deepest in the nature of the ultimately real.

It is no accident of history that consideration of this momentous possibility has long been a part of general philosophy, rather than something limited to theology. This is because the proposition outlined briefly above is manifestly important for all men and not merely for the devout or the believing. The question at issue is so far-reaching in its consequences that it includes every aspect of our total life. If God really is, then ours is one particular kind of world; if He is not, if all who have believed in Him have been deluded, then it is a totally different kind of world. The issues are so vital that no serious philosopher can afford to neglect them. To deal philosophically with the question of the existence of God is to stand aside, for the time being, from the emotional aspects of religious practice, and to use our minds in the effort to ascertain to the best of our ability what the truth in this important area of inquiry may be.

The Problem of Meaning

It is possible that God is not. Indeed, there are, in each generation, thoughtful persons who have come to this sad conclusion. Most of them are like Jean-Paul Sartre, who, in coming to this conclusion, admits that it is a saddening one. If they are intelligent, they recognize some of the consequences, most of which are inevitably depressing. It means, for example, that man has no spiritual power outside himself on which to depend and, if he is honest, he realizes that his powers are woefully inadequate to their manifest purpose. He realizes, too, that, with the end of life on this planet, or in our solar system, the human story will be over completely, since the denial of God entails the denial of immortality. He realizes that prayer, in the ordinary sense at least, would be, in the light of God's asserted nonbeing, a delusion and useless. Even Lord Russell, who almost flaunts his atheism, expresses his conviction of man's aloneness in somber overtones. At least he did this when he produced "A Free Man's Worship,"[1] and he has never publicly rejected it, though it was written long ago.

[1] B. Russell, "A Free Man's Worship," in *Mysticism and Logic*, Doubleday and Company, Inc., Anchor Books, 1957.

Now the point is that men like Russell and Sartre could be right. If there is any convincing evidence that they are right, the person of theistic faith, who is also an honest person, will accept the evidence and give up his faith. If the central religious conviction is not true, the effort to maintain it is manifestly evil. "Deliberately insincere, dishonest thinking," said Royce, "is downright blasphemy."[2] Many take this step of conscious rejection of belief in God and, in numerous cases, they are good people. Even those who suppose that their moral positions are of their own making, and therefore not based on something beyond themselves, seem to continue the effort to demonstrate a certain integrity or courage in their personal lives. The question, then, is not primarily the question of morality, and certainly not the usefulness of belief, but is solely the question of truth.

If we start with the clear understanding that, when we use the word God we mean an infinite Being, the Creator and Sustainer of the world, though transcendent to the world, the normal reaction is to say that belief in such a Being is either true or false. If Temple is right it is true; if Russell is right it is false, and there appears to be no middleground. The law of excluded middle would seem to apply here as elsewhere in all logical analysis of what is. There has been a tendency recently, however, to deny this analysis and to maintain a third conception, the conception that the idea of God is "meaningless." This position, which stems from logical positivism, is most clearly expressed by A. J. Ayer, though it is consistent with the thought of Carnap and others who have denied the possibility of meaning to any metaphysical proposition.

Ayer's central thesis is "to say that 'God exists' is to make a metaphysical utterance which cannot be either true or false."[3] Ayer is eager to make clear that he is not, by this dictum, upholding either atheism or agnosticism. The agnostic holds, says Ayer, "that the existence of God is a possibility in which there is no good reason either to believe or disbelieve," while the atheist thinks it is at least probable that God does not exist. The difficulty with both agnosti-

---

[2] J. Royce, The Religious Aspect of Philosophy, Harper & Row, Inc., Torchbooks, 1958, p. 5.

[3] A. J. Ayer, Language, Truth and Logic, Dover Publications, Inc., 1953, p. 115.

cism and atheism, as Ayer sees it, is the same difficulty that he finds with theism; they all believe that they are saying something when, in fact, they are saying absolutely nothing. "And our view," concludes Ayer, "is that all utterances about the nature of God are nonsensical." Ayer even claims to have overcome the conflict between science and religion by purporting to show that religious propositions are not in the same realm of discourse as scientific ones and that, therefore, they cannot be in conflict with each other. It is not likely, however, that any truly religious person will find any comfort in reading: "For since the religious utterances of the theist are not genuine propositions at all, they cannot stand in any logical relation to the propositions of science."[4]

If what logical positivists of this character have said is sound, it is perfectly clear that the whole discipline known as "the philosophy of religion" is a foolish waste of time and that all who have engaged in it, from Plato's beginning to the present day, have been entirely deluded men. This is a large claim and needs to be examined with the same tough-mindedness which it espouses. One who has done this most brilliantly is Morris Raphael Cohen, especially in a great essay on "Meaning and Implication." In this essay Cohen shows carefully what the contemptuous attack on all metaphysics entails, and that it is self-contradictory because it involves a metaphysics of its own. He concedes that the great philosophers of the past have often been doubtful about metaphysical issues, but notes that all have agreed that the effort to examine them is meaningful. The positivists may be right, he says, "But it requires a strain on our credulity to believe that the issues which have agitated humanity so deeply throughout the ages are entirely devoid of meaning, and that men like Aristotle, Plato, Lotze, Leibnitz, Kant, Spinoza, and others completely failed to realize this prior to its recent discovery by the logical positivists."[5]

It is understandable that many readers are so revolted by the limitless arrogance of Ayer that they do not stop to examine his evidence. If they would examine it, however, they would soon learn

---

[4] *Ibid.*, p. 117.
[5] M. R. Cohen, *A Preface to Logic*, The World Publishing Company, Meridian Books, 1959, p. 73. Reprinted by permission of Holt, Rinehart and Winston, Inc.

that it is not so fearsome after all. The only evidence provided is a reassertion of the positivist doctrine that nothing is meaningful unless it has empirically verifiable effects, and the trick is that "empirical" is arbitrarily limited to what can be experienced by the senses. It is, of course, easy, once the dogma of sense verification has been asserted, to rule out all experience of God, since no one claims that religious experience is sensory, but this is to get rid of a problem by a mere definition. Ayer cavalierly rejects the testimony of all those who, like Blaise Pascal, have reported a direct non-sensory experience of the living God, apparently with no real study of the data, though he makes some remarks about mystics. It is doubtful if he even understands what the French philosopher, Gabriel Marcel, means when he says "The mystics are perhaps the only thoroughgoing empiricists in the history of philosophy."[6] In any case it is not intellectually respectable to call oneself an empiricist and to rule out in advance an entire area of claimed experience.

Ayer's brief analysis of religious experience convinces him that the two propositions, "There exists here a yellow-coloured material thing," and "There exists a transcendent god," are not really parallel, because, though both depend on reported experience, the former is a true synthetic proposition while the latter indicates only a subjective feeling. This is where Ayer is most vulnerable. How does he know that there is a colored object? All that he has, by his own argument, is the subjective experience and it is just as subjective in regard to the physical object, say the legal pad, as in regard to God. In both cases there is an experience, and in both there is a reasonable postulation of that to which the experience refers. In both we are dependent upon corroboration. There is the same kind of verification of religious experience as there is of sensory experience. The chief verification in religious experience is that of the phenomenon of changed lives, which is something of which Ayer makes no mention.[7]

The intended proof that all metaphysical propositions are meaningless turns out to be extremely flimsy. Moreover, the positivists

[6] G. Marcel, *Royce's Metaphysics*, trans V. and G. Ringer, Henry Regnery Company, 1956, p. 12.
[7] I have tried to clarify this concept of verification in my Swarthmore Lecture, *The Trustworthiness of Religious Experience*, Allen & Unwin, 1939.

are caught in their own trap, because the assumption that there is nothing beyond the physical is itself essentially metaphysical. The penetrating remark of Charles S. Peirce is applicable in this connection. "Positivism," he said, "is only a particular species of metaphysics open to all the uncertainty of metaphysics, and its conclusions are for that reason of not enough weight to disturb any practical belief."[8]

Since positivism is based on a postulate, it cannot object to postulatist thinking. According to the great tradition of philosophy the meaningful need not be limited to the sensory, for it includes all that is intelligible. There is no way in which Carnap or any other thinker can verify, by sense experience, the idea that the earth was in existence before the advent of the human species, but the idea is a perfectly intelligible one, which we can discuss in reasonable terms.[9]

Few have argued more convincingly the meaningfulness of the proposition "God is" than that distinguished professor, the late Morris R. Cohen. He argued cogently that belief in God is intelligible, because of the difference it makes to men:

Certainly the man who believes that we have a Divine Father to look after us will see the particular events of human history in a different light than one who believes that the world is governed exclusively by physical forces. The two will certainly have different views as to the efficacy of prayer. The man who believes in the immortality of the soul regards life not only as continuing beyond death, but also as less dependent upon bodily phenomena even during our earthly existence. One may take the agnostic position and say that the evidence in favor of the existence of God or the immortality of the soul is inadequate to prove anything. Or one may take the position that what little evidence we have points more to a negative than to a positive answer. But neither position will justify the assertion that the question as to the existence of God or the immortality of the soul is altogether meaningless.[10]

There are, undoubtedly, meaningless propositions, and these

[8] C. S. Peirce, *Values in a Universe of Chance*, Stanford University Press, 1958, p. 140. Though Peirce directed his remark to the older positivism, it is equally relevant when applied to that which stems from the Vienna Circle.

[9] The positivist has not avoided the predicament by reference to fossils. It is possible, as Philip Gosse argued seriously, that the world was created with fossils in it.

[10] Cohen, op. cit., p. 75.

ought not to occupy our time. They are meaningless if their truth or falsity would have no conceivable bearing on our lives or on our conception of the universe. It is clear, of course, that verification depends on the ability of a proposition to be meaningful, in the sense of having logical consequences, but it is quite another matter to hold, as the early logical positivists did, that those consequences must always be of the kind which are involved in physical experiments and observations. There is good reason for a thinking being to doubt the metaphysical dogma that there is nothing meaningful in the world other than physical events and operations. The ease with which Ayer and his companions once disposed of difficult problems is now severely dated. Once he could say, with untroubled confidence, "We conclude, therefore, that the argument from religious experience is altogether fallacious," but that sentence, we must remember, was written in 1935. Perhaps Ayer had this kind of sentence in mind when, at the beginning of the Introduction to the revised edition of Language, Truth and Logic, he said of his work, "I have come to see that the questions with which it deals are not in all respects so simple as it makes them appear."[11] This is a tremendous advance, not unlike that attributed to the slave boy in the Meno, who was held by Socrates to have made signal progress because he first supposed that the questions asked of him had simple answers, but later realized that he did not know. "I think now," said Ayer, ten years after the first writing, "that much of its argument would have been more persuasive if it had not been presented in so harsh a form."[12] This applies more pertinently to the propositions about religious propositions than to anything else in the book. In any case, we need not be deterred from careful study of propositions about God's existence merely because of their alleged meaninglessness. That battle was only a skirmish and, so far as the main stream of philosophy is concerned, is already a thing of the past. We may consequently consider the question at issue without asking the permission of the logical positivists to do so.

The Problem of Language

Though logical positivism is now somewhat dated, and may

[11] A. J. Ayer, op. cit., p. 5.
[12] Ibid., p. 5.

therefore be mentioned chiefly in the past tense, there is a truly contemporary problem we must face, the problem raised by the members of the linguistic school. Though this school has its chief center at Oxford University, where its members hold important and honored academic positions, it is by no means limited to Oxford. The linguistic school raises a barrier to realistic belief in the existence of God that is, in some ways, harder to surmount than is the barrier erected by the strictly positivist position. In any case, the current influence is so pervasive that it must be examined.

The essence of the linguistic approach is that the only area of study for the philosopher is the use of language. His function is to analyze subtle differences of meaning, to show what it is that people are trying to say, and to emancipate mankind, consequently, from a number of confusions. The purpose of the philosopher is merely that of the diagnostician of and therapist to those errors in thinking which arise from misunderstandings of language. Philosophy, then, is not concerned with whether man's mind is free to make decisions, or whether God is, but only with what we mean when we assert these propositions. It is held by some that this approach to philosophy is epochmaking, that it gives philosophy an honorable role utterly different from that of science, and that accordingly it constitutes a true Copernican revolution.

Though linguistic philosophy is radically different, in some ways, from logical positivism it may be seen as its lawful heir. Both have one great feature in common, the rejection of metaphysics. According to both, the careful intellectual consideration of the truth or falsity of the great propositions that have stirred mankind from the beginning of serious thought, are really out of bounds. There is no use in asking, as old-fashioned philosophy did, whether the world actually contains universals or values. Instead, we are reduced to a sophisticated form of grammar.

The Marxians, the Freudians, and the linguistics present a doctrine of "withering away" by virtue of a therapeutic action. The Marxians expect the withering away of the state when the class struggle is resolved; the Freudians expect the disappearance of complexes when once they are brought fully to consciousness; the linguistics expect the pathology of metaphysical questioning to end once the impossibility of metaphysics is truly seen. The critics of all three point to such faith as fundamentally naïve, because they think they have evidence of the enduring nature of the problems thus so neatly by-passed.

We need to consider the relation of linguistic philosophy to religious belief. When we do so we soon realize that the position is not a simple one, as it was in the case of logical positivism. Anyone can see that positivism is completely and irrevocably antithetic to realistic theism. If Ayer is right, all believers in God are guilty of nonsense, but if believers in God are right, Ayer's philosophy is in error. The problem with the linguistics is different, even though the public tends to lump the two movements together, Whereas a positivist cannot conceivably be a believer, some linguistic philosophers are members of churches. The reason for this is their claim that they are merely studying language-usage and not truth. Therefore they leave equal room for belief and unbelief. The point is that philosophy has nothing that it can say on such august matters: this follows necessarily from the fundamental rejection of reason.

From the viewpoint of such philosophy it is impossible to take sides in conflicts, for the philosopher stands aloof in splendid isolation, continually analyzing words in their relation to one another. This looks like amazing tolerance, and it is, but this is no kindness. No deeply religious man is satisfied with a universal tolerance of religion, partly because, if his convictions are profound, he is so keenly aware of the terrible mistakes, intellectually as well as practically, which can be made in the name of religion. The truly religious man knows that we cannot responsibly state a faith unless we claim that it is true, and that we cannot responsibly claim that it is true unless there is some means of disproving it. The statement "God is" is a worthless statement unless there is an imaginable sense in which it can be held to be false. We know that some religious propositions are false because there are genuine contradictions. Complete tolerance, therefore, is not a mark of respect, but rather a mark of contempt. The keenest critic of linguistic philosophy has put the point so admirably that his words should be heeded, especially when he points out that the central thesis proves too much:

> For it proves the validity not of any one religion, but of all of them, and of all denials of any one of them, and indeed of any actually employed system of expressions (and is not the discussion of the relative merits of religion and atheism also a "use" of language?). The

trouble with Linguistic Philosophy is not, as is often supposed, that it is too restrictive, but on the contrary that it is far too permissive. It issues blank cheques all around. It allows everything that "has a use," except, perhaps, philosophy proper.[13]

What can we say of the considerable barrier thus erected? We can say of it, as in the case of logical positivism, that it does not seem so frightening when it is examined at close range, for it rests on nothing more serious than a definition. It represents only an arbitrary limitation of philosophy, and so runs counter to the weight of judgment of thoughtful men through the ages. If any of the professors at Oxford desire to limit themselves to language study that is their privilege, but they are clearly exceeding their prerogative if they try to make the rest of us believe that we have no right to deal with the fundamental issues of the objective world. Russell's dictum is likely to stand. "The later Wittgenstein," he says, "seems to have grown tired of serious thinking and to have invented a doctrine which would make such an activity unnecessary. I do not for one moment believe that the doctrine which has these lazy consequences is true." Linguistic philosophy rests on nothing better than a dogma which, says Russell, "it is not thought necessary to establish."[14]

The Problem of Existence

A more subtle approach to the philosophy of religion than that of either the logical positivists or the linguistic philosophers is involved in a significant tendency on the part of some philosophers to claim to believe in God, yet to deny His "existence." The most eminent thinker of this group is Paul Tillich who, fearing that the proposition "God exists" reduces God to the level of our finite, created world, prefers to speak of God as Ultimate Ground, beyond all existence. Religion, he holds, is "direction toward the Unconditioned." It is, says one of the most articulate of his translators, H. Richard Niebuhr,

the reference in all life to the ultimate source of meaning and the ultimate ground of being. This ultimate transcends experience and knowl-

---

[13] E. Gellner, Words and Things, Victor Gollancz, Ltd., 1959, p. 222.
[14] Ibid., p. 13 (Russell's Introduction).

edge though it is that to which all experience and knowledge refer. . . . Nothing temporal, nothing finite, no one object among other objects, or no one value among other values can be designated as the ultimate. It is always transcendent and therefore unknown, yet the reference to it is implicit in life and wherever there is any meaning this reference to an ultimate source of meaning is present.[15]

This position, thus so clearly expressed, is not difficult to understand or even to appreciate. It obviously arises out of a keen sense of reverence. Tillich's position, which he calls "belief-ful realism" has had a great appeal in the contemporary scene, as his large lecture classes at Harvard have shown. About the world and all of the things in it he is skeptical, tough-minded, unsentimental, yet he sees all objects as symbolic of "the eternal and unconditioned source of all meaning and ground of all being." His sense of the contrast between concrete objects which are epistemological referents, and God in His absolute transcendence is so great that he refuses not only to speak of God as a person, but even as a *being*. Though we can understand why such an extreme antilogical contrast is made, we have reason to doubt its adequacy.

Along with Tillich's refusal to speak of God as existent, there appears in many who have been extremely influential in our generation a complete rejection of intellectual proofs of God's existence, whether those of Thomas Aquinas or any others. It has been said, for instance, that nobody doubted the existence of God until Descartes tried to prove it. The fear is that a God whose existence is proved is one who is domesticated and therefore limited to our finite scale. This is the mood of Karl Jaspers when he says, categorically, "A proved God is no God."[16] The point made by Jaspers, as by so many existentialists, is that faith in God must be a starting point, never a conclusion. Existentialists naturally quote Pascal, when he makes God say to man, "Thou wouldst not seek me if thou hadst not found me."[17] Jaspers puts it this way: "Only he who starts from God, can seek him. A certainty of the existence of God, however rudimentary and intangible it may be, is a premise, not

[15] P. Tillich, *The Religious Situation*, trans. H. R. Niebuhr, The World Publishing Company, Living Age Books, 1956, pp. 11, 12.
[16] K. Jaspers, *The Perennial Scope of Philosophy*, Philosophical Library, Inc., 1949, p. 32.
[17] B. Pascal, *Pensées*, trans. W. F. Trotter, J. M. Dent and Sons, 1931, p. 149.

a result of philosophical activity." Jaspers is very clear, of course, that in his denial of the efficacy of proofs, he is not denying God or giving any comfort to the atheist. "For the nonexistence of God can be proved no more than his existence. The proofs and their confutations show us only that a proved God would be no God, but merely a thing in the world."[18] He holds that Kant radically confuted, once and for all, the notion that there can be "scientifically compelling proofs such as we find in mathematics or the empirical sciences." Jaspers' summary deserves careful study:

> The truth, as against all supposed proofs and refutations of the existence of God, seems to be this: the so-called proofs of the existence of God are fundamentally no proofs at all, but methods of achieving certainty through thought. All the proofs of the existence of God and their variants that have been devised through the centuries differ essentially from scientific proofs. They are attempts to express the experience of man's ascent to God in terms of thought. There are roads of thought by which we come to limits at which the consciousness of God suddenly becomes a natural presence.[19]

There is no doubt of the popularity of the existentialist view of the matter, thus expressed. When it is transmuted by the popular mentality it not only denies the possibility of absolute proof about God, but makes light of the entire philosophy of religion as something worthless. Religion then is "sheer faith" and not anything to be reasoned at all. When men quote the famous dictum of Pascal as showing that faith is sufficient, and reasoning consequently unnecessary, they seem to be unmindful of the fact that the entire book which Pascal was writing in his final illness, the proposed book for which what we call *Pensées* were mere notes, was to be devoted to an intellectual substantiation of the very faith which he espoused.

When men elevate the faith and neglect the reasoned examination they fall easily into the ancient heresy known as fideism. The basic trouble with this approach is that men can be in error about their faith, that they can have faith in the unreal and the nonexistent. A religion which is contradictory to fact is no better than any other delusion. But many modern writers neglect, systemati-

[18] K. Jaspers, *Way to Wisdom*, Yale University Press, 1960, p. 42.
[19] *Ibid.*, p. 42.

cally, this important point. They have an exaggerated sense of the possibility of proof in regard to science, and an exaggerated sense of the impossibility of proof in regard to religion. Even Nels Ferré, who criticizes Tillich for his rejection of "the classical confession of the personal God," nevertheless speaks of "fact" as belonging to science rather than to religion. "Fact," he says, "is the province of science; salvation is the domain of religion."[20]

The basic weakness of existentialism, in so far as the being of God is concerned, is that it has no intelligible theory of error. We need to stress again, as we have stressed in former chapters of this book, that men can be wrong, and they can be wrong even in their deepest convictions. Jaspers may be right that the conviction of God's existence may be more a premise than a conclusion, but there is no possibility of a sound logic unless we make a ruthless examination of premises, for premises may state what is not the case. Eichmann, at his trial in Israel, which led to his execution, defended his action in regard to deported and imprisoned Jews by reference to premises. There is no doubt that his action followed consistently from these premises, but most of us think that his premises were wrong. He had a faith but a *false faith*.

When we give our full attention to the possibility of error we are well on the way to a productive intellectual synthesis. It is true that real religion is a commitment to what is ultimate, but men can be mistaken about what *is* ultimate. The only recourse is to think, to think rigorously, and to think together. Now this is all that the so-called proofs claim to make possible. While I believe in God I realize that my belief may be a mere convention, or perhaps a pious heritage, and it is quite possible that I ought to get rid of it, as the intellectuals of the age of Socrates were getting rid of any serious belief in the divine inhabitants of Mount Olympus. God, when clearly understood, is either existent or nonexistent, and here the law of excluded middle obviously applies. We understand thoroughly what we mean by nonexistent. We can imagine a bearded old man who lives all year at the North Pole and who, on Christmas eve, distributes, from a sleigh pulled by reindeer, gifts to all

20 N. F. S. Ferré, "The Relation Between Religion and Philosophy," *Wesleyan Studies in Religion*, West Virginia Wesleyan College, Vol. 54, No. 1, p. 9.

good children everywhere, going down millions of chimneys simultaneously. The picture is clear and intelligible, but there is no evidence of the existence of this object of our contemplation, and much evidence that it is nonexistent. We must remember, in this connection, that we mean by "object" any referent.

If we refuse to discuss the existence of God we are simply avoiding the central issue, which is the issue of delusion. Lord Russell seems to believe that all of the millions who have believed in God have been deluded and he could be right. How are we to know? We do not find out merely by a new assertion of our faith or by an absolute leap after the fashion of Kierkegaard. What if it is a leap in the wrong direction? The fact that we cannot know beyond a shadow of doubt whether it is the wrong direction is no excuse for failing to do the best that we can, and the best we can will always involve the marshaling of whatever evidence we have. Once we rid our minds of the fallacious belief in absolute proof, we are better prepared to look carefully at what probable proof there is. The evidences for and against the being of God do not belong to the realm of absolute certainty, but to the realm of probability, which is the realm in which we, as mortals, are destined to live. What we must never forget is that this human predicament includes the facts of science as well as all other facts. The argument to this effect is the enduring contribution of the late Lord Balfour, particularly in his Gifford Lectures. It was not wholly unfair when wags said of him that he had demonstrated that scientific propositions are as uncertain as religious ones. What is important to know is that fact, anywhere, in any area of human experience, is distinguished from fancy by one method only.

Those who refer to Kant's demolition of the classical proofs of God's existence often exaggerate. Kant did, undoubtedly, destroy the naïve conviction that the existence of God could be demonstrated, but it must not be forgotten that he went on, in *The Critique of Practical Reason*, to present a powerful postulatist argument of his own. Indeed, the moral argument for God's existence, which has been brilliantly expressed by W. R. Sorley[21] and others in the twentieth century, is essentially Kant's invention. Kant did

[21] See W R. Sorley, *Moral Values and the Idea of God*, Cambridge University Press, 1919.

not claim to demonstrate, but he did claim to be able to show that the reasons for believing in God are good reasons and not merely unsupported leaps of personal faith. It may be noted in passing that philosophers of the stamp of A. J. Ayer, who hold that the proposition "God exists" is a meaningless proposition, do not object at all to a man who makes an unsupported leap of faith. This is because he is not dealing with the world of fact or of "what is" but only of his own inner emotion, which bothers nobody because it really says nothing about external reality. "As he says nothing at all about the world," writes Ayer, "he cannot justly be accused of saying anything false, or anything for which he has insufficient grounds."[22]

In this assertion Ayer is manifestly correct. If the man of faith is telling only about his own subjective state nobody cares, because what he says is of little importance. Everybody, including the most militant atheist, is tolerant of subjectivism, for the very good reason that it makes no significant assertions. What is important in religion is not the subjective quality of an experience which nobody doubts, but whether it refers to something that is truly objective. This is why the present fashionable depreciation of objective evidence is a serious philosophical mistake. Some subjective experiences have objective reference and some do not; we need to use our intelligence to distinguish between these. If we believe that our subjective experiences refer to what is objective then what we mean is that God is a veridical object. To call God an object is not to demote Him to the world of physical things, but to assert that He is real rather than fanciful.

In our contemporary study of logic we recognize that it is possible to use descriptions significantly even when they describe nothing that is. There can be the null class, such as that represented by "the present emperor of Mexico." We can describe unicorns with excellent intelligibility, even though no one supposes that there are unicorns in the sense that actually living creatures match this particular description. In short, we can talk and think significantly about the nonexistent. This is the real weakness of the ontological argument for God's existence, the argument, namely, that the idea of God must involve His being.

[22] Ayer, op. cit., p. 116.

What this means for the student of philosophy, above all else, is that he must recognize and learn to handle the ambiguity of "is." When we write "A unicorn is an animal with one horn," we are using a totally different meaning of "is" from that when we say "There is a unicorn now." It is important not to allow similarity in sound to disguise the difference in meaning. The five principal uses of the verb "to be" in modern languages, are as follows:

1. *Class inclusion*, e.g., Dogs are mammals.
2. *Class membership*, e.g., Socrates is a man.
3. *Existence*, e.g., Unicorns are.
4. *Equivalence*, e.g., The square root of 16 is 4.
5. *Predication*, e.g., The rose is yellow.

The ambiguity of the verb "to be" is an old theme in philosophy, mentioned specifically by Aristotle in *Metaphysics* VII, in a discussion which clearly refers to Plato's treatment of the subject in the *Sophist*.[23] Among the modern writers who have helped to clarify the issue are G. E. Moore, Bertrand Russell, and L. Susan Stebbing, each making a significant advance. Moore states the problem disarmingly by saying, "Why we should use the same form of verbal expression to convey such different meanings is more than I can say. It seems to me very curious that language . . . should have grown up as if it were expressly designed to mislead philosophers; and I do not know why it should have."[24] Part of the problem is that what applies significantly to a class may not apply in the same way to an individual. Russell illustrates this by the obviously invalid, though apparently genuine, syllogism: "Men are numerous; Socrates is a man; therefore, Socrates is numerous."

One of the best modern contributions to this important subject is that of Miss Stebbing in "The Systematic Ambiguity of 'exists,' "[25] a discussion in which she acknowledges her great indebtedness to G. E. Moore. She points out most helpfully the necessity of ascertaining the logical type of each assertion. Thus

[23] St. Thomas Aquinas deals with this problem in *Summa Theologica*, Part I, qu. 3, art. 4, ad 2 m.

[24] G. E. Moore, *Philosophical Studies*, The Humanities Press, Inc., 1951, p. 215.

[25] L. Susan Stebbing, *A Modern Introduction to Logic*, Harper & Row, Inc., Torchbook, 1961, 2nd ed., pp. 158-162.

"unicorns" and "numbers" are of totally different types. Any number is possible because number is a matter of syntax, whereas unicorns are necessarily referred to in the same way in which we refer to horses. The nonexistence of a number is a fatuous idea, but the same is not true of horses, for they might not be. Once mammoths were, but they are not now, i.e., they do not *exist*. I can think of unicorns even though there are none, and Lord Russell can think of God, even though he thinks that God is not.

If this general analysis is correct, those contemporary philosophers are mistaken who try to avoid the straightforward proposition "God exists." This is because He could be as unreal as a unicorn undoubtedly is. The problem of the existence of God is not at all like that of the existence of numbers or ideas. There is a world of difference between the idea of God and an existent referent corresponding to the idea. No one argues the existence of the idea, for that is obvious. What is at stake is the momentous question of whether God is more than idea.

It has long been time for some philosopher of great reputation to point out that the distinction between "being" and "existence" is really a distinction without a difference. Something of the need has been met by Jacques Maritain, who asserts that the notion of existence, like being, is "validly applicable to the uncreated as to the created." He goes on to say, with blessed clarity, "Those who think that one can say 'God is,' but not 'God exists,' maintain for being its essential analogicity but refuse it to existence—the strangest of illusions, since being itself is understood only in relation to existence. To say 'God is' and 'God exists' is to say exactly the same thing. One speaks the language of simple truth in speaking of the ways through which it is shown that God is or that He exists."[26]

Our analysis is at fault if we think of "existence" as merely the alternative to "essence" or to "ultimate ground." The significant alternative, if we stay close to the ordinary speech of ordinary men, as we ought to do, is "nonexistent." Jaspers is manifestly in error when he says a proved God would be no God. Provided we are aware of the limits of all proof, when we speak of a proved God we merely mean that we have more reason to assert His existence than

[26] J. Maritain, *Approaches to God*, Crowell-Collier Publishing Co., Collier Books, 1962, p. 26.

to deny it. The choice between the fanciful and the real is one which we make all of the time and we make it only by marshaling relevant reasons or evidence. If I hold, as I do, that.God really *is*, and is not merely a product of my fancy or my wish-thinking, I do not thereby mean that God is a thing or that He is a physical object. Only a little philosophical sophistication is needed to see that real existence is not equivalent to thinghood. If we say that God exists as truly and in the same sense as a stone exists, it is absurd to conclude that we think God is limited to space, as the stone is, or that God has mass. What we really mean is that we believe that propositions about God and about stones are of the same logical type, that they are genuine propositions, and therefore capable of being true or false. We mean that God, like the stone, might still be, even if all men were unaware of His being; we mean that, in regard to both God and the stone, the logic is identical even though the content differs; we mean that, in regard to both the stone and God, we have reason to believe that we are not mistaken when we assert genuine transsubjective reference.

What can the existentialist answer when someone asks him why he accepts one particular faith rather than another? After all, there are many competing faiths. Why not start with a bold faith in dialectical materialism? Some do. Jaspers' answer does not meet the inquiry, especially when he writes "God exists for me in the degree to which I, in freedom, authentically become myself. He does not exist as a scientific content, but only as an openness to existence." These words sound impressive, but, when carefully analyzed, they mean almost nothing. How does this conclusion differ from that of sheer subjectivism? Sartre seeks also to become authentically himself and announces, accordingly, that his freedom is purely his own, because God is not. Though much of modern existentialism seems to stem from Pascal, it must be remembered that such subjectivism is miles away from his final position. If God does not exist "as a scientific content," i.e., in objective reality, then He is hardly worth discussing. It is a truism that men have subjective faith and subjective feelings. This is so obvious that there would be no point in writing books about it. What is at stake is not a truism, but a possibility which may be false and may be true, but if true, is of momentous significance.

The Vindication of Belief

That part of philosophy which is devoted to the vindication of belief in God is impressive. It begins with Plato's formulation of the Cosmological Argument in Book X of *The Laws* and extends to this day. Many of the Gifford Lectures in the Scottish universities, still the most honored lectureships in philosophy, are devoted to this undertaking. An especially brilliant, though brief assembly of theistic evidence is that by the late A. E. Taylor, of the University of Edinburgh, in *Essays Catholic and Critical*.

There is increasing recognition in our day that the kind of evidence that makes the existence of God sufficiently probable to support faith in Him is not that of any single incontrovertible line, but rather the joint effect of several different arguments, which are powerful in conjunction. Since this conception of evidence was outlined in Chapter 6 it need not be elaborated here. The concept of cumulative evidence is part of the classical proof and is illustrated by the way in which Thomas Aquinas used five proofs together.[27] The modern cumulative argument is not identical with that of Aquinas, but, like his, refuses to limit itself to a single line of attack.

A. E. Taylor's significant presentation of the evidence is divided into three parts, which he terms "From Nature to God," "From Man to God," and "From God to God." The first of these three seeks to include all that is valid in the cosmological and the teleological arguments. The fact that there is an order in nature which is intelligible to mind is not an absolute proof of God's existence, but one that is extremely suggestive and is what we should expect if God is. If God is, and if He is the Author, both of the natural order and of our finite minds, it is not surprising that our minds, when they are most true to themselves, are amazingly able to probe the mystery of the natural order. The success of science indicates a kinship between mind and nature. But if there is a kinship between mind and nature, then the hypothesis that nature is the creation of the Infinite Mind, appears to have a certain verification. Charles S. Peirce put the argument aphoristically in his letters

[27] My own best effort in this connection is found in *The Philosophy of Religion*, Harper & Row, Inc., 1957, chaps. 7–11. The student may turn to this for a fuller discussion.

to Lady Welby when he said, "For to believe in reasoning about phenomena is to believe that they are governed by reason, that is, by God."[28]

No thinker in our generation has seen this important point more clearly than did the late Archbishop Temple, who, in his Gifford Lectures, said:

> But this fact of knowledge is more remarkable than all the varieties of known objects put together. For the mind which knows is in a perfectly real sense equal to what it knows, and in another real sense transcends it, unless what it knows is another mind which also knows. The mind of the astronomer is equal to so much of the stellar system as he grasps, and transcends it in so far as he knows it while it does not know him. That there should "emerge" in the cosmic process a capacity to apprehend, even in a measure to comprehend, that process is the most remarkable characteristic of the process itself.[29]

It is no diminution of Temple's contribution to say that the essence of it is found in Pascal's conception of the "thinking reed." The entire story of the success of natural science in the three hundred years since Pascal wrote the well-known words has served as a corroboration of his insight. Every would-be philosopher must meditate upon the question: What is involved in the fact that ours is a world in which science is possible? In many ways, science, properly understood, is not a barrier to realistic theistic faith, but instead is the first witness.

The contemporary conception of the relationship between ethics and religion is one which, because it is easily misunderstood, requires careful examination. This is what Taylor does in his second approach, called "From Man to God." Honest men do not believe in God because they need the existence of God to support the moral law. That would be to make God a pragmatic instrument and thereby to debase Him. The logical development comes from the other end of the series. We cannot fail to observe, with Kant, the extreme seriousness with which all normal men face their duty, even though they differ from one another in the details of what

[28] Peirce, op. cit., p. 400. The student will find in this book a much neglected essay from the pen of Peirce, "A Neglected Argument for the Reality of God."

[29] W. Temple, Nature, Man and God, The Macmillan Company, 1956, p. 129.

their duty may require. Now, if we pay attention to the moral law within, we may rightly ask what kind of a world it is which makes such a sense of oughtness reasonable. We certainly do not suppose that the source of the obligation is in ourselves, for then we could logically neglect what we arbitrarily produce. Nor can we suppose that the source is in the body politic or in the social order, because we recognize that the prevailing social order can be wrong. The point of every reformer is that it is wrong. The only possible locus of the moral demand is that which is transhuman, but nevertheless real, i.e., the living God.

The movement, then, in the second level of vindication of theism is *not from God to morality, but from morality to God.* We start with what we actually experience and we ask, logically, what this experience entails. If the first reasonable question is, as we have seen, "What is involved in the fact that ours is a world in which science is possible?" The second reasonable question for a philosopher to ask is, "What is involved in the fact that ours is a world in which a sense of oughtness is pervasive and universal?"

The third level of approach is that of the recognition of first-hand religious experience, which Taylor labels "From God to God." This is really the climax of the cumulative series of evidence and is obviously something of great persuasiveness in an age of science in which men are more concerned, they suppose, with experience than with speculation. One important fact about our world is that great numbers of men and women, perhaps millions, have reported a firsthand experience of God's presence and power in their lives. Because this impressive company includes people of many races, many religions, and many centuries, including those whom we have reason on other grounds to trust, they present the unbeliever with a really terrible dilemma. *Either God is or every one of those who have reported direct encounter with Him has been deluded.* This involves a cruel choice and not one which a thoughtful person will face lightly. It is, of course, logically possible that all of those who have reported their religious experience have been deluded, but the difficulty for the unbeliever is that this includes so many whom he has other reasons to honor. It certainly includes the great prophets of many generations, and it includes Jesus Christ. In the recorded prayer beginning, "I thank thee, O Father," we have an indication of a contact that is both immediate and intimate. On the cross He was not alone, though all the disciples but John were cowardly and therefore absent. And what shall we say of Socrates and the Inner Voice to which he listened with such respect? Or how shall we neglect the tremendous claim of Pascal to a firsthand experience of God so compelling that it altered the course of his career and dominated the final years of his life?

It is doubtful if most of those who discount, in advance of examination, empirical evidence of the kind just mentioned have any idea how abundant it is. Some apparently believe that it can be neglected because it is supposedly rare or limited to erratic people. Nothing could be farther from the fact. One source of reports, which is very impressive, is the vast body of autobiographical literature which constitutes a large section of the devotional classics. Characteristic in this area is the *Journal of John Woolman*, with reports of God's presence which are completely disarming because of the tenderness and modesty with which they are presented. We may hold, with some show of consistency, that the arguments from nature and from moral experience are not coercive, because they are, at best, speculative and postulational, but the argument from experience is obviously of a different character. It is not easy, provided we are thoughtful, to dismiss the humble yet self-critical man who says simply, "I have known Him; He has supported me in my darkest as well as my brightest hours." He is giving the same kind of evidence for the being of God that is given by a man who reports seeing the deer in the forest. Both may be wrong; both require corroborative evidence to convince the properly skeptical; but both are dealing with experience, which is the human starting point of knowledge. The fact that one of these experiences involves physical end-organs, while the other does not involve them, certainly does not settle the matter. Are we sure enough of ourselves and our world to be able to claim that the only valid experience is that which involves sight, touch, and hearing? These may, in fact, be but the narrowest of slits through which our contact with the real can take place. Only the philosophically naïve can hold that *empirical* and *sensory* are necessarily synonymous.

If the vast evidence which A. E. Taylor mentions in the third part of "The Vindication of Religion" is dismissed it must be done on one or more of the following grounds:

1. All of the reporters of direct religious experience are unbalanced and, therefore, unreliable as observers.
2. The reports are so varied that they do not provide the necessary basis for corroboration.
3. The reports can be denied objective reference because they can all be explained psychologically, as mere wish-thinking.

The person who tries to be philosophical about the matter will examine each of these hypotheses carefully, never judging the outcome in advance. The first of the three, we soon note, requires the least attention of any. On the face of the matter it could not be proved, because the critic could never be sure that he had examined all relevant cases. The scholar, such as A. E. Taylor, who has come to the conclusion that the empirical evidence is good evidence, cannot be forced into the position of having to assert that all reporters have been sound in mind. If even one is, the case is made. Either God is, we must remember, or *all* have been self-deceived. We must remember, also, that we are dealing with some of the most self-critical of minds and some of the most balanced. The late Rufus M. Jones (1863–1948), who taught philosophy at Haverford College for forty years and centered his entire career on the examination of the evidence of firsthand religious experience,[30] which he called his life-clue, was one who was perfectly confident of God's presence, yet a man whose character was marked by evident sanity and good humor. We do not have to know many such persons to see that the first hypothesis of dismissal cannot be sustained.

The second hypothesis of dismissal cannot be thoughtfully considered until we examine a good many of the reports of experience. Those who have given their lives to such an examination tend to conclude that the agreement in reports is really very great. It is as though, says Dean Inge, men had claimed to have experienced a

---

[30] Some of his most important books are *Studies in Mystical Religion, Pathways to the Reality of God*, and *The Double Search*. He was for twenty-five years chairman of The American Friends Service Committee.

far country and their neighbors doubt their veracity or even the existence of the country allegedly visited. They prove that they have been there, says Inge, by bringing back perfectly consistent reports of the country supposedly visited.[31] The reports may not be identical, as those of the deer seen by various observers in the forest, but we do not expect, in complex matters, the ease of corroboration which we find in relatively simple matters. What we do find is a genuine fellowship of verification over the centuries. Thus, in a significant sense, the reported experience of Blaise Pascal verifies that of Augustine of Hippo. The saints are not always good men and they have local differences, just as they employ different languages, but they tell, in essence, the same story.

The third hypothesis of dismissal is the most popular of the three, particularly among undergraduates, largely because of the influence of Sigmund Freud, who relied on this heavily. This argument, which Freud developed in *The Future of an Illusion*, is really a simple one. It states that, because men cannot bear reality in a harsh world, they project a father-image on the cosmos. The idea of God, then, is only a pleasing phantasy and men are not normally conscious that it is a mere projection. However popular this doctrine may be, its obvious fault is that it is too simple. It does not and cannot deal realistically with the many phenomena of religion in which men, far from pursuing their immature wishes, as Freud claims, are going directly against the demands of ease and comfort which, apart from God's leading, they would certainly follow. What can such a doctrine do with the tremendous fact of the Cross? How can the projectionist include the words, "If it be possible, let this cup pass from me; nevertheless not as I will, but as thou wilt." (Matthew 26:39.)

The wish-thinking hypothesis has the further difficulty that, if valid, it proves too much. It makes every human judgment suspect by the same standard, and this, inevitably, includes itself. Freudianism, if consistently applied, undermines Freud's own judgments, for what undermines everything undermines itself.

The weight of the evidence of religious experience is bound to seem greater as people of this generation become increasingly aware of the inadequacy of the grounds on which it is popularly dismissed.

[31] See W. R. Inge, *Christian Mysticism*, Charles Scribner's Sons, 1899.

Apart from these grounds, the argument should and probably will seem very important to an age which is increasingly scientific in its mentality. It was partly because his mentality was so deeply influenced by science that Charles S. Peirce could say, "The question of the truth of religion being a question of what *is* true, and not of what *would be* true under an arbitrary hypothesis, such as those of pure mathematics, the only logical proof possible is the testing."[32] Perhaps each person has only one significant book to write, the book in which he tells what has transpired in his own life and experience. It is, after all, hard to neglect the impact of the man who can say, sincerely yet modestly, "I was there." A classic foretaste of this scientific approach is afforded by the blind man of the gospel, whose only answer to skeptical inquiry was "Whereas I was blind, now I see."

The argument from experience may be strengthened by those from nature and from morality, as well as from aesthetic experience: we have not mentioned the latter for lack of space and because it is well developed in available works of reputable philosophers.[33] It is the combination which is powerful. The only evidence that can stand alone, or nearly alone, is the empirical evidence, as it is the only kind that is intellectually coercive, when rightly understood. The causal argument, as first formulated by Plato and carefully elucidated by Thomas Aquinas, is impressive, but it is no stronger than its major premise. This is the proposition that there is nothing in the effect that was not in the cause. This is sometimes called "the principle of sufficient reason." The problem is that this is something which we may believe, but cannot know. We take it essentially on faith and, if anyone wishes to deny it, we cannot dislodge him. Maybe there could be more in the effect than in the cause. With the argument from experience, however, we are on a totally different ground, for that is where we all begin.

The Character of God

The fact to which we must continually return, if we are to have an adequate philosophy, is the fact of personality. Contemplation of

[32] Peirce, *op. cit.*, p. 393.
[33] Especially in Lord Balfour's *Theism and Humanism*, George H. Doran Company, 1915.

this fact provides us with our only inside view. We do not know how large the physical universe is, though we are reasonably sure that it is larger than we think; neither do we know the age of the universe, though it is probably older than we suppose it is; but we do know that at one point in space and time in this amazing universe there has appeared a truly strange phenomenon. This is the phenomenon of a creature who can be aware of times long gone, of objects which are light years away, of purposes unfulfilled, of moral laws not fully obeyed. In short, though we do not know very much, we have knowledge that the actual world is a world with persons in it, *because we are persons.*

By a person we mean a being capable of comprehending both the self and the nonself, of entertaining purposes and of being truly creative, by means of ideas. There may be such beings on other planets which are in orbit around other various stars, but this we do not now know. Bergson argued confidently that the probability of the appearance of finite personality beyond the surface of our planet was very high. He held it "probable that life animates all the planets revolving round the stars." This life, he recognized, might take a variety of forms, some of which are remote from those familiar to ourselves, but all marked by "a slow accumulation of potential energy to be spent suddenly in free action." His basic reason for this speculation was his thesis that what appears in ourselves is not strange or accidental, but a true revelation of what there is. Bergson saw abundant reason not to regard "as accidental the appearance among plants and animals that people the earth of a living creature such as man, capable of loving and making himself loved."[34]

Whether persons exist on other planets or not, they are certainly on this one. What kind of a world is consistent with this undoubted fact? Perhaps it is barely conceivable that a world of unconscious forces would finally, by accidental measures, i.e., with no conscious purpose, produce beings capable of self-consciousness and purpose, but such an outcome would be strange indeed. The world may be mysterious, but is it *that* mysterious? The serious atheist must take his world seriously and must hold, on his thesis, that

[34] H. Bergson, *The Two Sources of Morality and Religion*, Doubleday & Company, Inc., Anchor Books, 1954, p. 255.

man's emergence is an absolute miracle, the result being out of all proportion to the causes. One reason why many of the ablest philosophers have not been willing to rest satisfied with atheism is that they have not been able to include, in a rational system, a miracle so great. Belief may be hard, they say, but unbelief is harder! The materialist who does not see this as an enormous difficulty is not really a thinker at all. It is conceivable, of course, that he finally rejects theism because of what seem to him to be still greater difficulties inherent in it, but he ought to begin by facing the forbidding nature of the difficulties in his own world view.

So far as the being of God is concerned, the major implication of the fact of personality is to be found in the problem of God's nature or character. It is very easy to believe in God, and yet mean so little by the belief that the matter is hardly worth discussing. Some, for example, think of God as an impersonal Force, somewhat like a natural law. Others, following the lead of Whitehead, think of God as the "Principle of Concretion." Those of Whitehead's school have fastened upon the level of organism rather than upon the level of personality. Others, like Paul Tillich, are willing to speak of God as "personal," but hesitate to speak of God as "Person" in the belief that this denies God's absolute transcendence of all human categories. Many hesitate to speak of God personally for fear of falling into the danger of anthropomorphism, a danger of which philosophers have been aware ever since the warning given by Xenophanes in ancient Greece.

The really insoluble problem, which all impersonal theists face, is the problem of making God inferior in some respects, to man. If we can know our friend and God cannot know him, then we are faced with the patent absurdity that the creature is at one point superior in awareness or comprehension, to the Creator. Those thinkers who do not hesitate to speak of God as truly personal and even as Person, are determined that, whatever their mistakes, they will not fall into this absurdity.

The fear that the ascription of personality to God means cutting God down to our size is really an idle fear. Those who speak of God in personal terms, as Christ did whenever He said "Thou," are not naïve enough to suppose that God is limited, in His personality, to our forms. They are simply rejecting the irrationality of seeing God as impersonal. Whenever we do so we are explaining the higher in terms of the lower. God may be *suprapersonal*; He may have characteristics far greater and richer than any which we, in our finitude, can imagine; but unless God, if He is, exhibits *at least* as much caring and concern as does a good man, the problem of His existence is hardly worth discussing. "Unless," says Josiah Royce, "the Absolute knows what we know when we endure and wait, when we love and struggle, when we long and suffer, the Absolute in so far is less and not more than we are."[35]

There are few philosophers who are not genuinely respectful of Alfred North Whitehead, so we must pay close attention to his insistence on the character of God as fundamentally organic. But the more we examine his expressions, the more we are impressed by how close his conception is to the conception of divine personality, outlined so persuasively by William Temple. Listen, for example, to words that are hardly meaningful except in the context of the fully personal, "The limitation of God is his goodness. He gains his depth of actuality by his harmony of valuation. It is not true that God is in all respects infinite. If he were, he would be evil as well as good."[36] It is not merely the use of the personal pronoun that is a giveaway; it is even more the unashamed ascription of goodness. What can be really good except a person? Even the famous passage about "concretion" sounds amazingly personal. "God is the principle of concretion; namely, he is that actual entity from which each temporal concrescence receives that initial aim from which its self-causation starts."[37] This is surely very close to the conception of a loving Creator whose conscious purpose includes the production of finite creators. Note, especially, the term "actual entity." Here is no nominalism, but the ascription of the same kind of objectivity which we rightly ascribe to objects revealed in science. Perhaps it is because Whitehead understood

[35] J. Royce, *The World and the Individual*, The Macmillan Company, 1901, Vol. II, 364.

[36] A. N. Whitehead, *Religion in the Making*, Cambridge University Press, 1936, p. 153. See also p. 61.

[37] A. N. Whitehead, *Process and Reality*, The Macmillan Company, 1960, p. 374.

science so well. There is much in his metaphysics that agrees with Peirce when he says, "Modern science, especially physics, is and must be . . . on the side of scholastic realism. So is religion."[38]

Lord Balfour contributed much to the clarity of mind of those who struggle for intellectual honesty concerning God, but perhaps his greatest contribution was in his ability to transcend a great deal of nonsense and explain the nature of the hypothesis being tested for its adequacy. In one of his Gifford Lectures he wrote:

When I speak of God, I mean something other than an Identity wherein all differences vanish, or a Unity which includes but does not transcend the difference which it somehow holds in solution. I mean a God whom men can love, a God to whom men can pray, who takes sides, who has purposes and preferences, whose attributes, however conceived, leave unimpaired the possibility of a personal relation between Himself and those whom He has created.[39]

If Lord Balfour is right, what is at issue is something of tremendous significance, not only to the professional thinker, but to the average man as well. God, in Balfour's sense, either is or is not. If He is not, we want to know it and end all the nonsense. If He is, that is great news, and news which bears on nearly all of the practical details of ordinary life. It bears, for example, on the probability of life after death and rational concern for it now.

The only important argument for conscious survival after the death of the physical body, which is what the plain man means by immortality, is that such survival is a logical corollary of God's existence. If God is, if He is personal in the sense of purposive, we must try to discover something of His purpose. The best hint that is available to us, as we see how life has emerged from matter, and how mind has emerged from life, is that God has been seeking all of the time to develop true personalities. It is one of the supreme marks of personality that the individual is of intrinsic value. The locus of value is not personality in the abstract, but rather the concrete, individual person. Our world, with all of its mystery and pain, makes sense if it has been so ordered that it becomes a theatre in which, at some points, there emerge finite beings able to love and

[38] Peirce, op. cit., p. 418.
[39] Lord Balfour, op. cit., p. 21.

to know that they are loved. If, as Plato suggests in the *Timaeus,* God created the world because His love overflowed, it is clear that God needs beings *to love.* Bergson has said this better than have most of his fellow philosophers:

> Nevertheless, it is hard to conceive a love which is, so to speak, at work, and yet applies to nothing. As a matter of fact, the mystics unanimously bear witness that God needs us, just as we need God. Why should He need us unless it be to love us? And it is to this very conclusion that the philosopher who holds to the mystical experience must come. Creation will appear to him as God undertaking to create creators, that He may have, besides Himself, beings worthy of His love.[40]

If the creation of creators, however slow and painful the process may be, makes sense, then it is not reasonable to suppose that the divine purpose will be defeated by the complete cessation, at the death of the body, of that which has come at so high a price. If death ends the story for each individual, there is a fundamental sense in which the whole process is frustrated at its climax. The believer in conscious survival, with the possible opportunity for completion of what is meaningful though fragmentary, is simply one who doubts the probability of the ultimate defeat of the apparent purpose. He does not claim to know, and he does not need to know, in his rational deduction, what the details of the future life are. He is consciously aware that the intellectual difficulties connected with any belief in immortality, which are severe,[41] are certainly no greater than are the difficulties connected with the emergence of spiritual beings in a world of chance. *Survival* may seem mysterious, but no more so than *arrival.*

The conviction that God is and that He is truly personal, involves not only important corollaries, but also important difficulties of its own. The chief of these is what is known, historically, as the problem of evil. "All simplifications of religious dogma," said Whitehead, "are shipwrecked upon the rock of the problem of evil."[42]

---

[40] Bergson, *op. cit.,* p. 255.

[41] For a brave statement of the difficulties see C. S. Peirce, "Science and Immortality," *op. cit.,* pp. 345–350.

[42] A. N. Whitehead, *Religion in the Making, op. cit.,* p. 77.

This is a problem which the atheist is not required to face, though he has other problems of an intellectual nature, but it is a problem which no theist can avoid and no honest thinker will try to avoid. In essence, the problem is that of the seeming impossibility of believing, without contradiction, in both God's love and God's power, which are necessarily involved in the view that God is real and also personal. It is a fact that our world abounds in examples of unmerited and even unredemptive or unprofitable suffering. The reader can supply his own examples and some will supply them from their own lives. It is one of the facts of life that absolute justice is not done here. This becomes a powerful argument for belief in the future life, because only on the hypothesis of its reality can belief in the final defeat of divine justice be avoided, but if we think only of this life, the problem of suffering sometimes becomes so severe that it makes thoughtful men reject the hypothesis of God's being entirely. The difficulty of theistic belief seems to them greater than the balancing difficulties of unbelief.

Though the problem of evil is never wholly resolved, it can be greatly reduced by careful examination. Two considerations have been discovered which make the problem a manageable one. The first consideration concerns *freedom*. If God is and if His purpose is to make finite creators, it is essential that they be free, in the sense of not coerced. But if men are to be free, really free, they must also be free to be evil, to make the wrong decisions. Otherwise the experiment is not genuine. If men are really free, some will choose wrongly. And when they do, dire consequences inevitably follow. If the alternative is a world in which all creatures are merely pawns, we cannot doubt that we prefer freedom, even at its fearful price. Forced goodness is not really goodness at all. This consideration does not explain sufficiently all aspects of the problem of evil, but it explains the worst aspects. Furthermore, it absolves God of the responsibility of human sin, for that is due to man's perverse use of his freedom. That freely chosen good is better than anything else of which we can think, there is no serious doubt.

The other valuable consideration arises from a deeper understanding of what a personal relationship is. It is not possible to think of a personal order that is not one in which the innocent suffer with the guilty. This is because personality is meaningless without mutual involvement. If God should rule against the emergence of any unmerited suffering, the result would be comparable to a round square—a contradiction in terms and therefore nothing. But, though a personal order thus comes at a high price, the price of temporal injustice, it is also the only context in which love can operate. In the mutual acceptance of one another's burdens we get a deeper hint of what a personal order is, and perhaps a hint of the deepest order in the universe.

Part III ～ VALUES

Chapter 11 ᗁ BEAUTY

The Science of the admirable is true esthetics.

CHARLES S. PEIRCE

IN HIS JUSTLY FAMOUS AND MUCH ADMIRED BOOK, Adventures of Ideas, A. N. Whitehead defines a civilized society as one which exhibits five qualities—"Truth, Beauty, Adventure, Art, Peace."[1] This list of qualities, which is surprising and unconventional, Whitehead defends with persuasive brilliance. It is not wholly strange, the student soon realizes, as he studies the various products of Whitehead's creative mind, that two of the five qualities belong to the aesthetic realm of human endeavor. Paul Schilpp, the editor of the great work on Whitehead in the Library of Living Philosophers, points out Whitehead's "constant and never subsiding interest in aesthetics."[2] The great man, being first of all a mathematician, and being consequently impressed by the beauty and harmony of mathematical forms, moved easily into the contemplation of the beauty

---

[1] A. N. Whitehead, *Adventures of Ideas*, The Macmillan Company, 1933, p. 353.
[2] Paul Schilpp (ed.), *The Philosophy of Alfred North Whitehead*, Tudor Publishing Company, 1951, p. 563.

of other forms, much in the style of his exemplar, Plato. When we consider this, says Schilpp, we see that his "predilection for the theory of beauty, and for the philosophy of art, is by no means out of line with his general position."

Every philosopher, whether he be also a mathematician or not, is bound to be deeply concerned with values, because, when he thinks of them, he is impressed both with their mystery and their importance. It is only by the careful cultivation of a sense of value, with all the labors which this involves, that human life can be kept from sinking "back into the passivity of its lower types."[3] Man does not survive at the truly human level by a mere concern for survival, but only by a concern for how he *ought* to think, for how he *ought* to live and for how he *ought* to be more sensitive to both actual and potential beauty. If man has any duty at all, he has the duty to reverence the truth and to honor beauty wherever they may be found. It is in this way that the ultimate values of truth, beauty, and goodness, all of which must be sought as ends in themselves, are indissolubly interconnected. This is why Clive Bell is not uttering a gratuitous paradox when he says, "To pronounce anything a work of art is, therefore, to make a momentous moral judgment."[4]

The field of aesthetics is one which we can neither master nor abandon. Discussion of beauty cannot have the definiteness which we introduce into natural science, and even the dialectic approach to the study of the admirable does not have the same sharpness which is possible in the study of moral values. Yet the concern for artistic production in a variety of media is so persistent and so profound that we could not avoid it even if we had any desire to do so. The haunting search for perfection of form seems to have been with man from his beginning, thereby providing us with our earliest evidences of human achievements. Aesthetics is a study in which both the importance and the difficulty must be recognized as equal. It is a field which is easily infected with subjectivism, yet one in which no one is willing to be satisfied with subjective reference alone. This is why the field of values, particularly the field of aesthetic value

[3] See A. N. Whitehead, *Aims of Education*, The Macmillan Company, 1959, p. 62.
[4] C. Bell, *Art*, G. P. Putnam's Sons, Capricorn Books, 1958, p. 84.

must be studied with all of the vigor which we can muster, and all of the help from one another that we can obtain.

The Negative Approach to Beauty

There is little doubt that it is far more difficult to speak with confidence of the aesthetic activity, than of the intellectual and the moral. Many suppose that it plays a smaller part than the other two, but this is probably an incorrect judgment. We are, as a matter of fact, engaged in aesthetic activity more nearly constantly than we are in scientific or ethical activity. The use of our eyes and ears in nearly all of our working moments leads to a steady process of aesthetic evaluation. We compare the shape of this tree with the shape of that tree; we hear and enjoy the songs of birds; we rejoice in a pretty face or form; we try, in spite of our ineptitude, to make some aspect of the world more beautiful than it would have been without our effort.

Our almost universal preoccupation with beauty has in it an element of pathos. Who is not moved by the window box of flowers in the slum? It is not utilitarian in any monetary or ordinary sense of the word, yet there it is, an object of loving care. Or consider the phenomenon of the rag rug. A humble woman collects individual rags, which are strips of old clothing, objects that, in most cases, have no beauty in themselves, and she braids them into rugs that give aesthetic delight to herself and to others. The final production may be stunning because it has about it the completeness and inevitability which the human mind requires for its highest pleasure. Indeed, one of the most hopeful facts about the ordinary human being is that, in spite of his many imperfections, he loves beauty and loves it for its own sake. Almost everyone, though he may not use such technical language, recognizes the great difference between terminal values and instrumental values. The latter exist as means to other ends, but the former are valued as ends. An object of art may have a commercial value, but if it is valued for this reason alone, it is not really an object of terminal value. Even persons who do not consider themselves intellectuals often understand this.

We cannot avoid the conclusion that beauty is the form of value which we meet most undeniably and most clearly. It is significant that Plato describes the form of the beautiful in greater detail than any of the others. He asserts, in the *Phaedrus*, that, among the forms apprehended by the soul, beauty alone is apprehended in the world of becoming as she really is.

But of beauty I repeat again that we saw her there shining in company with the celestial forms; and coming to earth we find her here, too, shining in clearest aperture of sense. . . . But this is the privilege of beauty, and that she is the loveliest and also the most palpable to sight.[5]

The paradox is that, though beauty is thus the most easily apprehended of all of the ultimate values, it is the one about which it is the hardest to speak with clarity. We can be helped at this point by Aristotle's recognition of the inevitability of different levels of precision. There are some subjects, he asserted in the *Nicomachean Ethics*, that "admit of much variety and fluctuation of opinion" and, in dealing with these, we must be content "to indicate the truth roughly and in outline." There is no doubt that, in dealing with the problems of ugliness and of beauty, we must be satisfied with relatively modest conclusions, because these are only conclusions which are appropriate to the subject. This is true because, as Aristotle says, in continuing the theme just mentioned, "it is the mark of an educated man to look for precision in each class of things just so far as the nature of the subject admits; it is evidently equally foolish to accept probable reasoning from a mathematician and to demand from a rhetorician scientific proofs." The fact that, in the study of aesthetics, we cannot get all of the help we desire is no reason why we should not welcome the help which we can get. This help is considerable, because philosophers have at least approached the subject courageously and tirelessly.

Though we all speak of beauty, whether it be in nature, or in human production, we have the greatest difficulty in defining it. This is true not only of ordinary persons, but of those who have given their most careful attention to the subject. So elusive is the concept of the beautiful that John Dewey, in the first few chapters

[5] Plato, *Phaedrus, The Dialogues of Plato*, Trans. Jowett, Oxford University Press, 1871, Vol. I, 250.

of his *Art as Experience*, deliberately avoids any use of the term. We have something of the same difficulty which comes to us when we are challenged to say what we mean by "truth" and "truly." We may remember, however, that we have found great merit, in dealing with the meaning of truth, in starting with "error." We know, as Josiah Royce taught us, that there is error, for everyone agrees that something is wrong, the reality of error following necessarily from recognition of the law of noncontradiction. We may not know which one is wrong, but we know that one is. Once we understand error, we are better able to understand truth.

That philosophers have long been aware of the wisdom of the negative approach to great problems, and especially to problems of value, is shown by the words of Aristotle in the *Rhetoric* when he says, "One line of affirmative proof is based upon consideration of the opposite of the thing in question." Why should we not try this method in our aesthetic inquiry? However unclear we are about the nature of the beautiful, we are remarkably clear about the nature of the ugly. Ask almost anyone for a vivid example of the ugly and you receive a quick and definite response. He is likely to refer, in the first instance, to a building. If he lives in London he is likely to point to the St. Pancras Railroad Station, or if he lives in Ohio, he may mention University Hall at Ohio State University. Nearly everyone is acquainted with some building so elaborately ugly that it seems to be a matter of genius. The stark and unrelieved ugliness of many military installations is something which is very familiar to many young men. Sometimes we experience a remarkable degree of ugliness in an otherwise beautiful scene. Thus, visitors to the famous Assembly at Lake Chautauqua, New York, can hardly fail to see the contrast between the beauty of the lake and the forest trees, on the one hand, and the ugliness of most of the Victorian houses, on the other. Only familiarity or affection could make one fail to see this.

In sentimental moods we tend to say that everything is beautiful, but when we become self-critical we know that this is not true. We need to contemplate the fact of ugliness, partly because it is so common. Lewis Mumford has forced us, in his books about cities, to realize how terribly ugly our cities usually are. There is not only the filth of the streets and the drab dullness of identical blocks of houses, there is, if only we could see it, real ugliness in some of the more pretentious buildings. In reference to Rome, Mumford speaks, for example, of St. Peter's as "a monument of spectacular vulgarity unredeemed by the Sistine Chapel."[6] Much of the ugliness of our surroundings is lost upon us because we are so accustomed to the scene. Thus we forget to note the ugliness of so many small towns which are made up of wholly inartistic houses jumbled together, the entire scene markedly inferior, aesthetically, to the rural expanse of well-kept farms and stately barns, beyond the town limits.

Not all ugliness is man-made. The ugliness of a valley which is left in complete desolation by a dam which beavers have constructed and then abandoned is something not easy to forget. Sometimes there is conspicuous ugliness of some isolated feature in what is, in general, a beautiful scene. It is possible, for example, to walk in the hill country of Texas, among the ubiquitous cedartrees with their magnificent odor, and come upon a goat with a large part of its head eaten away by maggots, though the animal is still alive. The goat, by the awful calamity which leads to the actual exposure of the brain, and terrible death, provides, in part, a single item in the problem of evil, but it also represents a conspicuous illustration of the problem of ugliness. We may not have any good explanation of this, but we need to face it.

Perhaps the clearest case of man-made ugliness is the dump heap or, specifically, the automobile graveyard. It is one of the unfortunate facts about American culture that we tolerate these ugly things in full view of all who pass. The jumble of rusty automobile bodies and isolated parts is so conspicuously ugly that one might suppose that we would hide such scenes behind high hedges, but we display them, presumably because it is more profitable to their owners for them to be seen by tourists.

Since the automobile graveyard is, apparently, recognized universally as something really ugly, a consideration of it may give us some hints concerning the nature of beauty, which is a quality it does not exhibit. Men may not agree as individuals or as cultures, about the nature of beauty or about particular objects of supposed

---

[6] L. Mumford, *The City in History: Its Origins, its Transformations, and its Prospects*, Harcourt, Brace & World, Inc., 1961.

beauty, but they can agree that ugliness is, and often they show great unanimity in judgment about ugly objects. The pile of abandoned and rusting automobiles is marked, above all else, by *disorder*. There is no inevitability about any location. The Buicks are not necessarily with other Buicks and the engines are not deliberately associated with other engines. There is no pattern of intelligibility which the mind can grasp. Sometimes there is color, but it is obviously accidental. Each car is the result, at an earlier period, of thoughtful planning on the part of both inventors and producers, but the combination now is not the result of planning at all. The scene is ugly in part because the mind cannot find anything in it to match itself.

Once we have a reasonably clear conception of what ugliness is, realizing that the essence of it is disorder, we have made a big step in our aesthetic quest. The ugly building has a false or meaningless decoration, a deceitful arch, a conflict of moods so atrocious that it cannot be seen as creative discord, but as discord pure and simple. When we see this we are on the way to an understanding of what beauty, the opposite of ugliness, is, much as we get light on truth from the contemplation of error. Ugliness means that something of value is being missed and that which is missed is beauty. Perhaps Clive Bell is right in his well-known claim that there are only two kinds of art, good art and bad art, and that the universal mark of good art is "significant form." It may, of course, take a long time for men to know what the details of such form, in any medium, are, but at least the proper task is thereby proposed.

In all of its features the ugly scene is the antithesis of any really great work of art. One of the chief indications of greatness, particularly in a musical composition, is its inevitability. As we come to the end of one of Beethoven's sonatas we finally realize, as a sort of afterthought that the final bars are what they must be, if the main theme is to be rightly developed. The chief point to observe is that the development is not arbitrary. One mark of the ugly is that it might just as well have been something else or in some other order. In the poor and shoddy book the chapters could have been in a different order without significant loss, while in a great scene of beauty we have the sense that any change, whether that of addition or subtraction, would be harmful. Nothing is beautiful unless it involves some kind of perfection. "A perfectly pure being," says Paul Weiss, "contains no trace of evil, ugliness, folly, of the chaotic, the conflicting. It exhibits a certain nature simply and completely."[7] Herein is wisdom. Beauty is one form of intelligible order.

Beauty is realized perfection, even though the realization is partial or evanescent. This realized perfection may include disharmony, much as the full dialectic includes, within a recognizable pattern, the clash of thesis and antithesis, or as the Gothic building includes, in one structure, the thrust and counterthrust of competing arches, which produce dynamic equilibrium.

One of the curious facts about ugliness is that, even when it is clearly recognized as such, it can be employed in a total aesthetic production. In the Poetics (1449a) Aristotle explains that there is a place for the presentation of the ugly, even in dramatic art. Comedy, he says, in its imitation of action, deals with the ugly, which is ludicrous. "For the ludicrous is that sort of mistake or ugliness which is painless and not destructive."[8] All who think about it are familiar with the way in which the ugly sight may be used constructively in painting and the ugly sound employed in music. Meditation on this theme led A. N. Whitehead to stress the importance of discord. "Progress is founded," he wrote, "upon the experience of discordant feelings. All realization is finite and there is no perfection which is the infinitude of all perfections. Perfections of diverse types are among themselves discordant. Thus the contribution to Beauty which can be supplied by Discord . . . is the positive feeling of a quick shift of aim from the tameness of outworn perfection to some other ideal with its freshness still upon it. Thus the value of Discord is a tribute to the merits of imperfection."[9]

The Issue of Relativism

Some people seem to suppose that they can avoid what they call value-judgments, but in this they are mistaken. Every human being

---

[7] P. Weiss, Man's Freedom, Yale University Press, 1950, p. 197.

[8] Aristotle, Poetics, trans. K. A. Telford, Henry Regnery Company, Gateway Editions, 1961, p. 10.

[9] Whitehead, Adventures of Ideas, op. cit., pp. 330, 331.

who engages in the exercise of his aesthetic powers is a critic. By this we mean that each person establishes some hierarchy of value and places particular objects of supposed beauty somewhere within a series. We do this every time we make a comparative judgment. The person who says that the "Mona Lisa" is more beautiful than a calendar print is acting as a critic, because he is asserting the existence, not merely of objects, but of value. Normally he supposes that he is making a judgment about something beyond himself, something that would be a valid judgment, whoever its author might be, and something about which people might reasonably argue. There is little doubt that the average person is, in this philosophical sense, an aesthetic realist.

The question whether the average person is right or wrong in his understanding of the nature of his aesthetic judgment is something which we need to examine. Perhaps he is not talking about the objective world at all, but only about himself. What is the object of the aesthetic experience and where is it? It is part of the task of philosophy to try to ascertain the locus or seat of value. Perhaps it is in the object; perhaps it is in the mind of the spectator; perhaps it is in the relationship between the two. Does the spectator discover the value, does he create it, or does he merely project it? At one extreme we have the doctrine of subjectivism, which holds that value is completely contingent upon the ideas, the standards, and the interests which the spectator introduces into the aesthetic transaction, while, at the other extreme, is the doctrine of objectivism, which holds that the object of beauty is as unaffected by the observer as would be a Platonic essence or form, and that the spectator is, therefore, either right or wrong, depending upon his ability to appreciate what is really there.

By relativism we usually mean any system of thought that holds that values are determined by the cultural or the socioeconomic position of the beholder. The ultimate ground of the doctrine of relativism is the obvious fact that people differ in their conceptions of what is beautiful. There are certainly people who prefer "Home on the Range" to one of Beethoven's symphonies. The "pop" concerts tend to draw larger audiences than the classical concerts. There are people who are terribly bored by art museums and who, when they view the remains of the classical architecture, wish they were back home. Some, undoubtedly, prefer the windows of the First Baptist Church of Clintondale to those of Chartres Cathedral. It is easy to show how standards of aesthetic taste have changed through the centuries, by thinking of Gothic architecture—once generally honored and later generally despised. A. O. Lovejoy showed how, with changes in philosophy corresponding to the moods of classicism and romanticism, people have at one time admired supremely formal gardens, like that of Versailles, while at another time they have admired the English garden, famous for its "naturalness." One has only to consider the appreciation of modern art and of jazz, both of which Mr. Khrushchev has denounced, to see how continuous this movement of apparent relativity is. The maxim that there is no disputing of tastes may be an idle one, since tastes are what people *do* dispute, but it is easy to see how the maxim arose. The fact is that judgments differ from person to person, from society·to society, and from age to age.

The tendency of the objective realist, who of course admits the facts of change and of lack of agreement, is to say that both the change and lack of agreement merely indicate that great numbers of people are not able to recognize beauty when they see it, and that the real test is the judgment of the qualified or "superior persons." To this point one of the able exponents of relativism has made an effective rejoinder by pointing out the fact that "the preferences of the so-called 'superior' persons vary from time to time, from place to place, from context to context, and are thus themselves characterized by a social-historical relativity. And this relativity makes it absurd to claim that the tastes of the 'superior' persons are certain or absolute."[10]

Few philosophers in our time have stressed the subjective side of the relativity of value more than has Professor George Boas of Johns Hopkins University. While admitting that, in the human race, some desires and some interests "are fairly pervasive," he holds that there are "none—not even those needed for self-preservation—which cannot be eradicated." He points out that, under the spell of our own subjectivity, we tend, in value judgments, to treat agreement with ourselves as evidence of the essential rightness of the

[10] A. Child, "The Social-Historical Relativity of Esthetic Value," *Philosophical Review*, LIII (1944), p. 8.

person who agrees. Essential to the argument of Boas is the following paragraph:

Yet an objective study of the history of taste, both within the growth of any individual and that of the race, shows that no desires are eternal and no standards universal. Standards emerge out of the confusion of appetites and acquire authority; they are neither omnipresent nor omnipotent. Their compulsive force is achieved by historical accident—in the Aristotelian sense of "accident"—and is not inherent in their essential nature. Thus people at all times and in all societies have treated the most diverse satisfactions as if they were rooted in the very nature of humanity, logically deducible from it, and necessary to its happiness. But as a matter of fact, even in primitive societies, there is a conflict of ideals and whatever uniformity has been attained is due to various repressive means, varying from taboos to moral suasion.[11]

When we have considered what Boas has said we have recognized nearly all that there is to say for relativism. The upshot of the argument is the simple fact that men have differed in the past and continue to differ today in regard to estimates of beauty, and that these differences are, in some way or other, relative to the accepted cultural patterns of each society or generation. But evidence of this kind, which everyone tends to recognize anyway, does not logically entail any denial of objective reference in the experience of beauty. For all that the argument necessitates, there could still be objective beauty in the world, with men varying from time to time and from culture to culture in their ability to recognize it. All realize that men have differed about the size of the moon or the distance to the fixed stars almost as much as they have differed about objects of aesthetic value, but no sensible person supposes that this variety of judgment involves the doctrine of subjectivism, denying an objective size and distance to the heavenly bodies. We must remember that it is only in the most recent chapter of history that this variation of astronomical judgment has ceased, and even now it has ceased only for educated people.

It is possible for the philosopher, therefore, to admit variety and change and still hold, as Arthur Child does, that there is an objective factor. While stressing the fact that an artist "will not create the sort of object which will not be found beautiful by the group

---

[11] G. Boas, A *Primer for Critics*, The Johns Hopkins Press, 1937, p. 141.

to which he at least ultimately appeals," he recognizes that there is an abstract "objective ground" which is relativized only when it is made concrete. "Clearly, then," he concludes, "we hold that the objective ground, though indeed a necessary, does not constitute a sufficient ground for the experience of aesthetic value." In this way the contemporary philosopher can, in upholding relativism, recognize both an objective and a subjective element, much as we do in regard to the existence and character of physical objects. It is usually held that the subjective factor is more potent in regard to judgments of value than in regard to questions of physical existence, because we are dealing with something more delicate and vastly more complex.

In spite of the apparent evidence in favor of subjectivism there is an important assertion of the objectivity of value, perhaps as strong today as ever in the past. The dialectic seems to move in three stages: the first, the plain man's assertion of objectivity; the second, the relativist criticism; and the third, the reinstatement of objective reference in a sophisticated fashion. The argument for the objectivism is both logical and empirical. We may profitably mention the empirical first. The point here is that we tend to exaggerate the lack of unanimity or agreement in our desire to maintain some form of relativism. Thus Child, while asserting the necessity of some social relativity, can say, "Although men do not always agree as to what is beautiful as to the degree in which beautiful things are beautiful, yet a comparatively large measure of agreement as to esthetic value—and, therefore, as to esthetic objects, does exist."[12] William Temple goes farther and makes an observation which, though it is at first startling, is bound to call attention to something which the student might otherwise miss. Scientific judgments, because they deal for the most part with measurables, often are regarded as exhibiting much greater agreement than do aesthetic judgments, but, when all the facts are considered, this is not so certain. Is it a fact that in science there reigns interior harmony, while in aesthetics there is nothing but chaos?

It takes a considerable time for a secure aesthetic judgment to be

[12] Child, op. cit., p. 7.

formed, and with regard to contemporary art there is much debate. But when a common judgment is reached after long periods of discussion, it is secure as scientific theories never are. Many may be uncertain in this second quarter of the twentieth century about the aesthetic rank of Epstein as a sculptor or of T. S. Eliot as a poet. But there is no serious dispute about Pheidias or Aeschylus, about Giotto, or Piero, or Botticelli, about Velasquez or Rembrandt, about Dante or Shakespeare. No doubt I "date" myself by the precise list which I select; there are some who put Euripides above Sophocles, some who prefer Beethoven to Bach; but every name thus mentioned is securely established in the list of Masters; and the actual works of the earliest touch us now as they touched the hearts of those who knew them first. . . . It takes longer for the aesthetic judgment to become stable than for the scientific, but when it reaches stability it also achieves finality as the other does not.[13]

What Temple is saying is shocking to modern man, but it is something which it is extremely hard to deny. And it is just as hard to deny in the third quarter of the twentieth century as it was in the second. We lose some of our superstitious reverence for the finality of science when we look at older scientific textbooks, including those of the recent past. We may be sure that our present scientific textbooks will soon seem equally quaint. But the remarkable fact about true classics, whether in art or literature, is that they do not seem quaint at all. There is nothing out-of-date about the statues of "David" in the beautiful city of Florence. Part of the evidence which the philosopher must always consider is the fact that ours is a world in which classics are possible. Art is really the most enduring rather than the most transitory element in our civilization.

With this empirical observation in mind, we are better prepared to study the argument for the objectivity of beauty. The argument has been made with great persuasiveness by many in our time, but never better than in the work of the late C. E. M. Joad. "I wish to imply," says Joad, "that beauty is an independent, self-sufficient object, that as such it is a real factor in the universe, and that it does not depend for being what it is upon any of the other factors

[13] W. Temple, *Nature, Man and God*, The Macmillan Company, 1956, pp. 158, 159.

in the universe."[14] Joad holds that, though obviously he has his own subjective feelings about beautiful objects, he is not talking about himself or his feelings when he speaks of beauty. He is, he believes, talking about something that would be even if he were not. Furthermore, he does not merely state this as a doctrine, but is prepared to give cogent reasons for believing that the conclusion which he has reached is a sound one, or in any case sounder than any known alternatives. The view that the value is objective is, incidentally, the view that is assumed by nearly every critic of the arts. Each believes that he is doing more than merely expressing his own opinions and he shows this by his willingness to give evidence, when it is required, concerning the rightness of his judgments.

Joad begins, as we might expect, by analyzing and exposing alternatives. One such alternative is that made famous by Tolstoy, who identified art with the communication of emotion. Since, according to Tolstoy[15] and all who accept his kind of subjectivism, beauty means nothing but an emotional effect on people, it is hard to avoid the conclusion that a work is better if more people like it, and Tolstoy did not hesitate to accept this monstrous implication. It follows, necessarily, that the peasant songs are superior to Hamlet, since more people like them. "Home on the Range" is really, on this basis, superior to the Ninth Symphony of Beethoven, since, if the test is that of counting heads, the cowboy song will win the competition. Likewise, the ubiquitous "western" of the television will win over a play like Macbeth, partly because it is sure to have a more pleasing outcome. Indeed, Tolstoy goes so far as to demote the Ninth Symphony. " 'What! the Ninth Symphony not a good work of art!' I hear exclaimed by indignant voices. And I reply: Most certainly it is not."

Joad has little difficulty showing the unsatisfactory conclusions to which mere subjectivism leads men. We are, indeed, in an unsatisfactory predicament when "we are reduced to the crude subjectivist position of assessing the value of a work of art in terms

[14] See C. E. M. Joad, Matter, Life and Value, Oxford University Press, pp. 129, 266.
[15] See L. Tolstoy, What is Art? Oxford University Press, 1924, especially pp. 171–174.

of the amount of pleasurable feeling it excites." Pornography, we are told, often excites great pleasure. One of the important facts which bears on the question at issue is the fact that people argue, that they argue incessantly, and that they argue about the beautiful. Of course, this may be a silly way for people to deport themselves, but they clearly do not think so, for they go right on, whatever philosophers may conclude.

The point to make clear to ourselves is that, unless there is some objective factor in the aesthetic experience, all people who argue about beauty are deluded by the supposition that they differ from one another. If John says the County courthouse is more beautiful than the new cathedral at Coventry, while Mary prefers the cathedral, and if both are referring merely to feelings within themselves, neither is contradicting the other. Both are telling the truth, which is that each gets pleasure out of what gives pleasure, and that is really the end of the matter. The only reasonable conclusion would be absolute tolerance of different judgments, since each is telling about himself. But it is notorious that this absolute tolerance is not what anyone is willing to practice and it is doubtful if its general practice would be compatible with civilization at all. We all know that people do argue about beauty, that the person who does not like Shakespeare is generally told that he should, and that, if only he were to pay attention to certain relevant considerations, he would. In short, all of our aesthetic arguments imply that there is a third reality, different from the subjective judgment of the man who judges, and equally different from the subjective judgment of his opponent, and it is this third reality which both are discussing. The hope of all argument is that we may get nearer to the truth about what we discuss. It may be noted that we find it extremely difficult to avoid the use of the adverb "really," and that every time we use it, we imply objective reference.[16]

[16] The student who wants to go further in this important issue cannot do better than to examine slowly, and more than once, an essay by G. E. Moore called "The Conception of Intrinsic Value," chap. 8 in *Philosophical Studies,* The Humanities Press, Inc., 1951. In this very carefully argued essay, Moore deals with both moral and aesthetic value, and makes a distinction between "intrinsic" and "objective" which is helpful. Moore believes that it is "intrinsic value" that the upholders of "objectivity" are really seeking to maintain.

It is reasonable to conclude that the truth about beauty is similar, in logical structure, to any other truth about the world: judgments are true only when they are independent of each observer. The essence of truth is that it is potentially public, even though it might, for a time, be recognized by only one or two persons. At the conclusion of his philosophic career, C. S. Peirce came more and more to think of truth, any truth, as that which fully alert and sensitive persons would reach. "But if Truth," he said, "be something public, it must mean that, to the acceptance of which as a basis of conduct any person you please would ultimately come if he pursued his inquiries far enough."[17] This conception has the great merit of being close to what the plain man means by truth, especially truth in regard to beauty, yet it is stated in a professional way. Does not this represent what most of us mean when we say that an object is really beautiful and not merely conventionally or superficially so? We mean that it would be appreciated by the person of the most refined, critical, and developed taste. We mean that it is the kind of beauty which can stand up under endless examination by the most demanding critics. There is one sense in which all beauty is in the eye of the beholder, when people see only what they are able to see, but this is a measure of our finitude. Unless all aesthetic discussion is fatuous, there is a right judgment in which all critics would agree, if all could see and hear what is to be seen and heard. The ages become the means of the objective test; the sincere critic believes that his judgment will be corroborated. This is what Walt Whitman is saying in the following lines:

> A hundred years hence, or ever so
> many hundred years hence, others will see them,
> Will enjoy the sunset, the pouring in
> of the flood-tide, the falling back to the
> sea of the ebb-tide.
> It avails not, neither time nor place—
> distance avails not.[18]

Now Whitman's hundred years have transpired. The aesthetic

---

[17] C. S. Peirce, *Values in a Universe of Chance*, Stanford University Press, 1958, p. 398.

[18] W. Whitman, "Crossing Brooklyn Ferry," *Leaves of Grass*, J. M. Dent and Sons, 1927, p. 134.

experience comes no longer on the ferry, but the enjoyment is the same. This is one of the reasons why poetry is possible. Aesthetics, whether it refers to the vision of poetry or the vision of art, becomes scientific in the only way in which it can be scientific, when it begins with some person's recorded experience, which thus provides our datum, and goes on to seek corroboration or dissent, with a reason for each. The purpose is to see what conception of aesthetic truth makes most sense out of the data.

If, when we speak of an objective order of beauty, we mean what the plain man means, to the effect that beauty is something actually discovered, we need not be at all surprised that the abilities to make this discovery are so various and that they appear with such painful slowness. Plato took great pains to warn his readers that the ascent of the ladder is difficult, and that normally it is necessary to take a step at a time. The vision of the form, he taught, comes not at the beginning of the learning process, but always at the end, and since in this life we do not reach the end, we should always expect differences of judgment. At the climax of the *Symposium*, which, though it is devoted to many subjects, is certainly concerned with the mystery of beauty, we learn that "at last the vision is revealed to him of a single science which is the science of beauty everywhere."[19]

In the light of this conception we do not merely note the fact of human variation and leave the matter there. We encourage, both in ourselves and in others, a course of training which at one stage will involve the exact sciences of measuring, weighing, and counting which are recommended by Plato. This is wise counsel, not merely for the practicing artist but for every sensitive person. The average man, who does not produce works of beauty, needs nevertheless to develop his aesthetic powers as fully as is possible, because otherwise he cannot appreciate what it is that the artist is trying to communicate. We cannot appreciate the beauty that others create unless we are all the time engaged, as thoughtfully as possible, in the aesthetic enterprise. Only a person who is himself something of a poet at heart can appreciate poetry, and this is possible for people who have never written a single line of verse.

[19] Plato, *Symposium*, trans. Jowett, Vol. I, 210.

The well-known and much admired statement of the principle of necessary kinship is that of Plato in the Seventh Epistle. He asserts that "neither quickness of learning nor a good memory can make a man see when his nature is not akin to the object, for this knowledge never takes root in an alien nature; so that no man who is not naturally inclined and akin to justice and all other forms of excellence, even though he may be quick at learning and remembering this and that and other things, nor any man who, though akin to justice, is slow at learning and forgetful, will ever attain the truth that is attainable about virtue."[20]

The objective reality of beauty is really a postulate of our experience. Our experience of course may be fundamentally delusive, but if it is dependable some conception of objectivity is hard to avoid. Provided we recognize that in aesthetic judgment it is really ridiculous to settle the matter by counting heads, we are bound to say that some opinions are more nearly right than are others. If we reject the notion that all judgments are equally sound, we cannot avoid the conclusion that some people are simply wrong. But if they are wrong, they are wrong in terms of something to which all are trying to refer. It is not an answer to say that they are wrong in terms of their own subjective culture or interests, for the subjective claim is that their decision is only a reflection of their own interests.

One significant conclusion of this process of reasoning is that there is uncontemplated beauty. We all believe that there are unexperienced objects, as was true of almost any piece of coal in current use, until a few months ago. It would not be so strange, then, for there to be unexperienced beauty. It would only be strange if, for some reason, beauty is unreal until it is admired. But would there be value in uncontemplated beauty? G. E. Moore has indicated his own answer, which comes as the direct result of much careful thinking, in the following paragraph:

Let us imagine one world exceedingly beautiful. Imagine it as beautiful as you can; put in whatever in the world you most admire—moun-

20 Plato, Epistles, trans. G. R. Morrow, Library of Liberal Arts, The Bobbs-Merrill Company, 1962, pp. 240, 241. The same theme appears in The Republic.

tains, rivers, the sea, trees, sunsets, stars, and moon. Imagine all this combined in the most exquisite proportions, so that no one thing jars against another, but each contributes to increase the beauty of the whole. And then imagine the ugliest world you can possibly conceive. Imagine it simply as a heap of filth, containing everything that is most disgusting to us for whatever reason, and the whole, so far as may be, without one redeeming feature. . . . The only thing we are not entitled to imagine is that any human being ever has or by any possibility can see and enjoy the beauty of the one or hate the foulness of the other. . . . Is it irrational to hold that it is better that the beautiful world should exist than the one that is ugly?[21]

Aesthetic Fulfillment

Man is a being who is addicted to the creation and enjoyment of art. Many of the oldest external evidences of human antiquity are objects which our ancestors made long ago, not merely or even primarily for use, but obviously because of a desire that unnecessary beauty be expressed and thereby made to endure. The vast amount of unnecessary beauty of nature reveals something important about the world as a whole, while the unnecessary beauty of art reveals something important about man. Flowers exhibit more beauty than is needed to facilitate pollenization, while the plumage of birds reveals more beauty than is needed to encourage sexual mating. A world wholly devoid of color is a logical possibility and seems monstrous to us only because we are so accustomed to the lavishness with which our world is painted. A world without art might be a highly efficient one, dispensing with a good deal of employment of energy which, from the utilitarian point of view, is now wasted, but it would not be our world. When we think of the similarity of natural and artificial beauty, we realize that the best evidence that man was created in God's image is found in the aesthetic order.

Art is serious business. It involves tremendous labors, continuous concentration over long periods, and much self-denial. Many men, now generally acclaimed, have worked without adequate financial rewards and without fame, simply because of a compelling vision

[21] G. E. Moore, *Principia Ethica*, Cambridge University Press, 1903, p. 83.

of perfection. Part of the importance of art is that, far from being a mere imitation of nature or of history or of society, it tends to influence the course of events. It establishes standards of conduct and of understanding by which ordinary life is understood and judged. It is not so much that art is "lifelike" as that life tends to be "artlike." We do not normally, in the western world, say that Hamlet is like our friend Mr. Jones; we say, instead, that Jones is like Hamlet. In short, we understand our neighbor, Jones, far better, because of the depiction of the Prince of Denmark which Shakespeare has made.

This can be put more vividly by saying that art, at its best, is always a revelation. Men have been heard to say that they did not know what joy was until they had listened attentively to Beethoven's Ninth Symphony. In a similar way we say that we do not appreciate sorrow adequately, by our own unaided efforts. We understand even our own moods better after we have been subjected to Milton's "Sonnet on His Blindness." Art, then, does not merely imitate; it organizes and informs and, above all, breaks down barriers to vision. The revelatory function of art is a strong hybrid, partly therapeutic and partly pedagogic. It teaches us to see, to hear, and to feel, what otherwise we should miss.

It is doubtful if any art is excellent which does not produce joy, including even the most tragic works. Interpreters of artistic experience have approached this important judgment in different ways, but there is a remarkable consensus of opinion. The joy which is recognized is seldom superficial happiness, for it comes often by our entering deeply into pain. We must not forget that sorrowful scenes lend themselves more fully to artistic treatment than do happy ones. It is no surprise, if we have some general knowledge of art, that Paradise Lost is a more significant poem than is Paradise Regained. It is no surprise that the Crucifixion is a more suitable subject for painting than is the Resurrection.

The joy which is compatible with a deep entrance into human sorrow is what Bernard Berenson calls "life enhancement." The commonplace is lifted out of triviality by contemplation of increasing perfection of form, and this is joy. It does not make for peace, at least not for a cheap or easy peace. We may remember Galsworthy's phrase, when, in connection with *The Forsyte Saga*, he spoke of a "disturbance that Beauty effects in the lives of men."

One of the ways in which art is a revelation of reality is the fact that often, especially in a poem or a drama, the meaning of the whole is not understood until we reach the end. Often only the end makes sense. The unity of the production is not static nor revealed equally in all of its parts, but appears in process and the unity cannot be appreciated until the outcome is seen. In short, the significance of a work of art is teleological.

That the meaning of a production is not known at the beginning is verified by countless authors. Josiah Royce is only one of many in telling us that in the composition of his serious philosophical works, his mind grew as he proceeded. This is why, according to various authors, the preface is not written until the very last. A man is in the grip of a vision which he partly understands, but only partly. Readers often suppose that an author knows, when he starts, the entire development of his creative work, but the evidence is that the public is wrong. One of the most remarkable facts about the production of a literary work, whether it be in poetry or in prose, is that the very act of writing becomes creative. New ideas, not even suspected in advance, appear miraculously as ink is applied to paper. The vision which is followed, even a little, grows and expands with the doing. If writing is thus truly creative, it is easy to see how the same is true in the painting of a picture, the composition of a symphony, or in the carving of sculpture.

This important fact of the creative nature of production leads to the conclusion that there is far more artistic talent in the human race than is recognized or developed. There must be great powers in the potential creation of beauty that are never suspected, even by their owners. We know that a good many people exhibit considerable skill in painting late in life. If this can be demonstrated in one art, there is reason to believe that it can also be demonstrated in others. Though people can appreciate the beauty of art without actually producing it, they might appreciate it more fully and deeply if they were trying to produce something at the same time.

For the most part, the arts which men have developed during the last few thousand years have been either visual or auditory, but we need to be reminded that we have other senses in addition to those of sight and sound. Perhaps there are unexplored possibilities in the experience of odor, which is relatively neglected. After all, odor stimulates our finest memories and gives some of our most intensive joys. While some odors are repulsive, others bring us close to ecstasy. Who, having once experienced it, can forget the aroma of the blossom of the wild azalea? To come upon it suddenly in the primeval forest, in the midst of summer, is to experience a new kind of joy, and to have in our experience a vivid illustration of what beauty is. In like manner, we probably underestimate the aesthetic potentialities of touch. A distinguished American, who has been blind from boyhood, has visited Greece and Egypt, to "see" the aesthetic monuments of the ancient world, and he sees them by using his fingertips. We understand something of the aesthetic possibility of touch when we give full attention, as we seldom do, to the joy of warm sunshine upon our flesh. We must, accordingly, beware of the danger of interpreting the aesthetic experience too narrowly.

Part of the task of philosophy in seeking to understand beauty is the examination of the conditions of aesthetic insight. Why do some see while others do not? How can more fruitful aesthetic fulfillment come in the life of the average person? There is a prodigal beauty in the world, but we can be sure that we have missed much of it utterly, because we have not learned to look in the right way. It has been the conclusion of more than one thoughtful student of the aesthetic experience that the prime condition for fulfillment is a certain kind of humility. Clive Bell's statement of this theme deserves careful attention:

And of one other thing am I sure. Be they artists or lovers of art, mystics or mathematicians, those who achieve ecstasy are those who have freed themselves from the arrogance of humanity. He who would feel the significance of art must make himself humble before it. Those who find the chief importance of art or of philosophy in its relation to conduct or its practical utility—those who cannot value things as ends in themselves or, at any rate, as direct means to emotion—will never get from anything the best that it can give.[22]

[22] Bell, op. cit., p. 55.

As Huxley taught us the best approach to truth comes when we sit down before the fact as a little child, and there is much reason to conclude that the same attitude is necessary in regard to beauty. The task is to be open-minded because we are truly humble, and then we have some chance of being rid of the prejudice which blinds us. It is no wonder, therefore, that we turn next to moral value. The step seems to be inevitable.

Chapter 12 ～ MORAL VALUES

If you want to swindle why do you want a moral sanction for doing it?
FYODOR DOSTOEVSKY

THE BEST THING WE KNOW IN THIS WORLD IS A REALLY GOOD PERSON.
A good person is manifestly higher in value than a lofty mountain
or a beautiful painting. But it is difficult to know precisely
wherein personal goodness consists, and it is still more difficult
to achieve such goodness in practice. The recognition of the preeminence of goodness, which is universal, requires that the nature
and conditions of goodness should become matters of careful
study. We do not expect, thereby, to be able to answer all moral
questions to the satisfaction of our neighbors, or even to our own
satisfaction, but there is much reason to believe that the study is
profitable in that it can set us free from many unnecessary confusions. In so far as we pursue this end we are concerned with
ethics, for ethics is the science of moral values. The philosopher
has a steadfast faith in the power of truth, relentlessly pursued,
to liberate men from moral confusion, provided they are willing to
inquire arduously and to subordinate their private interests and
opinions to what may be publicly intelligible knowledge.

Man's capacity for moral judgment follows logically from his
254

ability to view himself objectively, and apart from the rest of the world. This involves a certain detachment from the here and now and enables persons to view any act critically, whether it be the act of another or their own. Thus, man transcends the actual and asks what should have been as well as what ought to be. To say that man is generically ethical is not to say that he is good; it is to say that he is self-modifying. Man is always changing himself creatively by ethical reflection. Man is a creature who can be penitent and who can use his penitence to change future events, because a consideration of his total situation from an ethical point of view makes him decide to change. When men can formulate the ideal and judge the actual event by it, they are demonstrating the creative power of moral experience. One of the most distinguished of historical scholars has pointed to the crucial fact of the beginning of conscious character in the following sentence. "The marvel is that a creature rising out of animal savagery should have advanced to *begin* the great transformation at all, and it should give us little concern that in carrying on its further development man has at all times faltered, or even decidedly lost ground for a time."[1] The most significant fact about the human spirit, a fact which any man can verify in his own experience, is that man is inevitably restless because he is able to apprehend a perfection which he cannot achieve.

The study of ethics has attracted more careful attention than most subjects of inquiry, partly because it is so baffling and partly because it is manifestly so important. Since the production of Aristotle's *Nicomachean Ethics*, countless philosophers have followed in his path, each trying to make some significant addition to ethical knowledge. The result is that, though the problems remain different, some cumulative gains have been made and of these the contemporary student needs to be aware as he presses inquiries of his own.

The Possibility of Ethics

Though moral philosophy has long been an honored and serious endeavor, scientific in the sense of being carefully reasoned,

[1] J. H. Breasted, *The Dawn of Conscience*, Charles Scribner's Sons, 1934, p. 367.

there has fairly recently arisen a special philosophical school which denies the very possibility of ethics. The most extreme members of this school are the positivists, of whom Rudolf Carnap may be taken as representative. Any person who is seriously concerned with moral questions is advised to study Carnap's slashing attack on an intellectual enterprise which has been going on for more than two thousand years. The critical passage is the following:

The supposititious sentences of metaphysics, of the philosophy of values, of ethics (in so far as it is treated as a normative discipline and not as a psycho-sociological investigation of facts) are pseudo-sentences; they have no logical content, but are only expressions of feeling which in their turn stimulate feelings and volitional tendencies on the part of the hearer.[2]

This position, which Carnap owes in part to Ludwig Wittgenstein and to the Vienna Circle of the nineteen twenties, is intrinsic to all contemporary positivism and follows from the conviction that "scientific" sentences are the only sentences which have meaning. We must note that such a narrowing of intelligent discourse does not keep a man like Carnap from asserting that some men have performed acts which other men consider wrong. What he denies is the possibility of saying meaningfully that any act *is* wrong. He may note that, under Hitler, many Jews were exterminated, but the question whether this was right or wrong cannot even be discussed, for it is not, Carnap is bound to say, a "scientific" question.

What Carnap only infers, A. J. Ayer makes explicit. "The presence of an ethical symbol in a proposition," he says, "adds nothing to its factual content. Thus if I say to someone, 'You acted wrongly in stealing that money,' I am not stating anything more than if I had simply said, 'You stole that money,' in a peculiar tone of horror, or written it with the addition of some special exclamation marks."[3] The speaker can state an ethical proposition, says Ayer, with a tone of voice that reveals his feeling, but it is

[2] R. Carnap, *The Logical Syntax of Language*, The Humanities Press, Inc., 1951, p. 278.

[3] A. J. Ayer, *Language, Truth and Logic*, Dover Publications, Inc., 1953, p. 107.

not a genuine proposition, for it is neither true nor false and, indeed, does not say anything at all. "For in saying that a certain action is right or wrong, I am not making any factual statement," Ayer concludes, "not even a statement about my own state of mind." The same is true, this author claims, of all aesthetic judgments.

Though the positivist denial of the possibility of ethics is the most unequivocal attack which moral philosophy faces, other and not wholly different attacks are to be noted on other levels, such as that of behavioristic psychology. An extreme form of this attack is represented by Professor B. F. Skinner of Harvard University, who writes of "controlling agencies," but has practically nothing to say about the difference between acts which are only apparently good and those which are really good. We have some idea of the level of this discussion when Skinner deals with responsibility. "To say," he writes, "that a person is 'held responsible' for an act is simply to say that he is usually punished for it."[4] Most thinkers who have dealt with responsibility have held that a man is responsible even when he is not punished, or even when he does not act, for failure to act may have far-reaching consequences for good or evil. Most people suppose that a man like Eichmann was just as responsible before he was apprehended as afterwards, but strict behaviorism has no place for such sophisticated considerations. Indeed, the strict behaviorist cannot and will not discuss the question whether Eichmann was "guilty." All that he can report is that the man was apprehended, tried, and executed.

On wholly different grounds many contemporary psychiatrists tend to deny the possibility of rational discussion of strictly ethical questions. This is particularly true if the psychiatrist is a faithful follower of Freud, in his absolute determinism. If the patient did merely what he had to do, it is obviously idle to discuss whether he ought to have done it, since "ought" always involves an alternative possibility. Even the apparently noble stance in which a man admits that he has been wrong and deplores his act is necessarily seen as irrational. Why should a man denounce, either in himself or another, that which could not have been otherwise?

[4] B. F. Skinner, *Science and Human Behavior*, The Macmillan Company, 1959, p. 343.

That the denial of the very possibility of ethics has led to vigorous rejoinders on the part of philosophers is not surprising. Among the most vigorous of the counterattacks have been those of the late Morris Raphael Cohen and of Paul Weiss. One form which the counterattack takes is the effort to show that the very men who deny the possibility of ethics, themselves bring in ethical considerations surreptitiously or unconsciously. Psychoanalysis, for example, tends to claim a position of ethical neutrality, but the very drawing of a line between health and disease is a value-judgment and one which the therapist makes all of the time. The psychiatrist, like the surgeon, is in one sense a scientist, in that he studies a disease and develops a skill in dealing with it, but a distinction of great importance is added. The surgeon does not need to ask whether the inflammation of the appendix is genuine, but the psychiatrist is forced, constantly, to decide whether the sense of guilt is "real" or neurotic. Does the patient need psychotherapy for neurosis or does he need forgiveness for sin? A contemporary psychologist has stated the issue arising from the necessity of discrimination, as follows:

Making such discriminations obviously requires value judgments on the part of the therapist. What code of ethics is to be applied in arriving at such judgments? Shall he apply his ethical code or some other? Should he discard the patient's scale of values or abide by it? As long as he functions as a scientist, the psychiatrist can claim with validity to be ethically neutral, for science has no concern with values. When he begins to make value judgments, as he must in dealing with the complexities of human autonomy, the therapist forfeits a neutral status.[5]

Positivism does not escape judgments of value, but only hides them. Other terms, like "reinforcement," are substituted for standard ethical terms, but this is only self-delusion. Professor Skinner claims that he is writing merely as a scientific psychologist and without ethical judgments, but he is forced to evaluate contrasting experiments and admits that "in evaluating a particular cultural experiment we may, instead, ask whether that way of life

[5] O. S. Walters, "The Psychiatrist and Christian Faith," The Christian Century, July 20, 1960, p. 874.

makes for the most effective development of those who follow it."[6] Here is a glaring instance of trying to hide an ethical judgment, but doing it clumsily. What is the difference between "most effective development" and "best"? Writers on jurisprudence sometimes try to describe the law as it is and decisions as they have occurred with no reference to principles, but surreptitious ethical judgments are bound to enter. What, precisely, makes a law a law? Were the Aryan "laws" of Hitler really laws? M. R. Cohen, after analyzing such a revelation on the part of a leading French jurist, concludes:

The fact is that all people who pretend to be indifferent to considerations of right and wrong actually make judgments of right and wrong, implicitly if not avowedly, and these judgments are not better by reason of their failure to receive explicit critical examination—just as judgments of metaphysics are not sounder because they are unavowed. In short the fact is that we all do make judgments of value. As human beings we cannot avoid making such judgments. Is it not wiser to take the precaution to make these judgments as sound and as free of inconsistency as possible—as we do in all other fields of science?[7]

The supposition that we can handle all questions of conduct by the canons of chemistry or physics or biology will not stand under examination. Consider, for example, the question of selective breeding, which appears sometimes as a mere biological problem. The questions about fertility and inheritance are indeed *biological* questions, but the question of whether selective breeding is to be enforced is not a biological question. Who will decide which persons are to breed, and on what grounds? This is a problem with which Plato struggled as he wrote *The Republic*, but of course he faced it on avowedly moral grounds. Hermann J. Muller, Professor of Zoology at Indiana University, advocates controlling the genes of the population of the future by artificial insemination. Since Professor Muller is a Nobel prizewinner, his scientific data are assumed dependable, but that, anyone should be able to see,

---

[6] Skinner, op. cit., p. 445.
[7] M. R. Cohen, *A Preface to Logic*, The World Publishing Company, Meridian Books, Inc., 1959, p. 178. Reprinted by permission of Holt, Rinehart and Winston, Inc.

is not the end of the matter. On what grounds will he decide which genes we *ought* to breed out of the race?

It would be comfortable if we could fall back on natural selection and let it take its course, but this is what ethical man cannot do. He is bound to ask whether there is adequate ground for preferring one mode of survival over others. There are, in fact, several ways to survive, but Socrates set the stage for all subsequent moral discussion by showing that mere survival is not the primary question. Certainly we cannot settle for "naturalism" in the sense of following a natural course. "Anyone," said John Stuart Mill, at the close of his famous essay on Nature, "who endeavoured in his actions to imitate the natural course of things would be universally seen and acknowledged to be the wickedest of men." Man cannot be true to his own "nature" unless he tries to control the process in the effort to maximize value. "All human action, whatever," said Mill, "consists in altering, and all useful action in improving the spontaneous course of nature."

The best way for a philosopher to deal with the challenge of behaviorism is not by a defense of values, but by a frontal attack on behaviorism itself, which turns out to be surprisingly vulnerable. A striking example of such an attack is provided by Paul Weiss. He shows the alternatives which are open to the behaviorist, analyzes them, and shows the inadequacy or inconsistency of each. The essence of the attack, in the following paragraph, is really a reductio ad absurdum.

A purely behavioral account of man views all his acts as equally valuable, important, ultimate, good, interesting. It may note, but then without comment, that some take longer, that some are more familiar, that some have a wider scope, but it has no reason for selecting any one as being superior to the others. It is therefore unable to distinguish insane from sane men, the more perceptive or appreciative from the less, the perverted from the confused, except as men who, in different ways, behave as the rest do not and are rewarded accordingly. It has no right to say that one man had a better character than others; it cannot rightly condemn any act as wrong or mistaken. Criticism, reform, punishment, remorse, rewards, and education are for it arbitrary ways of making men change their behavior from one mode to another no less legitimate. A purely scientific theory which accepts all human activity without prejudgment or evaluation cannot cover all the facts. It has no place in its scheme for truth or right. Yet it claims to be true and requires other views to be false. Evidently it demands a dispensation for itself which it cavalierly refuses to any other view.[8]

Here is an example of what careful philosophical reasoning can do. It brings out implications which are often unnoticed by those who find the system in question superficially attractive. These implications are so serious and the inner contradiction of the system so glaring that the claim which it makes for the impossibility of ethics may be dismissed.

The Case for Objectivity

In the climate of opinion in which we live, particularly in colleges and universities, one of the most popular of all positions is that of ethical relativism. The usual argument runs somewhat as follows. There are many different cultures and civilizations in the world. Each of these has its own orthodoxy about human values, but they are in sharp conflict with one another. Hindus think it is immoral to eat meat or to kill a cow, while Westerners produce cows with the single purpose of killing and eating them. Each group thinks its position is right; therefore, moral values are merely relative to a cultural setting; therefore, moral values are purely subjective; therefore, one is exactly as good as another, for all are lodged merely in human minds and have nothing to do with objective reality.

Anyone who has not heard this argument many times has not been awake. It is often presented as a kind of revelation by those who have had a course in sociology in which they have discovered, for the first time, that there are people who do not see things in exactly the same way as we see them. How anyone could have postponed this rather obvious discovery so long is hard to understand, but apparently such delay is possible. Since the argument is so familiar, it needs no further statement, the task of the philosopher being to examine its logical structure. Perhaps there is more in the conclusion than the premises warrant.[9]

[8] P. Weiss, *Man's Freedom*, Yale University Press, 1950, p. 9.

[9] One of the most fair statements of the popular relativism, together with a careful critique from the point of view of a psychologist, is that of S. E. Asch, *Social Psychology*, Prentice-Hall, Inc., 1952, chap. 13.

Now there is no doubt that men differ in their judgment of what they ought to do, precisely as they differ about what is beautiful. Education plays an obvious part in moral judgment. The variety of judgment may not be as great as the popular form of the argument declares, but variety there certainly is. The difficulty lies, not, therefore, in the datum, but perhaps in the inferences which are drawn from it. The conclusion that, because moral judgments are in part relative to culture, there is no real right, is by no means the only possible inference. It is quite as logical to hold, as most philosophers have done, that the variety merely shows that the real right is very difficult to ascertain with certainty, and that some people differ from others because some are more perceptive than others.

Not only does this alternative inference follow with equal logic; it is exactly parallel to what we find in regard to the physical order. Our ancestors were not aware of the existence of Neptune, and we are, but this would hardly lead anyone to adopt the absurd conclusion that there is no objective truth about the distant planet. There may be millions of people living today who are unaware of Neptune's existence or who would even deny it, but this is a trivial consideration, because it is easy to see that they do not have the means of awareness. We have no hesitation whatever in saying that relativity concerns the ability to perceive, or that the variety is wholly compatible with an objective order which is, whether it is known or not. Thus, in the study of astronomy, we are thoroughly familiar with a knowing situation which involves both relativism and objectivism.

Suppose that, in the science of conduct which we call ethics, we deny that there is any objective moral order, comparable to the physical order. This would lead, inevitably, to the implication of ethical *nihilism*, i.e., that there is no moral truth at all. If, when we say Hitler did wrong to try to exterminate the Jews of Germany, we have nothing but a subjective reference, we are saying nothing at all about his act. As the positivists claim, ethical propositions are not genuine propositions for they cannot, on this basis, be either true or false. One result of this position is that no two people have ever really argued or even differed on a moral question. If John says, "I don't like carrots," while Paul says, "I like carrots," the boys are not arguing at all, for each is telling about his own subjectivity and probably each is telling the truth. *The statements are not in conflict because they do not have any common ground.* The only way in which they could have a common ground would be for a moral order to be a reality.

There is no doubt that men quarrel and that they quarrel about what is right. In fact, they quarrel about this more than about any other subject. Listen, for example, to a vivid quarrel about the recognition of Communist China, in which both parties, even when one is an ethical relativist, appeal ultimately to some moral law. Each says, "We ought, because . . ." It is important to realize that quarreling means, not trying to show that the other man fails to agree with you, which is too obvious to bother about, but rather that the other man is wrong.

A conclusion which makes nonsense out of something which all men do, and which they do even in their most thoughtful and self-critical moods, is one which is terribly suspect. And subjective relativism is precisely such a conclusion. Taken seriously, it denies not only the fact that men differ; it denies also the fact of moral progress. Once the slave trade was rampant, with as many as fifteen million persons exported for sale from the Congo, while now the slave trade is practically extinct. Most men believe that this represents progress, but, on the basis of subjectivism, it cannot be. Unless there is an objective moral order, in terms of which this change is to be measured, it is mere change. It is not progress unless there is a moral standard which we are approaching. But no thoughtful person will accept the notion that progress is impossible, no matter how vociferously he denies an objective right. Even the behaviorist believes that behaviorism represents progress.

The strongest arguments for ethical objectivity are not empirical, but always dialectical. When we face these carefully, noting that subjective relativism can be reduced to absurdity, we are driven to believe in an existent moral order, even though our understanding of it in any one period or in any one culture may be dim indeed. There is probably no one in our century who has presented this dialectical argument more brilliantly than has C. S. Lewis, of Oxford. "It seems, then," he says, "that we are forced to believe in a real Right and Wrong. People may be sometimes mistaken about them, just as people sometimes get their sums wrong; but they are not a matter of mere taste and opinion any more than the multiplication table."[10]

What, then, do we mean by an objective moral order? We mean that reality in reference to which a person is wrong when he makes a false moral choice, either in his own conduct or in the judgment of another. The conclusion that there is such an order, which the dialectic requires, is not the same as knowing precisely or even approximately, what the nature of the moral requirement is. Sometimes the philosopher is challenged to show what is right, beyond a shadow of doubt, and, if he cannot do so, the subjectivist critic declares triumphantly that this shows the nonexistence of the moral order. But this conclusion does not follow. We can know *that* it is before we know *what* it is. It may take a very long time before we know what is right in any concrete situation, because all of us are in the finite predicament and can never be sure that we are seeing the situation truly, but that is no reason for failing to come as close to the truth as possible. We do not know what is right about seating mainland China in the Security Council of the United Nations, and we argue vociferously about it, but there must be a right answer, if only we could know it. If there is not a right answer, our arguments are pathetic indeed, for they are then wholly pointless. What we all believe is that the very argument will help us to see the nature of the right, because the conflict brings out aspects which might not otherwise be recognized.

When men differ about moral standards, it does not mean that they should give up the struggle to learn what they ought to do. Instead it means that they must go on thinking and learning from one another, for, if there is a real right, all are far from it now. It is superficial to say that, concerning the sacredness of the cow, the Hindu feels one way and the western man feels another way, and leave the matter there. Perhaps the characteristic citizen of India will change his view in time, and perhaps the Westerner will change his. In any case, the matter should be argued as dispassionately as possible, with special reference to the effect on

[10] C. S. Lewis, *Mere Christianity*, The Macmillan Company, 1960, p. 6.

persons. If the protection of all cows harms human beings by reducing the food supply, this is a relevant consideration in trying to discover what the moral truth is.

As in considering beauty and truth, so, in considering the good, we are helped by the negative approach. We may have more nearly unanimous agreement on what is wrong than we can have on what is right. Thus, nearly everyone agrees that slavery is wrong now, and that it was wrong when it was widely condoned. But if there is something really wrong, then there must be a right which is missing. We can be more sure of error than of anything else, and this includes moral error. *The objective right is the bull's eye which moral error misses.*

When we speak of the moral law, as we must, we need to be aware that the object of our attention, though comparable to natural law, is not identical with it. In so far as we are physical beings we are all subject to natural law, such as the law of falling bodies. Human bodies fall from cliffs just as stones do. In the same way we are subject to various biological laws just as the animals are. The point to note about these laws is that we cannot disobey them, whereas the moral law is something which we can disobey. But a law which we can disobey is just as objective and real as a law which we cannot disobey. Neither one is anything which we can see or weigh or measure, but we are driven to believe in such realities by the power of rational thought. If there is no moral law, i.e., no ordered complex of obligations, there would be no sense in valuing St. Francis more highly than Nero.

Objective Relativism

While the case for ethical objectivity is a strong one, it must be recognized that relativism has a point. Some relativism is vicious and some is not. Morris Raphael Cohen refers to the vicious relativism which, by denying all universal principles and objective truths, would imprison each of us in an isolated subjective world.[11] But there is another relativism which is primarily a revulsion against an abstract absolutism, more concerned with inflexible rules than with changing circumstances. Much of the absolutism

[11] Cohen, op. cit., pp. 190, 191.

which the relativist rightly opposes is expressed by one side of the philosophy of Immanuel Kant. Kant held that the moral law is not only objective, but that it is absolute and inflexible in its demands. The most celebrated illustration of one of those demands is Kant's insistence that it is wrong everywhere and in all situations to tell a lie.

Kant believed that, in the moral order, reason could legislate without considering the historical context in which moral subjects have to act in concrete situations. The present philosophical position which rejects entirely this aspect of Kantianism is well represented by the contemporary French philosopher Gabriel Marcel. "What I want to stress, moreover," writes Marcel, "is not that it may be possible to introduce at this point a relativism which would, eventually tend to annul, to annihilate the affirmations of the moral conscience, but rather that the qualities proper to those affirmations and the way in which they should actually be considered, cannot be taken as independent of the concrete context which is their setting."[12]

There is a great revulsion against formal inflexibility, not primarily because of a denial of any objective order, but rather because there is a serious doubt that such a position reflects that order truly adequately. Consider the consequences of telling the truth in every circumstance. Suppose you are in a totalitarian country, in which a man of high principles and courage has been imprisoned. You happen to see him escaping down a certain street and soon afterward you notice that the prison guards are looking for him. You are reasonably certain that if he is caught and returned to prison, he will be tortured. You are asked whether you saw him go down the street, your only possible answers being Yes or No. What then, in this particular situation, is your moral duty? The people who doubt the validity of Kant's well-known answer are not doubting it because they fail to believe that something is right, but because they believe that Kant is wrong in his estimation of what is right. Maybe something in the world is more precious than abstract honesty. Perhaps concern for the welfare of a man or of men is a higher standard.

[12] G. Marcel, The Mystery of Being, Henry Regnery Company, 1951, Pt. II, pp. 93, 94.

The person who would lie to the police to save the prisoner from torture, because he believes that this is the best of all alternatives in that particular situation, is what we may call, in ethics, an "objective relativist." The correct moral choice, he believes, may differ from time to time and from place to place, not because values have subjective reference, but because the locus of every moral decision is always the concrete situation rather than some formal abstraction. A man's duty, then, is always his duty in the here and the now, and this depends upon the total context. *The object of the moral judgment is always the particular act.* The question whether to recognize a government cannot be settled in general, for there are conditions under which a government ought to be recognized and there are conditions under which it ought not to be recognized. Like the historical event, the right is always particular, though general principles, of various kinds, may be brought to bear on the decision. What is right, then, is the best possible alternative under the circumstances.

The more we examine such objective relativism, which is sometimes called "contextual ethics," the stronger its appeal is. Is monogamy always the absolute rule of right? If the fantastic situation should arise in which the only survivors of a holocaust were several women and one man, that man's espousal of monogamy, far from being a virtue, would be demonstrably evil. We usually suppose that the early Mormons in Utah were wrong in practicing polygamy, but, when we examine the situation and recognize the conditions, especially the presence of more women than men, we are not so sure of our doctrinaire position. It is recognized, of course, that the conviction that the moral situation differs when circumstances differ is, in some ways, dangerous, but the recognition of danger does not end a discussion. We are trying to see what the truth is. Life might be simple if there were inflexible rules which were to be discovered and followed, but ours does not seem to be that kind of world.

What looks, on the surface, like something entirely absurd in another culture, may turn out to be, under more careful examination, rationally defensible. History, says the Spanish philosopher Ortega, on showing the variability of human opinions, "seems to condemn us to relativism, but as it gives full meaning to each relative position that man takes, and reveals to us the eternal truth which every period has lived, it overcomes whatever there is in relativism that is incompatible with faith in man's extra-relative and, as it were, eternal destiny. For very concrete reasons, I hope that in our age the curiosity about the eternal and invariable which is philosophy and the curiosity about the inconstant and changing which is history may come together and embrace."[13]

The "best" in any concrete situation is identical with the "least evil." There is a certain evil in all lying, because it tends to break down the basis of trustworthiness, and there is evil in returning a good man to unjust imprisonment. The good man must weigh these as best he can, and the lesser evil is his duty, because *the only alternative is worse.* Often in such a situation, we wish we could avoid the cruel choice, but we cannot, for we are faced with what William James called a forced option. The very failure to decide is itself a decision and perhaps a decision for the worse of the only alternatives. The man who refuses to decide is not thereby freed from responsibility, but is obviously culpable. We are just as responsible for the evil we allow as for the evil we commit.

How are we to know, in a complex situation, what action is right, if we do not have some abstract rule on which to rely? Through the centuries, many moralists have considered this question with the general result that we see that we must rely primarily upon the *prediction of consequences.* Everyone knows that there are evil motives in human experience, but it is absurd to say that the evil of the tyrant lies wholly in his state of mind, rather than in the actual effect on suffering men and women. The greatest evil of the concentration camp lies in what it does to the inmates, though it may also harm the guards. Miss Stebbing has approached this matter with her usual clarity in showing what the locus of evil is. "I do not see," she says, "how there can be sin unless something other than the sinning is also evil. If I, an owner of a factory, taking advantage of certain economic conditions, force you to live in a slum, to work monotonously for long hours, and thus be deprived of the ability to develop as befits a

---

[13] J. Ortega y Gasset, *What is Philosophy?*, trans. Mildred Adams, W. W. Norton & Company, Inc., 1960, p. 27.

human being, then I harm you by creating for you conditions that are utterly unspiritual. I do you spiritual evil; since I am responsible for creating this evil, I thereby sin."[14]

Principles may help, but principles are always formal and what we need is something concrete. It is not enough, for example, to say that we must be loving. The principle of love may help me slightly when I am approached by the confirmed alcoholic and asked for money, but the principle alone is certainly not sufficient. Which of my possible acts is the loving one? If I give the drunk money, he may go to the bar and if I do not give him money, I may condemn him to hunger. Of course, I try to take a third way, but this, whatever it may be, is inevitably based upon some calculation of what the probable consequences of each possible action are. Love may provide the major premise, but the minor premise cannot be discovered except by a calculation of the direction in which each possible alternative is likely to lead.

A highly practical illustration of the necessity of such ethical thinking is the problem of maintaining Western forces in Berlin. There may be a few persons who are so fixed in their belief that all armed defense is wrong that they favor pulling out American and other defense forces from West Berlin now, but most people, no matter how much they hate war and preparation for war, would hesitate to make this choice, in view of the practically certain human consequences so far as West Berliners are concerned. Anyone who has been in West Berlin recently knows how terribly the citizens fear exactly such a departure.

Now the important point for the moral philosopher to make here is that a person cannot honorably make a choice without accepting, at the same time, whatever the choice may entail. There are people who say that they will do right regardless of the consequences, for which they are not responsible. It is difficult to see that such a statement, though it is often heard, means anything at all. Wherein does the rightness or the wrongness of an act lie, if not in what it does to people? It is easy to see why some people, including some philosophers, are in favor of unilateral disarmament—they believe that balanced armament strength leads to

[14] L. Susan Stebbing, *Ideals and Illusion*, C. A. Watts & Co., Ltd., 1943, p. 35.

conflict; but should those very people be convinced that unilateral disarmament would itself lead to war, then, if they are to be consistent, they would have to change their position. In short, the difference between the upholder of unilateral disarmament and his intellectual opponent is not a moral difference, but a factual difference of what the probable consequences would be. There is, of course, the man who says "I just have to do it! I don't know why," but such a person is not engaging in moral philosophy at all, and may in fact be very dangerous. Ethics is impossible unless it is brought within the universe of rational discourse.

The chief reason why it is not sufficient to say that we must act on principle, and neglect other considerations, is not that principles are nonexistent, but that they are *too numerous*. In almost every difficult decision there are several principles—some of them are in mutual conflict. Should we, for example, send surplus food to mainland China? One relevant principle is that of the duty of feeding the hungry, including those who hate us. But there are others which are likewise relevant. What shall we say of the principle that we ought not to bolster an oppressive regime and thus make liberation of the oppressed more difficult or practically impossible? We are always guilty of oversimplification when we stress only one of several relevant principles.

It is precisely because principles are so numerous that moral decisions are extremely difficult. Consider the physician, who is hurrying to the bedside of a patient who has had a heart attack and needs oxygen treatment. On the way the doctor encounters an automobile wreck in which people will die unless they have immediate treatment. What should he do? It is not enough to tell him to be loving, or to be just, or to do his duty! The question of what his duty is, is the point at issue. He must choose the most desirable of the available imperfections, and that is never easy. The fact that most of our decisions are not as obviously dramatic as that of the physician does not keep them from exhibiting the same fundamental pattern.

One of the most vivid illustrations of the nature of moral decisions is that provided by the choice before President Truman in the summer of 1945, when he knew that the atomic bomb could be used. He believes that its use was justified, grim as its consequences were, because he thinks that the alternative consequences of a much extended war would have been worse. General MacArthur, on the other hand, thinks it was not needed to end the war, but President Truman, we must remember, had to go on the basis of the evidence then available to him. This is a tragic example of the nature of all moral decisions, in that it must always be made before all of the evidence is available. It must be made in the midst of life and not in some speculative haven. We are often wrong, but moral decision in the light of the known context is the very stuff of man as man. It is imperfect, but it is the essence of the life we prize. One result of such an understanding of the moral situation is that it keeps us humble.

Happiness

It is well known that the first known human attempt to make ethics into a science, is deeply concerned with happiness. Aristotle dealt, not with what men ought to do, but rather with the nature of the good life and the rules of wisdom for its attainment. He saw that it is characteristic of human action that it points to an end, and this end, as he defined it, we usually translate by the English word *happiness*. Though the idea is a sound one, in that it can be defended with cogency, it requires analysis if the inherent ambiguity is to be avoided.

On the surface, the claim that men seek happiness as an end appears to deny really moral values rather than to uphold them. It appears to say that each person is self-centered and that this is the sum total of the truth on the subject. Some philosophers have, by their writings, given the superficial reader the impression that the emphasis on happiness, usually called hedonism, is incompatible with any ascription of reality to responsibility or a sense of oughtness. John Stuart Mill was responsible for some of this effect in his famous thesis that "desiring a thing and finding it pleasant are but different names for the same fact."

We begin to understand something of the ambiguity of happiness when we confront the "hedonistic paradox." This paradox, long acknowledged by philosophers, is the observation that the surest way to miss happiness is to seek it directly. When happiness comes to a person, it usually comes as a by-product rather than as something at which the individual directly and expressly aims. Often the most unhappy people in the world are those who are trying in a hectic manner to find happiness, going from resort to resort for recreation, for example, while the happiest people are those who never give happiness a thought. Such persons, the happiest ones, are usually engaged in work which seems to them of enduring value, and they give themselves to the task at hand with no ulterior motives. In short, it is part of the wisdom of the ages that the best way to get happiness is to forget it.

One of the most important sections of Aristotle's famous ethical treatise is that in which he shows what the conditions of happiness are, and he shows that they are similar to those just mentioned. The greatest happiness, he says, comes from production, when this means finding a task to perform which seems truly worthwhile, and trying to perform it with excellence. Man is made to make! The highest form of such production, he asserts, is that of contemplation, the creation of new thoughts. It is obvious that the great man was, in this instance, reflecting his own experience. The production of so many ideas, forming the basis of a number of our present sciences, must have been extremely arduous work, but Aristotle has found a way of telling us that it brought him very great personal happiness.

As soon as we consider the hedonistic paradox, we know that the problem of happiness is not a simple one and that it cannot rightly be identified with what is ordinarily called pleasure. Whatever else is problematic, it is reasonably certain that the truly good life does not come by self-indulgence or by any conscious concern for the self. Many of us can testify that the best and happiest hours of our lives have been those in which we have been engaged in some task, perhaps a mental one, which has been so demanding that we have not had a moment to think of ourselves, of our reactions, or the question whether we are happy. Later, however, as we have faced the experience in retrospect, we have tended to realize that the happiness of such moments has been very great.

Much confusion has arisen in the study of moral values by what is called "psychological hedonism." The popular inference of this term is to the effect that every act is the result of a personal desire, that this desire is for happiness, and that all human actions are therefore self-centered. Almost everyone has heard some variant of this doctrine and sometimes it seems hard to answer, though the listener senses that there is a fallacy. The fallacy lies in the fact that all that is presented is a tautology. It merely says that we want what we want, of which there is no doubt. What the statement fails to include is the known fact that what we want often refers to the welfare of others or to the achievement of ends which far transcend our own lives. It is easy to show, of course, that whatever a man does is the result of his desire, for, if he does not desire it, he will choose some alternative. In this sense the martyr goes to the stake because he desires to do so, for usually he can escape the violent pain of burning by recantation. To say this is not to say much—merely that we desire what we desire. The point to note is that our desires are extremely varied, and, for the most part, our desires are in competition with one another. The martyr, of course, desires surcease from pain, but he also desires integrity, and he may desire recognition after his death when he is not present to enjoy it.[15] There are, in the average life, both self-sacrifice and self-realization. The world is not in the least tidy or simple or unitary, and human beings are many-sided creatures. The simple answer is always wrong.

Among the men who have seen clearly the fallacy of psychological hedonism are the intellectual giants of the eighteenth century, especially Samuel Johnson and Bishop Butler. "The first motives of human actions," wrote Johnson, in *The Rambler* for September 4, 1750, "are those appetites which Providence has given to man in common with the rest of the inhabitants of the earth. . . . But as the soul advances to a fuller exercise of its powers, the animal appetites and the passions immediately arising from them, are not sufficient to find it employment." As a person grows he comes to have other desires than those of his animal nature or even of his childhood, desires connected with pride, with approbation, with the praise of peoples yet unborn, and even

---

[15] "The Desires of the Self-Conscious Animal," is an essay by A. O. Lovejoy precisely on this theme. See *Reflections on Human Nature*, The Johns Hopkins Press, 1961, Lecture 3.

with the quality which Adam Smith called "praiseworthiness."

The other great eighteenth-century thinker who detected the fallacy in the popular version of psychological hedonism, was Bishop Joseph Butler. Butler's major contribution was a careful distinction between the subject and the object of desires. He recognized, of course, that a man is always the subject of his desires, in that he is the person who does the desiring, but he was able to show convincingly that the objects of desire may be multifarious. It is possible, he pointed out, for a man to desire the welfare of another and to desire it so truly that he does not envisage, necessarily, his own participation in the promotion of that welfare. Can I, a thoughtful person must ask, ever desire the joy of another even when I am not auxiliary to it? The clear answer is that I can. Some philanthropy may be self-centered in the sense that the giving makes the donor feel big or generous, but there is desire which is purely objective, in that the donor does not think of himself at all. This may indeed be rare, but if it ever occurs, the universal indictment implicit in the popular form of psychological hedonism is not justified.

Charles S. Peirce gave his attention to the problem of happiness, as he did to almost all important problems, and came up with the realization that, among competing desires, we must distinguish levels. "The Will is Free," said Peirce, "only in the sense that, by employing the proper appliances, he [a man] can make himself behave in the way he really desires to behave."[16] Thus he connects freedom with the concept of levels of desire, and insists that the price of freedom to follow our deepest, instead of our most superficial desires, is the proper discipline. If a man becomes really disciplined, thought Peirce, he can subject his desire for individual pleasures to a desire for some end for mankind.

The fundamental mistake of hedonism is the mistake which G. E. Moore has termed "the naturalistic fallacy"—the fallacy to which many philosophers have succumbed, in supposing that they were defining "good" when they were only "discovering what are those other properties belonging to all things which are good." That the good happens to be pleasurable does not necessarily

[16] C. S. Peirce, *Values in a Universe of Chance*, Stanford University Press, 1958, p. 415.

mean that goodness is to be defined as pleasure. Pleasure may be a good, but this is by no means the same as saying that it is identical with good. We ought to be aware of this danger in the light of the known systematic ambiguity of the verb to be, but many have missed it. Moore held that good is intrinsically indefinable and said that, so far as he knew, there was only one previous ethical writer, Henry Sidgwick, who had recognized and stated this fact. We are driven to the indefinable character of good when we become fully aware of the naturalistic fallacy.

Moore makes his point clear by the analogous treatment of sensory characteristics.

When we say that an orange is yellow, we do not think our statement binds us to hold that "orange" means nothing else than "yellow," or that nothing can be yellow but an orange. Supposing the orange is also sweet! Does that bind us to say that "sweet" is exactly the same thing as "yellow," that "sweet" must be defined as "yellow"? And supposing it be recognized that "yellow" just means "yellow" and nothing else whatever, does that make it any more difficult to hold that oranges are yellow? Most certainly it does not; on the contrary it would be absolutely meaningless to say that oranges were yellow, unless yellow did in the end mean just "yellow" and nothing else whatever—unless it was absolutely indefinable.[17]

To recognize that good is indefinable, that it represents a point at which the road stops, is to make a very great advance. We can then discuss it intelligently, but we cannot reduce it to something more basic than itself. When we ask whether pleasure is a good we are not asking the tautologous question whether pleasure is pleasant. Whenever, says Moore, a person "thinks of 'intrinsic value,' or 'intrinsic worth,' or says that a thing 'ought to exist,' he has before his mind the unique object—the unique property of things—which I mean by good."

One of the chief ambiguities of the desire for happiness concerns the proper dating of the desire. A. O. Lovejoy dealt with this carefully in his writings, showing that, in most philosophical literature, it has been assumed that choice is controlled by "pre-

[17] This discussion appears in chap. 1 of Moore's Principia Ethica, Cambridge University Press, 1903. It has had a wide and profound influence among professional philosophers.

conceived future pleasurableness." He shows convincingly, by contrast, that the crucial factor in choice is "the present valued-ness of the idea, not the anticipated future value of the state-of-things."[18] We are concerned, of course, with the future, but we are concerned now, and it is now that the choice is made. It is the present pleasure of imagining future public recognition which is effective for the man who is at the moment maligned or un-popular. Only in the light of this is concern for posthumous repu-tation reasonable.

The emphasis on the present explains the effectiveness of final causes, in Aristotle's sense of the term. Lovejoy's conclusion is that, though final causes certainly have much to do with human action, "they can be seriously supposed to determine it only when they are translated into the present tense."[19] Desires are operative now, but they are of many kinds and they can be present desires regarding future events. They are always our own, but they can have reference to what is not our own.

Most of the confusion about happiness is dispelled if we recog-nize that happiness is not an end, correlative with truth, beauty, and goodness, and thus something to be chosen, instead of them. There are, by common consent, ultimate or terminal values, and these are always being denied if they are chosen because of any-thing else than themselves, even happiness. "If," says Clutton-Brock, "I aim at goodness so that I may profit by it, it is no longer goodness that I aim at, but profit. I may do what is right, but I do it for the sake of something else which I value more than doing what is right."[20] Happiness is not to be chosen instead of goodness, but it is a character of experiences which come when we are aware of, or even dimly glimpse, what are seen as ultimate values, whether of truth or beauty or goodness, and when we have some consciousness of fulfilling our duty concerning them. *Happi-ness is not another value, but something attached to values.*

Few, in our time, have seen so clearly the significance of the

[18] Lovejoy, *op. cit.*, p. 79.
[19] *Ibid.*, p. 74.
[20] A. Clutton-Brock, *The Ultimate Belief*, Constable & Co., Ltd., 1916, pp. 20, 21. The small book, which has been much neglected, presents one of the clearest statements in all philosophical literature of the contrast between ter-minal and instrumental values.

distinction just made as has Susan Stebbing. "Happiness," she says trenchantly, "is not an end to pursue; it is a sign, perhaps, that something worth while is being pursued, a characteristic of a state in which a human being's capacities are being fulfilled."[21]

Happiness is important, but happiness is not ultimate. Sometimes we ought to forego our own happiness, in the light of a larger end; in any case we should be unconcerned with it. Some of the things which make us happy are intrinsically evil. Some things ought to be done, even though we do not want to do them, and to miss this is to miss the whole point of the science of ethics. "Some of us," says Miss Stebbing, "find we are happy in managing a great business with a ruthless disregard of the welfare of those affected by our activities; others find themselves happy in dominating other human beings to their hurt."[22] One of the chief ways in which life can advance in excellence is by a radical change in regard to what makes us happy.

The Categorical Imperative

Once we recognize that moral choice is seldom simple and that it is always the concrete act that is the object of moral judgment, we have dispelled much confusion, but we still need to know how, in a concrete situation, we are to decide. Should we or should we not, for example, have contributed to the ransom fund paid to Castro as the price of liberation of the men who participated in the ill-starred invasion of Cuba at the Bay of Pigs? The choice was a clear one—to contribute or not to contribute. We are not talking about ransom in general, which is an abstraction, but about this particular ransom of these particular men at this particular time, in the light of all of the probable consequences. Clearly more than one principle is involved and the principles may be in direct conflict. How, then, were we to decide? We cannot decide in regard to this or any other concrete problem unless we act in the light of principles which seem applicable to the situation. The rightness or wrongness is particular if objective relativism is sound, as it seems to be, but we cannot settle for ethical atomism, be-

---

[21] Stebbing, op. cit., p. 76.
[22] Ibid., p. 78.

cause in that case there would be no reason for preference of one solution over another.

Here is a genuine ethical dilemma. Propositions such as "We must never pay ransom" are particularly unhelpful, since there may be exceptional cases when the reasons for paying ransom would overbalance our ethical repugnance to this act, but, unless there are some values to which we can appeal, we can give no reason at all, and then we merely toss a coin. Part of our decision rests upon knowledge—and we must agree with Whitehead that, where attainable knowledge would change the issue, ignorance is vice—but something more than knowledge is required. Even if we know that the prisoners are dying, that item of knowledge does not, of itself, settle the issue.

This is why the efforts to discover some universal law of right conduct have attracted so much attention. Among the most famous are the two formulations made by Immanuel Kant, of what he called "the categorical imperative." Kant understood the consciousness of morality as the consciousness of existing under an august obligation. What is required of me as a moral being, by virtue of my very being? Is there some inner command which transcends the merely conditional? Kant realized, of course, that most commands are conditional. If I propose to pass the bar examination I must do such and such legal work, but perhaps it is not my purpose to pass the bar; in that case the command does not apply. Is there, anywhere in experience, the unconditional imperative? Kant thought there was and he formulated it in two ways. The first formulation is the requirement that a man, as a moral being, be willing to universalize his act, i.e., that he not make an exception of himself. "So act," said Kant, "that thy maxim can be a universal maxim." This is really the logician speaking, asserting the principle of consistency. To require of others a standard which I am not willing to require of myself is to be guilty of a deep moral inconsistency; it is to break the rule of noncontradiction. The second Kantian formula is to the effect that we must treat each person, whether ourselves or others, as ends and never as mere means. This follows from the first formulation, as a kind of corollary, because each of us does desire for himself that he be treated as an end and not a mere cog in some other machine.

These formulations have often been criticized because of their formal nature, but it is difficult to see how they could be otherwise than formal if they purport to be universal. It may be freely admitted that such statements are not capable of producing ready-made solutions for hard moral problems. The question of application is always difficult and usually controversial. I must treat the imprisoned Cuban invaders as ends, but I must also treat as ends the ordinary Cuban citizens who may conceivably be hurt by any action which renders the present regime more durable, either in power, money, or prestige. I must not make an exception of myself, but as a matter of fact I may reduce to almost zero the class in which I am willing to universalize my act. I believe in traffic rules, but I may be willing to state my maxim as follows: "All men who have been held up by traffic and are rushing to catch a plane in order to fulfill a speaking engagement in a distant city, should exceed the speed limit."

Though the Kantian forms are open to abuse, and though they do not automatically solve problems, there is no doubt that they *help*. They become relevant considerations, along with others, in trying to see what, in a concrete situation, we ought to do, but they are even more helpful, negatively, in knowing what is wrong. If a man says, "I demand freedom of action on your principles and I deny you freedom of action on my principles," it is easy to see the great inconsistency. But even in positive matters we are actually helped, and sometimes we alter our intended decision. When I ask, "Am I making an exception of myself?" or "Am I treating this man as an end or do I see him as having only instrumental value for me?" I am less likely to make a rash decision.

As we continue the effort to philosophize about matters that are important, we must continue to search for principles which are relevant to as many different situations as possible. In short, we are always seeking for a more and more useful statement of the Golden Rule. We must, in trying to treat our neighbor as ourselves, not merely ask what he wants, for his wants may be perverted. We must not even be satisfied with asking what we would want, in his place, for our wants may be inadequate also. We must ask what we would want for him if we were perfectly loving and if we could know all of the consequences to follow from an intended act. These, of course, are impossible conditions, but they are not, for that reason, meaningless. Much of the glory of human life lies in the practical relevance of unattainable ideals. We do not achieve them, but they provide a beneficent disturbance and they indicate a standard in the light of which we can see that what we do is wrong.

No thinker of our century has worked more thoughtfully on the question of what the ultimate moral imperatives are than William Temple, who became the Archbishop of Canterbury, as his father did before him, but who was also an extremely percipient philosopher. He was deeply influenced by F. H. Bradley's essay "My Station and Its Duties,"[23] with its insistence on the conviction that, if I really know who I am, I know in greater measure what I ought to do. This is because what I am is determined by relations, and relations involve responsibilities. Thus the duty of the married man with children is not the same, in many areas, as the duty of the bachelor. Now the paramount fact about any man is that he is a person. Personality, as represented by himself and his fellow men, is the most precious reality which has emerged in the evolutionary process. Here, then, is a clue. Because we are persons we must treat others as persons. This will not solve all problems, but it serves as an efficacious negative factor, prohibiting many actions which might otherwise be adopted because they give us happiness. The student who wishes to understand Temple's profound principle must read and reread many parts of his Gifford Lectures, Nature, Man and God, but the vital passage is as follows:

The principle of morality is that we should behave as Persons who are members of a Society of Persons—a Society into which Personality is itself a valid claim of entrance. We are to treat all Persons as Persons, and as fellow members with us in the Society of Persons. Actual duties will depend upon actual personal relationship; there is a special duty of parent to child and child to parent; there is a special relation-

[23] Printed in Ethical Studies, The Liberal Arts Press, Inc., 1951, pp. 98–147.

ship between citizens of any one nation. . . . A man cannot do much to serve humanity as a whole directly; he must give his service to his own unit; but he can check the narrower loyalty by the wider, so that he will serve his family, but not at cost to his country, and will serve his country, but not at cost to mankind.[24]

It will occur to the thoughtful student that here, in Temple's reformulation of the categorical imperative, we are very close to what Josiah Royce meant by the "philosophy of loyalty." In any case we have moved a long way from simple self-centeredness, which, according to Royce and many others, is a denial of what it means to be a person. It is, as one of Royce's best contemporary interpreters has said, "to play with words to teach that the duty of the individual is to be himself, or rather, it is to be deceived by an abstraction. The individual is himself only by virtue of subordinating himself to willed purposes, by serving a cause."[25] The concrete order of society is, such philosophy teaches, "the only means of self-realization which can be granted to the individual." Thus the acceptance of the dialectic leads to the question of the social order, which is, accordingly, the subject of the next chapter.

[24] W. Temple, Nature, Man and God, The Macmillan Company, 1956, pp. 191, 192.
[25] G. Marcel, Royce's Metaphysics, trans. V. and G. Ringer, Henry Regnery Company, 1956, p. 110.

Chapter 13 ∽ SOCIETY

*My life means nothing, either theoretically or practically, unless I am
a member of a community.*

JOSIAH ROYCE

EVER SINCE THE GREAT DAYS IN ANCIENT GREECE, PHILOSOPHY HAS
been concerned, not merely with science and art and individual
goodness, but also with the life of man in society. The most
famous of all of the dialogues of Plato is *The Republic*; and his
pupil Aristotle, when he wrote his *Ethics*, wrote it as a kind of
preface to his *Politics*. The political life, he thought, is of major
concern, because the individual life of men, however good men
might be personally, would be very poor in a disordered or ill-
ordered political structure. Man, the ancient teaching declares, is
a social animal and, therefore, we need to put our best thought
into the questions which are involved when we undertake to improve society.

One of Plato's major motives was his desire to buttress the
Greek city-state, which, it was easy to see, was in danger of decay,
both from outside pressure and from internal confusion or dis-
loyalty. He cared for this ideal in much the same way that he
cared for the memory of his beloved Socrates, and the two mo-

tives combined harmoniously in his thoughtful work. *The Republic*, which is in some ways the crowning glory of Plato's career, combined his two dominant incentives to perfection. In his youth, Plato had come under the influence of Socrates, who, in the difficult days in the shadow of the Peloponnesian War, had engaged in a personal mission, which is described in the *Apology*. The heart of this mission was the effort to get men to think about the major question of what they should live for. Under this potent influence, Plato's thought was more and more directed to the values inherent in a good society. How could society be so refashioned that men might, with the least hindrances and with the utmost of assistance, realize the best that is in them? The enduring character of this aspect of Plato's thought is shown by the fact that his final work was the dialogue called *Laws*. Here the image of Socrates has ceased to dominate the pages; the theme of the good society is almost the only object of concern.

Beginning with this classic pattern, philosophy has had much to do with political life by the careful criticism of ideas and by the depiction of an ideal. In the seventeenth century, John Locke, who was certainly a professional philosopher and not merely a reformer, was the principal intellectual architect of the Glorious Revolution in Britain, and everyone knows of the influence of the French philosophers of the eighteenth century on the French Revolution. In America many of the formative influences on the thinking of Thomas Jefferson were philosophical ones. Philosophy, then, in dealing with questions of society, is not out of bounds, but in her natural territory. It is just as proper to have a philosophy of society, as it is to have a philosophy of science, or a philosophy of religion, or a philosophy of conduct.

The Reality of Community

It is usually a surprise to the modern student of philosophy to learn that Aristotle considered ethics to be subsidiary to politics. This seems to us the wrong order. We tend to say that a man must first be a good man and then should apply his goodness to a social setting, but there is much reason to conclude that Aristotle was right and that we are wrong. There is, of course, a certain responsibility which a man owes to himself, and even the Golden Rule, in its many formulations, never requires of a person that he prefer his neighbor's interest to his own. He is required only to put these interests on an equal level. But, after we have recognized this fact, we are bound to recognize also that most of our responsibilities are social. If there should be an atomic explosion that destroyed all human beings except one, most of the discussions of ethics would be wholly irrelevant to the life of the lone survivor.

No American philosopher has seen more clearly than did Josiah Royce that true individuality cannot flourish except in community. As he advanced in maturity of thought he said this even more cogently, but it is possible that the germ of the idea came from his contact with his contemporary at Johns Hopkins, Charles S. Peirce. This would not be surprising in view of Peirce's gift of originality. Very early Peirce had said, "Meanwhile we know that man is not whole so long as he is single, that he is essentially a possible member of society. Especially, one man's experience is nothing if it stands alone."[1] As the philosophic chain reaction goes on and Gabriel Marcel, in France, interprets Royce, the idea is enlarged. Marcel points out that, as a psychological fact, we become aware of the existence of others before we become aware of our own existence. We do not know ourselves first, and then postulate others by analogy. Knowing one's own existence is a great achievement, but is always a derivative achievement. The dialectic of personal discovery is not from self to others, but rather from others to self. We are social before we are individual.[2]

One of the clearest evidences of the preeminence of the social aspect of ethics over the merely individual aspect arises from a consideration of the relativity of duty. We have come to the conclusion in the preceding chapter that, in any concrete situation, there is only one right thing to be done, however difficult it may be to know what that is, but major factors that make one situ-

---

[1] C. S. Peirce, *Values in a Universe of Chance*, Stanford University Press, 1958, p. xxii.

[2] G. Marcel, *Royce's Metaphysics*, trans. V. and G. Ringer, Henry Regnery Company, 1956, p. 104.

ation different from another are factors having to do with society and, increasingly, with the political order. A man's duty in a Greek city-state, such as Athens under Pericles, a "fully developed democracy under the personal guidance of a disinterested states- man,"[3] is not identical with his duty in Franco's Spain, or in the Soviet Union in post-Stalin days. This is because the factors which constitute the situation are radically different in each case. Since it is partly by a person's membership in a society that his duty is determined, his duty may be different as his social relation- ships change. Temple has made this so clear that the reader is advised to consider his words with care.

It is evident that ethical obligations are always subject to modifica- tion by the group relationships into which the person concerned has entered. It may be right for a man on whom no one is dependent to throw up a lucrative employment in order to work in poverty among slum-dwellers. Is it equally right for him to do this if he is married? It can be so then only if his wife is willing to join in the same sacrifice. If both are agreed it may be a noble act. But now suppose that they have an infant child. Is it still noble? The child cannot give consent; and its whole future, even its physical health, may be jeopardized.[4]

We cannot with honesty separate ourselves from the groups to which we belong. It is pointless for me to say, "If I were a Nigerian." I am not a Nigerian; I am an American. My heritage I might intellectually renounce, but it is actually this heritage in which most of my responsibilities find root. It is the complex of social connections which make me what I am, and what I am helps me to know what I ought to do.

Our inevitable membership in many different societies demands participation in the management of those societies as part of our duty. Otherwise we are parasites. Participation in political life is a great risk, from which many persons naturally shrink, but it is a risk which must be taken at some point in life, if anything approaching integrity is to be maintained. We can be very glad, in this connection, that Plato has told us why, after much hesi-

[3] Plato, The Republic, trans. F. M. Cornford, Oxford University Press, 1960, p. xv.
[4] W. Temple, Christianity in Thought and Practice, Morehouse Publishing Company, 1936, pp. 90, 91.

tation, he accepted the invitation to go to Syracuse as counsellor and teacher to the young Dionysius. "Above all," he says, "I was ashamed lest I appear to myself as a pure theorist, unwilling to touch any practical task—and I saw that I was in danger of betraying Dion's hospitality and friendship at a time of no little real danger to him. . . . In so going I discharged my obligation . . . and cleared myself of reproach from philosophy, which would have been dishonored if I had incurred disgrace through softness or cowardice."[5]

In so far as a man has a clear vision of what he should live for, and accepts the responsibilities inherent in that vision, he will be involved in politics at some level. He will vote, not because he necessarily approves of any of the persons nominated for his choice, but because he knows that, even if responsible men do not vote, the irresponsible ones certainly will. He will accept office, not because he believes that he can stop all corruption, but because he has reason to conclude that the alternative may be greater corruption.

The true philosopher, when he gives his mind to political matters, is not so näive as to believe in the possibility of Utopia. He is convinced that life can be made relatively better than it now is, but he does not expect perfection. He recognizes that our world is intrinsically untidy and that something always comes along to sully the neat answers. This is part of what is meant by saying that the "best" is identical with the "least evil." There are evils in every kind of political system, but not all are of the same character and danger. This is the point of Churchill's famous remark to the effect that democracy is the worst form of government, except all of the others.

No system ever embodies all of the values which we require, and no system is ever free from inner dangers. The best that we can do is to recognize the dangers and to prepare for them in advance. This is what we are doing whenever we construct a system of checks and balances, in which the judicial branch, the executive branch, and the legislative branch each checks the others, while the electorate checks all. This is necessary because

---

[5] Plato, *Epistles*, trans. G. R. Morrow, Liberal Arts Press, 1962, pp. 220, 221.

no person and no group is good enough to be trusted with un-limited power. It is, as Niebuhr has said, man's tendency to injustice that makes democracy necessary, provided that we mean by democracy a system of mutual checks, which tyranny does not have.

Partly because she was a superb logician, Susan Stebbing was able to state with her characteristic felicity of expression something of the price which democracy entails.

Democracy, then, demands a great deal of the citizen. It demands self-discipline, submission to laws democratically established, willingness to participate in political discussion, willingness to serve others and thus to encourage in oneself those friendly feelings for other persons which find their highest expression in love. The sacrifices required of the individual by a community at war are hard to endure but they are not always hard to make; the sacrifices required in a democracy at peace seem easy to make because we have not seriously considered what they involve and how humdrum and irksome may be the enduring of them. To co-operate voluntarily with free men in a free community seems attractive because "to act voluntarily" and "to be free" are pleasant sounding phrases. Then comes the clash of interests.[6]

The fact that we do not expect Utopia provides us with no sound reason for any failure to outline the social ideal as carefully as possible. By clarifying the ideal we may be able to avoid some mistakes and thereby we keep before us a standard which avoids complacency about any of our actual achievements. If philosophy is devoted, in part at least, to clarification of meaning, the person who tries to be a philosopher can ply his trade in the field of politics as well as anywhere else. The need for clarity of thought is great, for the confusions which arise in political life from the use of cliches and slogans are legion. It is not enough to speak of freedom and justice, of equality and responsibility; it is necessary to make these concrete. If we are philosophers, we do not like abstractions! Miss Stebbing's advice at this point is obviously valuable. "My advice to myself as well as to others is," she writes, "Be definite. To formulate one's ideals is not to set out a string of maxims; it is to answer questions in the form: What is worth having in such and such specifiable circumstances?"

[6] Susan Stebbing, *Ideals and Illusions*, C. A. Watts & Co., Ltd., 1943, p. 55.

It is always possible to see a distinction between an idea as portrayed and the conduct which it inspires. An excellent and familiar illustration of this is the American Declaration of Independence, surely one of the major documents of human history. The authors and signers of the famous Declaration were not willing to assent to everything that their formula implied. They wrote about "all men," and the equal right of these men to the "pursuit of happiness," at the very time when a number of the signers held other human beings as property, which they could "sell." They clearly did not, therefore, include all races; they hesitated to include those without property; and the inclusion of women was extremely doubtful. Nevertheless, they were making a tremendous assertion that was practically certain to have more revolutionary consequences than they then realized or even desired. They declared, in essence, that: All men, of whatever race or color of skin, social standing, religious creed, mental or physical ability, ought to be allowed to live free and happy lives. This clearly meant that all ought to be free of external compulsion and able to shape their own ways of living in accordance with their own abilities, needs, and desires. However slow we may have been to see what this involves, or to put it into practice, the very declaration of the ideal constituted a tremendous advance for mankind. It does not, even yet, solve all of the old problems, and it raises some new ones, but it is, in any case, important.

Multiple Ideals

In considering the nature of a social ideal we soon realize that there are many relevant conceptions of what the good life together is, and that the very multiplicity of the relevant ideals provides us with some of our most difficult problems. Men ought, as the Declaration of Independence says, to be free, but it is equally true that men ought to have an ordered society, and the hard fact is that these are always in some conflict. Every thoughtful person recognizes that there are inherent limitations on freedom. When the founders of the American Republic drafted the First Amendment to the Constitution in 1791 they stated clearly "Congress shall make no law . . . abridging the freedom of speech or of the press," and this was probably wise, yet everyone knows that unlimited freedom of publication is not compatible with any good social order. There are sentences, including libelous and utterly obscene ones, which people cannot be allowed to print. Freedom is a value, but, since it is not the only value, it must compete with others. It is hard to believe that even John Milton favored unlimited freedom of printing, however noble an essay the *Areopagitica* is. The good society always involves, not the application of a single principle, but of many in conjunction and thereby in competition. There must be a system of checks and balances in our principles, as there must be in our forms of government.

In another, yet similar way, we can see that no single ideal is adequate in isolation, when we consider our manner of living. We try to have a society in which all are well fed, all are orderly, all are kind, but would we be satisfied with this if it were put into practice everywhere? William James dealt specifically with this question, and discovered, somewhat to his amazement, that such a society would be unsatisfactory because it would be boring and dull. Because many Americans, as well as foreign visitors to our country, are familiar with that peculiarly American institution, Chautauqua Lake, which still thrives each summer, the reference which James made to this institution is one which interests us. Much as he admired the Chautauqua ideal, he found it inadequate.

A few summers ago I spent a happy week at the famous Assembly Grounds on the borders of Chautauqua Lake. The moment one treads that sacred enclosure, one feels one's self in an atmosphere of success. Sobriety and industry, intelligence and goodness, orderliness and ideality, prosperity and cheerfulness, pervade the air. It is a serious and studious picnic on a gigantic scale. Here you have a town of many thousands of inhabitants, beautifully laid out in the forest and drained, and equipped with means for satisfying all the necessary lower and most of the superfluous higher wants of man. . . . You have perpetually running soda water fountains, and daily popular lectures by distinguished men. You have the best of company and yet no effort. You have no zymotic diseases, no poverty, no drunkenness, no crime, no police . . . you have, in short, a foretaste of what human society might be, were it all in the light, with no suffering and no dark corners. . . .

And yet what was my astonishment, on emerging into the dark and wicked world again, to catch myself quite unexpectedly and involuntarily saying: "Ouf! what a relief! Now for something primordial and savage, even though it were as bad as an Armenian massacre, to set the balance straight again. This order is too tame, this culture too second-rate, this goodness too uninspiring . . . this atrocious harmlessness of all things,—I cannot abide with them."[7]

The preface to James's book was dated 1899, but he added a footnote later indicating that the wars of independence in Cuba and the Philippines had shown that the rule of tameness had not wholly descended on the earth. What he would have said, if he could have seen the coming violence of two world wars, with the violent aftermath of each, we do not know. Even though we have had no serious danger of the dominance of the "Chautauqua ideal" in the years since James died, his warning still has point. There is something to be said for what Nietzsche meant by "living dangerously."[8] When we think of it seriously, we are bound to admire the lusty ideals of the high Renaissance, when the chief characters were far from moderate. Perhaps Whitehead is right in saying that a certain excessiveness is a necessary ingredient of all greatness. In any case, we must avoid boredom. A vivid warning in this direction comes from a somewhat unlikely source, the pen of T. S. Eliot.

People like license, and they like restraint. They like surprise. The one thing they do not like is boredom. And communism is successful so long as it gives people the illusion that they are not bored; so long as it can give them the illusion that they are important. For it has been shown again and again in history that people can put up with the absence of all the things that economists tell us they most need, with every rigour, every torment, so long as they are not bored. Why did the children of Israel murmur against Moses? Because they got tired of walking and seemingly arriving nowhere.[9]

[7] W. James, *Talks to Teachers on Psychology: and to Students on Some of Life's Ideals*, Holt, Rinehart and Winston, Inc., 1913, pp. 268–270.

[8] See the brief meditations from Nietzsche in *Existentialism from Dostoevsky to Sartre*, ed. W. Kaufmann, World Publishing Company, Meridian Books, 1956, pp. 101–112.

[9] T. S. Eliot, *The Criterion*, Vol. XII, p. 644.

The main problem raised by such serious thinkers as William James and T. S. Eliot is not the problem of violence, which all deplore, but the problem of zest in life. Men need food and clothing and sexual satisfaction, but, in the end, these do not satisfy. Men can be deprived of much and bear it, but that of which they cannot be permanently deprived is a sense of meaning in their lives. One of the most pathetic of facts about the recent past is that many people become genuinely nostalgic when they talk about World War II. Life was hard; hours of labor were long; danger was on every hand; but it was *not dull*. Everyone could sense a reason for living, and many experienced a community of feeling which they had never known in calmer days. We read, avidly, a short story such as Sartre's "The Wall," based on the Civil War in Spain and, though it is one sustained account of horror, we wonder, as we read, if there is any subject in our contemporary life that is as good.

Part of the reason why we now relive, so passionately, the American Civil War, after a lapse of a century, is that the period of that war seems to us to have been a much more exciting time than ours. We have fine cars, which we drive over smooth roads; we go to lectures and sit on soft seats in air-conditioned buildings with splendid lighting; we need never be very hot or very cold; but these things do not satisfy men and women, however they may be valued in a secondary fashion.

William James wrote wisely of "the moral equivalent of war," and this we may extend to include, not merely war, but any serious danger undergone for an adequate purpose. The ultimate enemy is not pain or cold or disease or physical hardship or even death. We know that we shall die sooner or later and all sensible people have accepted this as a fact long ago. We welcome death because the alternative would be an unimaginably crowded world. The ultimate enemy is not any of these things or events to which we usually refer when we speak of dangers. The most terrible enemy is *triviality*. No society will be a good one, no matter how adequately people are fed and clothed, if it is not a society in which men and women can be made to feel, without deception, that their lives are important. What many citizens of the West miss, when they contrast the Russian standard of living with their own and wonder how or why those people bear it, is the fact that millions in Russia actually believe that they are sacrificing current comfort for a more far-reaching and globe-encircling ideal. They are probably due for rude shocks, as they see Utopia postponed year after year and generation after generation, but, at the moment, the sense of meaning still exerts its marvelous power.

The ideal social order, then, must include many things, but three are preeminent. It must include freedom; it must include order; it must include a sense of meaning. And the greatest of these is meaning. Somehow life must be so organized to help men and women participate in some greatness of experience. The best known way in which this can be done is by commitment to a cause.

The Nature of Justice

The ostensible subject of Plato's *The Republic* is justice. If the famous dialogue deals, in its ten books, with a great many other subjects, this is partly because the question of justice is necessarily complex. In the course of the argument we deal with the possibility of nihilism, with whether there is a real right, with the contrast between instrumental and terminal values, with the educational process, with the equality of men and women, with the relationship between classes, with the idea of the good, with the parable of the cave, with poetry and immortality and comparative politics, and much more. The main question is "What does justice mean and how can it be realized in human society?" but in order to answer this basic question we necessarily deal with a multitude of other questions. The Greek word for "just" is like the English word "right," in that it has many senses. It covers the entire field of human conduct, in so far as it affects others, and especially as it affects others in a contrived social order, which every human society is.

It is clear that a society based upon justice, in this broad and inclusive sense, would be ideal. It would be ideal, not because it would belong to some other world of sheer imagination, but in the far more practical sense that it would provide a standard of perfection by which existing societies could be measured. It would provide a target at which to aim. *"The Republic,"* says F. M. Cornford, "is the first systematic attempt ever made to describe this ideal, not as a baseless dream, but as a possible framework within which man's nature, with its unalterable claims, might find well-being and happiness. Without some such goal in view, state-craft must be either blind and aimless or directed (as it commonly is) to the false and worthless ends."[10]

The influence of Plato's study of the ramifications of justice is so great and essentially so contemporary, that one of the best things which a teacher of philosophy can do is to direct his students to it, in such a way as to make them study it with avid interest. For this purpose Cornford's translation can hardly be surpassed. Contemporary philosophers need not suppose that Plato's work is beyond criticism, for it is not, but the more we read it the more we see that most of the problems of which we belatedly become aware, were already felt by the most gifted of the pupils of Socrates.

Whether we study the question of justice as Plato saw it, or in the light of subsequent thought and experience, we can hardly avoid the conclusion that absolute justice is not obtainable. Certainly Plato found that he could not produce it at Syracuse and everyone knows that it is more difficult in practice than in speculation. Every governmental officer finds a great contrast between the fair dream, which he outlines while he is seeking election, and what he is able to accomplish after he is elected. There are so many competing claims, so many inadequate persons who must be rewarded, so many interests that are incompatible.

But the apparent impossibility of absolute justice is not limited to the sphere of practice; it is found in the area of thought as well. Even in our fairest dream somebody is hurt. Aristotle saw nothing wrong with slavery, and even now, we have to admit that much of the excellence of Athenian society which we so admire seemed to require the bitter price of the denial of freedom to those at the bottom of the social pyramid. In our twentieth-century society, we never work out perfectly, even on paper, the proper representation of minorities, and we see inequities in the

10 Plato, *The Republic,* op. cit., p. 1.

system of taxation, however much we alter it from year to year. For example, members of a summer colony in the mountains, who normally occupy their cottages no more than two months out of twelve, and therefore make relatively slight use of public services, are required to pay as much in taxation as if they resided there for the entire year. These summer residents are required to pay a large proportion of the local school tax even though they do not have one child in the school. This is an obvious inequity, yet any alternative, partly because administrative difficulties arise when exceptions are made, would be worse. This simple illustration can be duplicated in essence at every level of the social order. Full justice is impossible because the world is not neat and tidy. But, though absolute justice is not possible, relatively better justice is possible, and to this wise people bend their best efforts, both in thought and in practice.

Plato's central answer to the question of what the nature of justice is may be stated as the vision of a society in which each one tends to his own business. This, of course, sounds too simple, and is, accordingly, rejected early in the dialogue in its most simple form, only to be reexamined seriously at a later stage. The good society, we are assured, is one in which each person finds what he can do; and, after adequate preparation in order that he may do it well, proceeds to do it with as little interference from others as is possible. Perhaps the chief glory of Plato's vision is that it is based almost entirely upon work. Though he did not say it as clearly as Aristotle said it later, man is created to create, and he finds his true life in making the contribution of which he is capable. Men have very different talents and capabilities, but whether they are the talents of the scholar or of the artisan or of the farmer, they are all needed; they must all be honored; and they must all be employed. One measure of justice, then, in a really good society, is the possibility of self-respecting employment for those who sincerely wish to be employed.

There is no possibility of justice, thinks Plato, unless we face resolutely the fact of inequality. Men are, in fact, not slightly unequal but extremely so. Some men are at least ten times as able as other normal men, intellectually or artistically or in practical skills. To deny this obvious fact is to condemn a society to injustice. This happens when the unworthy or the stupid person is put into a position of executive authority. It is like letting the glands guide us rather than reason. This is why, in important places in government, we do not want "common" or representative men, but "uncommon" men. The peril of democracy is always that it leans toward the common. Sometimes a man is elected, not because of excellence in those qualities which direction of a great society demands, but because, by the ordinariness of his speech and his complete identification with the thought processes of the masses, he is merely average. To elect him is little better than to choose by lot. In short, there is no possibility of the success of a democracy unless it has within it some way of encouraging a consciously self-developed aristocracy. This ought not to be an aristocracy of wealth or of inherited station, but rather an aristocracy of those who spurn the cult of the mediocre and pay willingly the price of self-discipline which the achievement of excellence, in any field of endeavor, requires.

Justice, then, will not come merely by a system in which every adult votes, even though that may be better than any alternative which we can now envisage. There are manifest evils in the existence of two parties, with fantastic expenses and many excesses for campaigns and elections, but there are worse evils in not having two parties. Justice will come, if it comes, by the permeation of society by certain intangibles, of which the idea of responsibility is supreme. The worker in the factory must have a sense of responsibility for the excellence of his product, even though he influences only a small part of it. We can have systems of inspection and systems of punishment for failure, but nothing external will ever take the place of the inner integrity. The same is true of every other occupation. The teacher will never help materially to overcome the shoddiness with which our education is plagued so long as he is chiefly concerned with hours and rate of pay. He must go on to see his teaching as something in which, in the pursuit of excellence, he can be a true aristocrat. He must be encouraged to take pride in his work.

The fact of inequality is in one way, simple, but in another it is very complex. No matter how realistic we may be about the fact that men differ in ability, in industry, in integrity, there is a sense in which all must be treated equally. We cannot have justice unless we have equality of opportunity. This we do not now have, even in our education, but it is a valid standard in the light of which we can measure both our failures and our approximations to success. Equality of opportunity is the keystone of the combination of aristocracy and democracy, which combination provides our best approach to justice. If we do not have equal opportunities we can never find out who the really "best" are. It is wholly possible, indeed it is likely, that some of those whom we most need in our effort to produce a more nearly just society are now in very poor homes. Education, then, is our means, both of discovering and of cultivating the talent without which we shall fail. The rule is that, in a just society no person is to be denied the fullest education of which he can make good use, merely because of lack of money. We dare not let poverty cheat us of the contribution of the ablest people wherever they are born. Whether the financial support of the potentially capable person comes from the state or from a system of private competitive scholarships makes little difference. The main point is that opportunity must be afforded for his discovery and development.

Justice cannot be separated from either intelligence or character. We shall approach justice as we put the wisest and most reliable persons in the places of greatest responsibility. But this is only a restatement of Plato's thesis, which, however hard it is to put into practice, is perennially valid. One of the clearest of the Platonic statements, which needs no change of any kind to be made relevant to our current situation, is that which we find near the beginning of the Seventh Epistle. After telling how hard it is to manage political or social affairs correctly, and how easily both laws and customs can be corrupted, he explains why he gave his mind unceasingly to the question of possible improvement. His basic answer is as follows:

At last I came to the conclusion that all existing states are badly governed and the condition of their laws incurable, without some miraculous remedy and the assistance of fortune; and I was forced to say, in praise of true philosophy, that from her height alone was it possible to discern what the nature of justice is, either in the state or in the individual, and that the ills of the human race would never end until either those who are sincerely and truly lovers of wisdom come into political power, or the rulers of our cities, by the grace of God, learn true philosophy.[11]

The Utilitarian Standard

Why should we wish to change a social or political order? There is, as everyone knows, a constant impulse to reformation, but how does it arise? Perhaps the urge comes, as Plato puts it, "from the height of true philosophy," and perhaps it comes from some other quarter. Possibly the continual effort to restate the vision of justice is sufficient, because the vision, when really understood, is always disturbing.

As we consider this important question we are driven to the examination of the answer of the utilitarians, who indeed have an answer. The answer is often neglected in contemporary philosophy for a variety of reasons. One is that the very name "utilitarian" is an unfortunate one, suggesting something less than noble. The name was given, almost by accident, to Bentham's system, when the young John Stuart Mill, a little less than seventeen years of age at the time, started "the Utilitarian Society." It was, says Mill, "the first time that any one had taken the title of Utilitarian; and the term made its way into the language from this humble source."[12]

Another reason for neglect of the utilitarian approach it that Jeremy Bentham's original statement of the thesis was couched in a clumsy manner. Bentham's book, the first edition of which was printed in 1780,[13] was unnecessarily verbose and artificially detailed. Much of it was based upon an inadequate and mistaken psychology. Bentham recognized some of the limitations of his work and mentioned in his Preface "the inordinate length of some of the chapters." (Chapter 16, "Division of Offenses," has 105 pages.) The style is, on the whole, almost as dry and uninteresting

[11] Plato, Epistles, op. cit., p. 217. Compare this with The Republic V, 473d and VI, 487e, 499b, 501e.

[12] See Autobiography of John Stuart Mill, Columbia University Press, 1944, p. 56.

[13] Bentham, Jeremy, An Introduction to the Principles of Morals and Legislation, The Clarendon Press, 1876.

as can be imagined. This makes it all the more surprising to the modern reader that the precocious Mill should have been so deeply moved by Bentham's work, but that he was moved is beyond doubt. Though he had been deeply indoctrinated in Benthamist thought by his father and teacher, James Mill, the first pages of Bentham's book burst upon him, he tells us, "with all the force of novelty." He believed that what he was reading represented a Copernican revolution. "The feeling rushed upon me," he said, "that all previous moralists were superseded, and that here indeed was the commencement of a new era in thought."[14]

What was this idea which seemed so revolutionary, to which Mill gave the name "the principle of utility"? As Bentham himself stated it, the test of the rightness or justice of any action, of a private individual or of a government, is whether it increases human happiness and reduces pain. This led naturally to the formula "the greatest happiness of the greatest number." Bentham's exact words are still the best introduction to the idea. "By utility," he wrote, "is meant that property in any object, whereby it tends to produce benefit, advantage, pleasure, good, or happiness, (all this in the present case comes to the same thing) to prevent the happening of mischief, pain, evil, or unhappiness to the party whose interest is considered."[15]

It is easy to see how such a statement has provided a rich field for analysis, enabling other men to make distinctions which Bentham did not bother to make. It is also easy to see that he laid himself open to possible criticism by his apparent emphasis upon pleasure, which seemed to give the entire system an air of frivolity, in spite of the dignified form in which it appeared. Even when Bentham spoke of happiness instead of pleasure, which he sometimes did, he failed to make adequate distinctions between the moral levels of happiness. He acknowledged that some men get pleasure out of dominating or persecuting other men, but he did not follow this up with any adequacy or admit that this constitutes a serious flaw in his system. If it is always our duty to give happiness, it must sometimes be our duty to encourage the person who rejoices in harming others. This is answered, in part, though

[14] Mill, op. cit., p. 46.
[15] Bentham, op. cit., p. 2.

not completely, by reference to the law of comparative numbers.

While we see that utilitarianism, either in its original Benthamite form or in Mill's development of it, involves genuine difficulties, the heart of the matter is amazingly invulnerable. *What it means is that the true measure of a just social order is what it does to people and nothing else.* It is people who count and their suffering is real. Suffering is not something to be condoned or explained away as somehow suitable to man in the light of his fallen condition. When we ask how we shall think of evil, the reasonable answer is that of L. P. Jacks: We shall think evil of it. Accordingly, we shall try to reduce it as much as possible, and this provides the strongest lever for social change.

Though Bentham and Mill and their many followers mention both pleasure and happiness prominently, we soon see that this is not the center of their motivation. John Stuart Mill tells us that his father, though a conscious disciple of Jeremy Bentham, "had scarcely any belief in pleasure." "He was not insensible to pleasures," writes Mill, "but he deemed very few of them worth the price which, at least in the present state of society, must be paid for them."[16] James Mill thought of human life as a poor thing at best.

In so far as utilitarianism brought a new note into social ethics, it was by a new sensitiveness to the evil of pain and suffering. Even when the philosophers of this movement seemed to be talking about the pleasures of life, they were really talking about conditions such as abject poverty and ignorance, which *deprived* worthy men of their rightful pleasures; in short, they were talking about misery and pain. What really moved them, and thereby rendered their position enduringly noble, was the fact that our world, after all the years of supposed civilization, is one which is marked by the prevalence of unnecessary human misery.

The misery which so aroused the thought and imagination of Bentham was not necessarily limited to the human race. A long footnote in chapter 17, which reveals the real depth of Bentham's motivation, is concerned with the suffering of animals. The philosopher agrees that it is possible to defend, on rational and even ethical grounds, both the eating of animals and the killing of ani-

[16] Mill, op. cit., p. 34.

mals. "The death they suffer in our hands commonly is and always may be," he writes, "a speedier, and by that means a less painful one, than that which would await them in the inevitable course of nature." According to our best evidence the *thought* of their death does not bother the animals, since they have none of the long-protracted anticipations of future misery which men have. While Bentham was thus completely tough-minded about animal death, he went on to ask a penetrating and embarrassing question. "But is there any reason why we should be suffered to torment them?" He ends the remarkable footnote with an eloquence which is hard to forget, partly because the style is in such sharp contrast to that of the book as a whole. "The question is not, Can they *reason?* nor, Can they *talk?* but, Can they *suffer?*"

The emphasis on the reduction of unnecessary suffering is a point which any philosopher, whether he calls himself a utilitarian or not, can make. If we are to have a good society we must have such a police system that we reduce or eliminate the vulnerability to attack suffered by innocent people on the streets. We must have swift and equal justice in the sense that we help the weak to be protected against the aggressions of the strong. We must find a way to eliminate the grinding poverty, which only degrades and does not ennoble. All of these actions have the same source—the desire to eliminate wanton cruelty and unnecessary misery. Some misery it may be impossible to eliminate, but no society is just unless an effort at elimination is sincerely made.

It is important to realize that Marxism, whether it be of the Russian communist variety or some other, achieves nearly all of its considerable moral leverage by the simple reference to the human misery that can be eliminated. Marx appeals to millions in the first instance simply because he points so clearly to *oppression.* Jean-Paul Sartre, who, though he is not a Communist, has made common cause with the Communists in France, has explained what the nature of communist motivation is more clearly than have most interpreters. "The revolutionary," he says, "adopts the proletariat's point of view firstly because it is *his* class and secondly because it is oppressed, because it is by far the largest class and its fate consequently tends to become fused with that of humanity, and lastly because the consequences of his victory will necessarily involve the suppression of classes. The aim of the revolutionary is to change the organization of society. And in order to do this he must of necessity destroy the old regime."[17]

It is not hard to see the evils which the revolutionary proposes to attack nor to see why he attacks them, even though we realize that there is a very good chance of his alternative bringing other and worse evils, like those illustrated in Cuba or in mainland China. One of the manifest evils which the revolutionary vows to destroy, and rightly so, is parasitism. If our brief analysis of the nature of justice is right, i.e., if it is based inevitably on work, then we can justify the maxim "If any one will not work let him not eat."[18] A just society has only one class, the class of those who toil, each seeking to give at least as much as he takes. The ideal of a classless society is a valid ideal. This can come about partly by legislation, but never wholly by such means. In the long run, it will not come about unless men have a cause to which they are committed, the cause of a society freed from unnecessary misery. The reason why such a society dare not have parasites is that all are needed.

When we try to evaluate the relative worth of the state and the individual, we are usually in some difficulty. We tend to say that the value of the individual is preeminent or sacred, but in doing so we run the risk of destroying or diminishing the means by which the worth of the individual is to be maintained. We are always in danger of distortion if we stray very far from Royce's teaching that both the community and the individual members are objects of infinite concern.[19] The life of the individual is greatly harmed if he is forced to live in an unjust or tyrannical society, while a total lack of order would endanger all personal freedom. The ideal, then, is never mere individualism, but an ordered society for the sake of the individuals who go to make up the society. Something other than individualism is necessary if the chief values of individualism are to be maintained. Thus we

[17] J.-P. Sartre, "Portrait of the Anti-Semite," *Existentialism from Dostoevsky to Sartre,* ed. W. Kaufmann, World Publishing Company, Meridian Books, 1956, p. 280.
[18] II Thessalonians 3:10.
[19] J. Royce, *Problem of Christianity,* The Macmillan Company, 1913, Vol. I, 98.

cannot give simple preference either to the individual or to society, for the twin values must be held together, and held in constant tension. The glorification of the state, in neglect of individuals, becomes tyranny, while the glorification of the individual, in neglect of the ordered society, becomes anarchy. It is hard to surpass the plain wisdom of Bentham when he says, "The interest of the community then is, what?—the sum of the interests of the several members who compose it."[20]

It may be said in conclusion that the motive emphasized in this chapter is either identical with or similar to what is usually known as love. It is also close to that which existentialism has made so prominent, namely, concern. This is not very surprising. Philosophy is, indeed, devoted to the life of reason, but reason can indicate to us the necessity of caring. The great advantage of the desire to eliminate unnecessary misery is that it avoids some of the vagueness and abstraction involved in our ordinary use of the word "love." If such definiteness can be given it, the word is still useful. Justice is none other than love distributed.

---

[20] Bentham, op. cit., p. 3.

Chapter 14 ∽ THE DEFINITION OF PHILOSOPHY

Philosophy is merely the attempt to answer such ultimate questions.
BERTRAND RUSSELL

IT IS WELL UNDERSTOOD IN MODERN CULTURE THAT THE DEFINITION of *anything* is a difficult and controversial undertaking. If we are at all sophisticated we are aware of the fallacy of the perfect dictionary. In no area is this fallacy more dangerous than in philosophy. *Philosophy*, though it is a term which almost all civilized persons employ, is notoriously ambiguous and sometimes there seem to be as many definitions as there are philosophers. It is obvious, therefore, that no simple definition, comparable to the definition of astronomy or geology, will suffice. The phenomenon which we are considering is too rich and varied to be adequately represented by some simple formulation. This is one of the chief reasons why, in this book, no attempt was made at the outset to give an adequate definition of the major theme. Definition at the beginning is impossible because of lack of experience. Until the problems have been developed and clarified, most of the words used, in even the best definitions, are essentially abstract. The only way in which they can be made concrete is by the actual undertaking, i.e., by the *practice of philosophy* rather than its contemplation from the point of view of the spectator.

There is one theory of definition, lampooned a hundred years ago by Lewis Carroll, to the effect that all definitions are arbitrary. All that a man needs to do is to make his own personal definition and stick to it. This, of course, is a logical possibility, but it is never worth doing because it indicates a failure on the author's part to have a decent respect for the opinions of mankind. Common sense may, indeed, be confused, but we are not likely to have much effect on our generation unless we try to begin, as nearly as we can, where the ordinary thoughtful man is willing and able to start.

In many ways the best definition of philosophy involves denotation. We are not far wrong if we say that philosophy is what Plato is practicing in his inimitable dialogues, or what Descartes is practicing in his development of the method of philosophic doubt, or what Lovejoy is practicing in his analysis of the predicament of the "thinking behaviorist." We learn what philosophy is, not by something seen in advance, but by watching philosophers at work and by participating, however modestly, in that work ourselves. The definition of philosophy is not a prefatory question, but it is not the subject of a postlude either. Entire books are devoted to this, because it is a live and central question which is far from settled. The way in which this question is answered determines much else.

The Attempted Reduction of Philosophy

When the definition of philosophy is hotly debated today, it is debated chiefly because there has been a concerted effort to reduce its scope more and more. Many have believed that the only way in which, in an age of specialization, the philosophical enterprise can be intellectually respectable is for philosophers to concentrate on some particularized field and there achieve genuine competence. Sometimes this strategy is referred to as the rejection of philosophy "in the grand manner." Once, in Aristotle's day, philosophy included all of the sciences, which was perfectly satisfactory when the specialized sciences had not developed their own techniques and equipment, but it would not be satisfactory now. It is surely the part of wisdom for each scholarly group to do what it can do best and not to spread its efforts over such a wide field that the results are superficial.

In an earlier generation it was customary for books of philosophy to begin by reference to the great and profound questions with which man on this planet is confronted. The purpose of the thinker was to help others, in the well-known phrase invented by Matthew Arnold, to "see life steadily and to see it whole." In short, even though different scholars might develop different and specialized skills in logic, or aesthetics or ethics or the philosophy of science, it was generally recognized that philosophy, in its essence, is metaphysics.

One of the striking movements of thought in our day, a movement with which every student who wishes to be contemporary must come to grips, is the movement which utterly rejects metaphysics. Though this tendency has already passed its apex of influence and is declining, it is something with which we must continue to reckon. If the antimetaphysical doctrine is sound, most of the issues with which we have tried to wrestle in this book are not even worth considering. To deal with them at all, we are told, is a waste of time. Problems about the relationship between mind and body, about the efficacy of purpose, about freedom and determinism, about the existence of God, are, we are assured, merely "pseudo problems."

The chief proponents of this antimetaphysical doctrine may be termed, with accuracy, the neopositivists. Most of these pay little attention to the work of Auguste Comte, but nevertheless their position is essentially his. What they have in common is the positivist faith in the methods of science and the conviction that problems which cannot be handled by laboratory technique are simply relics of an earlier, outgrown, and essentially childlike period of human thinking. The result is to bring about a radical reduction of both the number and the character of the questions with which a philosopher who understands his task, can deal. Collingwood puts this radical reduction into a syllogism which clarifies the stand which we are discussing. "Any proposition which cannot be verified by appeal to observed facts is a pseudo-proposition. Metaphysical propositions cannot be verified by appeal to observed facts. Therefore, metaphysical propositions are pseudo-propositions, and therefore nonsense."[1]

We get some idea how radical this reduction in the scope of philosophy would be, if neopositivism should prove to be generally acceptable, by listening to one of its most vocal exponents, A. J. Ayer. His opening sentence in Language, Truth and Logic, a sentence which, in spite of its apparently youthful arrogance, is retained, as we have seen, in the revised edition of this work, is as follows: "The traditional disputes of philosophers are, for the most part, as unwarranted as they are unfruitful." Most of the questions with which the great men of the past, such as Plato or St. Thomas Aquinas or Kant, have wrestled, we may now dismiss as pseudo-questions. It must be said for Ayer that he is not lacking in boldness. He asserts that his ability to point out the logical errors of his predecessors "will subsequently be found to apply to the whole of metaphysics."

A good example of a question which men of Ayer's persuasion now declare out of bounds is that of whether God really is.[2] There is literally nothing, these men declare, that can be said on this subject with intelligence, for the simple reason that "God exists" is only a pseudo-proposition. It is a pseudo-proposition because it leads to no verifiable sensory experience. If Ayer is right, and if people come to believe him, he will be doing an immense service to mankind in that he will be saving them from a prodigious waste of intellectual effort. The purpose of the reduction thesis is thus partly philanthropic and compassionate.

There are today two major branches of the school of neopositivism, one of which still tries to be loyal to logical positivism of the kind represented by Ayer, while the other makes an even greater reduction of scope by holding that the only valid area of

[1] R. G. Collingwood, An Essay on Metaphysics, Clarendon Press, Oxford, 1940, pp. 162, 163.

[2] Though the conflict between neopositivists and existentialists is, on most fronts, so fierce, they tend to come together on the impossibility of giving objective evidence of God's reality. We have seen already in Chapter 10, how Jaspers, who, in this regard, is simply echoing Kierkegaard, holds that a proved God would be no God.

philosophical inquiry is linguistics. This seems, at first, an extremely odd development, but the more we study the system, the more we see why it has moved in this direction. As early as 1936, Ayer spoke of "the kind of metaphysics that is produced by a philosopher who has been duped by grammar."[3] One of the paradoxes of the linguistic school, which, as we have seen, is now the dominant philosophical movement at Oxford University, is the fact that the whole movement started with an exaggerated emphasis upon science, while the pure grammarian is now far removed from science.

Far more serious than the removal from science is the removal from involvement in the great moral issues that so deeply affect mankind. When a man reduces his scope of inquiry, as these men do, he cannot concern himself with the rightness of the social order, the objective evils of an economic system, or any of the burning questions which divide mankind. The philosopher who has carried his neopositivism to its logical extreme removes himself from the turbulent world and analyzes "statements" to find their precise meaning. Whether they are true or false is a question which he refuses to try to answer.

We cannot understand this curious development apart from some kind of knowledge of the life and work of Ludwig Wittgenstein (1889–1951), whose influence now constitutes a cult. This strange man is the dominant figure, more than a decade after his death, in both branches of neopositivism. This seems surprising, in view of the obvious contrasts between the two schools, but it is accounted for partly by the existence of "two Wittgensteins," the earlier and the later. The earlier life included study at Cambridge University, the close association with G. E. Moore and Bertrand Russell, and the writing of a difficult work, Tractatus Logico-Philosophicus, during his service in the Austrian army at the time of World War I. He considered that this work had solved all philosophical problems and that there was no further need for philosophical speculation.

Wittgenstein's second public period, which included teaching for thirteen years at Cambridge University, involved his renunciation of the logical positivist position of the Tractatus, and the

[3] A. J. Ayer, Language, Truth and Logic, Victor Gollancz, Ltd., 1936, p. 45.

foundation of the linguistic school. His most important work, *Philosophical Investigations*, was published posthumously. His eccentricities were of the kind which, when combined with unusual fecundity of ideas, naturally led, among his devout philosophers, to a genuine cult, with many esoteric features.

What Wittgenstein taught in his second phase was that all philosophical problems are connected with language and, in fact, stem from it. Like the orthodox behaviorist, the disciple of Wittgenstein renounces any claim to know what men think, but he can hear and read what they say. Man is the language-producing animal and this gives us our only clue to understanding. The fact that language exists, plus some facts about language, are central for philosophy. Here, it would appear, is an area where philosophers can reign, even though it is a severely restricted one. Philosophy has found its own definition in a narrow field, which is not likely to be taken from it by one of the specialized sciences. What follows is that the proper and, indeed, the only task of a philosopher, as we have learned already, is to act as the diagnostician and therapist of those errors which arise, not from failure to accept objective truths, but from the misunderstanding of language. "Look on the language-game as the primary thing," said Wittgensten.

A clear illustration of the linguistic technique is the effort to show that a word like *exists* has more than one meaning. If we say "Houses exist," "Redness exists," "Number two exists," we are tempted to suppose that, since the sentence structure is similar, houses, redness, and the number two all have similar objective qualities. The reader will be reminded here of Aristotle's recognition of multiple meanings of *is* which we mentioned in Chapter 10. "Of course," says Wittgenstein in No. 11 of *Philosophical Investigations*, "what confuses us is the uniform appearance of words when we hear them spoken or meet them in script and print. For their *application* is not presented to us so clearly. Especially not when we are doing philosophy!" It might be supposed that, because there are many words and countless usages, the philosopher will never run out of work, yet the paradox is that the disciples of Wittgenstein expect a withering away of philosophy. This is reminiscent of the Marxian view that the state will wither away once the classless society is really established. If we become habitually careful in our use of words, fully cognizant of what is implied in ordinary speech, the pseudo-problems, which the faulty use of language has engendered, will obviously cease. The reduction of the scope will then be complete and the enterprise successfully finished.

Of course, it is obvious to the student of these matters that neither the Marxian state nor linguistic analysis does in fact wither away. Probably the cause of the failure of the prediction to come true, even in part, is the same in both instances: an oversimplification of the sources of evil. There are, in fact, more reasons for the need of a governmental system than the class structure, and there are more reasons for the need of careful analysis than the problems of language.

Though Wittgenstein is the chief inspiration of those who see linguistic analysis as the sole task of philosophy, there have been other strong influences, particularly those of G. E. Moore and Lord Bertrand Russell. The work of Moore has been admired by philosophers of various schools, especially because he has been such a strong exemplar and exponent of clarity. His essay, "The Refutation of Idealism," published in 1903, has become a classic in his own time. It is an instructive fact, however, that Moore is not strictly a linguistic philosopher. Neither is he a logical positivist, as one can see by noting Ayer's criticism of his ethical objectivity. It has been said that he practiced the art of linguistic analysis so well that he avoided the label. Lord Russell, who early became the leader of the movement concerned with the analytic approach to philosophy, has not only avoided the linguistic label, he has attacked the school with scathing contempt. He is especially critical of what he calls "The cult of common usage." C. D. Broad, who is himself highly skilled in analysis, both logical and ethical, has indicated his rejection of the strategy of reduction in an important address.[4]

All of neopositivism, of either branch of the movement, is essentially nothing more than an attempt to establish a radical nominalism. This is obviously all that remains, if there is no way in which we can have an intelligible discussion of objective reality.

[4] See *Inquiry*, Oslo University Press, Summer, 1958, p. 102.

If such nominalism is adopted as a creed, i.e., the creed of anti-metaphysics, the scope of philosophy is inevitably reduced to a game, which some call it, following Wittgenstein's lead. It is then an easy step to engagement in pretentious triviality. Historically, philosophy has been a discussion of *fundamentals*, including the central and enduring problems of the universe, of life, of man, of science, of causation. The major attack of neopositivism has been an attack on this conception.

Lord Russell, one of the most distinguished philosophers of the twentieth century, may not be sure about the answers, but he is very sure about the questions. He believes in dealing with important questions, and his strongest criticism of the philosophy now in vogue at Oxford is that it does not do so. "It excludes," he says, "almost everything that is of genuine interest, and prescribes either ineffable mysticism or dreary exegesis of the nuances of usage."[5] Russell employs in a telling fashion the epigram, "A cleric who loses his faith abandons his calling, a philosopher who loses his, redefines his subject."

Variety in Contemporary Philosophy

There could be no greater mistake, in the effort to understand contemporary philosophy, than the supposition that there is now one dominant philosophy that is new. There is no doubt that this impression has been received, partly because of the exaggerated claims of some of the particular schools. It is not very surprising that a person not well acquainted with the many developments of modern thought and noting the title of such a book as that by Professor Gilbert Ryle of Oxford, *The Revolution in Philosophy*, would suppose that some Copernican changes have already occurred. It is, of course, held by some that the meticulous study of language, especially of some hitherto neglected features of it, will completely transform our outlook. But this is something that can be argued. The works of the analysts can themselves be analyzed, for no one individual or group has a monopoly on the analytic process.

The branches of neopositivism, far from being the producers of

[5] E. Gellner, *Words and Things*, Victor Gollancz, Ltd., 1959, p. 14.

the revolution, represent only a relatively small segment of contemporary philosophy. The exaggerated claims, coupled with the fact that the leaders of the movement are securely established at Oxford, have overinfluenced some professional philosophers, especially those in whom any reference to Oxford produces a response that is mildly reverential. There *had* to be something to it! Now, however, with the avalanche of responsible criticism, the reverential mood is beginning to be dispelled. Without doubt the most vivid criticism is that of *Words and Things*. Gellner's book has had a wide reading on both sides of the Atlantic and provided the occasion for a series of articles in *The New Yorker*. The treatment is humorous as well as acute, giving delight by the way in which the author diagnoses the diagnosticians. His attack is both logical and sociological, the latter seeming to Lord Russell the more interesting. "For my own part," says Russell, "I find myself in very close agreement with Mr. Gellner's doctrines as set forth in this book."

It is doubtful if the movement thus criticized will recover entirely from this frontal attack, for it is especially vulnerable to ridicule. The chief linguistics may try to shrug off what Gellner says, but they can hardly shrug off what Lord Russell says. After all, he has been one of their heroes: he was Wittgenstein's friend; he invented logical atomism; he is the acknowledged leader of the analytic school; he produced, along with Whitehead, *Principia Mathematica*. Yet he denounces the reduction of philosophy in no uncertain terms. The fact that one of the chief members of the linguistic school, Gilbert Ryle, who is the editor of the periodical, *Mind*, refused to publish in that magazine in 1961 Lord Russell's review of Gellner's book has increased the impression that the school cannot take the kind of criticism which it loves to administer.

Gellner is not the first to accuse the contemporary grammarians of philosophy of concern for the trivial, but he is probably the most thorough in documentation. The fact that such philosophy claims to be therapeutic does not, he says, overcome its essential triviality. The curative aspect of the teaching is emphasized, not in order to enable men to deal with the great questions, but precisely to keep them from doing so. What is to be destroyed is not human perplexity, but the supposedly fatuous human belief that something can be done about such perplexity, a belief which Socrates shared. It is not surprising that the Oxford philosophers now encounter some resistance to their teaching, even among their own students. It is highly likely, says Gellner, that students who have to undergo great sacrifice to secure some education may "not wish to spend their studies acquiring techniques which only cure a conceptual illness from which they barely suffer, with which they have to be artificially infected so as to give the techniques something to work on."[6]

Perhaps the most damaging criticism that can be made of the linguistic school is its fundamental inconsistency. The various members of the school make a great point of saying that common speech of common men is sacrosanct. Philosophers are urged to note what the de facto rules of language are and to follow them. But the de facto meaning of philosophy, in common speech, is precisely what the linguistics will not allow it to be! There is no doubt that the average man expects philosophy to help in practical questions of value and in finding some meaning in the world, but these are the very subjects which are ruled out. It is not known how the contemporary neopositivists would deal with this obvious inconsistency, for, apparently, they have not noticed it.

The student need not be overimpressed with the claims of the disciples of Wittgenstein, for they are being answered and brought down to size. Bochenski's concluding remarks about the entire neopositivist movement are impressive. He shows, for one thing, that the representatives of the movement are extremely weak on the theoretical aspect, resting naïvely upon dogmatic presuppositions which they never examine, because they are taken for granted. Even worse, he says,

none of these philosophical systems have any answer to the great human problems with which contemporary thought is wrestling. . . . On account of their reactionary tendency, their theoretical weakness, and their failure before the great questions of human destiny, these philosophers are the least valuable in contemporary thought—with the exception of the purely methodological results of the analytical philosophers. Taken as a whole, contemporary philosophy has rendered

[6] Ibid., p. 246.

obsolete not only their conclusions, but even the way of formulating the problems.[7]

Bochenski, in his remarkably erudite book, presents six current tendencies: (1) the philosophy of matter, including the neopositivism already mentioned, (2) neo-idealism, (3) the philosophy of life, (4) phenomenology, (5) existentialism, and (6) the resurgence of metaphysics. Under the third of these he deals with the continuing influence of Bergson; under the fourth with Husserl and Scheler; and under the sixth, with Nicolai Hartmann and Alfred North Whitehead, as well as current Thomism. He deals but slightly with dialectical materialism because it has practically no academic representatives except in Russia and in satellite or associated countries, where it is the only philosophy that can be taught. Bochenski is concerned with those tendencies in philosophy which are international.

Whether we make our synopsis with Bochenski's help or in some other way, it is difficult to avoid the conclusion that ours is a time of "strenuous philosophical activity." The hundred flowers are growing and they are growing side by side. In the American colleges, partly as a result of the widespread revulsion against the production-line type of education, the interest in philosophical studies is increasing and the demand for qualified instructors seems to be greater than the supply. Published philosophical writings in journals and in books are numerous. Existentialist philosophy is unique in its ability to elicit interest at all levels, partly because it seems hard to understand and partly because its chief expositors, such as Jean-Paul Sartre, have employed successfully the novel and the play as ways of expressing philosophical ideas.

A movement which is increasingly influential, though it is not popularly recognized, as positivism and existentialism are, is that of the new metaphysics. A number of able scholars, especially in America, now find that the best forum for their mutual friction of ideas is the splendid quarterly The Review of Metaphysics. More than any other person, Professor Paul Weiss has been responsible for the success of this scholarly venture. Since most of the men who write for this journal are not in the least abashed by the

---

[7] I. M. Bochenski, Contemporary European Philosophy, University of California Press, 1961, p. 71.

confident claim, on the part of some contemporary thinkers, that the age of metaphysics is already past, they continue to think and write about the major issues. Some of their work may be the most enduring in our generation.

Almost as important as the recognition of variety, is the realization of the inadequacy of labels. The reader often desires to place philosophers in neat pigeon-holes, then he feels more comfortable, but nearly every first-class thinker defies simple classification. An able man may have some of the characteristics of idealism, some of realism, and some of pragmatism, for he may have found that the combination is richer than any alternative that he knows. This is not very surprising to us when we consider the probability that no particular position held by thoughtful people is likely to be utterly worthless. Most men who think deeply are eager to learn what they can from their critics. They are in the tradition of Copernicus who, in his letter to Pope Paul III said, "For I am not so much in love with my conclusions as not to weigh what others will think about them." In similar vein G. E. Moore, at the end of a carefully reasoned essay on "The Nature of Moral Philosophy," says, "It seems to me that Moral Philosophy cannot be merely a department of Psychology. But no doubt there may be arguments on the other side to which I have not done justice."[8] The active philosopher usually goes out of his way to reject labels. Thus both Jaspers and Heidegger assert that they are not existentialists, and Peirce, though he first introduced the term, said quite clearly that he was not a pragmatist.

One development which makes for both variety and depth in contemporary philosophy is the invention of the paperback book. Once college bookstores sold little more than textbooks, while now such stores, even in small institutions, stock thousands of paperback titles. This has constituted the true revolution in the teaching of philosophy, not a revolution in the growth of a single movement, but a revolution in the opportunity of the reader to come into firsthand contact with many kinds of intellectual greatness.

[8] G. E. Moore, *Philosophical Studies*, The Humanities Press, Inc., 1951, p. 339.

Serious Philosophy

"Of what is great," said Nietzsche, "one must either be silent or speak with greatness." That people will honor the vision of greatness is indicated by the fact that at least six of A. N. Whitehead's books are now in paperback editions. There is clearly a public need for philosophy, in the sense in which it has been understood throughout most of its history. Those who renounce this undertaking in favor of something else are free to do so, but it is less confusing to retain the historic word for the task of fundamental thinking about genuine alternatives in human life. Philosophy is not worth the trouble which is inevitably involved in hard and self-critical thinking unless it has to do with what we have reason to believe is real. We must be concerned both with concepts which denote essences and with propositions which point to genuine existence, i.e., the being of objects, whether physical or spiritual, in the actual universe. Here is an excerpt from a letter written by a thoughtful man connected with business, whose insight may be more significant, if philosophers will listen, than are many of those which normally find their way into printed books.

Have you ever noticed that periodically in the history of western civilization many of the professional philosophers become fossilized? As a result a great many ordinary people begin to pursue philosophy without even knowing her name.

This pursuit of philosophy by the common man nearly always winds up in the agora or its equivalent. People who have not studied philosophy formally have a way of coming back to the big questions concerning man and his destiny. When the schools become dominated by scholastics who are pre-occupied with nit picking, then the traders and merchants begin to take over.

This is something which trained philosophers will neglect at their peril. Some are so concerned with writing for one another that they tend to forget their chief function, which is to help to provide a critical and rational interpretation of experience for all who are willing to listen. Serious philosophy began in the person of Socrates, with a sense of mission.

It is easy to see why so many who, in Wittgenstein's phrase, undertake to "do philosophy" are attracted to the microscopic method. They think that they will achieve a higher reputation for scholarship among their fellow-philosophers, if they choose some minute problem and analyze it in meticulous detail. This effort is a surrogate of the scientific emphasis on specialization, and carries with it the same snobbishness and contempt for the general practitioner. Important as specialization is, it must be noted that its exercise is not at all incompatible with the development of skill in reaching the general public. Whitehead and Russell prove, in their own careers, that there is no such incompatibility. On the one hand they could produce the *Principia Mathematica*, but Russell could write lucidly *The Problems of Philosophy*, and Whitehead win a popular reading with *Adventures of Ideas*.

If philosophy is to be a really serious intellectual enterprise, particularly in our day, it will need to include both the specialized studies and the development of that discipline which enables a man to be understood by ordinary thoughtful people, without any superficiality. The easiest way to seem wise without being so is to adopt or invent a specialized jargon which has the effect of protecting the specialist because it intimidates the layman. But, however easy this method of security from criticism may be, it is unworthy. It is not decent to try to protect the castle of philosophy by the dragon of an esoteric terminology.

That the particular, specialized studies are helpful there is no doubt, and the meticulous work of some members of the contemporary Oxford school demonstrates this. For example, it is a real assistance to be able to show that Bishop Berkeley used *idea* in two ways, apparently without realizing that he was doing so. There is a crucial difference between idea as something in subjective experience and idea as objective reality, though the same word is used for both. Anything which makes for genuine clarity is good and must always be encouraged. It has, indeed, been encouraged from the beginning. "We must inquire," said Aristotle, "which of the common statements are right and which are not right."[9] And it must never be forgotten, if we are tempted to

[9] Aristotle. *Metaphysics*, trans. R. Hope, University of Michigan Press. 1960, 784.

suppose that the careful study of words is new, that this is how the discussions of Socrates in the market place began. Only, and this is important, Socrates was more concerned with *that to which* words refer than with the words themselves.

Philosophy, in the sense of the careful examination of fundamental issues, is not an option to be taken or rejected. If professional philosophers will not investigate the truth about great issues others will, and the fact that they will not do it carefully or skillfully will not deter them, because man is the kind of creature who has no choice about using his reason. His only choice, in this matter, is how well he uses it. If men do not philosophize consciously and in a disciplined manner, they will philosophize unconsciously and superficially.

A conclusion similar to what has just been said is now being made by so many that there is clearly a swing of the pendulum. In this the influence of the late Morris Raphael Cohen has been highly effective, partly because his conviction was so clear and unapologetic. "Just as there are fundamental principles," he wrote, "which enable us to systematize our judgments of perception and thus give us a theory of nature, so we can attain to certain principles which enable us to organize our judgments of value, ethical or esthetic, into a rational system of judgments on human conduct."[10] The publication of the Gifford Lectures of Professor John Macmurray of the University of Edinburgh, and their splendid reception, is evidence of the swing away from the trivial, and the renewal of metaphysical interest among thinkers in the United Kingdom. Macmurray has sought, by his emphasis on the self as agent, i.e., a genuine causal factor in events, to challenge the entire reductive trend of the recent past and to "conceive a personal universe." "This transformation," he says at the end of his lectures, "restores its whole substance to philosophy, which again becomes the intellectual aspect of the search for the real."[11]

If we need any other evidence of the swing of the pendulum in

[10] M. R. Cohen, *A Preface to Logic*, World Publishing Company, Meridian Books, Inc., 1959, p. 173. Reprinted by permission of Holt, Rinehart and Winston, Inc.

[11] J. Macmurray, *Persons in Relation*, Harper & Row, Inc., 1961, p. 224.

the direction of concern for great issues it is provided us in the generous public response to existentialism, in either its theistic or its atheistic form. Much of existentialism seems logically barbarous, to a careful logician. With its dark sayings and its frank avowal of passion, it seems to be the very antithesis of our dominant ideal of clear analysis. But the public absorbs it avidly because it is at least concerned with questions which the public thinks philosophy ought to try to answer. The power of existentialism lies almost entirely in the fact that it deals with ultimate situations. They cannot be denied, changed, or surmounted, but they can, says Jaspers, be acknowledged. Among these are the following:

I die.
I suffer.
I am subject to chance.
I am guilty.

These fundamental predicaments constitute, along with the Socratic sense of wonder, the most profound sources of all genuine philosophy. We may find Heidegger or Sartre hard to read, but we know what they are talking about, for we experience it every day. When Sartre makes his ringing avowal of his own personal responsibility, as against all seductive evasions, each of us stands a little straighter. What an intellectual and moral tonic it is to hear Gabriel Marcel say, "Such was my deed and I did it. Nothing in the world can deprive me of the duty or the privilege of saying that word."[12] It is a pity that existentialism generally is so unable to argue its conclusions, or to defend its central faith, but we are foolish if we let this fact blind us to the greater fact that it is dealing with the right subjects. "We are sluggards and cowards," said Royce, "if, pretending to be philosophic students and genuine seekers of the truth, we do not attempt to do something with these questions."[13] The aim of speculative philosophy is to reach general conclusions as to the nature of the universe and our posi-

[12] G. Marcel, *Royce's Metaphysics*, trans. V. and G. Ringer, H. Regnery and Company, 1958, p. 139.
[13] J. Royce, *The Religious Aspect of Philosophy*, Harper & Row, Inc., Torchbooks, 1958, p. 5.

tion and prospects in it. In this task we are never wholly successful, but if philosophy can be made cumulative and progressive,
each thinker listening humbly though respectfully to his predecessors, we can penetrate the surrounding darkness a little.

It is with shame that we have to report that college courses in
philosophy have often failed to present the history of thought as
a cumulative dialogue. A thoughtful woman writes in a letter
something which every teacher ought to take to heart. She says
that, while she had sensed progression in science, she had never
sensed it in philosophy. "Partly through a most stupid college
course, and partly through not finding the right reading, I had the
impression that Descartes, Spinoza, Hume, Kant . . . each went
back to the ABCs and rewrote them, each with a different slant.
I find it much more credible to think that many men, each loving
God and trying to make Him clear to men's minds as He is to
their hearts, have added on ideas until we now have a consistent
though incompetent whole."

One can nave considerable sympathy with this woman, in view
of the fact that some philosophers have claimed to make wholly
new starts. Wittgenstein provided a vivid example of this claim
when, in the preface to the *Tractatus*, he wrote, "On the other
hand the *truth* of the thoughts communicated here seems to me
unassailable and definitive. I am, therefore, of the opinion that
the problems have in essentials, been finally solved."[14] Descartes
and Kant also made claims of extreme breaks with the past, and,
as we have already seen, the youthful work of A. J. Ayer suggests
that nearly all of his predecessors wasted their time by dealing
with pseudo-questions. It is really not very surprising that the student sometimes gets the impression that my correspondent says
she got in college. But it is possible to show that the cumulative
development has actually occurred, and this is one of the reasons
why the highly developed discipline of the history of ideas is now
so important for philosophy as a whole.

If we look at the entire body of philosophers over the last 3,000
years, we find that it is fundamentally a fellowship of seekers.
There is one absolute test of genuineness in a philosopher, and

[14] Wittgenstein dropped this extreme claim of course, when, in his later
work, he sought to refute some of his former views.

that is humility. A good philosopher may be of any race or of any nationality; he may be an atheist; he may be a scientist or a humanist; what he cannot be is arrogant. The necessary humility must not be the insincere humility of one who retreats from great problems, but the more genuine humility of one who tries to handle what he agrees is too big for him, and thus becomes a fool for philosophy's sake. Herein lies the potent appeal of Socrates as Plato presents him. He stands at the beginning of a fellowship of those who are both serious and humble. As Cornford so well says, in his splended introduction to his translation of The Republic, "To possess this good would be happiness; to know it would be wisdom; to seek the knowledge of it is what Plato means by philosophy."[15]

Serious philosophy centers on the power of the question. Indeed, some of the best definitions make this the essential feature of the entire discipline. Thus one perceptive contemporary thinker defines philosophy as "the art of asking the right questions." Many of these will not be asked by the person who has not given long years to the search or, if they are asked at all, they are asked clumsily and ambiguously. Philosophy, instead of making questions easier, tends to make them harder. The recognition of this fact provided Bertrand Russell with a brilliant beginning for one of his most brilliant books.

Is there any knowledge in the world which is so certain that no reasonable man could doubt it? This question, which at first sight might not seem difficult, is really one of the most difficult that can be asked. When we have realized the obstacles in the way of a straightforward and confident answer, we shall be well launched on the study of philosophy—for philosophy is merely the attempt to answer such ultimate questions, not carelessly and dogmatically, as we do in ordinary life and even in the sciences, but critically, after exploring all that makes such questions puzzling, and after realizing all the vagueness and confusion that underlie our ordinary ideas.[16]

A great part of philosophy is the ability to recognize difficulties,

15 Plato, The Republic, trans. F. M. Cornford, Oxford University Press, 1960, p. xxix.
16 B. Russell, The Problems of Philosophy, Oxford University Press, 1959, p. 7.

especially in those areas of experience which, on the surface, seem simple. Growth comes when difficulties are faced in such a way that new depths of understanding are achieved. The depth of the synthesis is absolutely impossible apart from the prior grasp of real difficulties in both the thesis and its obvious alternative. An ideal example of this is found in ethics, when, before we can have a mature view, we must be forced to see the inadequacy of the naïve acceptance of the local mores on the one hand, and of a subjectivism which denies all norms on the other. The false gods have to be destroyed before the true God can be known.

Because most philosophers are teachers, it is wise for them to pay close attention to those generally recognized as master teachers. One of the finest of these, as members of various schools can attest, was Henry Sidgwick of Oxford, a philosopher's philosopher. Fortunately, Sidgwick put to paper his central concept of the teaching philosopher's task. Referring to the student he said, "Assuming him to be intelligent enough to feel difficulties, and as yet without the grasp of method necessary for solving them, the chief service that the oral teacher can render is to assist in their solution: first by mildly but firmly pressing the pupil to state his difficulties as clearly as possible; and secondly, by giving his own mind to the task of comprehending and answering them."[17]

Everyone knows that there is a great deal of confusion, for we always claim that our opponents are confused, even though we think we are not. But the worst confusions are seldom those of which we are fully conscious. Rather, they are the confusions of which we are either unaware or of which we are only dimly aware. This is why the thinker, who is seriously trying to help those who will listen, whether they be pupils or readers, must often be a gadfly after the fashion of Socrates, and must, accordingly, allow his first effect to be one of disturbance. There is no value at all in providing answers to questions which are not already vividly felt. It is perfectly all right to be in a fog for a while, but, says Sidgwick, if the fog is to be dispelled, it must be concentrated.

In the earlier stages of philosophical study, fog is sure to arise from

[17] H. Sidgwick, *Essays and Addresses*, Macmillan & Co., Ltd., 1904, p. 349.

time to time, in the perusal even of the best attainable books; from the obscurity of some statements, or their inconsistency with other statements of the same or other writers, or with the reader's previous beliefs. An intellectual fog, like a physical fog, is very pervasive, and liable rapidly to envelop large portions of a subject even when its original source really lies in a very limited and not very important difficulty. The great thing, therefore, is to concentrate it; and the most effective way of concentrating it is for the student to force himself to state the difficulty on paper.[18]

It is precisely because the concentration of intellectual fog is a difficult task, that we need one another. The dialogue itself, whether between teacher and student or between author and reader, is a constant encouragement to state our perplexities clearly and precisely. The very recognition of the pattern in its explicit form is a very great step toward an answer. Thus philosophy is intrinsically social, partly because we state our problems more clearly to ourselves when we are trying to state them to others. It is no accident that a good book of philosophy usually includes many quotations; this is because men's minds are aroused by the thoughts of other men. In his short autobiography, which is attached to the large work devoted to his thought, G. E. Moore reported his own experience in this connection. "What has suggested philosophical problems to me," he says, "is things which other philosophers have said about the world or the sciences."[19]

A philosopher is an ignorant man thinking, in the hope of communicating with other ignorant men. We must search constantly for the conditions under which the wisdom which we so sorely need is likely to emerge. We know that there must be times when we are alone, just as there must be times when we are with others. Socrates, we remember, was not only a convivial man; he was also a man who went alone for extended periods of meditation. One of these periods of aloneness, Plato tells us, immediately preceded the famous banquet at which the subject was the nature of love. We are not likely to do better than follow Socrates.

[18] Ibid., pp. 349, 350.
[19] P. A. Schilpp (ed.), The Philosophy of G. E. Moore, Cambridge University Press, 1943, p. 14.

The Future of Philosophy

There is no reason to suppose that philosophy will come to an end, and there are many reasons to suppose that it will continue to flourish. There was once an argument to the effect that philosophy deals with issues until there is some particularized science ready to take them over. This argument was given a certain credibility because of the fact that all that is now studied in the natural sciences was once called philosophy. It is well known that men of the character of Newton and Boyle were generally termed "natural philosophers." If such men are subtracted, in ever greater numbers in each generation, it would appear that eventually nothing would remain for the original discipline and that it would die a natural death. However persuasive this argument once seemed, it is so no longer, partly because of the fact that the presuppositions underlying all of the sciences are not and cannot be the sole responsibility of any science. The advance of the sciences, in their amazing complexity and compartmentalization, renders metaphysics not less, but more important. "Metaphysics is the science which deals with the pre-suppositions underlying ordinary science."[20]

It was philosophy in this primary sense that Aristotle stressed, even more than he stressed the particular sciences which he did so much to originate and to establish. The primary study he termed First Philosophy, Wisdom, or Theology. This is the subject matter which his editors called *Metaphysics*, because of where it stood in relation to *Physics*. There is nothing which has transpired in human thought to make this kind of study otiose or quaint. One reason for this is that there is no fundamental change in the human situation. We shall go on asking the same questions, not because the former answers are uniformly worthless, but because no answer is complete or, indeed, can be, and also because our deepest needs do not change.

The definitive answers in philosophy are always suspect. Our boldest assertions are sure to be challenged, perhaps by ourselves, as happened in the career of Wittgenstein. Verification is never

[20] R. G. Collingwood, op. cit., p. 11. See Pt. I, chap. 4, "On Presupposing."

absolute. It "only shows an hypothesis to be better than its alternatives because it explains something that the others fail to do."[21] Perhaps there will be new hypotheses, of which we do not now dream, which will explain our experiences better than they are now explained. Certainly the world is greater and more wonderful than anyone can possibly realize. This is why, from our point of view, it is always an open universe, and this sense of openness is a necessary element in any general philosophy which is worthy of the name. Even though what we know is slight, we have not, as yet, been able to reduce all that we know to a single coherent system. The continued significance of the problem of evil is a vivid reminder of this humbling fact. But the hope of greater integration sustains us. Metaphysics is therefore the pioneering area of philosophy. "Now metaphysics or general philosophy," says Cohen, "tries to formulate some world view using general principles to enable us to integrate all our knowledge. Its truth cannot therefore be conclusively tested by any one particular experiment, least of all by a purely physical one. Metaphysical propositions are perspectives. They determine the point of view from which all human experience or all our sciences and anticipations can be co-ordinated."[22]

Only those who do not face history tend to minimize the influence of philosophy on the course of events. That the philosopher may be a powerful force is shown by the example of Karl Marx. In our century, fascists, national socialists and communists have all referred, though in different ways, to the metaphysics of Hegel.

There is every reason to believe that philosophy will awaken from its antimetaphysical slumber, as it is already doing, and that it will rediscover great themes. Because no one philosophical phase is really permanent or continuous, there has to be the perennial task of rediscovery. Philosophy increases in excellence as it includes humor and passion and zest. Whenever the heritage of Socrates is restored, these characteristics begin to appear. We are more likely to restore this heritage if we meditate often on Plato's account of the true lover of knowledge, which we find at the heart of The Republic. The vision there is of "one born to strive

[21] Cohen, op. cit., pp. 73, 74.
[22] Ibid., p. 75.

towards reality, who cannot linger among that multiplicity of things which men believe to be real, but holds on his way with a passion until he has laid hold upon the essential nature of each thing with that part of his soul which can apprehend reality, because of its affinity therewith."[23]

Loyalty to such a vision will lead to many diverse tasks. One of these is criticism, including relentless examination of every idea presented. But if we stop with criticism we are unprofitable servants. We must also have the courage to propound our own ideas and thus submit them to criticism on the part of others. Somebody must make systematic and coherent efforts if our intellectual life is to have any wholeness. Those who are tempted to be satisfied to be mere critics need to be reminded, from time to time, of the strong words of Dr. Johnson on this subject.

Criticism is a study by which men grow important and formidable at a very small expense. The power of invention has been conferred by nature on few, and the labour of learning those sciences which may by mere labour be obtained; but every man can exert such judgment as he has upon the works of others; and he whom nature has made weak, and idleness keeps ignorant may yet support his vanity by the name of a critick.[24]

No single philosophy as represented by any one of the modern schools is likely to become dominant. This is because the problems are not simple enough to make such a development probable. Our greatest hope, and one that is already being realized in part, is that of the coming together of divergent schools in the willingness to learn from one another. For the most part each school has something positive to say and something that is needed, though each is incomplete. This is why we invoke the figure of Socrates at the end as we did at the beginning. Socrates loved clarity; Socrates studied words; but Socrates also had a sense of mission as he tried to convince his hearers of the existence both of a moral order and their own immortal souls. He gaily risked the obloquy of taking a stand, when convictions such as those which he held were not generally popular.

[23] Plato, op. cit., VI, 490.
[24] Samuel Johnson, The Idler, Number 60.

One of the saddest features of our age is that, in spite of our evident vitality, we have, at the heart of our intellectual life, a wholly unnecessary dichotomy. Walter Kaufmann has pointed to this lamentable division of our resources in a time when we need all the strength which mutual help can provide. He shows that, "on the one hand there are those whose devotion to intellectual cleanliness and vigor is exemplary but who refuse to deal with anything but small, and often downright trivial, questions; in the other camp are men like Toynbee and some of the existentialists who deal with the big and interesting questions, but in such a manner that the positivists point to them as living proofs that any effort of this kind is doomed to failure. Aware of their opponents' errors, both sides go to ever greater extremes; the split widens; and the intelligent layman who is left in the middle will soon lose sight of both."[25]

Socrates is sundered, and the result is tragic, because both sides of the Socratic heritage need each other desperately! They must be brought together, not merely as groups confronting each other, but as equally necessary elements in the lives of whole men. The future of philosophy, as something which makes a real difference in the counsels of civilization, depends upon the genuine union of clarity and passion.

[25] W. Kaufmann, (ed.), Existentialism from Dostoevsky to Sartre, World Publishing Company, Meridian Books, Inc., 1956, p. 51.

APPENDIXES

Appendix 1 ⁓ BIOGRAPHICAL NOTES ON PHILOSOPHERS

Anaxagoras of Klazomene (c. 500–428 B.C.) was the first philosopher to settle in Athens. There he lived until he was forced to leave under the charge of impiety. He was a great supporter of the doctrines of Parmenides. The emphasis seen in his philosophy, through the fragments of it which have come down to us, are on Nous or "mind," and the Greeks' fear of chaos. Socrates was greatly aroused when he first became acquainted with the emphasis of Anaxagoras on the ultimacy of mind.

Anaximander (c. 610–545 B.C.) was a prominent member of the school of Miletus and a pupil of Thales. In producing the first map, Anaximander showed his power of abstraction, and, in saying that man came into being from the fish, he gave the suggestion of evolution. Our knowledge of his philosophy comes from the writings of various ancient historians and philosophers. The fundamental stuff of the universe, he said, is "the Boundless."

Anaximenes (c. 550–500 B.C.), like Thales and Anaximander, was a Milesian. He maintained that the fundamental stuff of the Universe is air or "breath." By condensation and rarefaction, this basic stuff

329

becomes other things: by the former process, for example, it yields earth; by the latter, it yields fire. For our knowledge of Anaximenes' work in philosophy, we must rely on the reports of others, for his works are not extant.

Anselm (1035–1109), a contemporary of Abelard, was a realist and a deadly opponent of Roscellinus, another medieval philosopher who dealt with the problem of universals. As a realist, he maintained that universals actually do exist, and exist outside our minds. Anselm is also known for his contribution to theology, i.e., the ontological argument for the existence of God. The force of this argument depends upon existence being considered as a perfection. His chief works are his *Monologion* and *Proslogion*.

Aquinas, Thomas (1225–1274), the leading Roman Catholic philosopher. His great works are *Summa Theologica* and *Summa Contra Gentiles*, in the latter of which he develops five ways to demonstrate the existence of God. Strongly influenced by Aristotelianism, he faced a constant struggle with other philosophers of his generation who were chiefly Augustianian, drawing heavily upon Platonism.

Aristotle (384–322 B.C.) was the most famous of the students of Plato and was the founder of the Lyceum near Athens. He excelled not only as a philosopher, but also as a scientist and a logician. As a philosopher, he has given us, in his *Metaphysics*, many important doctrines; that of the four causes being only one. As a scientist, he provided the groundwork for the contemporary sciences of physics, biology, and others. And as a logician, he has given us the formulation of the syllogism, a contribution which von Leibniz has called the most beautiful single invention of mankind. His chief works are his *Organon*, his *Metaphysics*, and his *Ethics*.

Augustine (354–430), also known as St. Augustine, was made the Bishop of Hippo in 395 after his conversion from intense skepticism to Christianity. Of his many works, his *City of God*, *Confessions*, and *On Free Choice* are usually considered the most noteworthy. Augustine was perhaps the first philosopher to recognize the truth that man cannot doubt that he doubts, an idea usually attributed to the originality of Descartes.

Aurelius, Marcus (121–180 A.D.), was a Roman philosopher in the school of Stoicism. He formulated the Stoic concept of the soul. This soul, which consisted of the five senses, the organ of sound, and the faculty of reasoning, was considered to be the basic essence of man. When Aurelius inherited the throne of his father, it was widely believed that Plato's philosopher king had at last come to office. His philosophy is best known through his *Meditations*. A gigantic statue of Aurelius dominates the central point of the city of Rome.

Bacon, Francis (1561–1626), presented the possibility of an inductive rather than deductive means of discovering truth. The idea that the bulk of his work was in revolt against Aristotelianism and scholasticism is partly confirmed by the title of one of his most important works, the *Novum Organum*. His greatest concern, in this work and others, was for the source of the major premises of syllogisms.

Bentham, Jeremy (1748–1832), was the founder of the philosophical school of utilitarianism in England. By the doctrines of this school, the good for man is pleasure, and pleasure (or happiness) means the greatest pleasure for the greatest number. Bentham's moral philosophy was formulated in order to support his actions in English politics of the time. His chief philosophical work is *The Principles of Morals and Legislation*.

Bergson, Henri (1859–1941), was probably the most prominent of the philosophical vitalists and some of his most important work is in the area of metaphysics. He maintains that intuition, not reason nor analysis, should be used to find the Reality of things, because reason tends to distort the Reality of a thing by analyzing it into parts. Among his chief works are *An Introduction to Metaphysics* and *Time and Free Will*.

Berkeley, George (1685–1753), is best known for his philosophical idealism, although his work in religion through *Three Dialogues Between Hylas and Philonous* is also important. To Berkeley, the being or *esse* of a thing is its *percipi*. Matter, because all physical aspects of a thing can be reduced to the spiritual or mental, does not exist as such. Berkeley's philosophy is best illustrated in his *Treatise on the Principles of Human Knowledge*.

Boethius (470–525) is chiefly noted for his translation of Aristotle's *Organon* into Latin, because this translation made the work available to medieval scholars. He is also known for his principle of fusion, which he presented in his *Concerning the Trinity*. He wrote his *The Consolation of Philosophy* while he was in prison, under suspicion of treason.

Bosanquet, Bernard (1848–1923), as a neo-Hegelian idealist, maintains that Reality is one, all-encompassing, and completely rational. The aim of philosophy, Bosanquet believes, is to enter into the spirit of the Absolute, following its development through social and individual experiences. This "Pilgrim's Progress of Philosophy" is described in two of Bosanquet's major works—both being Gifford Lectures: *The Principle of Individuality and Value* (1912) and *The Value and Destiny of the Individual* (1913).

Bradley, Francis H. (1846–1924), is a foremost British dialectician. His main work in philosophy is a powerful attack upon the inadequacies of various hedonistic theories in ethics. He has also presented a new version of the coherence theory of truth through his theory of the degrees of truth. His principal works are *Ethical Studies* and *Appearance and Reality.*

Brightman, E. S., (1884–1953), is the leading representative in the modern world of the school of personalism, long associated with Boston University and the University of Southern California. Brightman had a deeply empirical orientation in philosophy; the most important experience, he believed, being the experience of *persons.* Like William James, he upheld the idea of the finitude of God.

Bruno, Giordano (1548–1600), was a monk of the Dominican Order whose opinions finally led to his being burned at the stake. Bruno maintained that God and the universe were no more than two aspects of one reality, the former name stressing the creativeness in all things, and the latter stressing the ultimate of the possibilities in which that creativeness might be manifest. His *De l'infinito universo e mundo* and *De monade* might be cited as his principal works.

Carnap, Rudolf (1891–), is most noted for his work in the field of modern and mathematical logic, and the application of the same to other fields such as epistemology, semantics, and the philosophy of science. He was active in the founding of the Vienna Circle, and helped Otto Neurath and Hans Hahn to write *Die wissenschaftliche Weltauffassung der Wiener Kreis.* His other major works have been concerning the empirical sciences.

Cassirer, Ernest (1874–1945), was born at Breslau, and studied at Berlin and Marburg. He left Germany in 1932 to teach at Oxford. In 1941 he came to America to teach at Yale where he remained until 1944. The last year of his life was spent as a visiting professor at Columbia.

He will be best remembered for *The Philosophy of Symbolic Forms* and *An Essay on Man*. His is a philosophy of symbolism.

Cohen, Morris Raphael (1880–1947), was born in Russia and came to the United States at the age of twelve. He was professor of philosophy at the College of the City of New York from 1912 to 1938. His reputation as a skillful logician rests upon the successful publication of *An Introduction to Logic and the Scientific Method* and *A Preface to Logic*. He was a vigorous critic of what seemed to him to be the exaggerated claims of positivists. His metaphysical work is *Reason and Nature*.

Comte, Auguste (1798–1857), is the father of the entire positivist movement of the last century. His work in philosophy, which glorifies science as something representing the maturity of mankind, is intended as a successor to both theology and metaphysics, now supposedly outmoded. His bold doctrine, which may be called scientism as well as positivism, appears in *Cours de philosophie positive*.

Croce, Benedetto, (1866–1952), represents Hegelian idealism in Italian culture. Much of his philosophical work is in the field of aesthetics. As a follower of Hegel he did a great deal in the philosophy of history, and in the relation of general human experience to historical experience. Among his major works are *Esthetics* and *History as the Story of Liberty*.

Democritus (c. 460–365 B.C.) was a pluralist following Parmenides and Empedocles. He maintained that the universe was composed of atoms which were hooked together by means of a cosmic swirl to form composites. He believed the atoms or elements to be unmodifiable. Democritus is considered a universal genius because of the great variety in subject matter of the fragments of his works that have come down to us.

Descartes, René (1596–1650), because his philosophizing differed so much from that of his medieval predecessors, is known as "the father of modern philosophy." His famous and careful method of doubting all that of which he could not be certain, led to the construction of his system of metaphysics and psychophysical dualism. His most widely read and studied works are the rather brief *Meditations on First Philosophy* and *Discourse on Method*.

Dewey, John (1859–1952), is one of the greatest of American philosophers. His work in the field of education has done much to advance the so-called "progressive education" in the United States and elsewhere. The most complete statement of Dewey's philosophy of education may be found in his *Democracy and Education*. Dewey is chiefly responsible for the establishment of the philosophy of instrumentalism. Among his many major works are: *How We Think, Reconstruction in Philosophy*, and *Art as Experience*.

Duns Scotus, John (1265?–1308?), was one of the most influential and able philosophers to come out of medieval Britain. Duns Scotus was a realist and was active in the medieval problem of universals. As a Franciscan, his philosophy was influenced by his Order; but he was also influenced by Islamic philosophy through Avicenna and by Aristotelianism. It was Duns Scotus who brought the word *real* into use in philosophy.

Empedocles (494–432 B.C.) was the first of the pluralist school and was subject to an influence by the earlier Pythagoreans. Empedocles' doctrine of the four roots or elements (i.e., fire, air, earth, and water) became the physics of his day. According to his cosmology, the objects or bodies in the universe are animated either by love, which unites, or by strife, which destroys the union. Only various fragments of his works have come down to us.

Epictetus (c. 60–110) was a Roman Stoic who was at first a slave, a fact which is indicative of the wide range of stoicism (q.v.). He was primarily concerned with ethical and moral matters, and offers only an incomplete metaphysical system. What man should do, according to Epictetus, is to strive to live according to Nature by virtue, and to accept all things with an untroubled mind. His principal work is the *Discourses*.

Epicurus (341–270 B.C.) is the founder of epicureanism, which served as a philosophic substitute for religion in a day when philosophy was a practical tool of life rather than a search for truth. His philosophy is a type of hedonism (q.v.), and presents a conception of pleasure that is similar to that of Aristotle. Epicurus founded his school in Athens about 306 B.C. Although only fragments of Epicurus' work remain, his philosophy is fully expounded by Lucretius.

Fichte, Johan (1762–1814), is considered the first great German idealist. He was very deeply influenced by the philosophy of Kant, especially that appearing in *The Critique of Practical Reason* and *The Critique of Judgment*. His *Addresses to the German Nation*, delivered during the French occupation of Berlin, reflects a great support for pan-Germanism. Some of his major works are *Versuch einer Kritik aller Offenbarung*, and *Die Bestimmung des Menschen*.

Hartmann, Nicholai (1882–1951), is considered by many to be the greatest moral philosopher of the twentieth century. His thorough work on the foundations of ethical thinking was brought to fruition during and immediately after World War I in Germany. Especially important is Hartmann's argument for objective reference in ethical propositions. Hartmann establishes the freedom of the will by a procedure similar to that which he uses to demonstrate that the object of knowledge exists in itself.

Hegel, Georg (1770–1831), is often considered one of the last great systematizers in philosophy. His writings, which should be looked upon as an inseparable union of doctrine and method, have had a profound and controversial effect on recent and contemporary philosophy. The philosophy of Marx, which followed that of Hegel, is said to be unthinkable without Hegel. Perhaps his greatest work is his influential writing on the philosophy of history.

Heidegger, Martin (1889–   ), is known both for his work in phenomenology and in existentialism. Prominent in almost all of his writings is a search for a new solution to the *Seinsfrage* or question of being, the primary question of metaphysics. His difficult works, some of which have only recently been rendered into English, include: *Being and Time, What is Metaphysics?*, and *Introduction to Metaphysics*.

Heraclitus (544–478 B.C.), because of the riddle-like fragments of his works that have come down to us, has been named "The Dark and Obscure Philosopher," "The Obscure," and "The Riddler." He is best known for his philosophy of change, in which he maintained that all things were in a state of constant flux. The fragments of his work indicate that he may have had a definite influence on Plato, the Stoics, Bergson, and Hegel.

Hobbes, Thomas (1588–1679), was a materialist and a skeptic. Most of his work was in the areas of the empirical sciences and history. In many ways he anticipated the works of philosophers subsequent to him. His distinction between primary and secondary qualities, for example, is an anticipation of the same distinction made by John Locke. His major works include *On Bodies, On Man*, and *On the State*.

Hume, David (1711–1776), was the greatest of British skeptics and empiricists. He is also considered by some the greatest of all philosophers in the Age of Enlightenment. The works of his immediate philosophical predecessors, Locke and Berkeley, served to influence a large number of his doctrines, such as his notion of causation, which is still of importance today. His principal works are: *An Inquiry Concerning the Human Understanding*, and *The Dialogues on Natural Religion*.

Husserl, Edmund (1859–1938), was the first to apply the title "Phenomenology" to an entire philosophy, his own. As a phenomenologist he was chiefly concerned with a descriptive analysis of the subjective processes. This philosophy of Husserl is having a profound effect upon contemporary phenomenology and existentialism. His major works include *Philosophie der Arithmetik* and *Ideen z. e. reinen Phänomenologie u. phänomenologischen Philosophie*.

James, William (1842–1910), is, without a doubt, one of the most colorful and influential of American philosophers. From the impression made on him by the essay of Peirce, "How to Make Our Ideas Clear," James went on to present an unequaled development of a recently important school of American philosophy, pragmatism. Among his major works are: *Pragmatism: A New Name for Some Old Ways of Thinking* and *Varieties of Religious Experience*.

Jaspers, Karl (1883–   ), has been much influenced by both Kierkegaard and Nietzsche, and their respective psychologies. The existentialist spirit of Jaspers, however, is more a scientific or analytic examination of man's outlook on the world. He stresses the need for a return to true philosophizing from traditional, stultifying, systematic philosophies. Among his major works, *Vernunft und Existenz* and *Existenzphilosophie* may be cited.

Kant, Immanuel (1724–1804), led a comparatively uneventful life, though he became one of the greatest of philosophers. In his entire lifetime he traveled scarcely more than forty miles from his home in Königsberg. The major works, resulting from his critical and rationalistic philosophical system, are *The Critique of Pure Reason*, *the Critique of Practical Reason*, and *The Metaphysic of Morals*. The influence of the Kantian system on recent and contemporary philosophers is great.

Kierkegaard, Sören (1813–1855), is often referred to as one of the two major forerunners of existentialism, the other being Nietzsche. His works, which indicate a pessimistic attitude toward society, have placed him with a group of men commonly referred to as "philosophers of protest." His major works include *Either/Or* and *Concluding Unscientific Postscript*.

Langer, Susanne K. (1901–), is an extremely active contemporary American philosopher. She studied under Whitehead and soon began to show the influence of Cassirer. She has won a great body of readers by her *Philosophy in a New Key*. Her most advanced work is her recent *Philosophical Sketches*, which she presents as a step in the development of something more ambitious. Her experience is rare among philosophers in that she has been the subject of a "Profile" in the *New Yorker*.

Leibniz, Gottfried von (1646–1716), is considered one of the most important philosophers of the seventeenth-century Age of Reason. His work extends not only to the area of philosophy, but also to that of jurisprudence, mathematics, history, theology. Through various political and academic appointments he was well acquainted with several of the seventeenth-century minds, such as Newton, Huygens, and Molière. He is best known as a philosopher for his metaphysical work, *The Monadology*.

Leucippus (c. 450 B.C.) was, according to tradition and various commentators, a disciple of Parmenides and possibly of Zeno, and a contemporary of Anaxagoras. He is supposed to have founded a school at Abdera. Extremely little is known of him, for, with the exception of a fragmented quotation, none of his written work has come down to us.

Locke, John (1623–1714), was the first philosopher in the English empirical tradition of Locke, Berkeley, and Hume. The ideas most often associated with Locke are (1) that the mind, at birth, is a *tabula rasa*, (2) that primary and secondary qualities are different in kind, and (3) that all knowledge comes by means of "representative ideas." His most important work is *An Essay on Human Understanding*. His other works include: *Reasonableness in Christianity* and *Two Treatises on Government*.

Lovejoy, Arthur O. (1873–1962), was for many years the dominant influence in philosophy at Johns Hopkins University. His teaching is associated with (1) an insistence on critical realism, (2) the importance of time, (3) the discipline known as the history of ideas, (4) the enduring validity of dualism. His best-known book is *The Revolt Against Dualism*. His death occurred December 30, 1962.

Lucretius, Carus (95–54 B.C.), was a Roman philosopher who is best known for his exposition of epicureanism in his didactic poem, *De Rerum Natura.* His natural science, the field in which he was most interested, was a purely mechanistic conception. Atoms, of which everything was composed, lacked, in his system, any "vital principle." His works were published in 54 B.C. by Cicero, after his suicide.

Marcel, Gabriel (1889–), is a contemporary French thinker who represents the theistic branch of existentialism, as Sartre represents the atheistic branch. His work can best be approached through his Gifford Lecures and his *Philosophy of Existence.* The influence of Josiah Royce on Marcel's thought is pervasive.

Maritain, Jacques (1882–), is one of the most outstanding Catholic and Thomistic philosophers of the present time. His philosophic system, which is constituted on Thomistic foundations without being simply a commentary on the same, is an illustration of one of his goals in philosophy: to apply Thomistic philosophy to contemporary problems. Among his major works is *The Degrees of Knowledge.*

Marx, Karl (1818–1883), is perhaps the most outstanding practical philosopher of the nineteenth century. His work is shot through with influence from Hegel and Feuerbach. Marx, in cooperation with Engels, founded the school of philosophy known as dialectical materialism. Although his work contains possibilities for development in almost all areas of philosophy, it can only be properly referred to as political philosophy. His major works include *Das Kapital* and (with Engels) "The Manifesto of the Communist Party."

Mill, John Stuart (1806–1873), probably did more for the full development of utilitarianism than any other philosopher. His work with utilitarianism was greatly influenced by Bentham. But Mill's utilitarianism differed so radically, in some aspects, from Bentham's that his position is often referred to as "Mill's heresy." Mill's principal works include *On Liberty, Utilitarianism,* and *Logic.*

Mirandola, Pico della (1463–1494), was one of the foremost philosophical humanists of the Italian Renaissance. The humanism he presented differed from that of most of the Greeks in that his was a theistic humanism. Pico died young, and his most widely read work, *An Oration on the Dignity of Man,* was completed while he was in his twenties. In this work is presented his conception of the uniqueness of man, as radically different from all other creatures.

Moore, G. E. (1873–1958), is a leading proponent of English realism. His editorship of *Mind* has done a great deal toward making him internationally known. Moore is to be credited as the founder of the neorealistic theory of epistemological monism in philosophy. His major works include *Philosophical Studies* and *Principia Ethica*.

Nietzsche, Friedrich (1844–1900), stands with Kierkegaard as being one of the most influential and important forerunners of recent and contemporary existentialism. Nietzsche's emphasis was almost solely on spiritual, intellectual, and physical power embodied in an ideal man, the Overman. His philosophy is best expressed in *Thus Spoke Zarathustra, Beyond Good and Evil*, and *The Antichrist*.

Ockham, William of (d.1349), presents a philosophy which is empirically oriented. He is well-known for his rejection of the problem of universals. He is also known for the principle of economy in argument, called "Ockham's Razor," although he certainly was not its inventor. This principle states that the existence of a certain number of entities or factors should not be postulated in an argument when a lesser number will do. This is known also as the "principle of parsimony."

Parmenides (fl. 504–500 B.C.) was a pre-Socratic monist *par excellence*. A great deal of his philosophical argument reflects his rejection of the earlier Heraclitean thesis of change. Maintaining that appearances, in the last analysis, cannot be trusted under any circumstances, and that only the use of reason can be trusted, Parmenides was the first clear-cut rationalist. His philosophical writings have come to us as fragments and as reports by his disciple, Zeno.

Pascal, Blaise (1623–1662), turned from his mathematical and scientific studies to a study of man and the solution to his problems through faith. Though Pascal is known more for his work in Christian apologetics and in theology than for his work in general philosophy, much of his thinking has a general application. His *Pensées* were put together, from scattered notes, after his death.

Peirce, Charles (1839–1914), is best known for his celebrated essay in *Popular Science Monthly* (1877–1878), "How to Make Our Ideas Clear." The content of his essay did a great deal to influence the formulation of pragmatism (q.v.) and instrumentalism (q.v.). He has been referred to as "the most versatile, profound, and original philosopher that the United States has ever produced." After teaching a short time at Johns Hopkins University, Peirce spent most of his mature life as a private scholar. Most of his work appears in essay form. These essays, including many not previously published, appear in *The Collected Papers of Charles Sanders Peirce*, edited by Charles Hartshorne and Paul Weiss.

Plato (428/7–348/7 B.C.) was the most famous student of Socrates, and subsequently the teacher of Aristotle. It is from Plato's *Dialogues* that almost all information to be had about Socrates has come. He wrote in almost every area of philosophy. A. N. Whitehead has said that all subsequent philosophy is a series of footnotes to Plato. His major dialogues include *The Republic, The Theaetetus, The Parmenides,* and *The Sophist.*

Plotinus (205–270) was the founder of the mystical and metaphysical school known as neo-Platonism or Plotinism. The psychology and metaphysics of Plotinus have had a great effect, through Augustine and others, on Christianity and Christian intellectualism. The *Enneads* of Plotinus, which are nine sections in six books, have come down to us through the efforts of Porphyry, the most active and devoted student of Plotinus.

Pythagoras (581–500 B.C.) established his school, which was essentially a religious brotherhood, in Croton, in southern Italy, in about 532 B.C. The religion most affecting this Pythagorean school was the Orphic religion of Greece. Because it was the goal of the Pythagoreans to free the soul of the impediments of the body by disciplined exercise of the mind, philosophy became for them the contemplation of pure mathematical essences. Pythagoras left no writings.

Royce, Josiah (1855–1916), is considered a neo-Hegelian idealist, but he was in actuality much more than this. Though American Hegelianism owes more to Royce for its development than to any other philosopher, Royce's interest turned from this type of philosophy to moral, religious, and social problems. His major works include *The World and The Individual, The Spirit of Modern Philosophy,* and *The Religious Aspect of Philosophy.*

Russell, Bertrand (1872–   ), is most widely known for his coauthorship with Whitehead of *Principia Mathematica,* and for his present political activities in England. His work toward the reconstruction of logic and his work in metaphysics have contributed much to contemporary philosophy. He invented the system known as logical atomism. *The Problems of Philosophy* and *Our Knowledge of the External World* are among his major philosophical works.

Santayana, George (1863–1952), is known not only as a philosopher, but also as an essayist and a poet. In maintaining that we are immediately conscious of the nature of reality, he presents a naturalistic and materialistic conception of philosophic realism. Among his major philosophical works are *The Sense of Beauty, The Life of Reason,* and *Realms of Being.* Early in this century Santayana taught at Harvard in the rewarding fellowship of James, Royce, and Palmer.

Sartre, Jean-Paul (1905–   ), might fairly be called the mainstay of French existentialism. His influences have come through Husserl and Nietzsche. As an existentialist, Sartre's major thesis is that man is free and that this freedom is inescapable. There is no exit from the assumption of responsibility of man, for there is no external authority upon which man may place responsibility. Sartre's major work is *Being and Nothingness.*

Scheler, Max (1874–1928), was the most striking character in German philosophy in the decade following World War I. He was called the "Catholic Nietzsche" and was, indeed, a colorful figure. Though he was considered a phenomenologist, he would not limit his interests to any sect. At the end he became convinced that the deepest of all philosophical problems is the problem of man's nature. The result of this conviction was the publication, in the year of his death, of *Die Stellung des Menschen im Kosmos.* This has appeared recently in an English translation with the title, *Man's Place in Nature.*

Schopenhauer, Arthur (1788–1860), is noted as being, with Nietzsche, one of the initiators of contemporary existentialism. In several of his works he presented an often caustic criticism of the Christianity of his day. His work as a whole is essentially deterministic and pessimistic. *The World as Will and Idea* is his major work. Popularly he is known for his low opinion of women.

Socrates (470–399 B.C.) was the greatest of the ancient philosophers who undertook to turn philosophy from a preoccupation with nature to a preoccupation with man. His way of life and attitude toward philosophy have been an example for countless numbers since his time. He was the teacher of Plato and, through Plato, influenced Aristotle and many others. He left no writings, and all we know of him comes from the writings of historians and from the *Dialogues* of Plato.

Spencer, Herbert (1820–1903), is noted for his works in ethics, psychology, biology, and sociology. The aim of his work, which seems to give strong support for individualism, was to formulate a mechanistic or material interpretation of life. He was greatly influenced by the Darwinian conception of natural selection. His major works include *The System of Synthetic Philosophy*.

Spinoza, Benedict (1632–1677), presented a monism in his philosophic doctrine which is often referred to as a philosophy of substance. Although it is a matter of some dispute, he is said to have been influenced by the works of the Arabic Aristotelians, neo-Platonism, and Descartes. His work was not confined solely to philosophy, for he also dealt with politics. Besides his *Ethics*, which is his major work, he wrote *Tractatus Theologicus-Politicus*, *Political Treatise*, and others.

Stebbing, L. Susan (1885–1943), was one of the most brilliant logicians toward the middle of this century. Well acquainted with the entire modern school of realism as well as with the work of Whitehead and Russell on the foundations of mathematics, she was prepared to present both modern and Aristotelian logic in a comprehensive fashion. Her chief works are *A Modern Introduction to Logic* and *Ideals and Illusions*, which is devoted to social thinking.

Thales (fl. 585 B.C.), the first philosopher of the West, maintained that the fundamental element of the universe was water, a deduction he probably made from the many states that water may take. It is said that he made the first accurate prediction of the eclipse of the sun in 585 B.C., although there is some doubt now that he could have done so. He is known as the founder of the Milesian school of philosophy and as one of the Seven Sages of Greece.

Tillich, Paul (1886–   ), is the author of a powerful religious existentialism. In one of his later works, *The Courage to Be*, Tillich asks whether man has the courage to be, even in the face of such an absolute threat to being as death. He has done a great deal of work with what he calls the "age of anxiety," or the postwar period in Europe and America. His major work is *Systematic Theology*. The final period of Tillich's teaching has been at Harvard where advanced students have flocked to his lectures.

Whitehead, Alfred North (1861–1947), is noted for his work with Russell in mathematics and for his work in logic and metaphysics. His metaphysics is unique in the degree in which he brings to metaphysics deep learning in the sciences. In his later life, the range of his work extended to education, religion, aesthetics, history, and history of science. His major work in metaphysics is *Process and Reality*. Other works include *Adventures of Ideas* and *The Function of Reason*.

Wittgenstein, Ludwig (1889–1951), is known as a "common language analyst." Before earning this title, Wittgenstein was a logical atomist, and a student of Russell. The great difference between these two schools of philosophy makes it necessary to refer to the early and the late Wittgenstein. His major works are *Tractatus Logico-Philosophicus* and *Philosophical Investigations*, representing his final position.

Xenophanes of Colophon (c. 570–480 B.C.) was a celebrated poet and philosopher of Greece. To him is attributed the founding of the Eleatic school of philosophy, and the ancients are said to have considered him the originator of the doctrine of the oneness of the universe. The works of Xenophanes have come down to us only as a few fragments of his poem on nature, which contained his philosophic system.

Zeno of Elea (c. 490–430 B.C.) was the supporting follower of Parmenides. He defended his master's teaching that changelessness was the whole of reality. His defense was by means of difficult paradoxes. Only since the new mathematics of the late nineteenth and early twentieth centuries have these paradoxes appeared less mystifying. Only fragments of his writings have come down to us.

Zeno the Stoic (c. 340–265 B.C.) founded the Stoic school in Athens. His teaching was according to the Stoic principle of submission to Nature or Providence, the order of which it was useless to resist. A brilliant modern interpretation of Stoicism can be found in Gilbert Murray's essay, "Stoicism."

Appendix 2 ⌒ NOTES ON PHILOSOPHICAL SYSTEMS

Agnosticism is based on the conviction that man either does not know or cannot know. It is usually more widely held as a theological doctrine than a philosophical one. In theology, the theory is that man cannot attain knowledge of God.

Analytic Philosophy is the name given to the current school of philosophy centered at the Universities of Oxford and Cambridge. It is primarily a method attempting to reduce complexities to their simpler elements. There are two specialized forms of analytic philosophy: logical analysis, which determines meanings of concepts by applying logical principles; and linguistic analysis, which examines both the common and ideal uses of language.

Determinism is a term applied to the doctrine of Thomas Hobbes to distinguish it from fatalism. It is the doctrine that all events of the present and future are necessarily as they are and will be, by virtue of past causes. The theory of determinism as a cosmology is that the universe is governed entirely by causal laws.

Dialectical Materialism is a philosophical position first developed by Marx and Engels. The word *dialectical* indicates the idea that the
344

universe is subject to constant change. This also shows the influence upon the school by Hegel. Dialectical materialism is primarily a doctrine of political philosophy, but it may also be developed as a social theory (termed historical materialism) and as an ethical theory (termed proletarian humanism). Dialectical materialism is the only philosophy which is encouraged in the Soviet Union.

Dualism appears in three different forms. In the first place there is psychophysical dualism, which involves the conclusion that there is a radical distinction between mental and physical functions. Dualism may also be epistemological, in which case the distinction is between the subjective knower and the object known. Metaphysical dualism teaches an ultimate bifurcation of reality.

Eclecticism is the practice of drawing from various philosophical doctrines in order to present a more complete view. The practice may be either passive or active. In the latter case, it is usually a deliberate attempt to present a synthesis of various positions. This may be accomplished with a great deal of originality, which a more passive effort lacks.

Empiricism is one of three chief methods of approaching philosophy, the other two being rationalism and intuitionism. The empiricist maintains that all knowledge comes from experience, that all true propositions are based on data gathered from experience, and that all true propositions of fact must be verifiable by experience. A good number of the contemporary schools of philosophy, such as the various forms of analytic philosophy, identify empiricism with limitation to sense experience, but other empiricists reject this limitation as arbitrary.

Epicureanism is the school of philosophy founded by Epicurus. It is usually referred to as a "pleasure philosophy," and, as such, is a type of hedonism. The primary concern of epicureanism centered on moral or ethical problems. It taught that the greatest good for man is pleasure, when pleasure is understood as a long, rather than short term or immediate state. The position is meant to inculcate a way of life and does not, therefore, concern itself with more speculative philosophy.

Epiphenomenalism is a philosophical doctrine presenting consciousness as no more than a by-product of psychochemical processes of the body. As such, consciousness merely accompanies these processes, and its presence or absence makes no difference upon them.

Existentialism is primarily a philosophy of man or a psychology in the broadest sense of that term. In general, existentialism is the theory that man's existence precedes his essence, or that a man is what he chooses to be. Because man is free, the responsibility for his actions, and for what he is, rests upon himself. Existentialism is usually classed as theistic, represented by Gabriel Marcel, or atheistic, represented by Jean-Paul Sartre.

Hedonism is a doctrine that makes reference to pleasure or happiness. It may take two forms. Ethical hedonism is the theory that pleasure or happiness alone is the supreme good, and goodness is determined either quantitatively or qualitatively by pleasure. The other form is psychological hedonism, which is the theory that all human motivation is, in fact, the desire to avoid pain and gain pleasure.

Humanism is any doctrine placing its primary emphasis upon human interests and values. Although it is often materialistic and atheistic, it need not be. Socrates is said to have been the first Greek humanist. The doctrine has been developed in the fields of religion, ethics (where it is often called humanitarianism), sociology, literature, and philosophy.

Idealism is the philosophical theory that reality is spiritualistic or of the nature of mind or idea. It usually is presented as a metaphysical or epistemological doctrine, and is often considered the antithesis of realism. One of the better known developers of idealism is George Berkeley.

Instrumentalism is actually a form of pragmatism developed by John Dewey. It is the theory that the mind serves as an instrument for the living organism. The position is similar to evolutionary philosophy, and has been influenced by the biological sciences.

Intuitionism usually takes the form of an epistemological doctrine in philosophy. The theory is that intuition is the basis of knowledge. Intuitionism is a highly developed doctrine in mathematics and ethics. As a theory of knowledge, it is opposed to both rationalism and empiricism.

Materialism is the theory that reality is ultimately composed of physical matter. Even mind and consciousness are considered to be either wholly dependent upon, or reducible to, matter. As such, the universe is entirely governed by the physical laws of motion and energy. Materialism should not be confused with either epiphenomenalism or mechanism.

Mechanism is the philosophical position that all phenomena may be explained by reference to the laws of cause and effect (usually by efficient causation). The position eliminates entirely all explanations of the universe in terms of purpose, final causation, design, etc.

Monism is usually a metaphysical position. As such, it is the theory that reality is either one thing or that it is one *kind* of thing (or collection of things), such as mind or matter. Monism is opposed to both dualism and pluralism.

Mysticism is the doctrine in philosophy that knowledge of reality cannot be had through any means (such as the means advocated by rationalists and sense empiricists) except a state of immediate awareness. In order to achieve this state, a great deal of discipline is necessary beforehand. In religion, the doctrine maintains that God can truly be known by a direct union or communion with Him.

Naturalism is the theory that the universe is explicable solely in terms of itself, i.e., an explication of the universe requires no concepts of final causation, supranaturalism, etc. The doctrine is somewhat similar to materialism, mechanism, and determinism. It is opposed to cosmological, teleological, and moral arguments about the nature of the universe.

Nihilism may deny the existence of reality, knowledge, or values, depending upon whether it is primarily a metaphysical, epistemological, or ethical doctrine. The theory is perhaps most widely developed as ethical nihilism, where the possibility of any distinctions among moral values is denied.

Nominalism is the doctrine limiting reality to physical particulars. The so-called universals are mere empty names, and do not belong to the class of real things or existents. Nominalism was one of the several positions taken in a philosophical controversy of the Middle Ages, known as "the problem of universals."

Panpsychism is the theory that reality consists of a plurality of psychic entities or minds. These entities may be of many levels. The most outstanding example of this position is the monadology of Gottfried von Leibniz (q.v.).

Personalism is based on the conviction that the world is best understood by concentration on the highest developments known, i.e., persons. Personality is seen as a means of understanding reality and as representing the utmost point of value. The founder of personalism as a philosophy in America was Borden P. Bowne, of Boston University.

Positivism is a highly specialized form of empiricism, maintaining the doctrine that all reliable knowledge is scientific knowledge and simple description. Metaphysical knowledge is regarded as impossible. The school began with the work of Auguste Comte (q.v.). Logical positivism is a contemporary variant of this emphasis, carrying the conception of scientism as far as possible. This school describes metaphysical statements as meaningless, due to the fact that they are incapable of empirical verification.

Pragmatism is the school which considers the solution of intellectual dispute and the determination of the meaning of intellectual concepts to lie in a consideration of the practical consequences that might result from the dispute or concept. The pragmatic theory of truth is similarly construed. Pragmatism was most fruitfully developed by William James (q.v.) and John Dewey (q.v.). Dewey's development of the theory later led to instrumentalism (q.v.).

Rationalism is the set of doctrine or method opposed to empiricism (q.v.) and intuitionism (q.v.). Propositions are established by deduction, and the premises employed in the process usually contain concepts or principles of a general nature. The emphasis of rationalism is always away from sensory criteria. Pure mathematics is usually given as the best example of the most specialized form of rationalism.

Realism is the theory that things exist independently of being known. As such, realism is opposed to subjective idealism. In the Middle Ages realism referred to the conviction that universals really exist and are not mere names. As such it is opposed to all nominalism.

Relativism usually takes the form of a theory of truth. As such, it is the theory that there is no objective standard by which truth may be determined, so that truth varies with individuals and circumstances.

Scholasticism is primarily a theological method which operates by deductive processes with premises usually derived from testimony of authorities. Scholasticism was most important and most active as a tradition in the medieval period.

Skepticism (also **Scepticism**) is the doctrine that any reliable or absolute knowledge is impossible. Knowledge about supranatural realities is also considered unattainable by man, or any knower.

Solipsism is the position held by an individual who maintains that he is the whole of reality, and that all other entities are simply products of his mental operations. The world, with its inhabitants, is considered to be no more than his private sense data, and, therefore, to have no existence independently of him. In logical positivism (see Positivism) a new form of solipsism, called linguisic solipsism, has been developed.

Stoicism is a philosophical school founded in Athens in about 308 B.C. by Zeno (q.v.). Stoicism was primarily an ethical doctrine and has left little work in other areas of philosophy such as metaphysics.

Subjectivism is primarily an epistemological doctrine that the knower (subject), rather than the object, is that which is known. In both ethics and aesthetics, the doctrine states that values have no importance independent of the relations or reactions of minds.

Thomism is the complete system of thought which stems from the philosophy of St. Thomas Aquinas (q.v.). It has the powerful backing today of the Roman Catholic Church as its patron. The system includes a realistic epistemology and rationalistic method of inquiry.

Utilitarianism is the philosophical and ethical theory that the good is that which produces the greatest happiness for the greatest number. This concept has been named the principle of utility. By reference to effects on men, actions are judged as good or bad. The best known form of utilitarianism was presented by Jeremy Bentham and by John Stuart Mill.

Vitalism is a doctrine, such as Henri Bergson's élan vital, which holds that living things are such because they are sustained by a "life force." This life force or vital principle of living things cannot be reduced to description by the same laws as those by which physicochemical phenomena are described.

Appendix 3 ∾ CLASSIFIED BIBLIOGRAPHY FOR STUDENTS

Though the page footnotes suggest many titles, there is need for a classified bibliography. This bibliography is not and ought not to be exhaustive. There are thousands of books that could be mentioned, but the result would inevitably be confusing. The purpose of the following list is to give the ordinary student, in or out of college, some idea of how to start. Most of the books mentioned have references in them to other books.

INTRODUCTORY WORKS

Joad, C. E. M., *Guide to Philosophy*, Dover Publications, Inc., 1936.
   This general introduction to philosophical thinking by a British author includes not only the author's own ideas, but analyses of the major ideas of Plato, Aristotle, Hume, and Kant. The concluding section on Whitehead's philosophy will give any beginning student a fair start on a difficult but important subject.
Klausner, Neal W., and P. G. Kuntz, *Philosophy: The Study of Alternate Beliefs*. The Macmillan Company, 1961.
   A new approach is made in this volume to the introduction to philosophy. The authors see very clearly that beliefs of many

kinds are important to men and that there are always competing reasons for choices.

Patrick, G. T. W., *Introduction to Philosophy*, Houghton Mifflin Company, 2nd ed., 1935.

> Though G. T. W. Patrick's famous textbook is now a little out of date, most of it is still extremely useful, particularly for the person who is studying philosophy for the first time. The book was long in standard use in colleges and universities.

Stroll, A., and R. H. Popkin, *Introduction to Philosophy*, Holt, Rinehart and Winston, Inc., 1961.

> In this book two professors have combined the presentation of the main elements of philosophy, such as logic, epistemology, metaphysics, political philosophy, ethics, and the philosophy of religion with a study of three types of contemporary thought—pragmatism, existentialism, and the analytic school.

Thompson, S. M., *The Nature of Philosophy*, Holt, Rinehart and Winston, Inc., 1961.

> Here the professor of philosophy in a small college presents what is obviously the material which he has found useful in reaching the minds of his undergraduate students. Both the various methods and the enduring problems of philosophy are expertly handled.

BOOKS OF READINGS

Beck, R. N. (ed.), *Perspectives in Philosophy*, Holt, Rinehart and Winston, Inc., 1961.

> A book of readings chiefly though not solely from contemporary authors and those of the recent past. These readings, classified by six types—classical realism, idealism, naturalism, positivism, analytic philosophy, and existentialism—are augmented by introductory essays.

Dewey, R. D., F. W. Gramlich, and D. Loftgordon (eds.), *Problems of Ethics*, The Macmillan Company, 1961.

> This is a comprehensive book of selections from 38 authors, ancient and modern. All of the major problems involved in moral philosophy are approached. The editors have added short introductory accounts where they believe that the student needs them.

Edwards, P., and A. Pap (eds.), *A Modern Introduction to Philosophy*, The Free Press of Glencoe, The Macmillan Company, 1957.

> This impressive book includes 46 selections from classical and contemporary sources. The eight major sections are devoted to standard questions, such as "A Priori Knowledge," "Determinism,

Freedom, and Moral Responsibility," "Verification." The book is made still more useful to the student by the addition of a detailed index. Famous works, such as G. E. Moore's essay on "The Indefinability of Good" are available in this collection.

Hook, S. (ed.), *Determinism and Freedom*, New York University Press, 1958.

Here are 27 particular statements, all by contemporary thinkers, including Brand Blanshard of Yale and Percy W. Bridgeman of Harvard. Especial attention is given to the ideas of responsibility in regard to law as well as ethics.

Mandlebaum, M., F. W. Gramlich, and A. R. Anderson (eds.), *Philosophic Problems*, The Macmillan Company, 1957.

This introductory book of readings is notable for its catholicity. On all of the major problems handled a variety of views by competent writers of many schools is presented. It is not a book to be read straight through, but to be used as a reference work when competing positions are studied.

Vivas, E., and M. Krieger (eds.), *The Problems of Aesthetics*, Holt, Rinehart and Winston, Inc., 1955.

This is a book of readings that covers all of the major issues in the field and represents a great variety of modern authors. The editorial prefaces are particularly helpful. Fortunately, Vivas does not hesitate to include a selection from his own work.

BOOKS ON LOGIC AND EPISTEMOLOGY

Broad, C. D., *The Mind and Its Place in Nature*, Routledge & Kegan Paul, Ltd., 1925.

One of the most careful works in recent philosophy. C. D. Broad faces the hard problems of which ordinary readers are generally aware, and helps to make them aware of others.

Cohen, M. R., *A Preface to Logic*, The World Publishing Company, Meridian Books, Inc., 1959. By permission of Holt, Rinehart and Winston, Inc.

An eminent logician deals with the recent additions to the science of logic with both appreciation of their novelty and respect for the older forms of thought. A sophisticated book.

Lovejoy, A. O., *The Revolt Against Dualism*, The Open Court Publishing Company, 1955.

This book, described in the subtitle as "An Inquiry Concerning the Existence of Ideas," is the most thorough defense of dualism in the twentieth century.

Montague, W. P., *The Ways of Knowing*, The Macmillan Company, 1928.

One of the most thorough treatments in print of the methods of both epistemology and logic. The chief methods studied are those of authority, of mysticism, of rationalism, of empiricism, of pragmatism, and of skepticism.

Moore, G. E., *Philosophical Studies*, The Humanities Press, Inc., 1951.

This book contains a number of influential essays, particularly "The Refutation of Idealism," which has had an enduring effect on epistemological discussion. Critical studies of both James and Hume are included.

Stebbing, L., Susan, *A Modern Introduction to Logic*, Harper & Row, Inc., Torchbooks, 1961.

Miss Stebbing, more than almost any other scholar, has been able to present fairly both the Aristotelian logic and the contemporary symbolic logic which has, to some extent, replaced it. The book is written with marked literary skill.

PLATONIC WORKS

Hamilton, Edith, and H. Cairns (eds.), *The Collected Dialogues of Plato, including the Letters*, Random House, Inc., Pantheon Books, Bollingen Series LXXI, 1961.

Unique among one-volume Platonic works in its completeness, this book makes use of many translators and shows in the Introductions the fine hand of that great American scholar, Edith Hamilton.

Plato, *Epistles*, trans. G. R. Morrow, The Bobbs-Merrill Company, Inc., The Liberal Arts Press, Inc., 1962.

This translation provides important sidelights on the more famous dialogues. The account of Plato's digression on knowledge in Epistle VII is especially helpful.

Plato, *The Republic*, trans. F. M. Cornford, Oxford University Press, 1960.

Though there are many translations and editions of this book, Cornford's is now recognized as one of the best. It includes an excellent general introduction as well as brief analyses at the beginning of each chapter.

Taylor, A. E., *Plato, The Man and His Work*, The World Publishing Company, Meridian Books, Inc., 1959.

A. E. Taylor, dedicating his great work to "All True Lovers of Plato, Quick and Dead," brought his great career to a climax by providing careful analyses of all of the authentic dialogues, as well as a substantial account of Plato's life.

METAPHYSICS

Berdyaev, N., *The Beginning and the End*, Harper & Row, Inc., Torchbooks, 1957.

This volume presents a metaphysics which might be called existential, but which the author, formerly a teacher of philosophy in the Soviet Union, calls "eschatological." The author is deeply impressed by the acute sense of evil which reigns in the world, but is not a pessimist.

Blanshard, B., *The Nature of Thought*, The Macmillan Company, 1940, 2 vols.

Brand Blanshard, now retired from the position of head of the Department of Philosophy in Yale University, deals in unhurried fashion with the major problems of metaphysics. He provides, among other things, one of the clearest defenses of the coherence theory of truth. The student concerned with this theory should turn to chapers 25, 26, and 27.

Collingwood, R. G., *An Essay on Metaphysics*, The Clarendon Press, 1948.

This is not primarily a book of metaphysics, but rather a book about metaphysics, and a very advanced one. The author explains what metaphysics is, why it is necessary to the well-being and advancement of knowledge, and how it may be pursued.

Heidegger, M., *Kant and the Problem of Metaphysics*, trans. J. S. Churchill, Indiana University Press, 1962.

This is the first time that Heidegger's work on Kant's *Critique of Pure Reason* has been made available in English. A notable feature is the discussion of being and existence, from the point of view of a scholar generally classified as an existentialist.

Royce, J., *The Religious Aspect of Philosophy*, Harper & Row, Inc., Torchbooks, 1958.

From its title the reader might expect this book to be devoted to the philosophy of religion. Actually it provides the basic statement of Royce's metaphysics, especially in regard to the importance of error. The essence of Royce's doctoral dissertation at Johns Hopkins University in 1878 is included.

Whitehead, A. N., *Adventures of Ideas*, The Macmillan Company, 1933.

A brilliant book, rewarding both to the beginner and to the advanced student. The way in which ideas grow and shape history is carefully shown.

Whitehead, A. N., *Process and Reality*, The Macmillan Company, 1960.

The definitive statement of Whitehead's famous philosophy of organism. This is his most advanced and difficult work, which should not be attempted until other works of Whitehead have been read.

MAN

Cassirer, E., *An Essay on Man*, Doubleday & Company, Inc., Anchor Books, 1944.

Beginning with the thesis that self-knowledge is the highest aim of philosophical inquiry, Cassirer defines man as the "symbolical animal" and develops thoroughly what is involved in man's ability to employ symbols.

Chardin, P. T. de, *The Phenomenon of Man*, Harper & Row, Inc., 1959.

The author of this book, a Frenchman and a Jesuit, deals with man on a firm basis of historical and anthropological knowledge, yet from the point of view of a philosopher. The author maintains that no philosophy can succeed if it avoids the central problem of what man is.

Lovejoy, A. O., *Reflections on Human Nature*, The Johns Hopkins Press, 1961.

The Emeritus Professor of Philosophy at Johns Hopkins gives the fruit of many years of reflection on man, his nature, his danger, and his hope.

Scheler, M., *Man's Place in Nature*, Beacon Press, 1961.

This is an English translation of Scheler's final work, presenting his mature conclusions on the central problems of philosophical anthropology.

Weiss, P., *Man's Freedom*, Yale University Press, 1950.

A Yale professor here presents a carefully reasoned account of how man, by his free effort "can become more complete and therefore more human." Even though it is clearly written, this is not a work for beginners.

PHILOSOPHY OF RELIGION

Balfour, A. J., *Theism and Thought*, Hodder & Stoughton, Ltd., 1923.

Lord Balfour, the versatile author who was a statesman as well as a philosopher, deals, in this second set of Gifford Lectures, particularly with methodological doubt, and shows how any meaningful belief can be substantiated.

Gilson, E., *God and Philosophy*, Yale Unniversity Press, 1941.
Etienne Gilson, in lectures given at Indiana University, shows carefuly the contrasts between the conceptions of God dominant in Greek philosophy and those which developed in Christian philosophy.

Herberg, W., (ed.), *The Writings of Martin Buber*, a selection, The World Publishing Company, Meridian Books, Inc., 1956.
The student interested in the philosophy of religion needs to know the works of Martin Buber, the eminent Jewish philosopher, and this compendium produced by Will Herberg, meets the need. Martin Buber is most famous for his book, *I and Thou*, in which he explains the theory of that name.

Temple, W., *Nature, Man and God*, The Macmillan Company, 1956.
One of the most comprehensive and dependable works of the twentieth century, this book, which consists of Temple's Gifford lectures, upholds with a wide variety of evidence the case for theistic realism.

Tillich, P., *The Religious Situation*, trans. H. R. Niebuhr, The World Publishing Company, Meridian Books, Inc., 1956.
This small book provides a satisfactory introduction to the thinking of one of the most distinguished contemporary theologians. Science, metaphysics, and art are treated, as well as religion.

BOOKS ON MORAL PHILOSOPHY

Bradley, F. H., *Ethical Studies*, The Liberal Arts Press, 1951.
This book of Bradley's essays is particularly valuable to the student who has read something in ethics and is ready to go farther. The famous essay, "My Station and its Duties," is in this collection.

Broad, C. D., *Five Types of Ethical Theory*. The Humanities Press, Inc., 1952.
This book presents the theories of Spinoza, Butler, Hume, Kant, and Sidgwick.

Moore, G. E., *Principia Ethica*, Cambridge University Press, 1903
This work includes Moore's celebrated claim, derived in part from Sidgwick, that "good" is intrinsically indefinable. The student who means to go far in philosophy must understand what Moore means by "the naturalistic fallacy," a fallacy which is exposed in this book.

Rashdall, H., *The Theory of Good and Evil*, Oxford University Press, 1924.

> An advanced book for students who have already faced the major problems of ethics and are ready for a detailed examination of alternatives.

Sidgwick, H., *The Methods of Ethics*, The University of Chicago Press, 1962.

> This is an acknowledged modern classic, especially notable for a balanced discussion of the arguments for and against determinism. Henry Sidgwick is the philosopher's philosopher, in both his precision and his fairness in discussion.

Stevenson, C. L., *Ethics and Language*, Yale University Press, 1950.

> A study of ethical issues from the points of view of the linguistic scholar. All of the major ethical terms, beginning with "good" and "bad" are meticulously analyzed.

BOOKS ON CURRENT TRENDS IN PHILOSOPHICAL THOUGHT

Gellner, E., *Words and Things*, Victor Gollancz, Ltd., 1959.

> This is the controversial book which criticizes severely the current linguistic school of philosophers at Oxford. There is an introduction by Bertrand Russell.

Heinemann, F. H., *Existentialism and the Modern Predicament*, Harper & Row, Inc., 1958.

> This book present existentialism as the philosophy of crisis, stated openly and directly, rather than covertly, as in many competing philosophies. The author asks primarily, not "What is existentialism?" but "What is its function in the present circumstances?"

Jacobs D. J. (ed.), *The New Communist Manifesto*, Harper & Row, Inc., 2nd ed., 1962.

> The useful volume contains the "Declaration" of representatives of the eighty-one Communist parties meeting in Moscow, November to December, 1960, along with related documents important for an understanding of the political philosophy of dialectical materialism in its current form.

Jaspers, K., *The Future of Mankind*, trans. E. B. Ashton, The University of Chicago Press, 1958.

> In this provocative book, Karl Jaspers, one of the most eminent of contemporary German philosophers, undertakes to study the philosophical issues involved in the creation and possible use of the atomic bomb. He faces the fact that the East has an ideology

while the West, having many, has none. An example of how philosophy can be applied to current problems.

Langer, Susanne K., *Philosophical Sketches*, The Johns Hopkins Press, 1962.

In this provocative book one of America's leading thinkers concerns herself with ideas which are still so pioneering that she calls her work a study-in-progress. Notable features are her consideration of "feeling" and her careful distinction between man and animal.

A LIBRARY OF PAPERBACKS

Guthrie, W. K. C., *The Greek Philosophers from Thales to Aristotle*, Harper & Row, Inc., Torchbooks, 1960.

A most able account of the rise and progress of Greek philosophy up to and including the greatest period in which it flourished. The movement from Socrates to Plato to Aristotle is skillfully presented, with no diminution of scholarship.

Highet, G., *Man's Unconquerable Mind*, Columbia University Press, 1960.

Excellent philosophy on the part of a scholar who is not professionally a philosopher. The sense of wonder, with which great philosophy began, is given a new meaning in this book, which has been written with passion as well as intelligence.

Kaufmann, W. (ed.), *Existentialism from Dostoevsky to Sartre*, The World Publishing Company, Meridian Books, Inc., 1956.

One of the best of the many contemporary books which help the modern student to know what existentialism is and what existentialists are saying. The book includes not only excellent selections from the most important representatives of the movement, but a carefully presented introduction by Walter Kaufmann.

Russell, B., *Problems of Philosophy*, Oxford University Press, Galaxy Books, 1959.

Written when Lord Russell was in midcareer and after his fruitful collaboration with Whitehead, this raises questions which would not otherwise be asked: he discusses them with admirable clarity and on the whole an absence of bias.

Sartre, J.-P., *Existentialism and Human Emotions*, trans. Frechtman and Barnes, Philosophical Library, Inc., Wisdom Library, 1957.

One of the best short statements of Sartre's general position, particularly in regard to responsibility. What Sartre is doing, in part, is defending existentialism against charges which have been made against it.

Taylor, A. E., *Socrates, the Man and His Thought*, Doubleday & Company, Inc., Anchor Books, 1956.
Probably the ablest short account in print of the first great figure in western philosophy.

Aristotle, *Poetics*, trans. K. A. Telford, Henry Regnery Company, Gateway Editions, 1961.
A wholly new and fresh translation of the work which has been so influential in all literary theory and criticism since Aristotle's day. Professor Telford's analysis helps the understanding of the average student immensely.

Whitehead, A. N., *The Function of Reason*, Beacon Press, 1958. By permission of Princeton University Press.
One of the shortest and most disturbing of all of Whitehead's works. The defense of the concept of final causation is included, with great success, in the critique of contemporary science.

INDEXES

INDEX OF NAMES

INDEX OF SUBJECTS